Praise for
THE DIARY KEEPERS

"An essential contribution to the history of WWII. Drawing from an archive of more than 2,100 wartime diaries . . . Siegal contextualizes her primary sources with exhaustive research and analysis of contemporaneous records. . . . A vivid portrait of the Nazi occupation as it unfolded, providing a wider lens than many Holocaust histories. . . . A treasure trove of firsthand perspectives."
—*Publishers Weekly* (starred review)

"Siegal intersperses artfully selected and translated excerpts . . . with interludes in which she explores larger ideas they raise, allowing the diarists to speak in their own voices while offering the necessary background to place them in context." —*Washington Post*

"Like an archaeologist excavating an ancient temple, Nina Siegal has dug up hundreds of stories of life under the unprecedented horror of Nazism, revealing the changing thoughts and shifting moods of heroes, villains, and victims. Until now, we only had a black-and-white image of these lives. Now, thanks to Siegal, we see them in living color." —Benjamin Moser, Pulitzer Prize–winning author of *Sontag*

"A vivid portrait of the daily lives of 'victims and collaborators, bystanders and participants.' . . . The author steps in frequently to summarize events and describe her own life (she is the granddaughter of Holocaust survivors), and she concludes with an insightful account of how postwar Holland recalled the experience, a section that includes a surprising number of interviews with survivors and their descendants." —*Kirkus Reviews*

"A beautiful, poignant book about the darkest period in modern Dutch history. . . . This book gives a powerful voice to forgotten witnesses."
—David de Jong, author of *Nazi Billionaires*

"The Netherlands was a nation of World War II diarists. . . . In *The Diary Keepers*, Siegal . . . uses a handful of those diaries—carefully chosen, translated, edited, and arranged—to describe the German occupation of the Netherlands and events leading to the murder of three-quarters of the country's Jewish population. She intersperses the diary entries with fragments of her own family narrative, as well as essays on the period, the diarists, the problem of historical memory, and the Netherlands' attempts to wrestle with a heritage of both rescue and complicity. . . . Her own writing is smart and on point." —*Forward*

"Nina Siegal has accomplished a remarkable feat. She has given us a day-by-day narrative of the Holocaust in the Netherlands by splicing together excerpts from a few of the hundreds of diaries stored in an Amsterdam archive. . . . With thoughtful and insightful observations of her own, Siegal helps us understand how 75 percent of the 140,000 Jews of Holland, a prosperous and cultivated Western European country, could have been murdered, posing a warning for our own deeply fractured country." —Joseph Berger, author of *Elie Wiesel: Confronting the Silence*

"The history of the Dutch Jews is one of the most disturbing of the Holocaust, but we must engage with it, and *The Diary Keepers* helps us do just that." —*Telegraph*

"*The Diary Keepers* is an astonishing, essential book that asks us to bear witness to an unbearable history, even as it invites us to think hard about what history *is*—how it gets written, and what stories it tells. This book is powerfully moving and necessarily terrifying. By way of rigorous research and intimate storytelling, Nina Siegal brings us close to her diary keepers—making it impossible to turn away from the difficult, necessary questions their lives raise about survival, suffering, complicity, and memory." —Leslie Jamison, author of *The Empathy Exams*

"*The Diary Keepers* is an important addition to World War II and Holocaust studies. It reveals, through the words of the people who were there, how any one of us might respond to unprecedented calamity.

And its coda is the unsettling reminder that nobody knows the ultimate ending to their story until it comes."
—*Washington Independent Review of Books*

"This moving and masterful book tells the history of those fateful war years, and their aftermath, in a wonderfully intimate way."
—**Margot Livesey, author of** *The Boy in the Field*

"This moving and riveting book is a revelation, providing a glimpse into life under Nazi occupation. At once epic and intimate, it merits comparison to Marcel Ophuls's classic 1969 documentary about life in occupied France, *The Sorrow and the Pity.*"
—*National Catholic Reporter*

"A work of orchestral power, moving among voices. I was riveted."
—**Patricia Hampl, author of** *The Art of the Wasted Day*

"A compelling look at the story of World War II and the Holocaust told through the diaries of Dutch citizens in firsthand accounts of ordinary people living through extraordinary times." —*Brooklyn Digest*

THE
DIARY
KEEPERS

THE
DIARY
KEEPERS

WORLD WAR II WRITTEN BY
THE PEOPLE WHO LIVED THROUGH IT

NINA SIEGAL

ecco
An Imprint of HarperCollins*Publishers*

HarperCollins books may be purchased for educational, business, or sales promotional use. For information, please email the Special Markets Department at SPsales@harpercollins.com.

Ecco® and HarperCollins® are trademarks of HarperCollins Publishers.

A hardcover edition of this book was published in 2023 by Ecco, an imprint of HarperCollins Publishers.

FIRST ECCO PAPERBACK EDITION PUBLISHED 2024

Designed by Angie Boutin

Title page background © LiliGraphie/shutterstock.com

Library of Congress Cataloging-in-Publication Data has been applied for.

ISBN 978-0-06-307066-0 (pbk.)

23 24 25 26 27 LBC 5 4 3 2 1

This book is dedicated to my grandfather, Emerich, my grandmother, Alzbeta, my mother, Marta, and all the Safar and Roth family members we lost in the war.

And it is also dedicated to the next generation of our family, my nephews, Joseph and Cameron, and my daughter, Sonia.

Everyone wrote. Journalists and writers, of course, but also teachers, public men, young people—even children. Most of them kept diaries where the tragic events of the day were reflected through the prism of personal experience. A tremendous amount was written, but the vast majority of the writings was destroyed.

—*Emanuel Ringelblum, creator of the Oyneg Shabes underground archive in the Warsaw Ghetto*

Nobody will ever tell the story—a story of five million personal tragedies every one of which would fill a volume.

—*Richard Lichtheim, from the Jewish Agency in Geneva, July 9, 1942*

CONTENTS

PART III: TOWARD LIBERATION, MAY 1944–MAY 1945

PART IV: THE WAR IN MEMORY, MAY 1945–MAY 2022

THE
DIARY
KEEPERS

Prologue

SEARCHING FOR EMERICH

Emerich and Marta Safar (later Marta Siegal,
the author's mother) in Hungary in 1942

When I was a girl, my grandfather Emerich would drive his silver Pacer over to our house in Long Island from Sunnyside, Queens, to take my brother, David, and me out to lunch. David's favorite spot was McDonald's on Northern Boulevard and mine was Friendly's on our town's main street, a kind of all-purpose American diner with bouncy leather seats. We'd alternate. Even weeks, McDonald's and odd weeks, Friendly's.

As with all good rituals, there was a catchphrase. Before we would step out of the Pacer and into the parking lot, Grandpa Emerich would turn to the back seat, narrowing his eyes. "Now, you can order whatever you'd like," he'd say with a mischievous glint in his clear blue eyes, "but if you don't finish it, I'm going to shove it down your throat with a rolling pin."

Even as we laughed nervously, we knew that this joke had a solid, indestructible core. Wasting food wasn't an option for Siegal kids, no matter where we ended up dining in junk-food America. A form of explanation would often arrive later, while we were seated at a sticky table fishing out the last greasy crisps of our fries.

"When I was in the camps," grandpa would start . . . What followed might be a story about coveting a hunk of bread in his pocket for days, and rationing it to himself over time to stave off hunger. Or how one could sip a watery soup slowly to make it more filling.

These narratives perplexed me, as a ten-year-old girl growing up on Long Island, because the word "camp" only conjured images of joyful canoe rides and marshmallows melting the Hershey's on s'mores. I remember the look of surprise on my grandfather's face when I finally mustered up the courage to ask, "Grandpa, if you didn't like the camp, why didn't you just go home?" There was a moment of silence, as his blue eyes scanned my young face and grasped that I'd missed a crucial point. Then he enjoyed a hearty laugh.

If he shared these anecdotal experiences with us quite freely, I don't recall him explicitly defining what "the camps" were, or how he'd come to be there. Although he'd sometimes begin a story with, "After I was arrested," I can't remember a time he'd indicated the reason. Somehow, I understood implicitly that he had not committed a crime, but the stories were never about that; they were usually about a cunning way he'd managed to outwit a guard or escape a perilous situation, using his smarts alone.

As I grew older, I accepted more easily that there were certain questions you didn't ask; or if you did, you couldn't expect an answer. Although I adored my grandfather, I saw that there was an ocean that divided us. His life had been back there in the "Old Country," across the Atlantic, a place that seemed to me to contain innumerable, unimaginable horrors. Czechoslovakia, Hungary, and Germany, to my mind, were nightmare places of forced labor, prison, random arrest, the Jewish camp guards known as Kapos, and the SS. I didn't know what all of these words meant, but they inspired fear. Nevertheless, I was assured that all of that was over.

What was important was to be vigilant, in various ways, so that we would simply be prepared if it would ever happen again. We should eat today in case we couldn't tomorrow. Our cupboards were stacked with canned goods; the "good silver" was hidden in the basement's dropped ceiling. I was made aware of certain portable valuables in particular closet drawers, just in case. In case of what? In case we had to flee suddenly?

When I looked around me, I saw only a quiet, lush, charming Long Island, with its views of the city across the Sound. Suburban ranch houses and mowed lawns with rhythmically hissing sprinklers. Purple and white hydrangeas like bursting bouquets across the fence of our sparkling backyard pool. Neighbors waved and called out friendly greetings when I walked my dog down the block. We were safe here, weren't we?

I CAME TO understand that my grandfather was what people called a Survivor, and that made him a rare and singular individual. He had fading blue ink numbers tattooed on his left forearm, testifying to his Jewish superhero status. People saw, and understood immediately, signifiers I was only beginning to grasp.

Grandpa Emerich, born on Valentine's Day, had at least two other names: Imre Sàfàr was his official name and his nickname was *Sanyi*. He spoke about seven languages, English with us, Hungarian and Czech at home. At least a little Yiddish, and enough Hebrew to lead our Passover Seders. I knew that he also spoke German, but he wouldn't use it.

Before the war, he had been a scholar, my mother told us, who'd been politically involved in the social-democracy movement in Czechoslovakia. She explained that his family owned a business, so they were relatively well off, but anti-Semitic laws made it difficult for him to find outside employment. They didn't live far from Prague, I understood, both before the war and after it. But I never heard the name of the town.

Grandpa was a handsome man with deep-set eyes, a sculptured jaw, and an expression of generous intensity. Years later, when I saw a picture of Franz Kafka, I thought I recognized my grandfather's face in his. I conjured a romantic image of a Czech intellectual, seated with men in gray caps at a smoky café table in Prague, slamming his fist down while making a trenchant point, to toasts and cheers.

After the war, once they'd left Europe for Australia, he'd become an auto mechanic to support his family. That skill seemed to translate across disciplines: he could fix pretty much anything around the house, and he was always coming by to help my dad with plumbing or electrical projects, like a skinny, white haired, Jewish MacGyver.

I was told that Emerich had thirteen brothers and sisters, who were all grown, and mostly married with children before the war began; or maybe he was one of thirteen brothers and sisters. I'm not sure. I only ever met two, Uncle Bumi, who had gone to work in Western Europe before the war broke out and emigrated to Queens, where he'd married another Hungarian, and had two children, my mom's cousins Fran and Stevie. In Hungary still were my aunt Blanca, who'd survived with her daughter, also named Marta. There was also a "cousin Mary" who I may have met but can't remember.

My mother told me that before my grandfather was arrested, he managed to arrange false papers for my mother and grandmother. They went into hiding with Blanca and Marta, in an apartment in central Budapest, which my brother thought may have actually been Blanca's home. My mother couldn't recall much from that period, but I remember a story she told about the women going out at night to procure food, and coming home with horse meat.

Once, when I described my mother as a Survivor, she quickly objected. That word, she explained in a hushed voice, was strictly reserved for those who'd endured the camps. She and her mother had only gone into hiding.

I took this response to be a rule of lexicography in a language that had a delicate precision. There were ways of articulating such matters, and if you didn't do it correctly, you might inadvertently detonate hidden emotional land mines. When periodically I wondered aloud about what had happened to this aunt or that cousin, for example, the answer I often received was that he or she had "perished in the war."

A lot of people seemed to have "perished." In my young mind, the word conjured a geographical or climatological event, maybe some kind of massive sandstorm that had ravished a continent. "Perishing" didn't imply violence or perpetrators. It suggested death in a natural disaster. In fact, World War II itself seemed to have been a cataclysmic force majeure, rather than a war of men, conjured entirely through the evil magic of Adolf Hitler.

The survivors I knew—and to me they were all survivors—never once sat me down to explain the broad strokes of history. The war was ever-present, and yet not discussed. Occasionally my mother would trot out certain stories, usually in questionable settings, like cocktail parties. She had certain go-to narratives I'd overhear in company, and that typically ended with a punch line. These were crafted, polished, palatable tales that might elicit laughter, but that had an unmistakable subtext of terror.

Yet, when I asked my mother, in private, quieter moments, to tell me about her childhood, she would swat the air, and say, "Oh, it's all too horrible. You don't want to hear about that."

What I felt without any doubt, was that something profound had occurred to my relatives, something that was in certain ways unspeakable. When it was spoken, it came out in a deranged form, like a demented, ratty doll popping out of the jack-in-the-box.

Whatever they'd lived through had fundamentally defined their characters. My grandfather, the personification of calm, was deeply, genuinely kind and unflappable. Jarring jokes aside, his company was always a gentle comfort. He always had time. Of course, by then, he was an elderly retired man, but there was something else. I had the feeling that after all he'd been through, he'd learned to live with everything, and nothing could faze him anymore.

IN SEVENTH GRADE, I got a little bit of clarity on the subject when another Holocaust survivor came to speak to our class. We were reading *Anne Frank: The Diary of a Young Girl,* and an elderly woman, who'd been a young woman in the war, would tell us her own experience of surviving Auschwitz.

I recall feeling slightly repelled at first: I already know all about *that,* I thought. Still, her testimony to our class had a deep impact on me. She spoke to us so clearly, so directly, telling her tale from the outbreak of war to her own liberation, mostly matter-of-factly. She was clear and straightforward, practiced but not in an effort to entertain us or soften the edges. She didn't get up and move around the room, nervously, distractedly. She sat still, looked us in the eyes, and told us what they had done to her. Sometimes tears came to her wizened green eyes, and I could feel how much courage it took to tell her story. She had tremendous dignity.

That same year, my grandfather Emerich died. I was thirteen, and David was fifteen. Grandpa had been doing his favorite thing, sitting at a card table at a Hungarian club in Manhattan, playing Gin Rummy, surrounded by friends. He just slumped at the table. I will never forget the plunging wail my mother let out when she got the news the next morning.

At the funeral, attended by about two hundred people, at least a half dozen weeping Hungarian women pulled me into a fierce hug and each one confessed that she'd been in love with my grandfather. Good for grandpa; even in his late seventies, he still had that charisma.

After his death, my mother told me more about Emerich's life. One story took place in the Hungarian countryside, where my mother and Alzbeta were in hiding with a family of farmers, after their hiding place in Budapest had been betrayed. My grandfather suddenly appeared, walking down the country road, seemingly out of nowhere. There were German soldiers standing nearby. My mother was maybe six years old at that time, but she already knew that showing affection for her father would put them all at risk. She managed to stifle the urge to run toward him and throw her arms around her father—an act that remains astonishing to me in its self-restraint.

I understood that her version of history was a combination of hagiography and mythology. My mother had been a mere child during the war years; what could she really have remembered?

Later, my mother had multiple sclerosis, a degenerative disease that can affect memory. Her stories became more hyperbolic, and she amped up their theatricality. Once, my grandfather had been in three concentration camps; now the number had jumped to four. Was this an emergence of new details, or was her memory becoming jumbled? Either way, it was increasingly difficult to parse facts from her embellishments.

By this time, I was an adult, living in other homes, other cities. I had a life I was supposed to be living in the present, for the future. The past was a horrifying morass. How curious was I supposed to be about the war, the Holocaust? Just because I came from a family of survivors, was I required to deal with that? Hadn't my family wanted desperately to "leave all that behind us" and "live a normal life." Normal was good, and for that, it seemed, forgetting was essential.

I LET IT go for a very long time, for decades. I had other things on my mind, other causes. I became a theater artist and then a journalist. Early on in my career, I wrote mostly about American social struggles: homelessness, incarceration, racism, housing rights, health care, domestic violence. I also wrote about the theater and the arts. Later, when I became a contract writer for *The New York Times*, my beat was Harlem and the Bronx; then I got a job at Bloomberg News, covering urban art and culture.

I didn't tend to identify as Jewish, even if I knew myself to be Jewish. To me, being Jewish meant being religious, and I was a secular atheist. I hadn't grown up going to synagogue or attending Hebrew school; both my parents were uninterested in religion, my mother avidly so. We did celebrate a few Jewish holidays, but around the table with family, not in the synagogue. When I attended Bar and Bat Mitzvahs, or family weddings and funerals, I felt like an anthropologist visiting an exotic culture: so *these* are Jewish traditions.

In 2006, I came to Europe. I was writing a novel about a dead man in a Rembrandt painting, his 1632 group portrait masterpiece, *The Anatomy Lesson of Dr. Nicolaes Tulp,* and had secured a Fulbright Fellowship to conduct research for ten months in Amsterdam. I would work with the world's leading Rembrandt scholar, Ernst van de Wetering, and spend almost a year living where the events of my novel unfolded in the seventeenth century.

My first apartment was in the Red Light District, around the corner from Rembrandt's former home and studio, and where the Rembrandt House Museum stands today. In the Dutch Golden Age, it was home to many Jews, which later gave it the nickname Jodenbuurt, or Jewish neighborhood. Sephardic Jews from Portugal and Spain had found refuge here since the Inquisition, and Ashkenazi Jews had arrived from Eastern Europe, fleeing pogroms. Jews had been granted citizenship in the Dutch Republic as early as 1616 and could practice Judaism in peace.

Rembrandt arrived in town from Leiden in 1631. As in many poor urban districts today, cheap rents attracted artists, foreigners, and low-wage workers. Rembrandt liked to sketch and paint his neighbors, right off the bustling local streets, and his subjects included both Africans and local rabbis. He incorporated Jewish faces into his so-called "history paintings," stories drawn from the Hebrew Bible.

Maybe I'd been trying to move away from my identity as a Jewish girl from New York, but here I was, right in the historical center of Jewish Amsterdam. Its main street, Jodenbreestraat, Jewish Broadway, was a minute from my apartment, which was in the converted storage attic of a former seventeenth century canal house, just like Anne Frank's secret annex.

Down the block from the Rembrandt House Museum, a restored 1606 mansion he purchased when his career and family life were both at their apogee, was the Jewish Historical Museum, built around a cluster of former synagogues. Among them was the glorious Portuguese Synagogue, lit majestically by gold candelabras. I learned that the local Waterlooplein Market, where I could buy secondhand jean jackets, colorful Rastafarian bags, and hookahs of every culture, had been famous until the war for its vast array of Jewish wares and foods.

I would walk up the Nieuwe Uilenburgerstraat, named after Hendrick van Uilenburgh, the art dealer who launched Rembrandt's career, passing the Gassan Diamond company, formerly Boas Diamond Grinding Company, once a workplace of hundreds of Jewish diamond cutters, polishers, and specialists, before the war. Adjacent was yet another quaint little synagogue adorned with a large star of David, hidden behind a high brick wall, the Uilenburgersjoel.

So many landmarks of Jewish life, Jewish history, Jewish cultural traditions. But where were the Jews? I moved daily through a neighborhood filled with monuments and museums for a Jewish community that seemed to exist as mere ghosts.

Not once did I spot a black-hatted Hasidim or even just men wearing yarmulkes or women in wigs and traditional orthodox garb, as I was used to in New York. The people walking in and out of the Portuguese Synagogue seemed to be largely tourists; the little synagogue near my office apparently hosted Muslim and Christian services, too. There seemed to be only one single Kosher restaurant on Jodenbreestraat, of the white tablecloth variety that was beyond my means. I couldn't find a decent bagel, a Jewish deli, or even a truly sour pickle in the Waterlooplein, once the central Jewish market square. Because my main cultural connection was always food, my stomach ultimately led me to the new center of Jewish life in Amsterdam, a district in the southern part of the city, Buitenveldert. There, I found two kosher butcher shops, a Jewish specialty store, and a supermarket that had a Jewish section that sold Israeli imports, including gefilte fish and matzoh meal. At last, I had the ingredients for Passover.

Even as I got to know the city better, and to widen my social circles, I found that Dutch people rarely identified themselves as Jewish. I became curious. Once, I saw a woman in my office who had strikingly similar features to my aunt, so I pleasantly approached and asked her if she happened to be Jewish. She blanched, stricken, offended. "Why?" she said, "Is it my nose?" And quickly walked away.

Another time, I was interviewing a couple who'd organized an exhibition about Nazi looted art, and when I tentatively inquired whether they had a personal connection to the subject matter—by then I knew not to ask directly—they waved me into a corner and whispered that they both had Jewish parents. "But please don't put that in your article," they said. "We don't want our neighbors to know."

Something was deeply troubling about Jewish life in the Netherlands. I observed as much to my friend Jenn, an older Jewish New

Yorker who'd been living in Amsterdam already for decades. "Ah, you've noticed," she said. "They say that the Dutch Jews are still in hiding."

WHAT CONTINUED TO boggle the mind was that, in the pre-war era, Amsterdam had a Jewish population that represented somewhere between 10 and 12 percent of the population. That starts to get close to New York's Jewish population today, which is about 16 to 18 percent of the city's residents.[1]

It seemed that Jewish culture may have had an outsized influence on Amsterdam culture, in much the same way that it has in New York. You can hear the traces of Yiddish, for example, in Amsterdam street slang, much as many New Yorkers know at least a few Yiddishisms (*nosh, schlep, schmuck*), regardless of their religion or race.

Amsterdammers pepper their conversations with words like *mazzel* (as in mazel tov), the Dutch word for luck. They'll use the same word for "crazy" that my grandfather liked to call my dog, Meschuga, spelled *mesjogge* in Dutch, and my daughter recently informed me that the word *smoezen* was Dutch, when I know it to be the English Yiddishism "schmooze." Lots of people still use the Hebrew-derived nickname for Amsterdam, "Mokum" proudly. In Yiddish, it's the word for "town"; in Hebrew for "place." This was their destination, their spot, their refuge, their home. Until it wasn't.

The penny finally dropped for me when I attended an art exhibition in the Jewish Cultural Quarter entitled, "Looted, but from whom?" An organization known as Bureau Herkomst Gezocht, or the Origins Unknown Agency (a Kafkaesque title if I've ever heard one) displayed fifty objects that the Netherlands had identified as works the Nazis had robbed from Jewish families. These works had been returned to the Netherlands, but not to their rightful owners. No one had yet come forward to claim them. By this point, sixty years had passed since the end of the war. Why hadn't people claimed their stolen art? Had all the former owners "perished"?

One fact shared in the exhibition's wall text shook me to my core: of the estimated 140,000 Dutch Jews, only about 35,000 survived World War II. Some 102,000, along with hundreds of Roma and Sinti people, had died in the Holocaust. Could that be right? That would mean that about 75 percent of the Dutch Jewish population was murdered in five years. In a single generation, the Nazis had managed to wipe out four centuries of Jewish tradition and culture in this city, in this Western European country? No wonder I felt that I was walking around in a void.

Although this won't come as news to most Dutch people, I found it surprising at the time because I'd always thought that Eastern European Jews had suffered the worst. The Dutch death toll was, I learned, extraordinarily high by Western European standards. In France, 25 percent of Jews were killed during the Holocaust;[2] about 40 percent of Jews from Belgium were murdered. The Netherlands holds the dubious distinction of having the lowest survival rate of all the Western European countries. In Eastern Europe, too, only a few countries fared worse, such as Poland, where 90 percent of the Jewish population, three million people, were wiped out. Hungary lost 60 percent of its Jewish population—and I'd always thought that was one of the hardest-hit countries.

Before I'd moved to the Netherlands, I'd thought of it as a progressive country, known for its famous "tolerance," its philosophical, scientific, artistic broadmindedness and receptivity. I'd gotten the impression, formed in large part by Anne Frank's diary, that the Dutch had sheltered their Jews. That the resistance here had been active and effective. How had I come to this misunderstanding? Where was I really living?

I STAYED. IT wasn't exactly intentional. The research for the novel that I'd hoped would be finished in ten months ended up taking six years; the book was eventually published in 2014. In the meantime, I'd got a job as a magazine editor, bought a surprisingly affordable apartment, learned the language so I could conduct my daily business in Dutch. My daughter, Sonia, was born in 2012, and that same year I started to freelance from Europe for *The New York Times* and art magazines.

Sometimes, when I thought about the fact that more than a decade had passed since I'd come for a "visit," I had a queasy feeling, like in one of those nightmares in which, no matter which way you turn, you can't find your way home. Other times, it felt like a conscious choice to live in a civilized country with universal health care and child-care subsidies, but often it was merely the decision not to go back to New York just yet.

In 2019, one of my brother David's sons got a school assignment to create a family tree. He'd asked questions about the Hungarian side of our family, which had prompted my brother to engage in a little genealogical research.

Although it seemed like my grandfather's story was by now merely the stuff of legend and fable, in the thirty years since his passing, a lot more information had become available to people doing genealogical research. And the internet had been invented. A number of research institutions could help people like us figure out lost family histories.

David contacted something called the International Tracing Service, as well as the Mauthausen memorial camp, and received a handful of official documents, including immigration forms that indicated Emerich's former addresses. Copies of yellowed hand-written customs forms, typed ships' logs, index cards scribbled in pencil, almost indecipherably. They were written in Czech, German, and Hungarian.

Nevertheless, I gleaned some basics: Emerich was born in 1905, the son of Samuel Safar and Fanny Eisenberg, in a town called Volove. He'd married my grandmother, Alzbeta Roth, in Vrable, Czechoslovakia in 1937, when he was thirty-two years old and she was thirty. Their wedding location was not far from Nitra, Czechoslovakia, where my mother, Marta, was born a year later, on July 19, 1938. She was their only child. Within a year or two, the family returned to Volove, where Emerich's family presumably still lived. (My grandmother died when I was two; I know almost nothing about her family history.)

That winter I took a long weekend break to Prague with my partner at the time. We visited the ancient Jewish cemetery, while on a tour of the Jewish Quarter. I read the names of the slanting ancient tombstones attesting to centuries of Jewish history in the city—stones dating back to 1439, just about the era of Richard III—and scanned the white marble mausoleum indoors for the name Safar, among Prague's World War II victims. I found Safars: Safar, Rudolph. Safar, David. Could these be some of our Czech relatives? How would I ever know?

Back at the hotel, I called up David's email with Emerich's immigration forms and asked the concierge if she could help me read the Czech. If this town, Volove, was near Prague, maybe we could make a side visit.

Leaning across the desk, the concierge informed me that none of the addresses on his list were anywhere near Prague. Volove, in fact, was no longer part of the Czech Republic, but now across the border in Ukraine. I went back upstairs determined, at long last, to stop being entirely ignorant about my grandfather's life, and stayed up late into the night in the hotel bed with my laptop, scouring the internet.

I learned that Volove had been invaded twice during the war years. In 1939, when the Soviets marched into Poland, the formerly Czech town became part of the Soviet Socialist Republic. The German army occupied the town in April 1941. By that time, Emerich, Alzbeta, and Marta, my mother, had already fled.

Not long after the Germans arrived, all the Jews of Volove were forced to move to the nearby town of Bibrka, where they were confined to a ghetto. In March 1943, according to eyewitness testimonies, German soldiers herded them into trucks and drove them to a brick-yard. They were told to undress completely and walk in pairs to a plank over a ditch. They were executed naked in groups of six.

"Someone shot them with a machine gun, and they fell into the pit," recalled a witness, interviewed by the organization Yahad in Unum, in 2009. "Some were wounded, others alive or shot dead . . . they were all in this pit." He added, "The little children were shot in the arms of their mothers. We could hear shots from the village."

The soldiers finished off with shovels all those who hadn't died from the bullets. Witnesses said they heard the cries until two in the morning.[3]

I shut my laptop. I decided I would put it out of my head and go to sleep. Lying staring at the ceiling, unable to close my eyes, I shuddered at the horror I had opened myself up to by looking into my family's actual past. Of course they had soft-pedaled the truth, and for good reason. Who wanted to know this kind of stuff? At the same time, I found myself marveling at my grandfather's foresight. How had he known to get his family out of Volove ahead of the Germans? Was he really the mythical superhero of the fables after all?

The next afternoon, we visited the Kafka Museum on the high bluff over the expansive Vltava River. Peeking into the spotlighted vitrines in the dark rooms, which showcased Kafka's first editions, journals, and love letters, I thought about how some men's lives are so well documented, and how others are lost to history. I reflected on the meager information that I had about Emerich and everyone else in my family. What kinds of lives are preserved and archived? What can we read if we want to understand the fate of an ordinary person?

When I got home to Amsterdam, I spent nights and weekends trying to puzzle together more pieces of my grandfather's story. It was, it seemed to me, far more harrowing than anything in my mother's oft-repeated tales.

About a month after the Germans invaded Hungary, my grandfather was deported to a forced labor camp in Szentkirályszabadja, a town on the eastern edge of Lake Balaton, where he spent about seven months. In October, the Reich toppled the Hungarian government, and thousands of Budapest Jews were murdered on the banks of the Danube. A month later, Emerich was transferred to another forced-labor assignment at a ship-building factory, Ferihegy Flugplatz Fertorakos, back in Budapest.

He spent the winter there, but in the spring, on March 31, 1945, he was deported to Mauthausen. A month and half later, on April 15, 1945, he was moved to a subcamp called Gunskirchen, in the woods.

He was probably one of the slave laborers who lived in tents while building the camp.[4] Three weeks later, on May 5, 1945, he was liberated by the 71st Infantry Division of the 3rd U.S. Army. Although some 90,000 people had died at Mauthausen and its subcamps, Emerich was one of 15,000 Gunskirchen prisoners who made it out alive.

The Swiss Red Cross took him to Hörsching, Austria, and from there on to the Jewish hospital of Budapest, where he was diagnosed with typhus. About a month later, he was released, and reunited with my mom and grandmother. By August 1946, they had established a home address in Budapest, but they later returned to Czechoslovakia.

I had some data, addresses, and dates. While I felt I was making some headway, the process of deciphering the information also felt strangely distancing. I knew the *where*, *when*, and possibly the *what* of things. But the *how* and the *why*—the crucial questions—had no answers. I couldn't reach into his world. There was no one left who could help me understand all of this data. I'd left it alone for too long; I hadn't asked the right questions when I still could have.

IT WAS A bright spring day in 2019 when I visited the NIOD Institute for War, Holocaust and Genocide Studies in Amsterdam for the first time. I was meeting two researchers there, René Kok and Erik Somers, who had curated an exhibition, "The Persecution of the Jews in Photographs: The Netherlands, 1940–1945." I was writing an article for *The New York Times*,[5] about how so many of the images had been shot by bystanders, ordinary Dutch people who had witnessed the roundups of their neighbors from their Amsterdam apartment windows.

I'd long been fascinated by the NIOD, both for its hallowed reputation as a center of war and Holocaust scholarship, but also for its very special building. It is housed in an exquisite double-wide mansion on the Herengracht, dripping with baroque design features, including cherubs and deities, and Romanesque soldiers whose heads pop out from columns and pilasters. Other impressive buildings situated along this Golden Bend of the "Gentleman's Canal"—one of the UNESCO Heritage canals that make up the city's picturesque *grachtengordel*—are nowhere near as ornate. They tend to be more faithful to a Calvinist tradition of stoicism and spare design, and the NIOD building flies in the face of those principles. I appreciated its interesting gaudiness in contrast to the otherwise austere canal mansions on either side.

I found that the interior also reflected the same kind of whimsical splendor, as its nineteenth century owner had decided on decorating it in a "potpourri of styles," in the manner of a seventeenth century castle,[6] hand-painted silk wallpaper, the Turkish-style mosaic tile encircling the sunken bathtub, the skylights that gave sight to the sun and moon, and the backyard complete with grassy lawn and horse stables, where the original owner had parked his carriage.

René Kok picked me up in the foyer and led me upstairs to meet Somers in a surprisingly nondescript conference room to talk about bystander photography during the war. While most of the surviving imagery we have from the occupation period in the Netherlands was taken by German or pro-German Dutch photographers for propaganda purposes, they explained, they'd been able to discover many new images taken by ordinary people who had clandestinely shot pictures out their windows, without getting caught.

I'd looked at the photographs in the accompanying book before the interview and spoken to Judith Cohen, the director of the photography archive at the United States Holocaust Memorial Museum in Washington, to ask how rare these were. She'd confirmed that it was very difficult to find images taken by "non authorized" photographers, especially of Jewish raids, or Razzias.

"We all know the who, what, when, and where of the Holocaust, but the why is a mystery still," she had told me. The "why," she elaborated, "is why so many people let it happen, why they collaborated, or watched from the sidelines, or made it possible in one way or another for the Nazis to round up and deport their neighbors. 'What were ordinary people thinking? What were they doing?' If you can get bystander photos, that explains a little bit of the why."[7]

I was riveted by this comment, which spoke directly to the questions I'd been considering while at the Kafka museum in Prague.

I told her that I'd been particularly struck by a snapshot on the cover of the book that accompanied the exhibition of a young Dutch couple strolling happily through Dam Square, next to the Royal Palace in Amsterdam, in January 1943.[8] They both wore the Star of David on the lapels of their winter coats, and yet they looked so happy, as if they were about to get married. (I would learn later, the couple, Ralph Polak and Miep Krant, became engaged that day.) I couldn't stop staring at their faces. The image just took my breath away. How could they be so vibrant and cheerful, while so clearly marked for death?

"It's important not to read history backwards," Judith Cohen said. "It's important to keep in mind that nobody knew how it would end."

The thought played through my head again and again as I spoke to Kok and Somers. The photographs, however, told a story of bystander fear, but also bystander complicity. One could look out the window, while drinking tea, and see their neighbors, marked, forced into public squares, driven into trucks, beaten, humiliated, deported. It had happened just outside their doors, outside their windows. Everyone could see everything.

Suddenly, René tapped me on the shoulder, breaking me out of my musings. "Before you go, can I just show you one more thing?" he said.

He led me down through the mansion's carved cherrywood staircase under a pendulous chandelier, through the modern study hall with its glass atrium below the carriage house, and down white marble stairs into the basement. There, he heaved open a bank vault door, one-foot thick, and pressed into the NIOD's archives, announcing that we were about to dive "below sea level."

The archive, stark and bright like a scientific lab, was filled with rows of metal filing cabinets. Using a hand crank, René Kok opened a single wall, revealing hundreds of camel-colored boxes. Inside these, he said, were personal diaries, written by ordinary Dutch people during the war. There were more than 2,100 of them.

"We opened the Institute three days after Liberation," he explained.

"We asked people to bring in their personal documents about the war. The diaries came pouring in."

In these files were the stories of shop clerks, resistance fighters, train conductors, artists, musicians, policemen, grocers. Anne Frank's diary was submitted here, too. He said the range of the collection was vast.

He pulled a file from the wall and opened it. The first thing that jumped out at us was a portrait of Hitler, pasted lovingly onto the black-and-white marbleized notebook cover. Inside, we found hand-drawn sheet music for SS marching songs. I'd never even imagined SS marching songs—but that made perfect sense.

"Did you say more than 2,100 diaries?" I asked.

René drew out another file from the wall. This one contained hand-painted watercolor illustrations. I gasped at drawings of Nazi soldiers standing in an open doorway, a civilian silhouetted in the hall. Another folder contained school notebooks filled with youthful poetry, pretty floral-patterned journals, bound, typed editions thick as textbooks.

Why was René showing me all of this? He explained that the Institute had recently initiated an "Adopt-a-Diary" program to make these journals more accessible to the public. His colleague René Pottkamp was coordinating a team of volunteers, who had already started to scan and transcribe them, and soon they would digitize them. Although they contained rich textures of the war, some of them were illegible or indecipherable.

"I see researchers coming in here and they're excited to read these diaries," he explained. "But you see after one hour"—he mimicked a person's eyes drooping—"And then another hour"—he pantomimed a head nodding, falling to a desk. "It's tiring to read someone else's handwriting."

Many of the diaries had been photocopied and the copies were poor, on cracked old mimeograph paper. Others had been preserved only on rectangles of microfiche, white text on a black background that could make one dizzy. Sometimes the copies were so small that they required a magnifying glass. By transcribing and digitizing them, NIOD was salvaging them from obscurity.

I could only stand and marvel. I felt that I had been introduced to a trove of writing that would give me direct access to the war period and an understanding of not only the facts—the *what, where,* and *when*—but also the *how* and *why*. How it felt to live through it, through the eyes of individuals from every walk of life.

It was neither the story of the Jews of the Netherlands, nor the history of their persecutors, nor exclusively the resistance story. It was all of them. Each of their voices was represented here, potentially offering perspective on the entire war generation. These diaries might be another way for me to read history forward, as Cohen had suggested, day by day, moment by moment, just as we all live our lives, without knowing what comes next.

Were these ordinary diary writers people like my grandfather, Emerich, facing the unknown, day to day? Would I be able to find him, somehow, here, amid all these pages? Or could I, at the very least, somehow use this material to get closer to his story?

Most important, was I allowed to read all these? And if so, how soon could I get started?

Introduction

"VAST QUANTITIES OF THIS SIMPLE, EVERYDAY MATERIAL"

Radio Oranje reporters, including Loe de Jong (center),
gathering around the microphone

On March 28, 1944, the crackling voice of Gerrit Bolkestein, Dutch minister of education, arts and sciences, came across the airwaves from London on Radio Oranje, the broadcast station for the government in exile. Ten months earlier, everyone but Dutch National Socialists and other German sympathizers had been forced to turn in their radio sets, under threat of punishment. But lots of people kept a hidden device, and on this occasion, those who had them huddled around their illegal transmitters in closets or attics or by the back door of the barn to listen:

"History cannot be written on the basis of official decisions and documents alone," Bolkestein told his listeners, who'd spent nearly four years living under German occupying forces. "If our descendants are to understand fully what we as a nation have had to endure and overcome during these years, then what we really need are ordinary documents—a diary, letters."[1]

He urged Dutch citizens to preserve their personal journals and other intimate correspondence that conveyed their private struggles and personal wartime ordeals—materials that the Nazi overlord did not even want them to have. "Not until we succeed in bringing together vast quantities of this simple, everyday material will the picture of our struggle for freedom be painted in its full depth and glory."[2]

Bolkestein and other Dutch officials had fled the Netherlands after the German invasion in May 1940 and had been operating in exile. It had been a painful four years, as they'd seen their country overtaken by fascist ideology and hundreds of thousands of their citizens drafted into service for the Nazis, deported to work camps and concentration camps.

By the spring of 1944, the end was in sight. At the very least, there was reason for hope. The war had reached a turning point at Stalingrad, the Allies were making clear advances, and the German army was finally in retreat. Even in pro-German circles, the general expectation was that an Allied invasion of Western Europe was only a matter of time.

On Radio Oranje, Bolkestein let the people know that the stories of individual struggles, personal experiences, written in ordinary peoples' own words, would be valued by future historians. He promised those listening that the government would establish a new national center for war documentation, and that it would collect, preserve, and publish this material, which would illustrate the character and stamina, the courage and endurance, of all of his countrymen and women.

A young raven-haired Jewish girl named Anne Frank, an aspiring teenage writer, was listening. She tuned in from her hiding place in an attic on the Prinsengracht, where she'd lived in fear for nearly two years, while the vast majority of her friends, schoolmates, and their families had been dragged away.

Anne had been writing in her diary since her thirteenth birthday, when she received it as a gift, and addressed it as "Kitty." That was just weeks before she, her father, Otto, her mother, Esther, and her older sister, Margot, had moved into the attic, which they would end up sharing with four near strangers.

"Mr. Bolkestein, the Cabinet Minister, speaking on the Dutch broadcast from London said that after the war a collection would be made of diaries and letters dealing with the war," she scribbled in her journal the next day. "Of course, everyone pounced on my diary. . . . Ten years after the war people would find it very amusing to read how we lived, what we ate and what we talked about as Jews in hiding."

The young diarist immediately set aside "Kitty" to begin a new, revised version she planned to call "The Secret Annex," which she hoped to publish as a novel. "The title alone would make people think it was a detective story."[3]

Anne Frank was among thousands of Dutch civilians tuning into Radio Oranje that night who dared to hope that the war would be over soon enough for them to publish their reminiscences. Some picked up their pens and started to jot down notes, inspired by Bolkestein's suggestion. Thousands of others had been recording daily wartime experiences since the first day of the German invasion. "Many people started these diaries from the tenth of May 1940, saying that they never had a diary before," said Kok.

WE TEND TO think of history as a story that is written at some temporal remove from the events described. Was it unusual that Netherlands' Minister had already obtained approval from the Dutch Cabinet to found an institute focused on a war that hadn't even ended? It would be another half a year before the Allies won any significant battles in the Netherlands, and fourteen months before the entire country would be liberated.

The idea to create a study center of the still-unfolding present had been conceived by exiled Dutch-Jewish journalist Loe de Jong, who had become a famous Radio Oranje voice out of London during the war period. Behind the scenes, it was De Jong who had convinced Minister Bolkestein to press for the initiative in the Dutch Cabinet. He also penned Bolkestein's March 29 speech.[4]

He was unaware that, back at home in the occupied Netherlands, another group of historians, led by an economics and social history professor, Nicolaas Wilhelmus Posthumus, was developing a similar plan. Posthumus, a scholar with a strong affinity for archival research, had already established several libraries and study centers to preserve documents about economic and social life, and by the end of his life he'd set up fifteen such institutions.

In 1935, he had established the International Institute of Social History in Amsterdam, "to acquire archival treasures from the possessions of the hunted and the defrauded," in a time of "political crisis and persecution" as the Nazis rose to power in Germany.[5] He'd also supported his wife, Willemijn Hendrika Posthumus–van der Goot, a Dutch economist, journalist, and peace activist, in establishing the International Archive for the Women's Movement, a feminist studies library, also in Amsterdam.

Almost immediately after the Nazis invaded Holland, Posthumus saw the necessity of an archive to collect evidence of the impact of the occupation, and he gave his first lecture on the matter in the May days of 1940. Two years later, he was fired from his professorial post at the University of Utrecht for his anti-fascist attitude. Later the Nazis confiscated large portions of his archives; twelve Rhine barges full of materials from the Social History institute were shipped off in 1944 alone.[6]

This did not stop him; Posthumus was already clandestinely collecting source material about the war and the occupation in 1942; working from an office at a publishing house in Leiden, he planned his "National Office for War Documentation," built a team of board members, and started fundraising.[7] In January 1944, this group met secretly in an Utrecht café to draw up the institution's research and publication plan.[8]

These were not the only historians on the European continent who were already thinking and planning ways to record the war for posterity. Before the 1942 liquidation of the Warsaw Ghetto, a group of writers, journalists, and archivists led by Polish-Jewish scholar Emanuel Ringelblum collected as much material as possible—photographs, memoirs, diaries, poetry, letters, children's drawings—and buried it underneath the ghetto. Today that extraordinary trove, Oyneg Shabes, is probably the world's largest recovered archive of Jewish pre-war and wartime documentation. Similar such collections were discovered from the ghettos of Vilna, Bialystok, Lødz, and Kornvo.

"In hundreds of ghettos, hiding places, jails, and death camps, lonely and terrified Jews left diaries, letters, testimony of what they endured," wrote historian Samuel D. Kassow. "For every scrap of documentation that surfaced after the war, probably many more manuscripts vanished forever."[9] The workers for the Oyneg Shabes realized, wrote Kassow, that they "might be writing the last chapter of the eight-hundred-year history of Polish Jewry."

Isaac Schiper, a leading Polish-Jewish historian of the inter-war period, understood the value of these materials not just for telling the Jewish side of the story, but for establishing the future of history.

"Everything depends on who transmits our testament to future generations, on who writes the history of this period," he told his fellow inmate at Majdanek concentration camp, not long before he was killed. "Should our murderers be victorious, should they write the history of this war, our destruction will be presented as one of the most beautiful pages of world history, and future generations will pay tribute to them as dauntless crusaders. Their every word will be taken as gospel. Or they may wipe out our memory altogether, as if we had never existed, as if there had never been a Polish Jewry, a ghetto in Warsaw, a Maidanek. Not even a dog will howl for us."[10]

The emphasis on collecting witness testimonies, first-hand memoirs, and other personal artifacts attesting to lives of those who would soon die, was not limited to Jewish communities facing extinction. A new form of "history of the present time" arose in the aftermath of World War I, wrote Egyptian-French historian Henry Rousso, out of a need to explain the vast destruction of civilian populations, attacks on noncombatants, massacres of prisoners of war, and demolition of nonstrategic urban centers.

"The terrible question had to be confronted: how to preserve the memory of the dead and disappeared without sepulchers," Rousso wrote, "how to come to terms with the collective losses, give meaning to events that seemed beyond the reach of reason?"[11]

World War II was not merely a military conflict but "an extraordinary assault on civilians," wrote historian Peter Fritzsche. Its ideological violence played out in urban centers, in public squares, on public transportation, and inside businesses and homes. Often, it was characterized by civilian betrayals among neighbors, even within families.

"The war erased whole horizons of empathy," Fritzsche wrote. It fundamentally altered human relationships, and as such, it was intimate, personal, and close to home.[12]

Historians recognized that they had a role in shaping the new "collective memory"—a term coined by French philosopher and sociologist Maurice Halbwachs between the two world wars—as a way not just to record events, but to transform human behavior, to try to heal society. This new way of writing recent history emphasized the "moral witness,"[13] voices of survivors who could speak on behalf of the dead, because the dead had a lesson to impart to humanity: we could do better, be better.

AS BOLKESTEIN HAD promised, the Dutch government founded the Rijksinstituut voor Oorlogsdocumentatie (RIOD), or Netherlands State Institute for War Documentation, (later renamed NIOD), on May 8, 1945, just three days after Liberation. People from all walks of life arrived to donate their notebooks, scrapbooks, collections of battered loose pages, index cards dug up from holes in the ground, unsent letters, drafts of memoirs, personal photographs, and notes scribbled on Monopoly money and cigarette rolling papers.

The Institute's founders actively solicited materials through a radio and poster campaign, too, and went door to door asking people to submit their personal documents. Loe de Jong,[14] who was appointed director of the Institute in October 1945, personally traveled across the country soliciting submissions, including from former collaborators, leaders of the Dutch Nazi party, the Nationaal-Socialistische Beweging or NSB, and the head of the German police in the Netherlands, SS Obergruppenführer Hanns Albin Rauter. Materials could also be dropped at the central office on the Herengracht, or at additional bureaus in The Hague and even in Batavia, the capital of the colony then known as the Dutch East Indies.[15]

The Dutch were the first to actively preserve such materials from the war era, wrote Rousso, but many other European countries quickly followed suit, including France, Italy, Austria, and Belgium. "Everywhere in Europe, often at the impetus of the state and on the margins of the academic world, history institutes and committees were created with the mission of collecting documents and testimony and of producing the first histories of an event that had only just ended," Rousso wrote.[16]

The Netherlands was certainly a pioneer in focusing on the individual, civilian, subjective experience of the occupation period. The Institute's archive represented a radically democratic source: the words of victims and collaborators, bystanders and participants, were all intermingled on the shelves. In the decades since, these sources have allowed countless scholars to explore the human side of war.

At the same time, the Institute became an authoritative center for war history. De Jong, its early director, would write a definitive national history, *Het Koninkrijk der Nederlanden in de Tweede Wereldoorlog*, or The Kingdom of the Netherlands in the Second World War, published from 1969 to 1988 in twenty-six thick volumes, which was preceded by a twenty-one-part television series he hosted, *De Bezetting*, or "The Occupation," broadcast on the country's only TV channel, from 1960 to 1965.

This "historian of the nation," through print and screen, thereby established a national narrative, which "quickly constructed a consensus about the war that was both public and popular," the British historian Bram Mertens argued.[17] It defined the collective memory of the post-war era. The nation's story, by his accounting, went something like this: The Netherlands was an essentially good country, with many resisters, who had struggled against a cruel invader, and ultimately prevailed. There were those who were "right in the war" and "wrong in the war"—in Dutch, *goed en fout,* according to De Jong, in the aftermath of the war.

From this narrative was born the Dutch "myth of resistance," as it has frequently been called, dominated by stories of heroic homespun defiance against Nazi efforts to destroy Holland's tolerant value systems. This dominant myth, however, faced clashing narratives that didn't achieve the same social traction. In that sense, the post-war memory culture was not defined by a single myth, but a "mythscape," as the political theorist Duncan Bell has proposed: a broader discursive landscape in which the nation struggled to define its national character in relationship to its wartime past—and continues to do so.[18]

DE JONG SET up a Diaries Department at the Institute in March 1946, led by his deputy director, A. E. Cohen, who strove to ensure that "all categories of diaries" would be represented among those preserved. This meant he wanted journals written by farmhands and school-teachers, wealthy landlords and poor ragpickers, Nazi sympathizers and communists—people from all walks of life. They "need not be many but they should be various," Cohen wrote.[19]

The Institute would read and review each submitted diary and decide whether or not to keep it, copy it, or return it. Jitty Sjenitzer-van Leening, a former student of languages and history at Leiden, was largely responsible for these choices, said René Kok. She wrote critiques of each submitted work, some as short as a sentence, and others as lengthy as three pages. Every diary handed in to the Institute, whether retained or not, received a number. By the end of the fifties, Sjenitzer-van Leening had logged #1001. Today, the collection consists of more than twice as many.

Anne Frank's diary was assigned #248, but Jitty's summary is one line long, a note that the Institute had "taken or intended to take steps to acquire the original."[20] Anne's father, Otto, had her writings at the time, and he was trying to find a publisher, which he eventually did. *"Het Achterhuis. Dagbrieven van 14 juni 1942 tot 1 augustus 1944,"* by Anne Frank, was first published in 1947. It subsequently became one of the most translated books in the world. When Otto Frank died in 1980, he bequeathed all of Anne's original manuscripts and three photo albums to the NIOD.

René Kok still remembers the day that November when a public notary arrived from Basel, Switzerland, with several boxes containing the materials. "For the Institute, it was like having the original Night Watch or the Mona Lisa in our hands."

I asked him once how he rated Anne's diary in comparison with the two thousand others currently maintained in the NIOD collection. He said that it is still a standout. "There were many people in hiding who wrote their own stories," he said, "but her talent was unbelievable."

The diary of Anne Frank was stored at NIOD for many years in the bank vault, then placed in a special safe in the archive cellar, but in 2019 was transferred to the Anne Frank House museum, just a couple of canals away, where part of it is usually on display.[21]

FOR THIS BOOK, I intentionally chose not to excerpt the best-known diaries of the Institute's collection, by Anne Frank, Etty Hillesum, Abel J. Herzberg, or other worthy diaries that have been previously published in full, such as camp diaries by Loden Vogel, Renata Laqueur, and David Koker. While they all deserve attention, each for its own sake, my goal here was to add new and different voices to the mythscape. Anne Frank's diary is a literary gem, but it is relied on too much to tell the entire story of the Dutch occupation and also the Holocaust. To me, it is one point on a map. More diaries, more perspectives, help us to get a far better sense of this geography and topography.

To find the diaries I would use in this book, I started by asking advice from the experts at NIOD, René Kok and René Pottkamp. Like A. E. Cohen, I was seeking a range of perspectives, not many but various. I wanted to juxtapose and balance voices from the occupation period and provide a rounded view of the war. I also hoped to explore gray zones, territories of moral indecision, and moments of social collapse.

I first asked René Pottkamp, coordinator of the Adopt-a-Diary program, to explore which diaries had already been transcribed and digitized, figuring that would make my translation go faster. At that point, about ninety diaries were finished and uploaded, but many of them were shorter diaries from 1944 and 1945, and I was seeking diaries that spanned the war. I had to expand my options.

Then I dove into the two large files of Jitty's summaries, finding her critiques quite charmingly specific: "Unimportant diary by a schoolteacher," read one. "Trivial commentary, and lots of inaccuracies." Or else, "Excellent diary of a tram conductor. It can be a bit monotonous, but the way he describes the atmosphere is outstanding." René Kok had pasted small yellow Post-it notes on Jitty's reviews of diaries that he found particularly interesting, so I paid special attention to those, which helped me narrow down my choices efficiently.

While I naturally sought well-written diaries, that wasn't my first concern. Some of the diarists were skilled writers, while others were untrained. My primary selection criteria was the diarist's ability to draw the reader into his or her world. Although this book started out as an effort to document "ordinary" lives in wartime, none of the individuals I ended up choosing was generic or quotidian. I found each one's life story to contain twists and revelations that were extraordinary.

Three of the diarists I've chosen are Jewish—one lives through the occupation in hiding, one writes from a concentration camp, and one maintains a life in Amsterdam for a while, as a member of the Jewish Council. Two diarists I've chosen were Dutch Nazis, one of them a police agent in Amsterdam and another the wife of an aspiring Nazi official, a socialite in The Hague. One diary writer is a member of a resistance organization, who saved many lives; the final diarist is a seventeen-year-old factory worker, with no political affiliation.

They are all, in one way or another, crucial documentarians of the Nazi occupation of the Netherlands, and their stories illuminate the private, personal war that every individual faced under the thumb of fascist oppression. Some of these voices have never been heard; others have been, but, in my humble estimation, not nearly enough.

Each of their stories shines a light into a dark corner of the war. We learn of the justifications and denials of a Nazi police chief who kept a rare 3,300-page, eighteen-volume scrapbook of the "New Order." We listen as a Jewish grandfather desperately moves his twin two-year-old grandsons from hiding place to hiding place. We see a young Jewish secretary's ethical struggles as she is forced into the untenable position of passing on the Reich's persecutory measures. We grasp what it takes for a grocer's family to provide shelter to dozens of Jews hidden in the woods. We witness the psychological unravelling of a Dutch Nazi wife, who'd pinned her hopes on an Aryan future that won't materialize. The diaries, running the course of the war, show us life-and-death struggle on a daily basis.

The French literary critic Philippe Lejeune has described the diary as "a daunting face-off with time." It forces us to read history forward, as Judith Cohen suggested, because "it is always on the very crest of time, moving into unknown territory." When we read diaries, Lejeune wrote, "we agree to collaborate with an unpredictable and uncontrollable future."[22]

The Dutch experience of war, its uncontrollable future, began, for most of these diarists, early in the morning hours of May 10, 1940, as the first German Luftwaffe paratroopers descended over Dutch soil, in and around The Hague.

They appeared at first as mere dots. Then, as they fell, separating, they became a kind of choreographed modern ballet midair: a thousand leaps followed by the fluttering of a thousand skirts. Anyone walking outside in the early morning hours and who happened to be looking skyward might have seen them. A sudden rain of sea anemones.

Many observers reported that the aircraft had at first seemed to be headed across Dutch airspace toward Britain. This was to be expected, as the Germans were already at war with England. But the bombers turned sharply over the North Sea and returned. Then there was a sudden barrage of paratroopers, bombs, and several bridges detonated. The morning's tranquility, and the illusion that the Netherlands would maintain the neutrality it had managed to preserve during the Great War, were soon shattered.

The diarists will take it from here. . . .

THE DIARISTS
(in alphabetical order)

Douwe Bakker (1891) was born in Nieuwer Amstel, present-day Amstelveen. In 1918, he became an inspector at the Central Criminal Investigation Department of the Amsterdam Police Department. When the Nazi Party came to power in Germany in 1933, he joined the Dutch National Socialist Movement, Nationaal-Socialistische Beweging, or NSB. During the German invasion, he was one of several Dutch NSB police officers arrested under suspicion of treason, but, once the Germans secured power, he rose quickly in the ranks of the police. In 1941, he was appointed to a special unit to investigate enemies of the German occupying forces, the Inlichtingendienst. In 1943, he celebrated his twenty-fifth year on the job with his wife, Agnes, and their two children. Beginning in 1939, he wrote in his diary nearly every day, paying special attention to the Nazi progress, air and sea battles. Ultimately, his diary amounted to just under 3,300 pages; the last book in the archive ends in October 1943.

Meijer Emmerik (1894) was a Jewish diamond cutter who worked in the Amsterdam diamond industry. He and his wife, Vogeltje (Fietje) Worms, had one daughter, Lena Emmerik (1918), who was married to Sam Vogel, another diamond worker. Lena and Sam's twin baby boys, Max and Loetje, were born in 1940. As a baby, Loetje had tuberculosis, and he required special medical care. Meijer's extant diary, a bundle of loose pages titled *"Mijn belevenissen"* (My Experiences), began in September 1943, when he arrived in the southern province of Limburg, somewhere between the towns of Helden and Beringe, to go into hiding with the help of a Catholic resistance organization. He had kept a diary before that, but he left it in Amsterdam when he fled, so the first part of his surviving diary recaps what he'd written in the lost one.

Inge Jansen[*] (1904) was a member of the NSB, married to NSB member Adriaan Jansen,[†] a tuberculosis doctor. Adriaan aspired to become a part of the German occupation's medical establishment, and Inge engaged in social networking to support his career aims. He briefly became an official at the Nazi Department of Public Health at the Ministry of Social Affairs. Inge wrote in her diary, a single hardcover book with lock and key, starting in 1941. She wrote infrequently and sporadically, and her entries were brief. The diary was largely a record of social engagements, but her contacts included many top-ranking SS occupation officials and NSB leaders.

Mirjam Levie, later Mirjam Bolle (1917) was raised as an observant Jew and became a Zionist in Amsterdam. After school, she met Leo Bolle, who was also a Zionist; they fell in love and got engaged. In 1938, Leo left for Palestine (then a British Mandate territory), and they planned that she would soon follow. In the meantime, she became secretary for the Committee for Jewish Refugees, an aid organization helping German Jews fleeing Nazism in Germany. When the war broke out, she was prevented from leaving the Netherlands, and they could not reunite as planned. Nevertheless, she began writing letters to him to describe daily life during the occupation. Because she could not send them, she collected them, and they became a kind of diary. (Here, she is referred to as Mirjam Levie, which was her name during the war period).

Elisabeth van Lohuizen (1891), and her husband, Derk Jan van Lohuizen, or Dick, owned a general store in Epe, a small town near the

---

[*] A pseudonym.
[†] Also a pseudonym.

Veluwe forest. Elisabeth was active in the Liberal Dutch Reformed Church in Epe. She was forty-eight when the war started and a mother of two grown children. Their son, Gerrit Sander (Ger), and his wife, Siny, were awaiting their first child. Their daughter, Maria Jacoba (Miek), aspired to become a pastor in the Reformed church. Elisabeth started writing her diary on May 10, 1940, and continued to keep a diary through the war, as she became involved in resistance activities, and went on writing after Liberation. In 1982, she and her family members were recognized by Yad Vashem as Righteous Among the Nations. She wrote in her diary nearly every day, ultimately 941 pages, which she kept hidden under a runner on the stairs.

Philip Mechanicus (1889) grew up in a poor family in Amsterdam's old Jewish Quarter; he had seven brothers. He became one of the most respected foreign correspondents in the Netherlands, covering Russia and Palestine as a reporter for a leading national newspaper, *Algemeen Handelsblad*. Later, he was the foreign desk editor and wrote a daily column about world affairs. He was fired in 1941 because he was Jewish. In September 1942, he was arrested for appearing in public without the Jewish star, jailed briefly, and then sent to Amersfoort concentration camp. In November 1942, he was transferred to Westerbork transit camp in Drenthe. He maintained a diary written in little cahiers he got from the camp's school. He wrote fifteen volumes at Westerbork, which he managed to smuggle to his ex-wife (who was not Jewish); thirteen of these survived the war. The first in the NIOD collection was labeled #3.

Ina Steur (1923) was seventeen years old when the war started. She had been raised in Weesp until age fifteen, and then her family moved to Amsterdam in 1938. They lived in Oost, a working-class area on the eastern side of the city. The eldest of ten children, Ina helped support the family as an office clerk at the machine and railway factory Werkspoor, where her father also worked as a sheet metal worker. Upbeat and curious, Ina jotted her observations in a single volume diary with a black-and-white marbleized cover. At first, she hid it in a linen drawer at home, but after she discovered that her siblings were taking it out to read aloud, she hid it under a hatch in the living-room floor.

SHORTER EXCERPTS

In some cases, I have added passages by additional diarists to fill in parts of the story that were not covered by the principal diarists. These excerpts were published originally in a compilation of diary entries in 1954 by RIOD and Veen Uitgevers, *Dagboekfragmenten 1940–1945*, or *Diary Fragments*, selected and edited by Jitty Sjenitzer-van Leening, with an introduction by RIOD director A.H. Paape.

Salomon de Vries Jr. (1894) was trained as a teacher and became a journalist and writer of radio plays. After working as a reporter for the *Groninger Dagblad*, he freelanced for various publications and wrote scripts for a socialist radio station known as VARA, the Association of Worker Radio Amateurs. Discharged in 1941 because he was Jewish, he later went into hiding and survived the war.[1]

Cornelis Komen was a salesman for an English asbestos company based in Amsterdam. Komen was forty-eight years old when the war started. He traveled a lot for business. Although we know his last Amsterdam address, near Watergraafsmeer in East Amsterdam, I was unable to trace his life after the war, and therefore could not print more of his work.

PART I

OCCUPATION

MAY 1940–MAY 1941

1

"PARATROOPERS CAME DOWN EVERYWHERE"

1940

German Armed Forces falling from the sky

Elisabeth van Lohuizen, 48,
general store owner, Epe

FRIDAY, MAY 10, 1940—Last night, we were awakened repeatedly by the roar of planes flying overhead, first at around two o'clock, and later around four. The second time, I went out to look, but I didn't see anything. I thought they were either German or English planes flying to fight their enemies. I tried to fall sleep again, but the noise continued. It was just so restless everywhere. Finally, I was awakened by shouting. At first, I thought it was workmen next door, but then I heard the distinct voice of Mies van Lohuizen.[*] "They can't hear anything!" So I got up and heard, "War! Can't you hear those airplanes?" I found it hard to believe, but I woke Cees, who immediately turned on the radio, and then we heard several messages from the air surveillance. It was a moment I will never forget.

I'd always assumed they wouldn't bother us. We had been completely neutral, and good for the Germans. I also called Miek.[†] For a minute, we all just stood there, stunned. My first thought was, "Our poor soldiers; so many will be killed." If only everyone had joined Church and Peace[‡] after 1918! In recent years, in particular, very few of the faithful have remained.

---

[*] Her sister-in-law.
[†] Her daughter.
[‡] A Dutch Christian pacifist organization, Kerk en Vrede, founded after the First World War.

After dressing, we quickly packed up everything that needed to go or be destroyed. We tossed the alcohol, which had to go.* Too bad because most of it was just sent here a few weeks ago. The workmen, who were at home, were asked to come. They were equally upset. War—we couldn't believe it. The weather was particularly radiant that day; everything in nature was so brilliant. . . . At around six thirty in the morning, . . . we started to see groups of people coming together. No one could believe it. Several branches of the armed services were already assembled at City Hall, awaiting orders. We were hearing constant reports from the air force.

Paratroopers were dropping everywhere, over Rotterdam, The Hague, (Bosje van Poot Park), and other locations. Sometimes they were disguised, wearing Dutch uniforms, clerical clothing, farmer's clothes and even women's dresses. Of course, many were "destroyed" as the radio put it, but oooh so many managed to land. Meanwhile, occasionally we'd hear a dull pop as the bridges across the IJssel and the canals were detonated.

We had a job to do, but our hearts were not in it. There were a lot of people in the store, trying to load up on supplies, but we were unaffected by them. For a while, we were concerned that something might hit us, but we mostly thought about Mother, who was either in Utrecht or Amsterdam, and about Siny.† [. . .] And it was our eldest's birthday that day.

All day, people were gathering in groups saying things like "They'll never take our country; our water defenses are too strong." And, "That's what we'd hoped but now . . ." Around four in the afternoon, the first people arrived in Epe from Oene and Welsum. The sight of these evacuees made me feel miserable—they were carrying children and elderly people on their bikes, along with all their basic necessities. Well, they'd known it was a possibility, but who would have actually believed it would really happen? . . . It was busy in the store all

---

* Rumors were circulating that the German soldiers would steal it.
† Her daughter-in-law.

afternoon, but it was hard to get anything done properly, both at the store and at home. In the evening, we sat in the dark and listened to the radio continuously. We went to bed very late, exhausted.

INA STEUR, 17,
OFFICE CLERK AT
WERKSPOOR FACTORY,
AMSTERDAM

FRIDAY, MAY 10, 1940—At about three o'clock in the morning we were awakened by strange banging sounds. We had never heard anything like it before so we didn't know what it was. I called out to father and asked him. "They're shooting," he said. The popping sounds just continued—one bang after another. So it dawned on me, We are at war.

Mother quickly turned on the radio in the hope that we would hear something, and yes, a few seconds later a strange voice echoed through the room: "Air Patrol Service here. Foreign planes are flying over our country. They are ejecting paratroopers." One message followed by another. Then, Heinkel[*] are spotted here, then other planes there, and the shooting just keeps going, as if it will never end. It is so horribly frightening. All the search lights in the sky, and the burning planes falling.

I feel small and vulnerable. The children[†] are sleeping through everything, including little Annie, who is a year and a half old. I don't understand anything. After a period of time, I go back to bed, and despite all the fear and excitement, I fall back asleep by morning. I wake up late and have to hurry terribly.

At seven o'clock father and I leave the house to go to Werkspoor. And there, we can't believe it: the whole of Oostenburgerstraat is

---

* German bombers.
† Her nine younger brothers and sisters.

crowded with people. We are let in the gate, but [made to enter] one by one. The Volunteer Citizen's Watch is stationed all across the company grounds. Everyone who has German or other foreign nationality is sent to the washroom. The others, including father and me, are allowed to go through, after an extensive check.

The morning is chaotic. Whenever the air raid sirens wail, everyone runs to the cafeteria. We stand there with about two hundred boys, girls, and a few men until we get the sign that it's safe to return to the work floor. The afternoon is just the same.

SATURDAY, MAY 11, 1940—The morning goes the same as yesterday afternoon. I don't believe that very much work is getting done at Werkspoor these days.

At home, I did a quick grocery shop for mother. Then Suze came over. She told me that paratroopers had dropped onto the railways. We wanted to see that. We walk out of Molukkenstraat, where we're halted by the police. When they aren't paying attention, we quickly run toward the tunnel. We stop on the bridge and look all around. But then we hear shots, and we know that we have to drop down into the dike. There are more people there. They tell us that the Germans are sitting in the trees further up, hidden by the dense foliage.

In front of me are a man and a boy; next to me is Suze. We are barely lying down when bullets start to fly past our ears. One bullet falls right behind my foot. The boy in front of me looks up over the dike and gets a bullet right through his throat. Within a few minutes he is dead.

Stiffened with fear, Suze and I look at each other, but there is no time to stand still, because we hear the roar of armored cars. They are our soldiers. As soon as they stop, they begin to shoot and promptly the Germans tumble out of the trees. There were only two.

Meanwhile, Suze and I crawl as quickly as we can to the bridge to take shelter behind the electrical transformer-house. How we succeed in all that noise and chaos, I don't know.

Late in the evening—it is pitch dark outside now—an air raid alarm. That's why father, mother and I quickly take the kids out of bed and dress them. We stand in the hallway, close to one another, but actually we don't know what we are supposed to do.

DOUWE BAKKER, 49,
DUTCH POLICEMAN, AMSTERDAM

SATURDAY, MAY 11, 1940—The Netherlands High Command says that any German soldiers who are found wearing Dutch uniforms (in whole or in part) must be shot immediately, on the spot. Chamberlain has resigned; Winston Churchill is his successor.

At 1:20 a.m., paratroopers descend from aircraft in several places, including Brouwershaven, Krabbendijken, and Soesterberg. Four German armored trains are destroyed, one of which was on the detonated bridge near Venlo.

This morning at 5:20 a.m., I'd been home already for about two hours[*] when we heard rumbling from anti-aircraft guns. We heard two violent explosions, as from high-caliber bombs. I stayed in bed but I couldn't sleep.

Up at 10:20 a.m. again, and I observe two German bombers at a distance of about 10 km southwest; two fighter planes attack. The lead fighter plane seems to be hit and crashes. This is the first aerial combat I get to see.

At 11:10 a.m., another German bomber. Later I heard at the desk that a few bombs had landed on one of the main post offices near the Twentsche Bank at Herengracht near Blaauwburgwal.[†] A house was destroyed with twelve victims. It's terrifying.

At 13:10: Three aircraft visible in the sky here in the South, headed

---

[*] He is apparently working the night shift, which starts at 7 p.m. and ends at 3 a.m.

[†] A Luftwaffe Junkers Ju 88 bomber dropped four bombs on Blaauwburgwal in Amsterdam, killing 44 and injuring 79 people.

Southeast. The last one looks to be a Hunter, but I can't be sure. We hear no air raid sirens. The air patrol service is continuously reporting that sixty to eighty paratroopers have descended in the vicinity of Rotterdam and Leiden. Not one report about the position of our military.

What's the situation in the North? Telephone connection with Leeuwarden seems to have gone dead. They haven't hit the post office, but three houses on the Herengracht were completely destroyed and now the house opposite those has been severely damaged. There will be dead and wounded.

In Rotterdam, several important locations are said to be in the hands of the Germans. The airport, however, seems to be back in our hands again.

When we were sitting down to eat, we heard more shooting. On the street, one can sense great agitation. Every now and then, there's a lot of shooting. After it has been silent for a while, I try to make my way to the bureau. It's almost seven. Suddenly, brisk firing again. On the Galileiplantsoen,* I see a soldier with a rifle at the ready. Allegedly, there are Germans near the railway tracks or the viaduct on Molukkenstraat. I drive back, trying to take a detour to Ridderweg by way of Transvaalkade, but suddenly I hear gunshots ahead of me in the Linneausstraat. People scatter, screaming. I see a few fall in the street near the police station.

I drive up the Transvaalkade. Mysterious goings-on near Amstel Station as well. Allegedly, Germans have been spotted there, too. Later, I hear from Bijlsma that two Germans had already been killed there, and four caught. They were dressed as civilians. In the Rijnstraat, anxious chaos; allegedly, there was a shooting there. A little while later, there's an air raid siren—a passing German bomber.

So, an exciting evening. Otherwise, it is calm, although there is a flood of warnings about suspicious persons. On the way to the bureau,

---

* In Oost, the eastern section of Amsterdam, near the Park Frankendael and a train station.

I also saw refugees coming into the city from the direction of Gooi*—trucks full of furniture, busses full of people; men balancing big boxes of household goods on their bicycles. The army bulletin reports that our army managed to push back at various locations.

SUNDAY, MAY 12, 1940—First day of Pentecost. I slept well for the first time in two days. In the morning, we heard several air raid sirens and planes flying overhead, but we couldn't see anything due to the blanket of clouds. In Amsterdam, there's rising unrest. Hundreds of unverifiable rumors about German activity in the city. Trucks full of soldiers, guns at the ready, are patrolling. It's not really possible to get a clear picture of the situation. Eight air raid sirens throughout the day. Returned to duty at 7 a.m.

I am interned† with Ponne‡ and Harrebomée.§ My weapon is taken from me, and I'm led to police headquarters where I'm brought before Mayor de Vlugt,¶ Attorney General van Thiel,** and Chief Commissioner Broekhoff.†† Had to answer all kinds of questions that were thrown at me. I'm told that I've been selected for internment.

Downstairs, . . . I'm reunited with Ponne and Harrebomée again. We are put into a prison car, under strict surveillance, and taken to Royal Marechaussee‡‡ barracks in Watergraafsmeer. Garrisoned in the throne room. Outrageously proper.

MONDAY, MAY 13, 1940—We spent the entire day in the interrogation room. I was permitted to write a letter home. Desperate thoughts

---

* The Gooi region is southeast of Amsterdam.
† Five members of the Amsterdam police corps were arrested on suspicion of sympathy for the enemy, Bram Harrebomée, Douwe Bakker, and Leen Ponne among them. Across the country, this number was 21.
‡ Leen Ponne, a Dutch police inspector.
§ Bram Harrebomée was a confirmed member of the NSB since 1933.
¶ Mayor of Amsterdam.
** Johan August van Thiel, attorney general for the Amsterdam Court of Appeals and acting director of the police in Amsterdam.
†† Amsterdam's Acting Chief Police Commissioner Karel Henri Broekhoff.
‡‡ Dutch military police.

make it hard to sustain morale. We think of our wives and children. How are they faring? We decide to stay strong and face the trials ahead. The food is quite good, but we are closely guarded, both by military police and a soldier with his carbine at the ready. In the late afternoon, the captain comes to tell us that we're being taken elsewhere. After dark, a military police officer, again with a carbine, puts us in a car and we are taken to the House of Detention. Then we were locked up there, just like any ordinary criminal suspects. . . . We spent the night there.

ELISABETH VAN LOHUIZEN, GENERAL STORE OWNER, EPE

MONDAY, MAY 13, 1940—This morning, in the drizzle, Dick and I biked to Apeldoorn. Nobody wanted to take us by car. Anna had forgotten her ID card, and she needed her eye drops and a few other necessities from home. So we had to go by bike, a trip we haven't made in years. It was okay. At the post office in Apeldoorn, we saw a German soldier standing guard, and we were not allowed to pass that way; we had to go through the Hoofdstraat to the market square. There was another blockade over there, but Dick was allowed to go to the pharmacy.

I stayed behind and chatted with one of the civilian guards. He'd seen German soldiers sitting on the café terraces and had seen Germans in cars. He'd heard that Apeldoorn was already occupied, that there was a battle in Ede, and that there were already evacuees in Apeldoorn, who'd come from Deventer and Zutphen on Friday and Saturday. I must say, I felt something snap when I saw the Germans myself. . . .

Dick returned with the medicine, and he was glad to be back with me. He said the area was full of German soldiers carrying machine guns and riding motorcycles. What is in store for us? We couldn't even buy a cup of coffee, and just biked back home. In Vaassen, they were saying that the Germans could arrive any second. . . .

Ger* got home around four. He had a good trip. He told us that all the bridges have been destroyed, and he saw German occupiers everywhere. We heard then, for the first time, that the rumors we'd been concerned about for a few months were confirmed. The army leadership had been betrayed from inside its own ranks. We also heard that ordinary Dutch citizens had committed acts of betrayal. Germans who have lived here for years fired at our soldiers in both Rotterdam and The Hague.

There were continuous news bulletins on the radio that made the situation seem dire. They announced that the Queen and the government had gone "elsewhere." Where is "elsewhere"? When we listened to our usual program at 10:20 a.m. from England, we heard that the Queen was already in England. The previous day the radio had said that the Princess, the Prince and their children had gone to England. We could understand that, but the Queen? Why didn't she stay?

TUESDAY, MAY 14, 1940—Last night, Ger was on duty again. I slept poorly and got out of bed very early. I couldn't tune in to anything on the radio. Later on, it turned out that some of the stations were down. . . . At 8 a.m., there was special broadcast, which was a morning service by a church minister, who spoke. The subject was, "Our hour of affliction!" One can only wonder what is in store for us—you got the feeling something else is coming.

Throughout the morning, it was terribly busy at the shop. We slogged through, but could not do any bookkeeping because we had to serve so many customers at the counter. Everyone wanted to stock up. Around midday, we received an order to shut the store. Luckily, we could work quietly. Dick had to attend a meeting of the Distribution Council at City Hall from 2 p.m. to 7 p.m. It seems that all businesses

---

* Her son.

must close on Wednesday, so we worked hard to get everything out of the shop, and managed to do so.

Around 7 o'clock, we could finally eat. Miek* had been listening to the radio the entire afternoon. It had regular reports from the air surveillance that were very concerning. They came from Rotterdam, Doorn, Mijdrecht, Sliedrecht, Dordrecht, The Hague, and Leiden. This made us extremely anxious. What does it all mean? The reporters from the ANP† always let their voices be heard so that we won't believe false news from other sources.

Then suddenly at 7 o'clock, there was a special announcement, a moment I will never forget. The commander-in-chief pledged to cease fighting. Rotterdam was already as good as destroyed by the bombing. If our forces continued to fight, he had been warned, The Hague, Amsterdam, and Utrecht would all suffer the same fate. This news moved me so deeply that I began to cry. We were not free anymore. That was because—Oh, we understood it all so well now—of the betrayal of our own people. We could not believe it, and yet it was so.

Everyone was glad that our soldiers would be spared death. But still, to become a part of Germany was terrible. What will the future bring? Poverty for our country. A dark time, and an uncertain future. It was as if there was a death in the family tonight. Everyone who comes in is quiet and anxious. I cannot feel relaxed; I just keep hearing the word "betrayal." We might not have succeeded against such a powerful enemy, but still this betrayal is so vile, it is odious.

WEDNESDAY, MAY 15, 1940—The shop was closed today as well. We should have been able to work, but we didn't feel like it. We only accomplished what really had to be done. Eggs are selling for 1½ cents, chickens for 25 cents each. . . . We have new rationing rules: every person can buy a 400-gram loaf of bread. Over two weeks, one can buy

---

* Her daughter.
† A trusted Dutch news service, akin to the Associated Press or the BBC.

a half a kilo of coffee or 1 ounce of tea, a half a kilo of barley, a half kilo of oatmeal, and a half a kilo of rice, plus a half a kilo of sugar.

Yesterday and today, everyone was angry at the Queen and the government for fleeing. . . . I think it is disappointing that she left. If I were her, I would have stayed, but I cannot judge.

Jan slaughtered chickens and brought home twenty-two of them. Tomorrow, I will go to Mother's house to make conserves. As of Tuesday, we are no longer allowed to bake white bread. We are only allowed to keep rye flour. The clocks will be set to German time from now on. . . .

This evening we had a lot of visitors. Everyone has their own opinions, but they all abhor the betrayal. German officers climbed onto the Moerdijk Bridge in Dutch uniforms, and when they reached our boys, they instructed them how to remove the dynamite under the bridge. The same thing at Westervoort. One of the women called it, "A black page in our history." But our day will come some day. I trust in that.

DOUWE BAKKER,
POLICE OFFICER, AMSTERDAM

TUESDAY, MAY 14, 1940—In the morning, Ponne, Harrebomée and I are placed in a cell for five, with an adjacent cell for sleeping. Our morale is put to an enormous test. The treatment is hellish. Our toilet is a latrine bucket; we have only a tin tankard for water, and a table with two hard wood benches for eating. We can't see outside through the narrow strip of window, because it is frosted over. There's only a small strip of clear glass at the top. Every once in a while, we hear air raid sirens, and we were briefly allowed out to get some fresh air. We have nothing to smoke, and we're not allowed to accept cigarettes from anyone else. We are all very worried about our wives and children. . . . It seems we were all betrayed by anti–National Socialists and Jews. Someone apparently sent in an anonymous letter saying that I was a member of the NSB.[*] That was apparently the only motivation for our internment. Van Thiel and De Vlugt drove the decision.

Ponne is a nervous wreck. Bram is pretty fine; we keep up our courage through continuous conversation. In the afternoon, we play dominoes and do some in-place exercises to try and stay fit. The food is abominable: coarse bread in the morning with a pat of butter, served with diluted milk. In the afternoon, brown beans from a tin can and plain fat. It's almost too disgusting to eat it, but we do so, just to keep up our energy. We now sincerely hope that the German troops advance quickly, because in our current situation, they'll be our liberators. At eight-thirty, it's bedtime, and we're locked into iron cages. Someone will pay for this. This situation is particularly painful; we need a lot of composure to deal with it. But we will get through the night. I'm rather optimistic.

Earlier in the evening, we saw a lot of refugees arriving in busses and cars from the Gooi, and to us that suggests that our army is in retreat. So they will certainly come, but what will happen if they don't come soon? Sometimes, I worry that the Jews will take excessive revenge on the Germans and NSB-ers if they were to find us before the Germans get here, or that the guards will want to take revenge on us.

We had only been in bed for a short time when I noticed a light outside. Bram was already asleep, but Leo saw it. We couldn't figure out what it was. . . . Then we heard steps in the hallway and a jangling of keys. The doors to our cell were opened, and two guards called out to tell us to get up because we would be freed. We were filled with great emotion. What joy!

They say there has been an armistice. The Dutch army could not hold its positions and fled, . . . and an avalanche of German armored

---

[*] Bakker joined the NSB party in 1933; in December that same year, a national ruling (*Ambtenarenverbod*) forbade members of the Dutch civil service (including police) from participation in the party. Bakker became an official member on July 9, 1940.

cars and tanks broke through the Grebbe Line.[*] Many poor young people were slaughtered, it was beastly. This is a crown of thorns that the Democrats will have to wear. Tens of thousands of our chaps dead,[†] and finally the democrats think it's okay to lay down our arms. Five days of terror for our country. But now we are free.

Albert Vis takes us in his police car to headquarters. We're received by De Vlugt, Versteeg and Van Thiel. They grovel and say they didn't know we had it so bad. I told Van Thiel that he was responsible and that I despised him wholeheartedly. He called Boss Versteeg by his first name, and said that Versteeg made the call and it broke his heart when he had to tell me. Anyway, it doesn't matter now. We are free, with our heads held high. . . . We are given our weapons back, and go home by car. Reuniting with the family is moving, seeing Agnes and the children again. Wink and Rie. Jos Fenningen and Catherien, his wife, also arrive. It's wonderful. Our suffering is over. Our day is coming. The city is illuminated, a luxury.

WEDNESDAY, MAY 15, 1940—The royal family has fled. They escaped with the government to London rather shamefully while our soldiers at home were being gunned down. They should feel at home there, among the traitors. What will happen now? I don't know.

I was back on duty again today, on my feet all day long. I witnessed the German troops marching into the city at the Berlagebrug.[‡] Great, just great! What beautiful troops and what artillery! The Maginot Line was broken in Sedan.[§] Hitler's new weaponry crushes everything that stands in its path. The end is near, I can feel it. Rotterdam is a great ruin. Our firemen are all going down there with equipment to help put out the fires.

---

[*] A key defensive line located at the foothills of Utrecht Hill Ridge, a moraine between Lake IJssel and the Lower Rhine River.

[†] It's estimated now that about 2,500 Dutch soldiers were killed during the four-day Battle of the Netherlands.

[‡] A bridge over the Amstel River.

[§] An important military victory for the Germans in France.

THURSDAY, MAY 16, 1940— . . . German time[*] was introduced. At night, everything needs to be darkened again. I had my first contact with a German officer, Lieutenant Ruge of the Field Police. It was a conversation about the German troops marching from Haarlem to Utrecht today. Spent a great deal of the day patrolling the Amstel near the Berlagebrug. German troops were passing by in all kinds of motor vehicles. It was overwhelming. I saw an armored division belonging to Führer Adolf Hitler himself, and many others with large SS markings on the side. . . . In Haven, eight of our NSB men were held in one small cell . . . for three consecutive days without food, water, or the opportunity to use a toilet. . . .

The German army is on the rise. German soldiers, supported by their exceptional air force, have been entering France and Belgium at an unprecedented rate since they broke the Maginot Line. . . . The French armies are withdrawing . . . while there is fierce fighting against combined French and English troops at the Antwerp-Namur Line. What has been achieved in the last six days surpasses everything known so far in military history. Throngs of German soldiers pour across the continent like a gigantic avalanche.

TUESDAY, MAY 21, 1940—Finished the night shift. The weather remains beautiful. In the afternoon, I went to buy a new hat at Swaart's. When I returned home, I had a warm reunion with G. van der Mark, a first lieutenant from the infantry, in uniform. We have both been through a lot. He was in Delft and fought against paratrooper divisions.

Later I saw Schmuck, who told me that he had been arrested; someone also tried to shoot him; there were bullet holes in the front of his own shop. The Gestapo has arrived. Justice will be done. . . . The German army is advancing at a breathtaking pace. Their achievements are incredible. They've taken Amiens and Abberville, on the coast of the English Channel.

---

[*] One hour later.

GERMAN TROOPS ARE ON THE CANAL . . . The verdict on the accursed plutocrats has been delivered. There have been a great number of suicides[*] among the guilty Jews and anti-fascists, including a member of parliament, Prof. van Gelderen,[†] as well as Prof. Bongen and Alderman Boekman.[‡] Lie and deceit, Judaism and capitalism are going to get their comeuppance. The genius of Adolf Hitler will crush them.

---

[*] In the early days of the German invasion, dozens of Dutch Jewish citizens committed suicide, often as whole families.

[†] J. Bob van Gelderen was a member of the Social Democratic Worker's Party (SDAP) and a professor. He and his wife and two children committed suicide on May 14.

[‡] Emanuel Boekman was an Amsterdam alderman, writer, and member of the SDAP and friend of Van Gelderen. After the invasion, he tried to flee the Netherlands and was unsuccessful; then he and his wife committed suicide on May 15.

2

"ONE SHOULD MAKE
THE BEST OF IT"

Ina Steur

The German army bombed Dutch forces into submission within five days. After the decimation of the historic port city of Rotterdam, the Dutch army, with Queen Wilhelmina and the Netherlands' Cabinet leaders safely in Britain, surrendered on May 15, 1940.

Several thousand civilians had attempted to flee before the borders closed, including masses of Jewish Amsterdammers, who'd rushed to IJmuiden harbor, hoping to get on one of the last steamships to England. Only about 2,000 managed to escape. Others, who didn't possess the right visas or diplomatic papers to board the steamships, returned, terrified, to their homes. Seeing no other means of escape, more than 1,000 Dutch people committed suicide—388 in the month of May alone.[1]

Hitler immediately appointed former Austrian Minister of the Interior and Chancellor Arthur Seyss-Inquart as Reichkommisar, or Imperial Commissioner, of the Netherlands. Seyss-Inquart informed the Dutch population that he'd assumed "supreme control of government and civic affairs" ten days after capitulation.[2] Occupying German forces quickly filled the power vacuum left by the departed Dutch leaders, setting up a civil administration, rather than military control, leaving the vast majority of Dutch public servants in place.

For the next nine or ten months, many Dutch people were surprised by the mildness of the occupation.[3] Some historians have described this as a "honeymoon" period between the SS and the nation. One saw this as merely a "wait-and-see approach" while another characterized it as "opportunistic accommodation."[4] Since the German authorities "had not yet revealed their hand," wrote historian

Jennifer L. Foray, it was not surprising that "leading political figures and civil servants expressed their desire to work with the occupiers."[5]

As part of a "long-term racial ideological goal"[6] Seyss-Inquart hoped to Nazify the Dutch people—or rather, he hoped they would self-Nazify,[7]—so they would fall in line without any need for totalitarian control.

To be sure, there were plenty of Dutch supporters of National Socialism already; in some parts of the country, arriving German soldiers were welcomed with flowers, gifts, and local girls' kisses. More than 100,000 Dutch people were members of the fascist NSB party, founded in 1931 and led by the popular Dutch Nazi Anton Mussert. But they never represented more than 4 percent of the Dutch population.[8] There were also many smaller fascist parties across the land, with thousands more members.

After the invasion, a new party, Nederlands Unie, emerged with the goal of joining the Germans to build a new society in line with National Socialist ideals, while simultaneously preserving Dutch cultural values and traditions. Within a year, some 800,000 Dutch people had registered. Later, as many as 30,000 Dutch young people would volunteer to join the Waffen-SS.

Hein Klemann, a Rotterdam-based economic and social historian, explained that many Dutch administrators and much of the population had an essentially defeatist attitude in the early stages of the war. Nazi Germany had successfully invaded France, Belgium, the Netherlands, and Scandinavia. By the summer of 1940, all had capitulated to Hitler's army. Mussolini controlled Italy and Franco Spain; Eastern Europe was overrun by the Reich. The only holdout at that point was Britain, which could not match Germany's military might.

"The war was lost," Klemann wrote with his co-author, Sergei Kudryashov, in the 2012 book, *Occupied Economies*. "Those thinking that the United Kingdom still had a chance to win lived on another planet." Hendrik Colijn, five-time former Dutch Prime Minister, penned an essay arguing that his countrymen should expect Berlin to decide their future perhaps until the year 2000.[9]

Figuring this to be likely, Dutch companies stepped into line with the Reich. By the end of 1943, the nation's industry had fulfilled 84.4 percent of German orders—more than any other occupied country, including France, which achieved 70 percent.[10] By the spring of 1944, more than 40 percent of Dutch industry worked for the Germans.

Dutch legal historian Joggli Meihuizen, author of 2003's *Noodzakelijk kwaad* (Necessary Evil), found that leading manufacturers in the Netherlands also agreed to German demands very quickly. "The first business sector to give in reluctantly was the metal sector," he wrote. "Thereafter, the building and textile industries, the Dutch Railways, and finally the major weapons industry followed in rapid tempo."[11]

The "cardinal decision" to comply came when the occupation was no more than a few weeks old. In late May 1940, "meeting after meeting took place with German authorities and leading industrialists," Meihuizen wrote. The participants included Werkspoor chairman Marinus Hendrik Damme Sr., Dolph Kessler, the founder and director of leading Dutch steel manufacturer Koninklijke Hoogovens, and Dirk Christiaan Endert Jr., director of the Rotterdam-based shipbuilding company, Rotterdamsche Droogdok Maatschappij, as well as directors of the Fokker aircraft factory and shipbuilding and ship-repair giant Wilton-Fijenoord. All agreed to "align" with the Reich's business goals.

Werkspoor did so within two weeks. On May 28, 1940, Damme penned two letters indicating his clear intention to cooperate. The first, written to SS officials, helpfully provided them with an overview of Werkspoor's employees and current projects, including defense orders it was processing for the Dutch government (two cruisers, floodlights, and airport tankers) as well as its weekly capacity for building railway wagons and locomotives.

A second letter, circulated to all members of the Metal Guild in North Holland and Utrecht, encouraged them to follow his example. "You would oblige us by sending it soon," he added. A post-war investigation of his behavior found that both Damme, as an individual, and

Werkspoor, as a company, had cooperated with the Nazis "from the outset" and "with a certain eagerness." It also found that Werkspoor's contributions had substantially strengthened the Nazi war machine from early on.[12]

WORKERS FOR THESE industrial companies, however, didn't necessarily strive to "align" with National Socialism. Many were subscribed to one of the three major communist and socialist parties—the Communist Party of the Netherlands, the Social Democratic Workers Party, and the Revolutionary Socialist Workers Party—which in July 1940 were placed under the "supervision" of the NSB, but not outlawed until the following year.[13] Labor activists continued to organize and produced a slew of widely read clandestine newspapers, such as *De Waarheid* (The Truth, put out by the communist party), *Het Parool* (The Watchword), and *Vrij Nederland* (The Free Netherlands), among the most read.

Ina Steur's family, working-class Catholics, were similar to thousands of others who served the metal and shipbuilding industries in Oostenburg, an industrial wharf area known today as the Eastern Docklands, not far from the Jewish Quarter. Werkspoor, founded as a repair shop for steam engines in the 1820s, was by the 1930s the largest steel manufacturer in the country, building bridges, locomotives, and freight carriages. It was also Europe's foremost supplier of diesel engines. Its headquarters were in Amsterdam, but much of its manufacturing was based in Utrecht.

In the decades just prior to the war, Oostenburg had the "dynamism of a bustling harbor city," wrote Dutch historian Geert Mak. "Worn out freighters, a tug boat belching smoke as it tows a line of barges carrying cargo. Ferries moving to and fro; a ship laden with ore, lying low in the water."[14]

Ina Steur came from a large, poor family, which was struggling to get by in a post-Depression economy. Her father, Hein, worked for the company, as did several of her cousins. But his income couldn't sustain a family with nine children. Ina went to work after finishing primary school. "The day after you turned fourteen, you had to go to work," she said in a 1995 interview.[15] As the eldest child (her mother would give birth to a tenth in 1942), Ina was expected to help raise her siblings. When she was ten years old, and her mother was hospitalized with sciatica, "I took care of the whole family for weeks."[16]

She remembered her family home as "full of love and care," because her parents were devoted to one another, and her close family bonds "filled me with warmth and joy." Her father, Hein, she wrote, could sing anything the pianist was bound to play, from classical to popular music, and she remembered his "beautiful baritone—a voice that is enshrined in all of our DNA and collective memory."[17]

She also found time for her private joys, "reading and writing stories and poems, and writing in my diary. I loved beautiful clothing, scents and colors."

It is clear from her diary entries where her political sympathies lay—positions she expressed primarily through wry sarcasm about the German invaders. Her focus in her diary was on how the occupation affected her family, her work, and her social life. Years later, she would tell an interviewer that the Nazis stole her youth. But in the moment, she seemed to want to get as close to the action as possible—so close a German bullet tore through the neck of a boy behind her. As such, she played a crucial role as a bystander and eyewitness—but as a seventeen-year-old, she was largely impotent in the face of war.

ANTI-SEMITIC MEASURES DIDN'T fall into place immediately. It wasn't until October 1940 that a Nazi ordinance required all Dutch public servants to submit paperwork concerning their "racial" heritage. Gentiles filled in Form A, the "Aryan Declaration." Those with Jewish ancestry had to use Form B, non-Aryan, which required them to indicate whether they had one, two, three, or four Jewish grandparents.

The registration process would become crucial to the Nazi genocidal program, but for the vast majority of people who registered at the time, this act seemed to be relatively harmless. "We signed, but none of us really knew what we were doing," wrote historian Abel Herzberg.[18] Dutch civil servants then marked index cards in the population register and identity cards with a "J." A month later, all Jewish civil servants were fired. In January 1941, the Aryan Declaration was mandatory for all Dutch citizens.

In Amsterdam, where eighty percent of the country's Jewish population lived, the tensions were rising. People knew what had happened in Germany: to ordinary Jewish citizens, to businesses, to synagogues. They'd heard horrifying stories from the German Jewish refugees who'd fled their homeland to the Netherlands since 1933.

Such nightmares were about to play out in Dutch streets. Hans Böhmcker, the capital's top SS official, an avid anti-Semite who reported directly to Seyss-Inquart, asked city officials to provide him with the "precise boundaries of the Jewish neighborhoods," and notified Berlin that his intention was to "arrive at some form of ghetto."[19]

Amsterdam mayor Willem de Vlugt felt the idea was "unpalatable," but nonetheless instructed his staff to draw up such a map. Böhmcker was impatient, however, sensing that the Dutch public servants were dragging their feet. He wanted to foment a disturbance that would make the process of segregation and ghettoization move faster.

Local Dutch Nazis were invited to watch anti-Semitic propaganda films and were given "Jews Not Wanted" signs to post in local cafés and shops.[20] Members of the NSB's paramilitary unit, known as the W.A.,* started beating up Jews in public places. Members of the National Socialist Dutch Workers Party forced their way onto a tram in the city center demanding that the conductor force all Jews off. When he refused, the group assaulted passengers they assumed were Jewish.[21]

Fighting erupted in early February, when Dutch Nazis infiltrated the Rembrandtplein, close to the Jewish Quarter, distributing signs

---

* *Weerbaarheidsafdeling* or "Resilience Department."

and telling pub owners and shop keepers to eject Jewish patrons; off-duty German soldiers would enforce these actions, when necessary, promised Böhmcker.

The following Monday, rumors circulated that the Dutch Nazis planned to attack the Jewish Quarter. Jewish men and boys armed themselves with whatever they had on hand—iron bars, hammers, clubs, rubber hoses—and prepared to defend their neighborhood. The men formed self-defense groups, one with about fifty fighters, and they trained and worked in shifts, wrote historian Ben Braber. On February 11, about forty uniformed National Socialists marched into the Jewish Quarter across the Amstel River at the Zwanenburgwal. Jewish fighters were already there, at the ready, hidden in doorways and alleys around the Waterlooplein market square.[22]

3

"ANGER BLAZED IN YOUNG HEARTS"

February 1941–March 1941

SALOMON DE VRIES JR., 48, JEWISH JOURNALIST, AMSTERDAM

FEBRUARY 1941—It began Sunday evening. A group of NSB-ers and their crazy bitches and, allegedly, several German soldiers walked along the Jodenbreestraat. The ladies used axes to smash all the windows while passing. It was dark and quiet on Jodenbreestraat. The windows shattered, clattering into the shop displays and onto the street. That was the first assault on the Jewish Quarter, supposedly a "demonstration" to show the Jewish proletariat how they felt about them, that was the surprise. The gals were screeching and the guys were roaring with laughter all the while.

The elderly trembled in fear, young hearts blazed in anger. The director of the Tip Top theater had the lights outside turned off and the gates closed. Director Kronenberg took the stage to beseech the audience not to leave the theater during the intermission. There was a feeling that they were in the midst of a pogrom.

Monday, a sense of resilience was awakened, and the young Jews began to organize themselves. There were fellas on Jodenbreestraat, trained wrestlers and boxers, who dared to look these men in the eyes. By Monday afternoon and evening, they fought back, using iron rods or whatever they could get their hands on. But some of the NSB-ers who showed up were carrying revolvers. Several people were killed.

Tuesday, the neighborhood seethed. A number of groups formed. Scared people and brave people. The scared drifted off, but the courageous stayed. There was fighting on the market square. Guys from the Jordaan area showed up to support them if it was needed. It was needed.

It's better if we take up your cause than you do it, said one of them.

Doesn't matter, answered a young Jew. Whether you do it or we do it, we'll be blamed.

On the corner of Zwanenburgwal, near the Tram 8 stop, a man selling mussels was yelling NSB slogans. A pair of strong Jordaaners picked him up, beat him, and threw him and his cart into the canal.

Another NSB-er shouted insults down from the second floor of an apartment building. A few men went upstairs, smashed things up, and put him in hospital for at least a few months.

On Tuesday and Wednesday nights, shots were fired and there were casualties on both sides. The Green Police* began what they called an investigation. In truth, they helped the NSB members. The brawls lasted through the night.

On Wednesday, the Jewish Quarter was closed off from the rest of the city. The bridges were hauled up and Amsterdam traffic cops were posted at key positions. People were saying that Green Police with ma-

---

* These are members of the German *Ordnungspolizei*, or Order Police. Because they wore green uniforms, many people referred to them as the "Green Police." Dutch police uniforms were black, and Dutch police officers were often called "Black Police."

chine guns stood guard within the Jodenbuurt. The Amsterdam police did nothing! They just closed the neighborhood. On whose orders? No one is allowed in or out. What's going to happen inside that restricted zone? . . .

Now it's Wednesday, ten thirty p.m. It was incredibly silent in the city all evening. Those few who walked the streets spoke very softly. Hardly any passengers on the trams. There is a sense of menace in the city. The atmosphere feels tense. There is fear and anger, and hate dominates. People are waiting. But nobody can say precisely what for. Rumors are going around that the NSB are preparing for attacks in Zuid. People are on their guard.

DOUWE BAKKER,
POLICEMAN, AMSTERDAM

TUESDAY, FEBRUARY 11, 1941—In a communication issued to the corps today, the German SS High Command and Police Führer outlined the relationship between the Dutch police and the W.A. The police will offer the W.A. protection, but not to the extent that one would get the impression that the W.A. is part of the police. All actions must be taken in mutual cooperation. Members of the W.A. may not bear weapons, but may act when there are potential acts of war. . . .

At 9:45 a.m., Bram calls and announces that there has been fierce fighting in the Jewish Quarter. Two comrades' shops were destroyed on the Kromme Waal, and then the W.A. was summoned and they penetrated into the Jodenbuurt. Fights ensued in which one W.A. man was quickly and seriously injured. The German Schutzpolizei also engaged; there was shooting, and then the Jewish Quarter was cordoned off.

It is foggy and yet every now and then we hear the roar of engines and, here and there, the firing of anti-aircraft guns.

WEDNESDAY, FEBRUARY 12, 1941—The night quiet; the weather pretty good; slightly colder. It now seems that there was a disturbance last night in the Jewish Quarter. A few hundred Jews stormed Comrade Linssen's paint shop on the Oudeschans and got in, even though it was heavily barricaded. They used cleavers, hammers and axes. The door was bashed down with an iron-studded wooden post. Old Linssen himself was beaten unconscious, but then help arrived. W.A. and German Schutzpolizei intervened.

The [Dutch] police did not show up. A group of more or less forty W.A. men was attacked by hundreds of mad Jews by the playground, so near the police bureau, on J.D. Meijerplein at around seven. A fierce fight ensued. Without the police even raising a finger, the W.A. and the Jews battled for about twenty minutes. Someone hit comrade Koot from the W.A. on the head with an iron bar. He will probably die. A Jew sat on top of him and hit him anywhere he could manage to hit. W.A. men have beaten this Jew to a pulp.

A car also drove through the crowd and the Jews jumped onto it. The driver, probably one of the National Socialists, drove full throttle into the crowd. One person was run over and dragged along. This man (a comrade) may also have died. The German police then closed off the Jodenbuurt between the Piet Heinkade, the Amstel and Nieuwmarkt by pulling up the bridges, and closing the streets to all traffic. No one is allowed in or out. There's a curfew from 7 p.m. to 8 a.m. We have received a heavier shift, namely, we have to work until 11 p.m., and in uniform. We're once again required to wear helmets.

ELISABETH VAN LOHUIZEN, GENERAL STORE OWNER, EPE

WEDNESDAY, FEBRUARY 12, 1941—There are already disturbances in Amsterdam. The NSB-ers are dragging Jews and anyone wearing Queen's pins from restaurants, and beating them up. The boys from

Kattenburg and from across the IJ have gone to support the Jews, but there are fatalities. The bridges to the Jewish Quarter have now been raised, and nobody is allowed in or out. Several NSB-ers were thrown in the canals. There is palpable tension in the streets and the Jews are blamed for it.

DOUWE BAKKER,
POLICEMAN, AMSTERDAM

FRIDAY, FEBRUARY 14, 1941—The night was quiet, the weather was pretty good, but foggy, clearing up later, with mild temperatures and a southeasterly breeze. W.A. sergeant Koot has died. He was so badly beaten by the horde of Jewish beasts that he was unrecognizable. That's the umpteenth victim on our side. Where are the victims among our opponents? . . .

Yesterday afternoon, Jews from the barricaded area around the Diamond Exchange convened a meeting, at which Abraham Asscher[*] spoke. About 4,000 Jews were in attendance; there had to be two groups. Asscher warned his audience that any future attempt at revolt would have most serious consequences. He told them that all weapons, of any kind, should be handed in at the Meijerplein police bureau on Friday. Many weapons were handed in. Meanwhile, many Christians have indicated that they want to leave the neighborhood.

SUNDAY, FEBRUARY 16, 1941—The night is quiet again; the weather bad, rainy and cold.

I went into town with [a friend] in the afternoon to see the Dutch SS parade. When we arrived at the Kleine-Gartmanplantsoen, from which they were supposed to depart, we found that most of them had already left. Later, we watched them march along the Rokin. There

---

[*] Owner of one of the largest diamond factories, and a Jewish community leader.

were not many, a few hundred. Afterward, we went to De Kroon for coffee. This café has now also been declared closed to the Jews, so we sit where the ostentatious Jews used to sit. Lots of National Socialists, W.A. and SS in the city today.

ELISABETH VAN LOHUIZEN, GENERAL STORE OWNER, EPE

WEDNESDAY, FEBRUARY 19, 1941—One NSB man was killed during the riots in Amsterdam and of course they blame the Jews. Someone said in a eulogy that thirty Jews attacked him, but he will surely be avenged.

FRIDAY, FEBRUARY 21, 1941—The Jews are not allowed to use the slaughterhouse anymore in Amsterdam and they will make sure that there won't be any Jewish butchers anymore within two months. Now, Jews are also not allowed to take up a course of study at the university. These men act as if they are already the bosses in our country.

SALOMON DE VRIES JR. JOURNALIST, AMSTERDAM

SUNDAY, FEBRUARY 23, 1941—At first, it was quiet after the horror show of the burial of W.A.-man Koot, but the locals knew that something else was coming. After all, the trick is old and familiar. . . . The Jewish-owned cafeteria on Rijnstraat,[*] which already attracted

---

[*] He's referring to the Koco ice cream parlor, which had two locations in Amsterdam, one on the Rijnstraat and another on the Van Woustraat (Braber, 105).

the catastrophic attention of the W.A. thugs several times, has another branch on Van Woustraat. Thursday evening, about twenty of
the thugs moved in and demanded entry there. The owner and his
staff managed to keep the uniformed mob outside and locked the
door. Then the Green Police showed up and they shot off the locks
with a revolver. The W.A. barged in, but the owner, who immediately
understood their aim, sprayed them with ammonia and they quickly
peeled off. After a little while, the Green Police came back wearing gas
masks. They shot, hit and destroyed . . . The W.A. was free to do its
thing. Then the owner and his entire staff were arrested. They're still
in jail; the case is closed. . . .

That was the prologue. This drama played out yesterday and
again today in the Jewish Quarter. Yesterday (Saturday) afternoon,
the Green Police suddenly showed up with police vans and took all the
young Jewish men captive. They invaded homes claiming they were
searching for weapons. They forced everyone out of the Tip Top Theater and loaded the young Jews into trucks. They ordered them to run
from one place to another and then wait with their hands up, until
another truck came.

That's how it was yesterday from 4:45 p.m. until 6:30 p.m., and
that's how it was again today (Sunday)! The Amsterdam police had to
shut down the whole district so that the Greens could do their work
unhindered. Jaap told me that one of the policemen almost cried in
anger and outrage, but what could he do?

Jaap said again, "Now, I have seen what kind of beasts they
are, how they whip and kick. *The Veensoldaten,* exactly as in *The
Veensoldaten!*"[*] It's the Jewish proletariat who are whipped and
beaten so badly. Only because they didn't want to helplessly put up
with the terror of Mussert's crooks; only because they wanted to defend themselves. It has nothing to do with Jewish innocence or Aryan

---

[*] *De Veensoldaten* was one of the first eyewitness accounts of a concentration camp, written
by the German actor and director Wolfgang Langhoff, published in 1935, and translated
into Dutch.

culpability. It's about people. And no one is doing anything. No one can do anything.

MONDAY, FEBRUARY 24, 1941—Notices posted all over the Jewish Quarter read "The Crackdown Is Over!" The families of young people who were arrested should not worry, because the "hostages" (as they call those who have been arrested) are in Schoorl. The residents of the Jewish Quarter have been urged to go about their business as usual.

Throughout the neighborhood, great sorrow and bitterness. The multitudes of Amsterdam are simmering with anger and hate. Now people see, even if they've only heard about it. Now they know that the stories that once seemed unbelievable, are true in every sense.

Tonight, messengers biked through Jodenbreestraat and the surrounding streets and alleys, crying out: Keep a supply of water! Tomorrow the workers from the gas and electrical and utility companies will go on strike! Protest against the persecution of the Jews! We can't but wait. Tomorrow we will see. Is the poster that reads, "Don't worry" a result of the Germans' fear of the response of the Amsterdam workers?

INA STEUR,
FACTORY OFFICE CLERK,
AMSTERDAM

TUESDAY, FEBRUARY 25, 1941—General strike of the big companies such as gas, electrical, tram, and train personnel, ship builders, Fokker,[*] Werkspoor and others. Businesses will be closed at ten-thirty.

This afternoon I went into the Indischebuurt,[†] where it was terri-

---

* An aircraft manufacturing company.
† A neighborhood in the eastern part of Amsterdam.

bly busy. In the Javastraat, there's a pub owner who is a member of the NSB. Some kids had thrown bricks and smashed out his windows. In the Wagenaarstraat, another NSB-er who had a photo of Uncle Adolf hanging in the window had his windows smashed too, and that beautiful portrait torn. Everywhere, there was still fighting and crowds gathering. On the Dapperplein, there was a potato seller who refused to shut his shop, and a group of women went and stood in front and wouldn't move until he locked it up and went home. There was still a whole band of people there in front when suddenly a Green Police officer came riding up on a motorcycle . . . and the whole group went running, except for a few boys—the Heroes!! At about six p.m., it was announced widely that we were not allowed on the street after half past seven. Really comfy, huh?

WEDNESDAY, FEBRUARY 26, 1941—Eight thirty in the morning at the factory, all the workmen stood outside talking. They disagreed about what to do because we had said it was going to be a twenty-four-hour protest strike and now we were supposed to start working. One says, I'm going back home. And another said, Come on guys, let's go into the factory. That's how it was everywhere; people just didn't know what they should do, and that was mainly because there really is no organization to this all anymore.

- One third went home
- One third stayed at the factory
- One third just stood in front of the factory gate

At about nine-thirty, the factory council and the board of directors had a conference and they decided then that we would strike until Feb. 27, at eight-thirty.

That was greeted with general enthusiasm. I was back home at around ten a.m. By midday, I went outside and saw a huge crowd of people, so I ran over. A group of men and boys were trying to lift up a tram. I threw myself into the group and helped with the lifting. Yes, very slowly it went up and over. There it lay, the conductor lying close to Mother Earth. A hurrah arose from the crowd, followed by the cry "Green Police!" and then everyone ran away.

I hid in the entrance of a shop, and that's why I could see what happened next. A car stormed up with about a dozen Green Police inside. They jumped out with their rifles at the ready, running up the Insulindeweg, shooting at imaginary perpetrators. Those idiots couldn't shoot a sitting duck, so that was not so bad. They set off across the area hoping to find something, but found nothing. At one o'clock, the tram was finally hoisted over.

At three o'clock, I went to the Dapperstraat for groceries. There, I saw another police vehicle with a dozen officers. They stopped at the corner of the Commelinstraat and detained a man. Immediately, the wagon was surrounded by residents and bystanders. The Krauts got angry, and one of them started to threaten us with his handgun. Nobody was very impressed. He took something out of his pocket that looked like a box of cigarettes. He got out his lighter, held it to the box, and then threw the box into the crowd. We rushed off in all directions and within a split second, the whole street was empty. Just in time, because that thing made a thunderous bang. It was a hand grenade! Then the rotten bastard had a big grin on his face when he walked right into the middle of the street. He raised his hand, as sarcastically as possible, as if to say, "I let you get away, didn't I?" Then he stepped back into his car and rode off, together with his mates and the man that they'd picked up.

For the whole rest of the day, they patrolled the streets everywhere and stood watch. In the evening we heard that everyone had to be at home by seven thirty p.m. Nice, huh? The curfew is going to last for five days, and on the sixth day we have to be home at eight thirty and a few days later at nine o'clock and so on, back to midnight. Woe to whoever isn't home by then. They'll be picked up by the Green Police and taken to some place like the City Theater and forced to do some strange kinds of exercises, like marching up and down or that sort of fun, and if they make a wrong move they'll be corrected by a bayonet. We hear that such antics go on from seven thirty at night until four o'clock in the morning.

ELISABETH VAN LOHUIZEN, GENERAL STORE OWNER, EPE

WEDNESDAY, FEBRUARY 26, 1941—A protest strike started in Amsterdam yesterday, because they deported many Jews, with the excuse that Jews killed a W.A.-man. Martial law was declared, trams were halted, all stores were closed, and nobody was allowed on the street after seven-thirty. Tonight the papers reported that the Germans have retaken command, and martial law was declared in the whole of Noord Holland. Everyone had to go back to work. Anyone who continued to strike would be punished with fifteen years in prison; anyone working at the "essential companies" could get the death penalty. . . .

Whenever a few people gathered anywhere, they'd shoot and throw hand grenades. One policeman told Miek that it was a spontaneous strike. Rumor is that Verkade and the Fokker plant were also on strike. We heard that there was tension all across Holland.

SALOMON DE VRIES JR., JOURNALIST, AMSTERDAM

WEDNESDAY, FEBRUARY 26, 1941—To the fighters! For now, this is what they are—they who have proved themselves worthy of this badge of honor. For justice, for the love of mankind, for a fair, true society.

These are the facts. The strike began on Tuesday. A few municipal utility companies started it. The city sanitation department, the electricity companies, the gas and water services, tram. It spread like an oil stain. In factories, workplaces and offices of individual companies, people cried: "Strike!" And then throngs of workers, office workers, workshop girls, left their workplaces.

The message went by word of mouth across the city: "They're striking everywhere, the Amsterdam dockworkers, the shipbuilders, De Vries Lenz, Fokker! The ferries are stopped! The trams aren't running!"

People flocked into the streets. Many of them wept with happiness and emotion. They cried out to one another. They talked, offered instructions. Everyone had the feeling that he had to *do* something! *Do something,* even if it was only to trot from one group to another!

Empty streets. No trams, almost no cars. Many workers and drivers for both large and small shipping companies joined the strike. Almost everywhere the shops were closed. Strike—a general strike! Against persecution of the Jews, against the inhumanity, against the W.A. men and Mussert's crooks taking over our streets.

Empty streets. Until ten o'clock. Then, all of a sudden, one of the trams rode out of the Kromme Mijdrechtstraat depot. The public stormed over to the depot from the Amstellaan and the Rijnstraat. This morning another one had already tried and failed. A driver from Tram 16 tried to drive out, but an old conductor had thrown himself over the rails in front of the tram!

"Drive then, if you dare, fascist! Traitor!"

The man had *not* dared and just drove back. And now, suddenly again!

Hundreds of tram drivers and conductors were in the depot. A director stood in front of them, making a speech full of threats. He was an NSB-er. But his speech wasn't effective. The men continued to stand on the rails. Then the NSB-er summoned a policeman to clear the rails. The policeman first checked with a senior police officer, who was standing further down. Then it happened, the rails were cleared and the tram rode out.

Again, all kinds of messages traveled by word of mouth: "We've

lost the strike! All the trams have driven out of the Havenstraat depot!" It was a lie, spread by the fascists, but it worked. There were
men with two decades of service behind them among the strikers, and
they all knew what they were risking . . . But the rumor was quickly
determined to be untrue and put to rest. "Back!" came the call. "It's
not true! They're still on strike in the Havenstraat! Get the boys back!
Get the trams off the street!"

People ran from traffic island to traffic island. There were some
tram drivers who didn't want to believe the signals and kept driving.
Others nodded: understood! Right in front of my house I saw a Tram
25 pass by. Several men from the sewage company—strikers—flocked
into the street and sat down on the rails. The driver rang his bell. The
men ignored him. He rang the bell again.

—Do you really want to ride while we all strike?

The tram returned to the depot.

At around ten-thirty, various trams returned via Amstellaan to
the depot. Trams 3, 5, 18, 22, a strange sight to see, as they normally
run down different routes! Across Berlagebrug and back into the depot. They went out on Kromme Mijdrechtstraat, and then back in at
Amsteldijk. We won. Silence returned! The streets were empty. People
ran through the streets; people who had never met before, embracing
one another. We've won!

—We're going to win, said an old driver who joined me walking
down Rijnstraat. We must win. The public has to understand: we are
not fighting for ourselves!

The public does understand it, thank God! Some people wanted
to jump on the few trams that were running, but they were either held
back or dragged off by those who had more understanding and feeling
and a sense of solidarity.

Empty streets! And all these people, people who spoke their minds
for the first time in months, really shouted out their opinions, defi-
antly, self-assuredly. This is our day! Our day! Our day! "We will show
them who is boss here!" a man shouted across the crowded Willinkplein
square.

Douwe Bakker,
policeman, Amsterdam

WEDNESDAY, FEBRUARY 26, 1941—The night is quiet, the weather is good, colder and freezing. When I cycle to the office through Sarphatistraat, I don't see any trams at first, but then I start to see more and more. . . .

Later in the morning, it turns out that troublemakers are still trying to disrupt everything; trams are stopped; the public has been told, sometimes threatened, not to take a tram. There are big gatherings in different neighborhoods, resulting in the Germans taking action. DEAD AND INJURED. In the Jordaan, the Kinkerbuurt, and on Albert Cuyperstraat and its surroundings, hand grenades and rifle fire are being used. A lot of casualties. On Van Woustraat, some twenty of those wretches tried to stop a tram; at that exact moment a German car full of soldiers arrived. Four men were seized. Apparently there was shooting, but no casualties.

In the afternoon, civil authority was withdrawn and handed over to Christiansen,[*] the military commander. General Schumann entrusted Mag Bendzko with the supreme command of the police, giving him orders to quell the disturbances. Henceforth, the entire police force, with the exception of the purely administrative female personnel, must be employed continuously, taking breaks to eat in turns.

When I'm home for dinner, we see a column of the German SS passing by on Radioweg. It's equipped with light cannons and soldiers holding machine guns.

Straw bags are delivered to the bureau for beds, but I doubt whether they'll be used. After half past seven, no one is allowed to be on the street anymore. . . . Bergsma, Bonarius, Berends and I play cards (bridge) in the evening. Jansen tells me that the Germans are taking lots of rich Jews away in police cars from the Beethovenstraat

---

[*] Friedrich Christiansen, Supreme Commander of the Wehrmacht in the Netherlands.

area. It's about time. According to him, seven people have been killed in recent months and sixty or more seriously injured. . . .

We spend the night at the bureau, and we don't get much sleep. From 6.30 a.m. to 8 a.m., I sleep a little, but it isn't much. I was reading and writing a letter until half past three. The night is quiet, by the way. After dark, we didn't hear any British planes.

THURSDAY, FEBRUARY 27, 1941—Today, as far as is known, work has resumed everywhere. The Democrats' friends set up a useless riot, leaving nine dead, or probably more, and sixty wounded. From 9 a.m. to 10 a.m., I go for a bike ride through the district. It is very cold again and there is a strong wind from the southeast. The streets are peaceful. But there are still patrols. The morning paper contains an official announcement about the incidents in Amsterdam and Christiansen's proclamation. . . .

During the course of the day, our shift becomes such that two of us are always at the bureau. So it's sixteen hours on and eight hours off. Bergsma goes home at night to look after his wife, who isn't so well, mentally speaking. Bonarius and I will stay. So that is from yesterday morning at 9 a.m. to 8 a.m. tomorrow, all within 47 hours. It's still okay. Bonarius downs a cognac and then we'll sleep. Everything is quiet in the city all day long. Work has resumed, but we notice a distribution of pamphlets for another strike that's planned for March 6.

WEDNESDAY, MARCH 19, 1941— . . . Had a 10 a.m. meeting this morning with the Police Senator Schröder,[*] along with comrades Ponne and Harrebomée at the Beauftragte.[†] It was a two-hour interview, during which we discussed various situations within the Amsterdam police and the attitude of the various leaders. Later, Major Leisner and Major Arnele joined in these discussions. Senator Schröder works for the Chief Commissioner. We felt it was a most satisfactory meeting. We

---

[*] Walther Schröder was a German SS official who worked briefly in the Netherlands in 1941 as police president and SS-Oberführer.

[†] Reichskommissariat, or German administration of the Netherlands.

expect there to be major changes: the reorganization of the police department must be in effect by January 1, 1942. . . .

In the evening, there was very strong attendance at the group meeting; the mood is good.

TUESDAY, MARCH 25, 1941—Restful night; rainy weather. THE DIE HAS BEEN CAST: I was summoned this morning to the senator,[*] who informed me that it is his intention to dedicate the leadership of the police Criminal Department to Comrade Krenning, while he will assign me the leadership of the Political Department. This is an offer that fulfills one of my dreams. Spoke further with Chief Commissioner Broekhoff, who says that further instructions will follow.

SALOMON DE VRIES JR., JOURNALIST, AMSTERDAM

WEDNESDAY, MARCH 19, 1941—With a heavy thud, the door to the building just slammed shut. It is a quarter past twelve, and at midnight everyone must be indoors. It shoots right through you: "They're here!" Footsteps on the stairs. They stop outside our door, then continue. Up to the next floor. It was just someone who was naughty,[†] and didn't get caught. And still . . . You wait, put your book down, listen carefully. Nothing. You laugh softly. Not yet.

There are some prisoners who have returned, others are still in jail. Now they are arresting others. Often in the night. Usually between midnight and 1 a.m. The door to the building will click shut just like it just did, and there will be the sound of footsteps on the stairs, just like the ones I just heard . . .

This is the atmosphere at the moment. Detective stories?

---

[*] Presumably Schröder.
[†] Broke the curfew.

Not in the least. It is the sinister truth. When we take leave of each other these days, we don't say, "See you later!" We say, "Courage!" and "Stay strong!" We don't know what comes next, we know even less about tomorrow. We hear stories about "what happened there." A police van pulled up in front of the house, and a few men stepped out. Most people didn't even have time to properly put their clothes on. One woman was punched just because she wanted to say goodbye to her husband. That's how it goes.

We know and we are prepared. Anyone who isn't affected is lucky. And beyond that? Beyond that nothing. We wait. But if, in the night, we hear a door slam and the sound of heavy footsteps on the stairs, we listen. I listen. Ultimately, I sit—dissecting my thoughts—and wait for the pop of a hand grenade that is used to burst open the front door. Because that's how they do it. We all know that. Such are the times, such is the atmosphere. Thousands have been captured this way. No one has heard anything from most of them since.

ELISABETH VAN LOHUIZEN, GENERAL STORE OWNER, EPE

MONDAY, MARCH 31, 1941—Went to Amsterdam today and walked for over an hour, but I could not find a restaurant anywhere that didn't have a "Jews Not Wanted" sign in the window. I asked at a hotel, where we at last took a seat, and they told us that they were required to post such signs, under threat that their property would be destroyed. Later, the waiter came to show us a photo of the new princesses.

4

"NO GRAVES, NO GRAVESTONES"

February Razzia

On Saturday, February 22, and Sunday, February 23, after at least a week of street fighting in the Jewish Quarter, the *Ordnungspolizei*, German Order Police, stormed the district. Known locally as the Green Police (*Grüne Polizei*), owing to their long green coats, with high leather boots and military hats, these German officers were an intimidating presence, far more frightening than the local NSB thugs, the so-called W.A. men, that the Jews had been battling for days. Some 300 to 600 of them arrived in military trucks, armed with police batons and rifles, blackjacks, and vicious dogs.

David Meents and his brother-in-law, David Kropveld, who'd spontaneously decided to catch a show at the Tip Top Theater, were ambushed by Green Police in the foyer, and lined up in the streets with several other men who'd planned to see the performance. Louis Gosler, out walking arm-in-arm with his wife, Beppie, was torn away from her. A trained wrestler, Gosler fought back while Beppie dove into the ice-cold canal, but the Germans got him anyway. Joseph Nijkerk was headed to the Jewish bathhouse on the Nieuwe Uilenburgerstraat when he was picked up. Loe Peereboom was going to celebrate the birthday of his musician friend, Nico Gerritse, on the Jodenbreestraat. Both men were grabbed by the Green Police.[1]

Jewish men were nabbed, assaulted, and forced into two squares, Jonas Daniël Meijerplein, next to the Portuguese Synagogue, and Waterlooplein, the market square, where the humiliation and beatings continued for hours, while the public watched. "Standing by the window, we witnessed a scene I'll never forget," Mirjam Levie wrote in her diary. "More Greens showed up and they were asking every passing man: Are you a Jew? And when the answer was 'yes' they were grabbed and kicked about, in the most literal sense of the word, and sent to Meijerplein." She added, "I never imagined such ghastly scenes."[2]

Salomon de Vries Jr. continued in his diary: "They were flogged and kicked and beaten to the ground, and then dozens of them were loaded into trucks and driven away. To where, no one knows."[3]

In the course of two days, more than 400 men disappeared. City residents were outraged, especially those who had heard the eyewitness reports, and soon the communists, who had already been discussing a worker's walk-out, announced that municipal workers would strike. The two-day work stoppage, which spread across the country and ultimately included more than 300,000 Dutch citizens, was a landmark event in Dutch history, known as the February Strike.

It is recognized as the only popular protest of non-Jews against the persecution of the Jews anywhere in Europe during World War II, and its reputation has since grown into "an act of resistance of almost mythical proportions," wrote historian Annet Mooij.[4] It has been commemorated on February 25 with a parade and gathering in Amsterdam. Queen Wilhelmina inaugurated the event in 1946, calling Amsterdam, "heroic, determined and merciful," for its courage in facing off against the occupiers, which became the city's official motto.

Since the 1950s, a throng has gathered each year at the Dockworker's monument, a bronze statue of a burly stevedore, standing proudly with his fists clenched, in Jonas Daniël Meijerplein. The fact that this is a site of atrocity—the first roundup, mass assault, and deportation of Jewish civilians, marking the beginning of the Dutch Holocaust—is usually only briefly mentioned, as a prelude to the celebration of the bravery of the resisters.

For eighty years, no one even knew what had happened to the disappeared men. Their families, frantically seeking news of their whereabouts, received no straight answers from either Dutch or German officials. Some said they'd been taken to Schoorl, military barracks in the dunes of the North Sea; others said the men had been imprisoned at Buchenwald.[5] Within a couple of weeks, "The death notices started coming in," Mirjam Levie wrote. "One person after another received news that one of their relatives had died in Mauthausen from the most implausible illnesses."[6]

"Ulcerative colitis" was one of the supposed causes of death in the camp written on one such report, along with "general sepsis," a rare overall inflammatory infection; others said the men had died from reproductive system diseases that only affect women.[7] Simon Groen, a gymnast who'd trained as a tailor but worked in the furniture trade, was picked up for no reason just three weeks after he'd married Voge-lina Kroonenberg: the granddaughter of Joseph Kroonenberg, direc-tor of the Tip Top Theater. His death notice, which was sent many months later, said he'd died of multiple sclerosis.

Some families posted obituary notices in newspapers: "Today we received the sad news of the death of our beloved son and brother, An-dre Duitscher, a medical student who died on May 28 at Mauthausen at the age of 20," read an *Algemeen Handelsblad* of June 6, 1941. "Today my best friend, Jacob de Vries, died in Germany at age 21." "Our sweet son, brother, brother-in-law and uncle, Gerrit Gobes, died at age 23 on July 23."[8]

MOST PEOPLE UNDERSTOOD that the sweeps, or Razzias, were re-taliation for the death of NSB "comrade" Hendrik Koot, whose pic-ture was plastered across the front pages of all the German-controlled mainstream press and the Nazi propaganda papers.

But the Germans announced that the "hostage taking," as authori-ties called it, was to be blamed on the Jewish resistance, which refused to back down. As the W.A. and NSB seemed to be losing, Böhmcker had ordered the whole district closed, and demanded that local Jewish leaders "restore peace" in the Quarter. He also announced that non-Jewish residents of the neighborhood would have to move out, so that Jews from other parts of the city could move in. A Jewish Council,

Joodse Raad, would then take over administration of the anticipated ghetto.[9]

He appointed Abraham Asscher, owner of the district's largest diamond factory, as chairman of a new organization, and ordered him to force the local resistance to surrender its weapons. Asscher's name appeared on an official flyer posted and circulated on February 13, "on behalf of the Amsterdam SS Beauftragte" (Böhmcker) urging submission of "firearms, clubs, knifes and other weapons"[10] to the local police station, promising impunity to those who did so before Friday afternoon.[11]

Hardly any weapons were handed in; the Jewish resistance would not give up. Fighting continued for another ten days before the Green Police were deployed. But in the meantime, Böhmcker had achieved at least one of his aims: a partial segregation of Jews, though he would never get an official ghetto.

The newly formed Jewish Council, Joodse Raad, would soon become the occupier's primary tool for controlling not only Amsterdam's Jewish population but also all 160,000 Jewish residents of the Netherlands—including German Jewish refugees and Dutch Jews who had all been rendered stateless—across the country. But no one knew that at the time.

Asscher asked David Cohen, a classics professor at the University of Amsterdam, to work with him as co-chairman of the Council. The two men were already recognized community leaders, and, though they came from different disciplines, shared an interest in the welfare of Jewish people. They asked others to join as well; two days later, at the Amsterdam Jewish Council's first official meeting, twenty men were in attendance who would officially become the organization's board.

Although they agreed to be representatives for the community, many of the board members voiced concerns about their role in the occupation administration; all resisted the idea that they worked for Böhmcker. They wrote up a set of governing principles, which included the assertion that they would, "not go as far as accepting tasks that are dishonorable for Jews," although this later proved far more difficult than anticipated.[12]

Mirjam Levie, who'd been a secretary for the Committee for Jewish Refugees, an aid organization for German Jews, described in an interview she gave in 1999 how her work was transferred over to the Council without any warning.

"On March 20, 1941, I went to my office but I wasn't let in," she said. "The Germans had taken over the whole building. Because I was a secretary, I was allowed to enter, but there was no point because I just sat on my chair and had no idea what was happening."[13]

The Committee for Jewish Refugees, established in 1933, was the largest of several Dutch charitable organizations set up in the pre-war period to aid some 15,000 German Jews fleeing Nazi Germany across the border. In early May 1938, the Dutch parliament decreed that no more Jews from Germany would be admitted. The justice ministry issued new instructions: "A refugee shall (henceforward) be considered as an undesirable element for Dutch society and therefore as an undesirable alien, who will be therefore kept out at the border, or if found in the country, escorted to the border."[14]

Hendrik Colijn, who'd been prime minister at the time, justified this decision in a speech to parliament, paradoxically arguing that it was better for the Dutch Jews if the government would limit German Jewish emigration because such an influx could boost anti-Semitic sentiments in Holland. "If we were to admit here an unlimited stream of fugitives from abroad," he reasoned, "the necessary consequence of this would be that the feeling in our own country with regard to the Jews would swing in an unfavorable way."[15]

The government then built a refugee camp in the damp, cold, eastern province of Drenthe, close to the German border, called Central Refugee Camp Westerbork. The state, however, sent the bill for its construction to the Committee for Jewish Refugees, which also acted as its administrating office. Westerbork opened its doors on October 9, 1939, as a state-run refugee camp financed by Dutch Jews. This was an early indicator that the Dutch government expected the Jewish community to fend for itself, freeing the state from the "Jewish problem."

The Nazis tapped into this system in 1941, transforming existing Jewish community structures into a single Council, and severely constricting its autonomy. Many of its workers that were folded into the Council, like Mirjam Levie, had a background in community service and charitable work, and they felt that it was their duty to try and continue to help as many Jewish people as possible.

David Cohen, the co-chairman, for example, also had deep roots in community service. As a teenager growing up in Deventer, he, his brothers, and some friends of theirs would wait at the local train station to greet Jewish refugees who were fleeing the Russian pogroms, on their way to England or the United States. They would arrive with buckets of hot tea and mugs, which they'd pass through the windows as they offered the travelers encouraging words. This childhood experience, he would later explain, had a lasting influence on his desire to ameliorate Jewish suffering.[16]

Alongside his studies in classic letters and literature (Greek and Latin) at the University of Leiden, Cohen continued his service-oriented work for Jewish refugees from Eastern Europe, becoming secretary of the Nederlandse Zionistenbond (Dutch Zionist Union), and organizing talks on the subject of a Jewish homeland, with the Dutch Zionist Student Organization. In 1926, he was named a professor at the University of Amsterdam, where he worked for twenty-seven years in the Classics Department, and in 1933 he helped establish the Comité voor Bijzondere Joodsche Belangen (Committee for Special Jewish Interests), becoming its secretary.

This was the umbrella organization for the Committee for Jewish Refugees, for which Cohen served as chairman. Asscher, too, had a long track record of serving the Jewish community and aiding refugees. Before the war he was a prominent liberal politician and president of the Nederlands-Israëlitisch Kerkgenootschap, which represented Dutch Jewish synagogue congregations.[17]

Like Cohen, Asscher, and Levie, many people who had come from such a background naturally found it loathsome to be folded under the arm of the German authorities. Mirjam's future brother-in-law, Max Bolle, also active in the Council, had been part of the Dutch Zionist Association, while others had promoted Jewish cultural life through the academy, journalism, the arts, medicine, and science. Working for the Nazis was antithetical to their beliefs, to their tradition, and to their personhood. Nevertheless, few of them quit the Council. Cohen had an opportunity to escape the Netherlands before the capitulation but refused to leave the refugees; Asscher, too, had a chance to flee to Switzerland, but similarly refused to go.[18]

Mirjam explained one of the practical reasons she stayed: "There were no other opportunities to get a job at that time," she said. "I couldn't get a job at a non-Jewish association or a non-Jewish company, because they were not allowed to hire Jews. All Jewish businesses had been put under *verwaltung*, Aryan management. I wouldn't be accepted there either. It never occurred to me to say, no, I'm not in it anymore. I couldn't afford that."

Many agreed to work for the Council because they were sure they could play a protective role. Abel J. Herzberg, a legal scholar who was one of the editors of *Het Joodsche Weekblad* (The Jewish Weekly), run by the Jewish Council, clearly understood that the publication had been turned by the Nazis into a mouthpiece of the German administration. Most of its staff had formerly worked for *Nieuwe Israeliëtisch Weekblad,* a weekly magazine on Jewish issues. Now, it had almost no autonomy and was censored of any content that didn't serve occupation aims. Yet Herzberg maintained after the war that it served as the "last means of communication among the deserted and isolated."[19]

Others thought the organization would be a buffer, an intermediary, between the harshness of Nazi reign and the increasingly vulnerable community. Cohen articulated their aims frequently as an attempt "to prevent worse" calamities for the Jewish population. NIOD researcher Erik Somers, Cohen's biographer, characterized this position as "probably näive," while NIOD researcher Laurien Vastenhout, who specializes in Jewish Council history, feels they did what they could under the circumstances. "From their viewpoint, there weren't any alternatives but to cooperate and try to prevent any retaliations," she said.[20]

By October 1941, Seyss-Inquart had banned all national and local Jewish organizations, and the Amsterdam Jewish Council became the only intermediary between the German authorities and the Jewish communities in the Netherlands. After these other organizations were gradually dissolved, the Council became the sole representative for Jews and the only institution they could turn to for all their needs.

It granted travel and relocation permits, collected taxes, and provided financial and social support to the poor, as well as vocational services to the unemployed. When Jewish children were banned from public schools, the Council coordinated and oversaw the newly formed system of Jewish schools. Although many people regarded the Council, even in the early days, with great suspicion, many sought some form of connection to the organization. After all, anyone who worked for the Council, Seyss-Inquart granted, would receive a Sperre, or stamp, on their identity card, which protected them against deportation—for as long as that lasted.

WHILE ALL OF this reorganization was taking place within the Jewish community, families of many of the 400 disappeared men from the roundups of February 22 and 23 had learned little about their fathers, husbands, cousins, and sons.

"The most incredible stories did the rounds about German soldiers visiting the relatives of those who had died in Mauthausen, saying they weren't dead," Mirjam Levie wrote. "Today nobody believes that these young men were not, in fact, tortured to death. We may never know what really happened."[21]

Eighty years later, we finally do know what happened to each one of the victims, thanks to a Dutch historian, Wally de Lang, who made it her mission to learn the fate of every single man.[22] "So much research has been conducted about this brave resistance on February 25," she told me, "but so little is still known about what caused it." [23]

De Lang began her research in 2017, and by 2021, on the eightieth anniversary of the events, had been able to track down the biographies, and fates, of 390 men caught up in the raids. She published a book about her findings, which were also featured in an exhibition at the Stadsarchief, Amsterdam's city archive.

The first thing she had to do was to figure out exactly who had been taken; De Jong had reported 425, and that number had been used for years, but other historians said 400 or 380. A series of twenty-one photographs shot that day by an unknown German soldier had survived the war, because it had been sent for processing at Fotohandel Capi-Lux, a photo studio on the Roelof Hartplein, where the workers, who were members of the resistance, secretly made an extra set of prints.

"There was no single list," De Lang told me. "No German list survived the times. Nothing from Schoorl. I have no idea where the original lists are. So I had to reconstruct them, from all kinds of different angles." She combined six archival records to discover that 403 men had been taken; thirteen were almost immediately sent back to Amsterdam because they were suspected of having tuberculosis, and 390 were sent on.

De Lang found that these were mostly young, working, and poor men; many were getting by as ragpickers and junk-metal sellers. De Lang describes them in her book as "43 hawkers, 66 market traders and 33 tailors." Dozens of families had lost two or more of their male relatives, and collectively, the victims had left behind twenty-four pregnant wives.

The first Razzia group arrived late Saturday night and Sunday afternoon at the Schoorl barracks, which had been converted into a prison camp. They only had the clothes on their backs, which were often light, though the temperature had dropped below freezing. Elias

Kloos, who had been taken from the café where he'd been working, was wearing only his white server's uniform. They slept on iron beds without mattresses and were subjected to constant verbal and physical attacks by Camp Commander Johann Stöver, who was nicknamed *"de Blaffer,"* the barking dog.[24]

They stayed until February 27, when they were awakened early in the morning, driven to Schoorl train station, and transported via Alkmaar, then Kassel, to Buchenwald in Weimar, Germany, a trip of twenty-four hours. Camp Buchenwald was in the middle of a forest, about five miles from the train stop, and the men were forced to march a path known as "Blood Street."

In Buchenwald, the Amsterdam men were put to extreme endurance tests. They were forced to stand still for hours in the freezing cold in thin prison pajamas. In the mornings, they were harnessed like horses and forced to pull a "Jew Wagon."

Within three months of arrival at Buchenwald, forty-seven of the men from the group had been murdered by various means. Two survived by luck: Gerrit Blom, a communist who was suspected of helping to organize the general strike, was sent back to Amsterdam, where he was tried as a political prisoner. He was convicted and sent again to other concentration camps, but managed to survive the war. Max Nebig, who'd been arrested while buying a birthday present for his brother, survived Buchenwald because he hurt his foot and was transferred to the infirmary; despite then being subjected to horrendous medical experiments, other inmates protected him, and he was not sent on to Mauthausen.

On May 22, 1941, all of the remaining members of the Razzia group were put on a transport to Mauthausen, a concentration camp in Austria, not far from Hitler's hometown of Linz.[25]

I VISITED MAUTHAUSEN in the 1990s with my mother as part of a family root-finding trip to Eastern Europe. She hadn't traveled to Hungary or Czechoslovakia since she'd fled as a ten-year-old girl to

Australia, by way of Italy, in 1949. After the Berlin Wall fell in 1989 and the Iron Curtain with it, she was interested, somewhat tentatively, in exploring the Old Country her family had left behind.

Unlike some of the concentration camps that were razed or otherwise destroyed by retreating Germans at the end of the war, Mauthausen was relatively well-preserved. What was memorable to me were the high, medieval style fortress walls, the barracks with creaky wood bunk beds where prisoners slept side by side, and the central feature, a massive stone quarry where they were worked to death.

We opted for the guided tour so that we could be silent and quietly listen. I remember the guide's explanation of the "stairway of death," made of steep, uneven stone. They were built this way intentionally so slave laborers would trip and fall when forced to run up or down, and be stampeded. Usually, they were chased by snapping dogs and flanked by SS wielding whips and pistols. If they fell, so be it. The weak had to be replaced. The other prisoners would then have to carry their dead bodies up the steps.

I recall that when we were standing in the bowl-like base of the quarry, gazing up at the jagged cliffs, the guide explained that most of the inmates died of starvation and overwork, but there were other tortures, like being stripped naked and doused with ice-cold water, or forced to stand for hours during a head count in the dead heat of summer or the freezing winter wind. He also mentioned that some prisoners, the Dutch in particular, were marched over the side of the cliff.

For some reason this fact about the Dutch Jews stayed with me. I remember wondering then whether I'd have preferred to be killed that way, smashed to pieces in the quarry, or whether I'd have been able to endure the torture of hauling stones like Sisyphus or been stampeded running up the stairs of death. I imagined Emerich there, hauling stones and gazing up to see the Dutch Jews plummeting to their deaths.

But was the guide's story accurate? Dutch historian Geert Mak mentioned something about this in his book, *Amsterdam: A Brief Life of the City.* Four days after their arrival at Mauthausen, Mak wrote, "Ten men jumped to their deaths in a deep stone quarry, holding one another by the hand."[26] This version sounds more romantic but also dubious.

I asked De Lang if her research indicated that some of the Razzia group victims died this way. "They were pushed to jump or forced to jump, or sometimes just encouraged to jump," she answered. "Sometimes they preferred to jump, because at least that would be quicker than being worked to death."

Five of the Dutch men from the Razzia group died within five days of arriving at Mauthausen in May. Another five died in June—forty-one in July and thirty-five in August. Then, all of a sudden, in September, 190 died all at once, according to official death notices. What was even stranger was that they seemed to have died in alphabetical order. On September 1, twenty-seven men whose surnames all began with A, B, or C. The next day, twenty-four men with surnames starting with C, D, and so on. This continued until September 6, when the last of the group, twenty-eight men, died at once.

These men, overworked and nearly starved, had been taken from the quarry of Mauthausen to the nearby Castle Hartheim, in Alkoven, Austria, a Nazi euthanasia center, De Lang had discovered. The castle had previously been used to murder disabled people with lethal gas, in a Nazi program known as Aktion T4. In 1941, the program changed to Aktion 14F13, with the aim to kill camp prisoners who were no longer able to work, making space in Mauthausen for new slave laborers. The men from Amsterdam were its very first victims.

"Most of these men have no graves, no gravestones," De Lang told me. "Their names are not even mentioned in history."

ALTHOUGH ALMOST NO one in the Netherlands had even heard of Mauthausen before 1941, the very word became, for them, synonymous with erasure. Dutch Jews nicknamed it "Moordhuizen," a pun, combining the words *Moord* meaning murder, and *huizen*, meaning houses. Murder houses. After the Strike, Jewish people who didn't immediately comply with Green Police orders or Nazi regulations were told they would be sent to Mauthausen—a terrifying prospect. "'Mauthausen' was the threat that hung over anyone who resisted, and everyone knew that 'Mauthausen' meant death."[27]

Loe de Jong once observed in a lecture, "Jews in the Netherlands were convinced that to be sent to Mauthausen was tantamount to a death sentence. So in July 1942, the Germans' announcement that Jews (they did not say: *all* Jews) would be sent to labor camps in Eastern Europe ("labor camps," mind you!) was accompanied by a statement by Himmler's personal representative in the Netherlands that every Jew who was detected in hiding would be sent to Mauthausen."[28]

The Razzias of 1941 were not a prelude to a stream of Mauthausen deportations, however. Just five transports went from the Netherlands to the Austrian camp, all of them that year. Some 1,750 Dutch Jews would die there in 1941 and 1942—a small fraction of the 102,000 killed in the Dutch Holocaust.

By mid-1941, the SS administration in The Hague was already at work on its far more comprehensive "Jewish removal" plan, directed toward two much more efficient killing centers equipped with new technology to wipe out thousands at a time. The Nazis used what they'd learned from their experimentation with gassing in 1940 and 1941 at Hartheim Castle, and other such smaller testing grounds for murderous methods. Now they were prepared to implement it on a much broader scale.

De Lang pointed out that Hartheim was not only a useful place for testing chemicals, but also for laying the foundation for other aspects of large-scale death machinery: recruiting the right kind of doctors and other personnel, figuring out how to deceive victims, and learning how to dispose of corpses. These were technical lessons for the mass murder to come, which would take place in locations such as Sobibor, Treblinka, and Auschwitz.

To start moving the population of Dutch Jews toward these death centers, the occupier needed a collection point in the Netherlands, preferably far away from the potential witnesses. For this purpose, the Germans took control of the former refugee camp, Westerbork in Drenthe, and expanded it to serve as a "transit" camp.

Dutch contractors were commissioned to build twenty-four large wooden barracks, to fit two to three hundred people each. The Dutch national railway, N.S., was also commissioned in 1941 to build a rail link from the camp to the Hooghalen station. Jewish inmates were used to construct the new railway line, and Jewish assets, sold at the Dutch stock exchange, would fund the deportations. The whole system was ready to move Jews to "extermination" camps in German-occupied Poland as efficiently as possible.

5

"NOW THE GAMES CAN BEGIN"

Douwe Bakker during the raid of a café
in the Jewish Quarter in April 1942

How did the Dutch civil administration respond to this harassment, assault, and arrest of its Jewish citizenry?

"What should we do, what can we do?" Johannes Boot, the Dutch mayor of a small town called Wisch, wrote in his diary in August 1941. "No people is more debased than the Jews. They should get help in order to save them from the terror."[1]

Some local Jewish residents had already gone into hiding, and one man from his town had attempted suicide twice. Boot discussed his feelings of impotence with Secretary General of the Ministry of the Interior, Karel Frederiks, who talked him out of resigning.

"In the opinion of Frederiks, accepting discrimination and humiliation of Jewish citizens for the time being was 'the lesser evil' that had to be accepted in order to do a proper job under the German occupation," wrote historian Peter Romijn. This was emblematic of a belief many Dutch authorities held at this stage: Dutch public servants had to think of all the other citizens who relied on them, and not focus on "the Jewish issue."[2]

The administration's "lesser evil" reasoning, Romijn argued, was the basis of a strategy for dealing with the occupier that muted the Dutch response and discouraged it from fighting back. Until 1943, the civil administrators, he concluded, "managed to convince the majority of the Dutch population to refrain from resistance."

The February 1941 worker's demonstration in support of the Jewish compatriots, as ebullient as it seemed from the ground, did not penetrate the hearts of those in the upper echelons of industry. Companies such as Werkspoor, Fokker, Wilton-Fijenoord, and the Dutch national railways continued to comply with the Reich, in spite of the mounting persecution.

A 1949 investigation of Werkspoor's wartime dealings with the Nazis, conducted by special Attorney General A.H. van de Veen, concluded that the steel manufacturer's work for the Germans was "unquestionably" of a military nature and "served the war purposes of the enemy." In the employ of the Nazis, Werkspoor manufactured turbines, boilers, and other machinery for destroyers, minesweepers, and warships. They made camouflage aircraft and reclining devices for gun racks, as well as railway carriages for troop transport. They also assembled an airplane hangar for the Germans at Volkel Nachtlandeplatz, a diversion airfield the German Luftwaffe built in a nature reserve in the Netherlands, later a Luftwaffe base.[3]

After the war, Damme claimed that the company had only complied with the German requests "under duress." But Attorney General Van de Veen was unconvinced by his arguments. Instead, he found, "Werkspoor treated the Germans with the kind of courtesy that is entirely customary towards normal business clients." Based on the "enthusiastic" attitude toward the occupier, he added, "it is difficult to speak of observing even the necessary reserve vis-à-vis the enemy."

He concluded, "This is more than mere culpable complacency." The company's chairman, Marinus Hendrik Damme, had been "eager" in his work with the occupier, according to the investigation.[4]

Some workers secretly joined the resistance, participating in various kinds of illegal work. If discovered, however, they faced more severe penalties than (non-Jewish) people who worked in any other trades, because their companies were so instrumental to the German war effort.

As soon as the February Strike had come to an end, a "Proclamation" was posted across the nation, threatening workers with fifteen-year prison terms for walk-outs. The worst penalties were reserved for employees of companies that were "important to the Wehrmacht, which includes all essential businesses."

"If you are important to the German Wehrmacht, a strike can result in the death penalty," a twenty-five-year-old typist in Amsterdam reported accurately about the notices in her diary of February 26. "Now we know. And I hope that the Netherlands will go back to work. But I'm glad that the strike was so spontaneous and universal, regardless of whether it was sensible or not. The Netherlands has shown, spontaneously, that it will not allow itself to be messed with, that we will stand up for our fellow citizens, no matter what their race. . . . What do the Germans think of us now?"[5]

WHAT DID THE Germans think? They immediately fired more than seventy Dutch city administrators and dismissed the Amsterdam municipal council. While Seyss-Inquart and other SS leaders may have been surprised by the workers' support for the Jews, they were dismayed that the Amsterdam police had—apparently quite intentionally—failed to defend the NSB.

Mayor de Vlugt was deposed and replaced with the pro-German Edward John Voûte. German SS Oberführer Walther Schröder was appointed as a "special envoy" to find a replacement for Amsterdam Police Commissioner Versteeg. He settled on Sybren Tulp, a former lieutenant colonel from the Royal Dutch East Indies Army, a "convinced National Socialist," with "internalized anti-Semitic ideas."[6]

Chief Constable Tulp, charismatic and popular with his men, didn't transform the entire force, but he added "new units that operated independently under his personal authority."[7] Within a few weeks, Tulp had arranged to meet Willy Lages, the German chief of the Sicherheitsdienst, or S.D., the Nazi intelligence agency of the SS, in Amsterdam, to discuss how they could best organize the police department so that this fiasco wouldn't happen again. They needed to get Dutch civilians on their side, and to combat any forces of resistance. To do this, they needed a pro-German Dutch entity that would serve as an intermediary with the public.

"A lot of Dutchmen did not want to go to the Sicherheitsdienst in Euterpestraat," to report suspicious activities, Lages explained in postwar testimony, because this would mean reporting to the Germans, an idea that even many complicit civilians felt would be traitorous. The idea was to establish a police division manned by Dutch agents, where Dutch people would feel more comfortable delivering tips and submitting official police reports against their neighbors.[8]

This was the first step toward the creation of the Inlichtingendienst, or Intelligence Agency, a Dutch political investigations department that served the Sicherheitsdienst. It would be located just outside the Jewish Quarter at Nieuwe Doelenstraat 10, over the bridge and down the street from the Hotel L'Europe, then the headquarters of the SS Air Force command.

SS-Oberführer Walther Schröder conducted interviews with various local policemen to staff the department, seeking pro-German and NSB members, among them Douwe Bakker. Ever since he and his two colleagues, Bram Harrebomée and Leen Ponne, had been released from internment in the May days of 1940, the three police officers had openly affirmed their Nazi affiliations. Prior to the arrival of the German forces, civil servants, including policemen, had been barred from joining the party, but the occupiers allowed it.

"For NSB sympathizers in the Amsterdam police force, a new and surprising era dawned after capitulation," wrote police historian Guus Meershoek. Their non-collaborating superiors treated them with greater caution, but granted them more freedom.[9]

Together, in the first summer after the occupation began, the same three officers took the initiative to organize an NSB member organization within the police department, called Rechtsfront. NSB party leader Anton Mussert immediately endorsed the plan, and appointed Bakker as head of the Amsterdam division's "political" wing, while Ponne and Harrebomée also attained key positions. Mussert even gave Bakker his own headquarters on the Reguliersstraat, where he worked with volunteers to publish the magazine *Recht en Orde* and organize "comradeship evenings" every fortnight with lectures and German propaganda film screenings. Later, the Amsterdam Rechtsfront offices would host a well-attended German course.[10]

Schröder, no doubt impressed by this enthusiasm for the Nazi cause, interviewed all three men March 19 for two hours, Bakker noted in his diary. They discussed police "attitudes" and the "reorganization of the department," according to Bakker, who found this conversation "very satisfying" and left in a good mood. It must have been clear to Bakker that the police reorganization would favor him, because he wrote in his diary that day: "Now the games against the scoundrels can begin."

Four days later, Schröder summoned Bakker back and offered him the top job. "THE DIE HAS BEEN CAST," Bakker reveled in all caps in his diary.

Tulp appointed Harrebomée as Bakker's deputy at the Inlichtin-gendienst, and together they hired about twenty subordinates, most of them members of the Rechtsfront, their new association of NSB members who worked in law enforcement. This appointment marked the start of Bakker's ascension within the Nazi police hierarchy. Although he didn't always get along with his German bosses, he nevertheless rose through the ranks by virtue of his commitment to Nazi ideology. After leading the Inlichtingendienst, he later attained posts as chief of the Documentatiedienst (Documentation Service), chief of the Vice Squad and chief of the Social Police—all high-ranking jobs in specialized collaborating divisions of the Dutch police.

In his first role as a police chief, however, Bakker would soon find himself caught between competing objectives of the Dutch police department and the German Sicherheitsdienst. Behind the scenes, Tulp and Lages had made a deal about the Inlichtingendienst. "All important political matters" had to be referred directly to Sicherheits-dienst headquarters, Lages had demanded, "while the smaller matters would be handled by the Bakker Department," as Lages called it.[11] It is unclear from the record whether Bakker was informed of this arrangement.

As Inlichtingendienst chief, Bakker's primary responsibility was to quash anti-German activities, and any resistance efforts that undermined the occupation. These were outlined as, but not limited to, "listening to English radio broadcasts, making propaganda positive to the royal family, insults against the German Reich and Hitler, possession and distribution of illegal pamphlets, printed matter and writings of communist activity, prohibited possession of weapons and trade and affairs concerning the Jews."[12]

A series of black-and-white photographs of Bakker during a police raid on a "Jewish café" at Nieuwmarkt 15 that April shows the chief inspector in action.[13] In one of the images he looks like a classic gumshoe detective straight out of a 1940s film noir. Dressed in a trench coat, suit and tie, his fedora is slightly askew, and a cigarette dangles from his mouth.

Surrounded by six other identically clad police agents, he stands out in a pale jacket, while the rest wear dark coats, behind the open doors of a paddy wagon. A crowd of onlookers gathers in the street around the café,* a billiards bar called Café Hartlooper. The Amsterdam city archive noted, "items considered black market trade were seized. The traders were arrested and deported."[14]

EACH WEEKDAY MORNING, at 9 a.m. roll call, Bakker doled out assignments at Nieuwe Doelenstraat 10.[15] Sometimes they came from Lages or Tulp, and sometimes from tips received from civilians. Although he was supposed to send "important matters" over to Lages, Bakker often overstepped his bounds, as far as the German S.D. chief was concerned.

In September 1941, for example, Bakker took it upon himself to launch an investigation into the murder of W.A.-man Hendrik Koot, the NSB's street fighting martyr. He proudly cited his agents for a commendation, announcing that they had arrested eight suspects, "6 Jews and 2 Aryans," who he'd handed over to the S.D. While the general Amsterdam police department's earlier investigation had come to a dead end, his own agents, Bakker boasted, "succeeded in elucidating this matter almost completely."[16]

---

* Owned by W. Hartlooper, according to the Stadsarchief.

The next month, he filed for commendations for two agents who had arrested members of seven anti-German resistance organizations, including De Geuzen, De Leeuwengarde, Het Oranjefront, and De Oranjegarde.[17] His men went after clandestine newspaper *Vrij Nederland,* repeatedly, and arrested forty-two communists in a single raid.

In August 1942, he told his men to raid the Fotohandel Capi-Lux on the Roelof Hartplein—the shop that had surreptitiously copied prints of the February Razzias—ostensibly for stocking copies of *Vrij Nederland.* One of his agents, Johan Ros, recalled how Bakker had provided extremely precise instructions: "He told us that in a corridor wall, which was located on the left before entering the main room, we'd find a hanging tapestry, and behind it a wall safe."

Indeed, it was exactly where Bakker described. Agents broke into the safe and found two firearms and illegal pamphlets.[18] The shop's thirty-eight-year-old owner, Richard Voitus van Hamme, handed over to the S.D. by Bakker's men, was imprisoned in the Oranje Hotel, sentenced to death, and shot by a firing squad on November 4, 1942.[19]

It is hard to know which of Bakker's activities most irritated Lages, but it is clear that the Dutch detective, who was supposed to be a subordinate, was getting under Lages' skin. Lages installed a German police agent, Kurt Döring, as an "intermediary," insisting that Bakker discuss any potential cases with Döring before proceeding. This arrangement also didn't yield the results Lages desired.

"Lages always told me that he was not satisfied with the Bakker Department," Döring testified. "This was because Bakker always worked too independently and worked out things that he had not discussed with me beforehand."[20]

Lages also complained after the war about Bakker's insubordination. "Right from the start of the work of the Bureau Inlichtingendienst, things did not go as I had hoped," he said. An "unpleasant relationship" developed because "Bakker did not want to submit to my orders," and "wanted to be the head of his own office."[21]

Tensions escalated, and the "Bakker Department" wasn't long for this world. By February 1942, Lages had offered jobs in the Euterpestraat S.D. office to almost all of Bakker's detectives, poaching them from under him, and then he suggested folding the entire bureau into the Sicherheitsdienst. Bakker would get his own desk, Lages promised.

Frustrated, Bakker turned to Chief Constable Tulp and asked to be relieved of his position as Inlichtingendienst chief. Tulp kept him in place, and Bakker continued to run investigations with a much smaller team—but he soon developed a reputation for slapping and punching suspects. Lages saw to it that the "Bakker Department" was officially shut down in September 1942.

"That's the final verdict," Bakker wrote in his diary, "and also the end of many illusions."

IN THE MEANTIME, Sybren Tulp had set up another new department across the street, at Nieuwe Doelenstraat 13: the Amsterdam Bureau for Jewish Affairs. This unit, established in June 1942, and run by "rabid anti-Semite" Rudolf Wilhelm Dahmen von Buchholz, became the largest of several specialized police units set up across the country that spring and summer, explained historian Ad van Liempt, as the Nazis began to coordinate plans to address the "Jewish Problem" with Dutch civil administrators.

By establishing specialized units to handle Jewish arrests, Dutch police officers who found the work distasteful could "keep their hands clean," Van Liempt explained. But these units were then able to act with near impunity, directly for the German occupiers, and they took full advantage of this status to behave sadistically, he said.

Police historian Guus Meershoek, however, said that the division of the force didn't ultimately matter much because, in the end, "ordinary Dutch police officers" also did much of the dirty work. They also arrested Jews, ensured that they complied with their deportation call-up notices, requisitioned homes, and cleared out their possessions.

"Basically, if you just count numbers, you can be sure that at least two-thirds of the Amsterdam police force participated in arresting Jews and collaborating in the deportations," he told me. Lages, too, testified after the war that without the Dutch police involvement, not even ten percent of the country's Jews would have been captured.[22]

The Dutch police, too, enforced increasingly rigid Nazi regulations. Jewish children were expelled from public schools and forced into hastily constructed segregated schools. Jewish employees were fired; licenses for Jewish professionals were withdrawn, Jewish businesses were forced shut, and their goods either sold for a pittance or transferred to non-Jewish *verwalters,* "administrators" who took their earnings. Jews could no longer own bicycles, radios, or telephones.

They were forbidden from using public transportation. They were only allowed to shop between 3 p.m. and 5 p.m. and had to be indoors before the 8 p.m. Jewish curfew. Jews had to deposit all their money and assets into a single bank, and were allowed just 250 guilders at any given time. Any other money or valuables could be confiscated.

In April 1942, it was announced that Jews age seven and older must wear the Star of David, a yellow six-pointed cloth about the size of an adult's palm, with the word "Jood," in the middle. The Jewish Council was forced to distribute the stars, with strict instructions on placement: clearly visible on the left side of the chest, on all outerwear.

All of these measures were enforced by the Dutch police.

PART II

PERSECUTION AND DEPORTATION

APRIL 1942–FEBRUARY 1944

6

"IT'S SO HARD TO KNOW WHAT TO DO"

April 1942–December 1942

INGE JANSEN, 36, HOUSEWIFE, THE HAGUE

SUNDAY, APRIL 26, 1942—This morning I escaped to the sitting room upstairs and relaxed there for a while, before I did some administration. In the afternoon, heard the Führer's very long, serious speech. How terribly tough it must have been in Russia and what a struggle it has been! This is all such grief for Hitler. He is going through hell.

Adriaan is ashamed that he so desperately longed for a holiday. More and more people are escaping The Hague, and I can hardly express in words how cowardly and despicable I find this attitude. "These people don't need to come back," Adriaan says. I enjoyed the sun on the terrace; the forsythia is beautiful; tulips and daffodils are finally beginning to bloom.

INA STEUR,
FACTORY OFFICE CLERK,
AMSTERDAM

TUESDAY, APRIL 28, 1942—The Jews are once again the scapegoats. Now, they must walk around with a star on their clothing. A big yellow star with the word "Jew" written in the middle. And starting at seven years old. They are no longer allowed to go to the market square, parks, cinemas or theaters, into cafés and so forth. They can't leave the city without a pass. There is only one theater they're allowed to attend. The one on the Plantage Middenlaan, where it will naturally become very busy. As many Jews as possible are being sent to concentration camps, where they are treated terribly. Lots of work, little food, and less rest.

DOUWE BAKKER,
POLICE DIVISION CHIEF,
AMSTERDAM

MONDAY, APRIL 27, 1942—The night calm, the weather pretty much the same. A strong East to Northeast wind, dry and sunny. In the afternoon at 3 o'clock, we raided two cafés on the Nieuwmarkt, using about twenty men. One Jewish café and another café where we body-searched everyone; we took everyone and everything to the Doelenstraat. We hoped to nab some ration card traders, but we didn't succeed. We did manage to find a few people whose papers were not in order, along with packets of coffee, tea, chocolate, and cans of food that were squirreled away, and which we confiscated. All in all though, the action didn't yield much. Comrade Captain Dahmen von Buchholz was there; he wanted to experience what a raid was like.

WEDNESDAY, APRIL 29, 1942—JEWISH BADGE INTRODUCED[*]—
The night quiet, with a stormy wind from the Northeast to the
East. Edeus and Ros confiscated about 150,000 guilders' worth of
gold and silver objects and jewels from several Jews who'd hidden
them with an Aryan. Scheikelen, who buys drills and electrical materials for the German Wehrmacht, also made a good deal, worth
about 60,000 guilders. He caught some black marketeers, who
didn't know who they were dealing with. One guy even expressed
his opinions of NSB members, saying he'd rip open their bodies and
tear out their hearts if he could. We'd be happy to relieve him of his
burdens. If only the S.D. would lock this guy up in a concentration
camp.

Effective May 2, all Jews over six years old who are on the street
or other public places must wear a Jewish badge on their left breast,
a yellow Star of David the size of a palm with a black cross (Jewish),
and the word "JEW."

THURSDAY, APRIL 30, 1942—The night quiet; the weather unchanged, cold with wind from Northeast, but less powerful. Today
was another very busy day in the bureau. . . . Cases are just pouring
in at the bureau; it's late when we get home, after stopping off first
at Comrade Smaalders' for a few plates of excellent pea soup, albeit
without a bone. Tomorrow we'll be on standby while a number of
workers at a few large factories such as Werkspoor and the Dutch
dockworkers are fired and sent to labor service in Germany. This
has already created a lot of waves at the factories. In a monster trial
against a bunch of thieves and dealers who stole one million ration
cards, the eight main suspects have been sentenced to death, which
they duly deserve.

SATURDAY, MAY 2, 1942—The night quiet; a little rain in the morning, but it cleared up later. Wind northern to western. Now there are

---

[*] Written in the margins.

friends of the Jews who also want to walk around wearing the star. Today we caught one such joker.

Elisabeth van Lohuizen,
general store owner, Epe

SUNDAY, MAY 3, 1942—This morning, Ger[*] arrived at church wearing the Jewish star. I was worried that he was taking too great a risk. I'm willing to go to prison for my convictions if necessary, but I feel that this action does very little to help. If everyone did it, perhaps it would make an impression, but there are so few. When I spoke to him this evening, he said he'd taken it off this afternoon, because one of Dr. Loeff's granddaughters was already arrested for wearing it. It's so hard to know what to do.

MONDAY, MAY 4, 1942—Today was a very emotional day. For the first time, we're hearing reports of executions: 102 officers and intellectuals. The newspapers have reported seventy-two, but we learned that more people have been killed by firing squad in Brabant. The families of the victims were informed by telephone that sentences had been executed. It seems these people had done illegal work. The paper described it as "a dark day." On the radio, Max Blokzijl[†] said, "Since May 14, we have continued to live as if there was no war and no occupation. But this summer we will certainly notice the war." There were also mass arrests across the country today.[‡]

---

[*] Her son.

[†] Max Blokzijl was a Dutch radio personality and NSB member who broadcast pro-Nazi shows on Radio Hilversum (Philip Rees, *Biographical Dictionary of the Extreme Right Since 1890,* 1990), 37.

[‡] On May 4, 1942, the Germans imprisoned 460 prominent Dutch people as hostages, including politicians, mayors, professors, clergymen, lawyers, writers, and musicians in the Beekvliet Preparatory Seminary in the Dutch town of Sint-Michielsgestel.

In Epe, a member of parliament (Mr. Van Steen, S.D.A.P.) was arrested, but he was let go later the same night because he'd suffered a heart attack. Other members of Parliament, such as Joekes, Kranenburg, Banning, and so on, as well as physicians, pastors, lawyers—all intellectuals—have been taken hostage as well. What does this forebode?

WEDNESDAY, MAY 6, 1942—The Queen gave a radio address again tonight and offered a eulogy for those who were executed. After that, she cautioned us to be very careful, saying the telephone is not safe and letters can be opened. She also said we must be cautious when speaking in public. She added, Holland will rise up again.

INA STEUR,
FACTORY OFFICE WORKER,
AMSTERDAM

TUESDAY, MAY 5, 1942—Military officers, sailors, and midshipmen are all required to report for call-up notices now. They too will be detained. It seems like they'll lock up all able-bodied men eventually.

FRIDAY, MAY 8, 1942—They've issued new regulations. Werkspoor has to send a hundred men to work in the Borsig factory in Berlin. A hundred unmarried men between twenty-one and forty years old. How many of them will ever return? It is extremely dangerous. They must be there before Ascension Day, which is in six days. And the Jews are no longer allowed to marry Christian men and women. They're not even allowed to apply for any kind of marriage license at all unless there's an urgent necessity.

SUNDAY, MAY 10, 1942—It's already been two years since the war broke out. Oh, how crazy and overjoyed we would be if only there were peace again. So many families are missing one or more people already, because of death or labor service. Yesterday, again, more shootings. This time seventy-two people, most of them from Naarden and that region. Seven people, thankfully, were pardoned and instead of death got life in prison. We hope that we won't have to wait another two years for liberation.

ELISABETH VAN LOHUIZEN, GENERAL STORE OWNER, EPE

TUESDAY, MAY 12, 1942—There is a lot of talk that Mussert[*] will take office this week. The mood is tense all over. Many NSB women from the west have moved into the villages around here. On the radio, Blokzijl says it's a shame they've had to do this, but by talking about it, at least he admits that it's happening. They must be afraid of riots or an invasion. There's a charge in the air, you could say. In recent weeks, the British Royal Air Force has bombed several German cities, including Augsburg and Pilsen. They did a great job. The Americans have bombed Tokyo for the second time.

In Amsterdam, six people have been shot dead for committing some kind of swindle with ration coupons. These Germans shoot so easily. But the Dutch, at least, have retained a sense of humor. After the introduction of the Star of David, they're calling Jodenbreestraat the Milky Way. Waterlooplein is now nicknamed *Place d'Etoile* and Amsterdam Zuid has been called Hollywood.

---

[*] Anton Mussert, founder of the Dutch Nazi political party, Nationaal-Socialistische Beweging, or NSB.

INGE JANSEN,
HOUSEWIFE, THE HAGUE

THURSDAY, MAY 14, 1942—Ascension Day, Milda's[*] last day, I find it terrible that I'll now be here alone. We were both in tears. She really spoiled me. Such a sweetheart. I just can't imagine that she is really gone. She was such a trusted hand in the house. This afternoon I ate early and went to the cinema for the *Wochenschau*.[†]

FRIDAY, MAY 15, 1942—Luckily my new cleaner, Dien . . . , has arrived. She was with me all day. Wim treated me to a delicious lunch at Lensveld.[‡] He told me that various people have taken him to task for keeping in touch with us. Ans is so very anti-German that she no longer wants to have anything to do with us! Alas, there are thousands who think this way.

SATURDAY, MAY 16, 1942—They are indeed holding active servicemen in various barracks; I was very surprised because I didn't expect that. About 2,000 people have been arrested. It is also scandalously shameful that so many Dutch officers (40) have broken their word of honor to the occupiers; one cannot blame Germany for losing faith in our army. The mood is terribly bad in our country and the hatred is enormous. How are we ever going to come to positive results, with so many troubles? Those with the best of intentions have to suffer a great deal.

SUNDAY, MAY 17, 1942—Adriaan left early with Van Stockum for Mussert's swearing in by Reichsführer Himmler at the zoo.[§] I went

---

[*] Perhaps her maid.

[†] The German *Wochenschau*, or Weekly Review, were weekly Nazi propaganda newsreels presented in movie theaters.

[‡] Lensvelt-Nicola was a German-owned bakery and tea room in The Hague, frequented by politicians and NSB members.

[§] On May 17, 1942, in The Hague, 800 Dutch SS men took an oath to serve Adolf Hitler in the presence of SS Reichsführer Heinrich Himmler.

to the parade on De Plaats;[*] I found most of the young men had a very poor bearing. The Germans walk much better and they also look healthier and stronger. Avoided the Kochs as much as possible. Afterward, we went with Mies van Stockum to the zoo to hear speeches and to see the swearing in of Feldmeijer,[†] the new foreman.

I spoke with Siep and Jessy Tulp[‡] for a while; they are very satisfied with their new home. Siep does have many political complaints. He also made my acquaintance with Mrs. Strak. It seems that Conti[§] will soon come to Holland. He is also enthusiastic about Wagner's plan for the Health Insurance Fund. He is the one that Keijer wanted to introduce to Adriaan. He could be useful to Adriaan. I also heard that, at the last moment, Mussert forbade them from using the Binnenhof[¶] for the swearing-in, apparently because he wanted to keep that specifically for the W.A. (or his headquarters!). Rudi[**] told me that Mussert would only walk in the Hitler Youth and the National Youth Storm parade, so not "next to" the Reich Commissioner, Seyss-Inquart. What a lot of fuss!

TUESDAY, MAY 19, 1942—Juul[††] is extremely busy trying to investigate the reason that Adriaan was not accepted by the Waffen-SS. She spoke with two staff members at the office of the Reichsführer-SS and they were quite amazed to hear the whole story and they said they would look into it all immediately. Very sweet of Juul!

---

[*] A square.

[†] Henk Feldmeijer was a Dutch NSB member, who established the Dutch SS.

[‡] "Siep" is probably short for Sybren Tulp, chief constable of the Amsterdam police department. He attended with his wife, Jessy (also Jessie).

[§] Leonardo Conti was Reich Health Leader and head of the National Socialist German Medical Association. "He was jointly responsible for forced sterilization, abortion and euthanasia," writes historian Ernst-Alfred Leyh. "His involvement in human experiments is also undisputed." *Der Spiegel*, by Solveig Grothe, May 31, 2008.

[¶] The historic, central square at the seat of government in The Hague.

[**] Last name redacted.

[††] Inge did not identify Juul, but this appears to be Julia op ten Noort, a Dutch National Socialist activist and a co-founder of the National Socialist Women's Organization (NSVO). She was known to intimates as Juul.

Elisabeth van Lohuizen,
general store owner, Epe

TUESDAY, MAY 19, 1942—This morning at 4:30 a.m., Marja Elisabeth, our first grandchild, was born. Seeing that newborn in the nursery, surrounded by so many beautiful bouquets of flowers, and seeing my children so happy, it feels as if I'm in another world entirely. It feels so strange that such a miracle can still occur in wartime.

Inge Jansen,
housewife, The Hague

MONDAY, MAY 25, 1942—Mien and Wim came this morning for coffee, which was pleasant, but it is still almost as if there were strangers visiting. Ans says she will only visit me on my birthday if there are no "comrades" at the party. Pretty cheeky!

Mien said, according to a reliable source (!), the great conspiracy of the Dutch officers wasn't directed against the Germans; in other words, it was organized against an anticipated Mussert government.* That much is clear. The Hennigs have been evacuated. I saw that coming, as they live so close to the lighthouse. I'm slowly becoming very tired—still no maid.

MONDAY JUNE 1, 1942—Adriaan was summoned by the SS office, and he's going there tomorrow. Tonight, there were a lot of jets flying overhead and gunfire. I was awakened in the night very frightened, which is unusual for me. I don't yet understand why I saw Jesus so clearly. I'm grateful that I did, but I still don't understand the meaning

---

* Many people assumed that Anton Mussert, head of the NSB party, would be given an official role in the national occupation government.

of it. I am certainly very active and happy that I can do so much for other people. It is also wonderful that summer is coming.

TUESDAY JUNE 2, 1942—Adriaan went to the Erganzungstelle* at 10 a.m., and indeed the examination determined that he *can* become an officer with the Waffen-SS right away. When the embarrassed Dr. Reuter† then told him that there was no place for him here in The Hague, although he was very much needed, I felt so sorry for him. But now it seems that everything will be in order within a few days or a week. Juul was most amused about it all.

THURSDAY, JUNE 18, 1942—We were sitting around listlessly today, when suddenly we got a call from SS officer Graf. He said, *"Berlin stellt sehr viel Wert darauf, dass Sie eingesetzt werden,"*‡ whereupon Adriaan asked him to personally contact the Reichskomissariat§ and to speak with them on his behalf. It is very nice that this has happened, that Adriaan's status was given a great boost. Now, we must just wait and see how it will play out. Either he will be appointed immediately, or else he will be sent elsewhere by the SS staff who, quite rightly, don't want to waste his talents. Krista van Dijk¶ visited us; she was very excited with the news that Voorhoeve** read a secret order at her group meeting last night, saying that all "pro-German elements" had to be removed, and so forth . . .

FRIDAY, JUNE 19, 1942—Krista van Dijk came over again to tell us that Voorhoeve has now been banned from public speaking, as of yesterday morning. He might be arrested. It also seems that Ober-

---

* Ergänzungsstelle Nordwest was the recruiting office for the Waffen-SS in The Hague.
† Dr. F. Reuter was chief of the Department of Public Health under the Nazi occupation's General Commissariat (*Abteilung Volksgesundheit* of the *Generalkommissariat für Verwaltung und Justiz*), and later Red Cross supervisor under Seyss-Inquart.
‡ German: Berlin finds it very important that you be deployed.
§ German administration of the Netherlands.
¶ A pseudonym.
** Ernst Voorhoeve was the NSB's propaganda leader.

gruppenführer Rauter of the Dutch SS has forbidden him from getting sworn in a second time, whatever the cost. It seems like there will be more tension.

I had a delicious lunch with Adriaan at Lensveld; tried their famous Merlan fries and polonaise* pastry (filled with ice cream). Berman will come here on Tuesday night. I am so curious whether Adriaan will be offered a position within the Dutch SS soon. . . . Adriaan went to the Ergänzungs official to discuss the matter in person.

Just now, at a quarter past three, Gräf called up to say that they can't do without Adriaan here, and he will be appointed to a position within fourteen days. They will also keep a place open for him in case he wants to join the service later. Now at last we know where we stand.

TUESDAY, JUNE 23, 1942—Adriaan had a long two-and-a-half-hour meeting with Secretary General of Social Affairs Verwey† and chairman Beuning stopped by to make his acquaintance as well. Really, the nicest man. . . . We dined first at Gerzon's and after that we went to the Cineac‡ and I treated Loes first to cakes and soup and later to a delicious strawberry ice cream at De Kroon. I was very thirsty because of the uncommonly warm weather. We spoke very briefly with Hertman, who was with Oberstführer Sprey and another German, who complimented me on my German pronunciation! . . .

The situation with the NSB leadership is becoming increasingly difficult.§ Presumably, the German side will now withdraw, or at least will take their distance. Commissioner Schmidt seems to be going. There is also a rumor going around about a possible NSDAP membership in some time. Blokzijl is not Aryan and Van Hees is half Jewish.

---

* Meringue pastry (filled with fruit or ice cream).
† Robert Antony Verwey, Secretary-General Ministry of Social Affairs, August 1940 to May 1945.
‡ Movie theater.
§ There was a lot of infighting within the NSB, struggles between Mussert, who sought more Dutch Nazi leadership, and NSB leader Rost van Tonningen, who sided with the Germans.

In fact, almost none of the leading figures can be, either morally or through pedigree, maintained over time. Adriaan is going to begin on Wednesday, the first of July.

MONDAY, JUNE 29, 1942—It was an unusual birthday, not entirely pleasant. Adriaan was out the door by eight-thirty to be assessed by Hamberg, the one-quarter Jewish internist. In the afternoon he had to come back for a photo and he was very outraged when he was told that he was not eligible for a permanent position.

I received beautiful flowers from Zus K. and Etty B.; water lilies from Krista van Dijk, a visit from Jo S., Zus S., Ans + Simonette van H., Joep van R., the van S.s, Han and Bert, Rietma, Ans K. and a home-baked cake from Zus Ooster van V.!* Lous was a terrific help. It was boiling hot all day. Because I didn't have sugar, I couldn't offer tea; luckily we had lovely lemonade and a piece of cake for everyone.

---

* Names have been abbreviated to initials.

7

"LIKE A GOOD GARDENER"

Propaganda poster for the NSB Dutch Nazi movement, encouraging
women to join: "The Woman Who Thinks Also Votes for the NSB"

Inge Jansen kept a diary in a single hardcover blank book known as a *"gedenkboek,"* or "memory album." Its brown leather front cover was illustrated with pastel-colored flowers. Each new month opened with a pre-printed poem by the Dutch nineteenth-century poet and theologian, Nicolaas Beets, and a line or two of spiritual wisdom. "The Lord protects your comings and goings," for example, in January. Inge's writing focused on her social calendar and periodic concerns, with short entries rather than long, intimate reflections.

She wrote infrequently, filling in the pages of her blank book haphazardly. The page for January 1, for example, was filled in on Monday, January 1, 1945, while the next page, January 2, was filled in on a Saturday in 1943. Her entries were jotted in tiny scrawl, the words scrunched together at the top of the page, leaving the rest of the paper blank. None of her entries filled more than a single page, and rarely did she write twice on the same page, although the war lasted five years, giving her opportunities to return to a single date repeatedly. After shuffling the entries into a more logical order, it became clear that the first entry was dated December 12, 1941, and her last May 3, 1945.

I cannot share Inge Jansen's real name, because of Dutch privacy rules that protect the descendants of former Nazi collaborators, nor can I convey very much of her personal history, as giving such details might also indicate her identity. In any case, I could find very little by way of information about her life in public archives, either before or after the war. She was not a famous NSB-er in her own right, but it is apparent that she had friends in high places in the Nazi regime.

Public records indicate that Inge was born in Amsterdam in June 1904 to a prominent, upper class family. At age twenty-three, she married thirty-five-year-old Adriaan Jansen—also not his real name—a divorced tuberculosis specialist from Wageningen, who'd started his career in Dordrecht. Both Jansens appear to have been members of the NSB party prior to the war, but I could find no record of their membership dates. During the occupation period, Adriaan became an SS Unterscharführer, or junior squad leader, and an ascendant member of the German medical establishment.

When Inge began writing her diary, the couple was living in The Hague, and during the war they moved to Amsterdam, near the Amstel River. Inge noted that the house at Handelstraat 17 had been "requisitioned" for them, very likey meaning that another owner was evicted to make way for their arrival. Stadsarchief records indicate that it previously belonged to a twenty-two-year-old recent medical school graduate, Adolph Roozendaal, who was working as a nurse at the Nederlands Israelitische Ziekenhuis, the Jewish hospital. In 1943, Roozendaal, who was Jewish, was arrested and deported to Auschwitz, where he died on December 31, 1943. She mentioned a "Jewish boy" named David who may make a claim to the property, but it isn't clear whether this is Adolf or someone else. Whatever the hassle, from Inge's perspective, Inge and Adriaan managed to take over the apartment, and remained its owners at least until the end of the war.

City archives also note that Inge spent a month in Germany, from May to June 1944—a trip she never mentioned in her diary—and then returned to Amsterdam. After the war, she moved to a small town on the Rhine River in the province of South Holland. Newspaper obituaries relate that she died at age seventy-five in 1980.

Inge Jansens' diary was among the first 500 collected by the NIOD before 1946. In her critique, Jitty Sjenitzer-van Leening wrote that Jansen was "clearly stupid; she doesn't really understand politics. She has 'visions' and 'sees' Jesus sometimes, and dreams about a 'ruddy stranger' as well as her dead mother, father and husband." Jitty concluded that Inge was, "a somewhat wild yet insignificant personality," but she nonetheless decided to retain the diary for the Institute's collection.

I tend to disagree with Jitty in this case. While Jansen was neither a brilliant writer nor a great intellectual, she is not quite "stupid" and her diary certainly not insignificant. It takes readers into a world of Dutch high society, within a culture of German and NSB socialites that isn't often reflected in wartime literature. Her diary is a rare document of this social *metier.* Inge tours us through dinner engagements with Nazi couples, engages in outings and tea parties, all the while name-dropping so much that we start to understand how one Nazi figure relates to another—especially the women. By connecting the dots in her network, we can get a sense of the whole constellation of German and NSB figures in wartime socialite circles in the Netherlands, and how the Nazi wives played a role in the movement.

Inge recorded seeing Jessy Tulp, the wife of Sybren Tulp, Amsterdam's Police Chief—Douwe Bakker's boss—on a regular basis. She was acquainted with them enough, apparently, to call him by his nickname, Siep. At the swearing-in ceremony of NSB member Henk Feldmeijer, commander of the Nederlandsche SS,* the Tulps updated her about their new home and introduced her to other Nazi notables. Later, Jessy loaned Inge an umbrella, and she also informed Inge that her dog, Tipsy, would have to be put down.

Inge frequently mentioned how "pleasant" Dr. F. Reuter, chief of the Occupation's department of Public Health was when he stopped by for coffee, and how she enjoyed the company of his wife, "cheerful" Frau Reuter.

On another occasion, Inge wrote of enjoying a "blissful vermouth and cookies with Fraulein Schmidt," the widow of German commissioner-general for Political Affairs and Propaganda Fritz Schmidt. Schmidt, one of Seyss-Inquart's four national commissioners, was a rabid anti-Semite who declared to the nation in the summer of 1942 that the Netherlands would be free of Jews within a year.[1]

---

* The Dutch extension of Heinrich Himmler's SS.

Eight days before that "blissful vermouth," Fritz Schmidt fell out of a train window on his way to Paris. The cause of the deadly accident is a mystery that has never been solved.

In addition to her own social engagements, Inge regularly noted in her diary Adriaan's important NSB functions. He attended Anton Mussert's swearing in, conducted by Reichsführer Himmler at the zoo in The Hague, while she enjoyed the Nazi parade on De Plaats.

For Inge, attending such events was not merely about connecting to like-minded socialites—although improving her social status was evidently a primary goal. She was performing her wifely duty to help secure her husband, Adriaan, a comfortable position in the SS medical authority in the Netherlands. Her diary entries suggest that this goal consumed much of her thoughts.

Although the couple were repeatedly frustrated by setbacks, and the process took some time, Adriaan ultimately achieved his goal. With the help of their connections, he was appointed to a high-ranking position in the Department of Public Health at the Ministry of Social Affairs. Inge deserved no small credit for this feat, it seemed. She actively cultivated social relationships with well-connected Nazi women; she charmed new male SS acquaintances with her proper German pronunciation, and she leveraged those contacts to help remove obstacles to his career advancement.

One subject that Inge never discussed in her diary was the substance of the work that Adriaan aimed to do. Her primary concern was his career advancement, not his objectives for the medical establishment. Adriaan's work, as it turned out, would be to promote Nazi medical and scientific ideology.

Interviewed for an article in the official NSB newspaper, *Het Nationale Dagblad,* at the time of his appointment to the health department, he talked about his goals for improving the national well-being. In addition to boosting preventative care and expanding treatment for tuberculosis, Dr. Jansen said that he would devote serious attention to "eugenics, genetic research and the protection of the species."

He explained that "cross-breeding" of races was, in his opinion, "undesirable" because it "degraded" the quality of both races. To focus on improving genetics as part of national health practice, he explained, "fits entirely within the framework of preventative medicine." One of his priorities would be to promote the marriages of "young, healthy people." A doctor, he told the newspaper, "like a good gardener, must take care of his crops, in order to reap a bountiful harvest."[2]

Adriaan's position on human genetics, as briefly outlined in the newspaper, was very much in line with Nazi ideology, which aimed to create a "racially pure," biologically superior "master race." Inge similarly appeared to be concerned about Aryan "purity" in the Nazi leadership in the Netherlands. She commented in her diary: "Blokzijl is not Aryan and Van Hees is half Jewish. In fact, almost none of the leading figures can be, either morally or through pedigree, maintained over time." In the following entry, she describes an intern as "one-quarter Jewish"—a calculation for which she provides no source.

Women, naturally, played an important role in genealogical engineering, as producers of the newly dominant "Aryan" species, and the SS even meticulously vetted prospective SS brides for their biological, political, and social fitness.[3] As Gudrun Schwarz explained in a groundbreaking 1997 study of women in the SS,[4] the Nazi party understood itself not to be an exclusively male fraternity, but a *Sippengemeinschaft,* or "family institution," whose job was to create the master race. Women played a crucial role in supporting the Nazi family structure, not merely as "keepers of the race," but also as stabilizers of a home environment that would act as a "normalizing" environment. As Schwarz put it, they were to "establish a normal family life . . . in order to make the crimes their husbands committed . . . appear like an ordinary job."[5]

Vetted and approved Nazi wives "recognized their contribution as an integral part of the battle to cleanse and renew the fatherland and vowed unconditional and eternal loyalty to their husbands in an oath undertaken during SS marriage ceremonies," wrote religious studies professor Katharina von Kellenbach, who explored relational dynamics in such families, through their post-war contact with prison chaplains.[6]

Nazi marriages were thus organized quite strictly along conventional gender roles. Husbands performed in the public realm, and wives remained fixed to the domestic domain. The wives were not mostly blind or unaware of their husbands' role in genocidal work either, she found. In fact, most often they were informed, and condoned this behavior, as it advanced the fascist cause.

Even after the war, when wives learned of atrocities some of their men had committed, Von Kellenbach discovered, they rarely expressed shock or moral revulsion. Instead, as steadfast companions in the cause, they offered ongoing support and devotion, as they'd been taught. Von Kellenbach found this "nexus of private decency and public atrocity, female nurture and male violence," to be the sustaining formula for Nazi relationships.[7]

IN THE NETHERLANDS, about one-third of the members of the NSB party were women, according to Zonneke Matthée, who has studied this contingent in depth. Seven years after Anton Mussert founded the Dutch Nazi political party in 1931, the National Socialist's Women's Organization, or NSVO, was established as a subsidiary wing for women. Its co-founders were Julia op ten Noort and Elisabeth Keers-Laseur, who were both actively involved in the fascist movement in the Netherlands from its early days.

Inge had close personal ties to both the leading women of the NSVO. In one of her first diary entries, she mentioned "Juul," who was helping to investigate "the reason that Adriaan was not accepted by the Waffen-SS." Juul went out of her way to plea Adriaan's case to the office of the Reichsführer-SS, Heinrich Himmler; his staff promised to "look into it immediately." Her intervention apparently had some impact, because two weeks later, Adriaan was admitted into the Waffen-SS, and "Juul was most amused about it all." Later in her diary, Inge mentioned that she caught a train with Juul and her mother, Mrs. Op ten Noort, to Amsterdam from The Hague in a torrential rainstorm the day she and Adriaan moved house. In another diary entry, she noted that Keers-Laseur (who she calls Bets Keers), "stayed faithfully beside me" at an important funeral.

Julia op ten Noort, known among her friends as "Juul," was prized in Nazi circles in the Netherlands and Germany as an Aryan beauty, "infamous for her carnal way of life," according to historian Jan Meyers, who described her in his biography of Mussert. Another friend said she had a "regal" bearing. In the 1930s and '40s, she traveled, as a single woman, to Berlin with both Mussert and co-NSB leader Rost van Tonningen, and helped connect the two Dutch Nazis with Hitler's top political leaders. She had a particularly intimate relationship with Heinrich Himmler, who became known as her ally and "protector." In 1944, as yet unwed, Op ten Noort gave birth to a son, whom she named Heinrich, rumored to be Himmler's child.[8]

Interviewed at her home in the Netherlands in 1990, Op ten Noort continued to refute the rumor. She explained that she joined the Nazi party in the early 1930s because she felt that the Netherlands was too socially and politically divided. "We wanted a new world, based on a Christianity without sects," she said. "We envisioned a new global community." Jewish people didn't have a place in her idealistic Christian vision, but while she knew about persecution of Jews, she claimed she "never saw it."

"You must understand," she added, "I had nothing against Jews, but among the Jews there were many materialists, and I scorned that."[9]

"Bets" Keers-Laseur, the wife of a high ranking NSB-er, was appointed as the first national leader of the NSVO after the German invasion. At its triumphal membership meeting on October 25, 1940, she presented the gathering with the first edition of its new propaganda publication, *De Nationaal Socialistische Vrouw*. NSVO women should, she said in a speech, "think, not what can this offer me, but what can I contribute?"[10]

Serving the "public good" rather than the "private interest" was a core principle of NSVO membership. Its women were encouraged to take German folk dancing lessons, German language, and sewing courses. In the winter month, they formed knitting circles to make ear-muffs, mittens, and socks for soldiers on the Eastern Front. "Women must feel the great Germanic solidarity," read a pamphlet for NSVO members, most likely penned by Op ten Noort. "And she must take responsibility, alongside men . . . for the moral and physical well-being of her people."[11]

Keers-Laseur lived to be 107 years old, the Netherlands' old-est person at the time, and was nicknamed the "black widow of Bloemendaal," where she lived. She never disavowed her involvement in the NSVO, and continued to argue that "fables about the gas cham-bers were spread by the Allies."[12]

Unlike the larger NSB party, the NSVO saw an uptick in mem-bership during the German occupation. In 1939, it had no more than 1,000 members, found Matthée, but by 1943, that number had risen to 20,000. During that growth period, the National Socialist's racial ideology and its anti-Semitic rhetoric had become far blunter and more blatant, winning over more NSVO adherents. Its membership only declined once the Germans started to lose the war. Still, the NSVO remained in existence until the Netherlands' liberation.[13]

Not every female adherent to the NSB party was an NSVO mem-ber. There were many women who merely supported their husbands or fiancés, but weren't politically active. These women often felt that they need not operate in the political arena as their primary domain of influence was in the home. "Women had a clear role in National So-cialism," explained Op ten Noort. "We could contribute to the unity of the people, a unity that naturally began with the family."[14]

Although we tend to regard genocide as "men's work" and see women's roles as more obscure or indirect, there is mounting evidence that women were substantially complicit in the Nazi genocide proj-ect. In her book, *Hitler's Furies: German Women in the Nazi Kill-ing Fields,* American historian Wendy Lower found that, contrary to popular conception, hundreds of thousands of German women went to "the Nazi East," as she called it, and were "integral parts of Hitler's machinery of destruction."[15]

Von Kellenbach found that whether women were combatants, nurses in euthanasia centers, or housewives, their adherence to Nazi party ideologies and acceptance of subsidiary roles undergirded the regime. "I look at women's support, love, and loyalty as an integral element of the genocide," Von Kellenbach wrote. "Although most women did not directly participate in the violence, their intimate involvement with the perpetrators makes them more than 'innocent bystanders.'"[16]

Lower found that in the popular imagination, Nazi women tend to fall into "two pretty extreme categories": either the passive woman who served as "Hitler's babies machine," on the one hand, or the sadistic "bestial" female concentration camp guard, such as Ilse Koch, the "Beast of Buchenwald," or Irma Grese, the "Hyena of Auschwitz," who were either denuded of their femininity or sensationalized as eroticized examples of deviant femininity. But there were many female Nazis who conformed to neither of these tropes.[17]

Inge Jansen exerted some influence over her husband and she held fast to her Nazi principles. In her diary, she wrote about a friend who was so anti-German that she could no longer associate with Inge, but Inge didn't experience this as problematic. Her response: "Alas, there are thousands who think this way."

Throughout the war, however, Inge worked hard to keep in step with her German cohorts. She took German lessons, and attended the weekly Nazi film reels at the Cineac, as well as concerts of German-approved classical music. At the Schubert song night at the Concert-gebouw, featuring Austrian opera singer Isolde Riehl, she noted that Seyss-Inquart was in the audience.* She admired men who represented the Nazi ideal: tall, blond, blue eyed, and, of course, uniformed. She wasn't merely keeping up appearances to appeal to the overlords; she was entranced and convinced of the cause until the bitter end.

---

* Noted in her diary on November 23, 1942.

As the bright Nazi future began to dim in her eyes, Inge Jansen's mental landscape also declined, along with her social and economic prospects. She experienced a personal tragedy, the Reich lost its grip, and the whole New Order she'd pinned her hopes on unraveled. Her decline mirrored the dissolution of the Nazi dream, in a way that no collaborator—least of all Inge herself—had anticipated.

8

"WAS THIS FORCED LABOR OR SLAUGHTER?"

A "Jewish District" sign on the corner of Jodenbreestraat, in 1941.
Rembrandt's former home and studio is in the background.

In a nook of her dining room in her home in Amersfoort, Rebecca Emmerik leaned down over a small desk, while her crown of dark curls fell across her face. She was checking for something on her computer in her cramped office space, cluttered with photo albums, folders, and binders.

She removed her thick glasses when she looked back up at me, pushing back her curls. "I've been working on my family tree," she said. "It's been going on for a while. My mother came to me one day, and she showed me a picture and she said, 'That's my uncle.' I said 'uncle'? I never knew that my grandfather had any brothers or sisters. Then I got multiple sclerosis and I had some time, because I couldn't work, so I thought I'd figure it out."

Rebecca is a goldsmith by profession, and when she was twenty-nine she began to lose sensation in her fingers. Eventually, she was unable to practice her trade, and went on disability.

I wanted to ask her questions about how it had started and how it had progressed. My mother had had numbness in her legs at first, and gradually lost her ability to walk, but the MS had spared her hands. It was already something of a coincidence that her family name was Emmerik—no relation to my grandfather, of course—but wasn't this also an odd and unlikely echo?

It turned out that Rebecca was trying to figure out how to call up an MP3 file. She wanted to play me an audio recording she'd made during the commemoration of the seventy-fifth anniversary of the liberation of the Netherlands at Camp Westerbork.

There had been a ceremonial reading of names of the 102,000

victims who'd been transported from there to the East, and never returned. The reading started on January 22, 2020, in the evening, continued through the night, and lasted six whole days, ending in the afternoon of January 27. Some 830 readers had taken turns.

"When they got to my family's names, I taped it," Rebecca told me. Then she clicked Play.

A woman's voice, somber and monotone, pronounced each name carefully: "Abraham Emmerik, 35 years old. Abraham Emmerik, 36 years old. Betje Emmerik, 17 years old. Betje Emmerik, 27 years old. Betje Emmerik, 57 years old. Betsy Emmerik, 20 years old. Branca Emmerik, 9 years old. Branca Emmerik, 24 years old. Branca Emmerik, 30 years old. Clara Emmerik, 17 years old. David Emmerik, 15 years old. David Emmerik, 34 years old. Dientje Emmerik, 22 years old. . . ."

"It goes on like that for about four minutes," she said, taking off her glasses again, this time to pat tears from her eyes with a cloth. "I still get emotional," she said, lowering the volume. "That's only the D, and they go to V. Vogeltje is the last one." Vogeltje, Meijer's wife.

This single family list contained the names of grandmothers and grandchildren, brothers and sisters, uncles and cousins, several name-sakes from an extended family, across generations.

"I had family of 156 people," Rebecca said. "Twelve survived the war."

Rebecca never knew that all these people even existed until that day, about twenty years ago, when her mother mentioned her great uncle. Since then, she had traced her genealogy to the seventeenth century. She learned that two French brothers from a town called Metz moved to Amsterdam in 1760, establishing a family line in the Netherlands.

"I kept doing research on family members and I found a lot of people in my family, but in the twentieth century they were mostly murdered, so it stops there," she said.

Abraham Emmerik, a cousin, was probably the first. He was picked up in the February raids of 1941, and is on Wally de Lang's list.[1]

Abraham was the ninth of ten children in the family of Jacob Emmerik, an Amsterdam fishmonger, and his wife, Branca Fortuijn. After completing six years of primary school, he became a butcher's apprentice and married a "cardboard worker," Betje Engelsman, who lived down the block. They had three children, Japie, Mozes, and Branca. During the 1930s Depression, they fell deeper into poverty, and received government aid. They earned extra money renting a room to Abraham's brother, Joseph.[2]

On February 22, Abraham was walking with Betje's brother, Nathan Engelsman, through the Jewish Quarter and they were both caught in the sweep, and both sent to Mauthausen. Nathan was a victim of the Hartheim Castle gassings, and Abraham lasted a few more months and died in the camp at age thirty-five.[3] Betje was informed verbally, but never knew the details. Two years later, she was also arrested and deported to Sobibor, along with Mozes, 13, and Branca, 9, where they all were killed on arrival. Japie, 13, survived the war. All but one of Abraham's brothers and sisters were also murdered.[*]

Uncle Joseph, their sometime tenant, was the sole surviving child of Jacob and Branca. He was spared because of his "mixed-marriage" to a non-Jewish woman. Their son, also named Joseph, born July 4, 1938, was also safe as a non-Jew. He was Rebecca Emmerik's father. Joseph Jr. was in his eighties when I met Rebecca. I asked her if he'd be willing to talk to me about his childhood and his life. He declined, telling her that he found it "too hard." She told me, though, that Joseph still had vivid memories of his childhood in the Jewish Quarter, even if he won't visit his old neighborhood anymore.

"He can't handle that," Rebecca told me. "We used to do that in the old days. I went in the car with my father and since he was kind of like a street kid, he was always telling great stories about all the things that happened to him in his childhood."

During the occupation, his mother would ask him to stick his head

---

[*] Stadsarchief, Emmerik bio.

out the window, look down the street, and see what was happening. He did this regularly for about two years.

"He'd look out the window and yell back to his mother, 'I see movement!'"

But little by little, the neighborhood was cleared. Because they were non-Jewish, they were some of the last of the old residents left.

One day, his mother sent him out to look, and he went all the way down the block. He came back and told his mother what he'd seen. "Mom, nothing. Nothing. Everything's empty. Everyone's gone."[*]

THE FIRST JEWS to be sent to "labor camps" were German Jewish refugees, who had never been regarded as Dutch citizens, and unemployed Dutch Jewish men, who were out of work because they'd been barred from holding jobs or running businesses. Their deportations were handled by various Dutch government bodies, such as the Labor Office in The Hague and the Amsterdam Labor Office, with some involvement from the Jewish Council.

A Central Bureau for Jewish Emigration was set up in Amsterdam at the end of March 1941, and at first it was mainly concerned with Jewish registration and applications for emigration abroad. After Nazi leaders agreed to implement their "Final Solution" at the Wannsee Conference in January 1942, it was moved to Adama van Scheltemaplein in Amsterdam Zuid and renamed the *Zentralstelle*. From then on, it focused on "Jewish removal," under the command of SS Hauptsturmführer Ferdinand Aus der Fünten, chief of the Bureau for Jewish Emigration, the *Zentralstelle*. The German SS mounted its pressure on the Dutch civil administration, police, Dutch railways, and also the Jewish Council, to enforce compliance with deportation efforts.[4]

The Jewish Council had no authority of its own and made no decisions about who would be sent away, or when. It is a common

---

[*] Emmerik interview.

misconception, still frequently re-reported, that the Jewish Council drew up deportation lists. This is not true. Aus der Fünten obtained cooperation of the Council, however, by handing out exemptions, which the Council could use to protect people from "labor duty." At first, he granted the Council 17,500 such exemptions, for people who were "deemed indispensable to the Jewish community."

"I received a call-up to go to the *Zentralstelle* to be exempted," Mirjam Levie recalled. "Eitje added that my parents and Bobby[*] would also be exempted. . . . I was completely overjoyed. I . . . briefly stopped by Father's office to tell him the news. We were so happy that day. At the very least, we'd be safe for the winter months, or so we thought."

Anyone who was granted an exemption got a stamp on their identity card, which indicated that they were barred from deportation. The word for stamp in German is *Sperre*, and soon, any form of exemption from deportation was "a Sperre."

Working for the Council served as sanctuary, and so the Council hired as many people as it could, as quickly as possible. "The most implausible jobs were created," wrote Levie.[5] By 1943, it had 8,000 employees, each holding a Sperre that (theoretically) barred not just the individual, but their nuclear family, from deportation.

The German authorities at first also allowed for medical exemptions, which initially could protect the physically unfit from deportation, especially with the help of sympathetic Jewish doctors. Later, only Aryan doctors who'd been approved by the Germans were allowed to sign such examination forms, but they usually overlooked even legitimate ailments, in order to facilitate the process of deportation.

Early on, government officials, too, sometimes found ways to sabotage individual call-ups, by either forging identity cards, fabricating doctor's certificates, or sending Jews to the East as "Aryans," which allowed some to survive.[6]

During the first half of 1942, the call-ups came in relatively small

---

[*] Her sister.

batches of mostly able-bodied young adults—500 to 1,000 at a time—who were sent to various small work camps on Dutch soil.

But the rules kept changing, and the screws were always tightening. Generalkommissar for Political Affairs and Propaganda, Fritz Schmidt, announced as early as August 1941 that the Führer no longer sought "rehabilitation" of the Jews, but their exclusion from European society. This was slightly premature—five months before German Nazi and SS leaders met at the Wannsee Conference.

"The death blow" for the population of Jews in the Netherlands "followed at the end of June 1942," wrote Mirjam Levie in her diary.

It was a Friday evening, the beginning of Sabbath. The phone rang at the homes of Jewish Council members, and each one was told to report at 10 p.m. at the *Zentralstelle* offices for a meeting with Aus der Fünten.

The Council's Co-Chairman David Cohen had a premonition that something terrible was about to occur, but he tried to "take solace in the beautiful summer evening, and the singing of birds all around."[7] Asscher and other board members assumed it was a routine meeting, and didn't attend, so only Cohen and two other board members, Edwin Sluzker and Abraham de Hoop (director of the Cinema Association), faced Aus der Fünten. The Hauptsturmführer chief informed them that Jewish men and women aged sixteen to forty would henceforth be sent in "police-controlled" groups to Germany for labor service.

Cohen was "extremely shocked," and objected, calling such a plan a violation of international law, according to a memoir he wrote later. Aus der Fünten answered, according to Cohen, "It is we who decide what is international law." He added later, "We are the winners."[8]

The co-chairman said that he continued to protest, but did not make headway.* The following day, the larger Council board met again to discuss how to proceed. Some members rejected the notion of

---

* There are competing narratives of this meeting; no minutes have survived—probably none were taken—so it is impossible to know which version is correct.

any cooperation, and others felt that, if the Jewish Council served as an intermediary, it could delay implementation, forestall deportations and "prevent worse" harm to the Jewish people.

Aus der Fünten's *Zentralstelle* made up the deportation lists, but it offered the Jewish Council a consolation: an additional 25,000 *Sperren* to distribute. The Germans reserved the right to veto them.[9]

A few weeks after the Council's board meeting, Mirjam Levie wrote in her diary that "Jews, men and women between the ages of 16 and 40, would be sent to labor camps in Gross-Deutschland,* probably in Upper Silesia," and she "assumed we would be put to work in factories in areas that were most heavily bombed."

Dutch Jews from other parts of the country were soon forced to leave their homes and relocate to Amsterdam, as part of a consolidation process, but others were deported from their hometowns. Anyone who received a "labor camp" call-up in the capital was first processed through the Hollandsche Schouwburg, a former national theater, which had been converted into a central deportation center.

After spending a few hours or several days at the Schouwburg, Jews were transported to Westerbork. For a period of fourteen months in 1942 and 1943, the theater temporarily housed 46,000 Jewish people, although it had no sleeping, dining, or facilities for basic needs. When it became overcrowded, children were taken across the street to a Jewish day care center, from which the resistance could sometimes spirit them away to safety.

At Westerbork, they joined German Jewish refugees who hadn't been granted permission to naturalize, and were now officially prisoners of the Reich. Until the end of June, Refugee Camp Westerbork was still under Dutch control and manned by Dutch military police, the Marechaussee. On July 1, 1942, a German camp commander was installed, and it was officially renamed: *Durchgangslager* Westerbork, Transit Camp Westerbork.

Those who didn't comply with call-up notices faced police raids

---

* Greater Germany.

of their homes. Sometimes, police would take the moment as an opportunity to raid the whole street, regardless of their call-up or Sperre status. During one such raid in August, Levie was called into the Hollandse Schouwburg in the middle of the night to type up petitions for members of the Jewish Council who had been hauled in at random. She witnessed Aus der Fünten lining up Council employees against a wall, and doing preliminary "selections" of potential deportees. She noted the complete "arbitrariness" of such decisions, made while he was "often stupid drunk."[10] She typed up as many exception cards as she possibly could, and was "pleased to learn the following day that all the cases I had typed up had turned out all right."

In these and other ways, she and other Jewish Council staff members tried to intervene wherever they could. Sometimes this meant rushing off to someone's house at night to help them pack, make sure they had winter clothes, or prepare sandwiches for the journey. Although she had a Sperre that protected her parents and her sister, Mirjam's extended family was still vulnerable to deportation; Green Police came to their door several times, and twice they were rounded up.

Other people tried to avoid deportation by petitioning against their categorization as Jews. If they only had two Jewish grandparents, for example, or if they'd been baptized into the Christian faith, or were married to a non-Jewish person (known as a "mixed marriage") and had "mixed" children, they could apply for an exemption. These requests were sent to The Hague registration office, where they came under the purview of a German civil servant, Hans-George Calmeyer. Seyss-Inquart gave Calmeyer until December 1942 to decide on ambiguous cases, and in that time, Calmeyer was able to save somewhere between 2,000 to 3,000 people by "downgrading" their Nazi-defined Jewishness.

"The office was inundated with pleas and requests, most of them transparently bogus," wrote historian Bob Moore, "and there was clearly little that Calmeyer could do with these."[11]

Applications for any kind of Sperre were usually submitted through the Jewish Council offices, at a specialized department, the

Expositur, led by Edwin Sluzker with 150 employees. The letters that informed applicants of the Germans' decisions were also distributed by the Council. This gave many people the wrong impression that it was the Council that made such fateful decisions, and the organization was also frequently blamed for the outcomes.

The Expositur was the Council's direct liaison with the *Zentralstelle*; when it could, it tried to help people avert summonses. De Jong described Sluzker as someone who was "equally obliging to everyone who visited him," but who "did not overestimate his position." He became both loathed and beloved, depending on how effective his intervention was, but De Jong asserted, "He tried with patience and kindness, but also with cunning, to gain margins of favor for this or that."[12]

Dutch historian Jacques Presser characterized the Sperre system as the Germans' "cat-and-mouse game" with the Jews. "Their main object was to get rid of the Jews smoothly and by stages, so as to cause the minimum disruption in Dutch public life," he wrote. "To do that, they needed the cooperation of the victims themselves—by granting temporary privileges to a minority, they succeeded in liquidating the rest without too much fuss or bother. . . . Hence the Jewish Council became inextricably involved in a *danse macabre* with Satan calling the tune."

This dance of death often included German concessions to the Jewish Council, to give its members the illusion that they maintained a degree of control over the situation. For example, in June 1942, Aus der Fünten wanted to begin the deportation process by calling up 600 people a day. The Jewish Council, hoping to forestall at least some call-ups, managed to negotiate him down to 350 a day. He conceded, under the condition that at least 4,000 people would be sent to him by mid-July.

On July 5, 1942, a Sunday, Amsterdam police agents delivered "labor duty" call-up notices to Jewish men. The *Zentralstelle* had selected the victims based on a list drawn up by Mayor Edward Voûte.

This list was handed over to the Jewish Council, which managed to exempt an unknown number of people from deportation. Its staff typed the names and addresses onto pre-printed cards. Tulp's Jewish Affairs Bureau at Nieuwe Doelenstraat 13 received these cards and distributed them to the police stations across the city, giving them to policemen whose job it was to hand them out.[13]

"Nobody knew: Was this forced labor or slaughter?" Levie wrote in her diary.

The call up notices read: "Summons! You are called up for forced labor in Germany under police supervision and you must present yourself for personal and medical inspection at transit-camp Westerbork."

You must be present at . . . . date: . . . .
    hour: . . . . place: . . . .

As luggage, you are allowed:

1 suit-case or rucksack

1 pair work boots

2 pairs of socks

2 pairs of underpants

2 shirts

1 overall

2 woolen blankets

2 sets of sheets

1 bowl

1 mug

1 spoon

1 pullover

towel and toilet things

also victuals for 3 days and all your food coupons.

A few other instructions about identity documents and suitcase labeling followed. The notices concluded: "The home must be left in good order, closed and the key must be taken with you. No pets are allowed."[14]

The police would make arrangements for Jewish families' abandoned household pets, Meershoek said. They would be cared for by non-Jewish volunteers.

Few people who had received their notices showed up as instructed. The Germans, infuriated by this non-compliance, responded with a raid on July 14, randomly arresting 700 Jews. They announced in a circular that all of these "hostages" would be sent to Mauthausen if all 4,000 people with summonses didn't report for "duty."

NEVERTHELESS, BY MID-JULY the occupiers had sufficient numbers of people in transit camp Westerbork to begin its "Jewish removal" project. On July 15, a Wednesday, the first transport of 1,135 people left for Auschwitz from Camp Westerbork. They had to first walk three miles, carrying babies and baggage, to Hooghalen train station, a march of about two hours, before embarking on a twenty-four-hour train journey with no breaks.

The very next day, Thursday, July 16, 895 more camp residents followed in their footsteps—also lugging blankets, sometimes wearing heavy coats in summer, because they were unable to carry them, and hoped these would come in handy when the weather turned cold. Then again on Tuesday, another 931 people were marched out of Westerbork three miles to Hooghalen, and forced onto trains. Sometimes these were third-class passenger cars, but often, the people rode in freight boxcars, occasionally equipped with wood benches, and sometimes they were forced into livestock carriers, where they sat on the floor among the luggage, on a little bit of straw, with a bucket in the corner to serve as a latrine.

Then, Friday, July 17: 1,000 more.

Monday: 1,010.

Friday: 1,007.

And so it went, every few days. Another 500 to 1,000 people would be notified that their name was on the list. They would be leaving the next morning, so they'd better pack their bags. Awakened around 6 a.m. or 7 a.m., they marched two hours, boarded a train for a full night and day, and were mostly never heard from again.

By the end of August—in just six weeks' time—fifteen such transports had already departed for Auschwitz, containing a total of 12,800 men, women, and children. The last train to Auschwitz from Hooghalen station left on October 30, 1942. Some thirty-two transports of 31,000 people, already gone, mostly murdered on arrival.

After that, the process was simplified. The Dutch national railways had finished building the rail link from Westerbork to Hooghalen. No more long marches. Those listed for transport could board a train from the very heart of the transit camp on the so-called *Boulevard des Misères,* with no return ticket. Westerbork, once a refugee center for German Jews fleeing persecution at home, was now essentially a railway depot on a transit line to death.

The departures were regularized to once a week. Mostly on Tuesdays, very early in the morning, those on the list would be roused from their bunks to board the trains. Beginning in March 1943, a new destination was added: Sobibor in German-occupied Polish territories. It would be an even more brutal train ride of nearly four long days. The vast majority of passengers would be gassed on arrival.

9

"A KIND OF
GATHERING PLACE"

Hanukkah in Westerbork, photo by Rudolf Breslauer

In the winter of 2020, while the Netherlands was in its second pandemic lockdown, the friends who made up our "Corona bubble" invited us to join them at a Dutch holiday park in Drenthe, where we could all stay in separate small cottages and let our kids play together in a quiet, natural setting. Without the option of leaving the country to visit family for the winter holidays, I jumped at the idea.

I booked one of many cottages nearby theirs from the lots of ticky-tacky houses, near a well-equipped playground and indoor swimming pool. The concept behind such parks, as far as I can gather, is that they centralize activities for children so that parents can sit in their yards and relax to their heart's content. Normally, this kind of park is not really my style, but on this particular occasion, it promised just what I was looking for: a break from isolation.

On the day of the booking, I plugged the address of the holiday park into the GPS of my rental car, without even glancing at a map. I didn't think about where we were headed until I started to see familiar names along the highway: Epe, Apeldoorn, Wezep, Hooghalen. I was musing about my unshakable faith in modern technology right up until the moment when we made the final turn onto the long road that led to the holiday village. Street signs informed me that if I turned left, I'd come to our destination. If I turned right, I'd arrive at Memorial Camp Westerbork.

As soon as we had stepped into the driveway of our holiday house, still trying to recover from the chill that had shot through my bones, I quizzed my best friend: "Did you know that we were so close to Westerbork?"

She blanched. "I didn't want to tell you because I was afraid you wouldn't come. I thought you'd probably figure it out before you booked."

So, there we were, vacationing adjacent to a concentration camp, the terrors of which I had been reading about for months. I had not yet visited; I hadn't been sure I wanted to. But at that moment, I made up my mind that this was no real coincidence. It was necessary for me to see Westerbork at some point for my research, and now was as good a time as any. In fact, maybe it was an ideal time. Although it frightened me to think of walking there, onto that ground where tens of thousands of people had faced deportations, I knew I had to do it.

We waited until the last day of our trip, postponing what we felt sure would be an unsettling experience. As was perhaps inevitable, it was pouring rain that day, an unrelenting downpour. The children stayed with one of our friends, and a group of us adults put on our rain gear and tramped out onto the dirt roads that led from the parking area into the memorial park, dragging along my soggy, miserable dog behind us.

Drenthe's landscape is both surprisingly stunning and deeply dreary. Evergreens stand tall and lofty, and there is a lush, forested underbrush. The sky is wide, by turns slate blue and granite gray, as the weather continuously changes. The earth under our feet was mossy, muddy, and sodden. When we were there, in December, it was dark nearly all of the time. Sunset came at around 4 p.m., but it hardly made a difference because of a nearly omnipresent blanket of dark clouds.

To get to the camp from the parking lot was a two-mile hike; we took the circuitous paved path through the woods, which were largely serene and unremarkable, until we suddenly came upon a sprawling Radio Observatory, a long row of monumental radio telescopes reminiscent of the first scene of the movie *Contact* with Jodie Foster. This surreal, space-aged feature to the landscape provided an unexpected twist to our journey, and we marveled for a moment, snapping photos with our phones, before we continued on to the camp.

At about the point that we could see the barbed wire from the distance, we encountered a series of five enormous stone, coffin-shaped blocks. Inscribed in each one was the name of a destination camp and the number of Dutch people murdered there. The memorial stone for Theresienstadt read 175; for Mauthausen, the death toll was 1,749; the number on the Bergen-Belsen stone read, "more than 1,700." Curiously, the stones for the camps where most Westerbork detainees died were no larger, though the number of deaths they represented were vastly higher: Sobibor, 34,313; and Auschwitz-Birkenau, read 60,330, including 200 Sinti and Roma people.

Next, we passed the only preserved building on the site, the former residence of the German camp commander, a stately green country house that was fully encased in misted glass. Because of Corona restrictions, it was temporarily closed.

Then we entered the main gate, surrounded by barbed wire fencing, and stepped into a large open field where hundreds of barracks once stood. On either side were large fields, both the size of soccer pitches, with a path cutting between them. Grass was trying to grow, but only half-heartedly, and it was mostly coming up in brown, mangey patches.

I knew from my reading that Camp Westerbork once housed not only scores of sleeping barracks but also an operational hospital, factory buildings for everything from shoemaking to scrap metal production, as well as a school, outdoor recreational facilities, and even a restaurant. There was a weekly cabaret, which took place on a stage—suggesting there may have been a theater at the camp. None of these structures remained. After the war, Westerbork served many purposes, first as a prison for suspected Dutch collaborators, then a military camp, and later a "reception center" or internment camp for Moluccans and Indo-Dutch attempting to repatriate to Netherlands after Indonesian independence.[*] The last of the World War II camp barracks were demolished in 1971, long before the Remembrance

---

[*] A story from another complicated chapter of Dutch history.

Center was established in 1983 and apparently there have been scattered, desultory efforts to make monuments here since.

A half shell of one barrack had been restored to give a sense of the space hundreds of Jewish inmates inhabited, but it was perplexingly unfinished. There was only a small illustration of three-high bunks crammed up against each other, and the stoves on which dozens of people jostled to cook.

The camp itself was an inconceivable 119 acres when it was operational, I'd read. Walking around the memorial grounds, enclosed by barbed wire, it felt like it couldn't be more than four or five acres. Where were all these other acres? Were they where the radio telescopes stood today? Where was the heath where they strolled in the summer, as I'd read about in the diaries, that had once been teeming with lupins in bloom?

The paved path cut right through the heart of the camp, known as the Boulevard des Misères, where the train once pulled in to collect its "cargo." But here, too, only a fragment remained: two red box cars. In between them, a small video monitor, which might've told a story, was turned off.

To the right was another monument to the dead: a multitude of red bricks of various heights, scattered across the paved ground. My friend whispered in my ear that if I looked at it from above, I could see that these formed a map of the Netherlands, with each section revealing how many Jews from each province had perished. Each brick, topped with a Star of David, stood for a single Jewish victim, and those with metal flames on top represented Roma and Sinti.

At irregular intervals, a photograph stuck out from the brick, with an image of the victim, or a family of victims. The heights of the bricks varied, from about an inch off the ground to about a half a foot. I grasped that these heights depended on the age of the victim: the older the victim, the taller the brick.

But none of these bricks were very tall, and I found it very uncomfortable that they were all lying on the ground, as if discarded materials from a construction project. As I gazed upon them from above, I wondered if other visitors to this site also felt the urge to step on them, to walk across them, as if they were mere stepping stones. How had so many people been reduced to stepping stones under foot?

We continued walking through the endless downpour, each of us separately, and silently, lost in our own thoughts. I tried to imagine what it might have felt like to be an inmate here, with the damp and the cold and the raw elements—but mostly the horrifying uncertainty. Eventually, at the end of the boulevard of misery, under a black wooden guard tower, we stood before the rusted steel remnants of railway track, with its ends bent unaccountably skyward. This monument was built in 1992 by a Jewish survivor, I read later, who'd boarded one of the departing trains from here as an infant. Yet another fragment.

"WESTERBORK WASN'T REALLY a concentration camp," one of the Dutch men on the trip tried to explain to me, before we visited. "It was just a kind of gathering place, collection point, before people were sent on."

This is correct, in a sense, as far as it goes. Westerbork certainly wasn't a killing center or a place of terrible hardship. Inmates at this camp were often shocked when they witnessed the degradation of prisoners transferred in from other Dutch concentration camps, such as Amersfoort and Vught, where torture and abuse were more common.

In fact, there are a surprising number of surviving photographs[1] from Westerbork in which people appear to be having fun. We see images of men playing soccer in their sports clothes, smiling women carrying baskets across a farm, a violinist playing for a group of rapt children, and a crowd gathered around a menorah, lighting candles for a Hanukkah celebration. The camp cabaret produced enough songs that someone, more recently, made an entire CD of them (which I once received as a gift) and someone else compiled a small book of fairytales for children, also composed at Westerbork.

No one wore striped pajamas, but instead went about in their own street clothes. Their faces in the photos were not gaunt, and their bodies were not skeletal. If these were not black-and-white photos, one would be sure that the people strolling down the camp paths or doing calisthenics in the yard would be ruddy-cheeked. There is one photograph of a dentist's office, in which several people are having their teeth checked and cleaned.

Who can make sense of any of this? Why would people be having dental work done when they're about to be shipped off to be murdered? I found the incongruity rather perverse. But I was reminded of Ralph Polak and Miep Krant striding across Dam Square with the yellow stars on their coats, and Judith Cohen's caveat: "We have to be careful not to read history backwards."

While these images conveyed a misleading narrative about Westerbork, diaries revealed another: The Nazis had created a simulacrum of normalcy undergirded by the false hope that, with a little luck of the draw, one could live out the war under poor but adequate conditions. However, for anyone who watched the trains depart again and again, the terror the deportations instilled must have been tantamount to psychological torture.

What can we make of the happy pictures of Westerbork, then? Are they propaganda shots similar to the staged documentary film that was made at Theresienstadt, the Nazis' "model camp" in German-occupied Czechoslovakia? Were the inmates forced to look joyful? Or did these pictures reflect peoples' last-gasp efforts to enjoy what there was in life? Could they have been glad only that, at least, they were still on Dutch soil, and had not yet been added to a list? Or did they show that people were utterly unaware?

In March 1944, Westerbork's German SS commander, Albert Konrad Gemmeker, decided that he wanted to make a documentary film about Westerbork. His plan was to share it with top Nazi officials in Berlin, to convince them that he was running the Dutch project efficiently and that the camp was still useful for its industrial output. By that point in the war, 90,000 Dutch Jews had already been transported East, and Gemmeker was concerned that the camp would soon be closed because it had lost its primary purpose. If it was closed, he would likely be sent to the Eastern Front, a future he did not relish.

Gemmeker assigned the filmmaking project to Rudolf Werner Breslauer, a German Jewish camp inmate from Leipzig who'd worked as an art photographer and lithographer before the war. He had moved his family to the Netherlands, as refugees from the Reich in 1937, and had worked for printers in Utrecht, until 1942, when German officials came to the door and said they would be requisitioning his house. Then he and his wife, Bella Weissmann, and their three children, Ursula, Mischa, and Stephan, were put on the train to Westerbork.

By the time Gemmeker commissioned the film in 1944, Breslauer had already worked for some time as the camp's official photographer, responsible for identity-card portraits, and also pictures of official camp functions, such as SS parties for German officials at the Commander's mansion. He also took snapshots of the camp's shop and check-ups at the very modern dentist's office.

Breslauer was not paid for his photography or filmmaking work, but Gemmeker must have promised that he and his family would not be put on a transport list while the film was in production. All materials needed for the film would be supplied and paid for by the SS.[2]

Over the next two months, Breslauer managed to shoot more than two hours of raw documentary footage. He captured inmates engaged in all manner of labor, in a carpentry workshop, making furniture, in an aircraft scrap yard, taking apart fallen jets, and in a leather studio, making shoes and bags—even researchers working in a scientific laboratory. All of this footage might have worked as marketing material for Gemmeker.

But, Breslauer took an extraordinary risk: he filmed eight minutes of footage of the trains transporting Jews, two in March and one in May. Two were incoming trains, bringing Jews from Amsterdam and Camp Vught, and one was an outgoing train, rather atypically headed for two different destinations. Third-class passenger cars in the front of the train were headed for Bergen-Belsen; freight boxcars at the back were destined for Auschwitz. Whether Gemmeker knew at the time that Breslauer was shooting that day, May 19, has never been established.

Researcher Koert Broersma interviewed Breslauer's daughter in the 1990s, and she said the footage was made without the commander's approval, and Gemmeker was unhappy about it.

"She told us that her father was determined to leave an eyewitness account on film," Broersma told me. "He was eager to shoot images of these transports because they were a definite proof of the Holocaust."[3]

The film reels, smuggled out, and later preserved at NIOD, have provided posterity with some of the only surviving moving-image documentation of Nazi transports. "The Westerbork Film," as it has become known, was never really edited, but pieces were spliced together to create an eighty-minute piece of film material. The transport section has been used in countless films about World War II, and it has come to represent the Holocaust itself. It is one of the most-requested items from the collection of the Dutch national film archives, which preserves the original film material. It was featured in Alain Resnais' famous 1955 war documentary *Nuit et brouillard* (Night and Fog), one of the most important Holocaust documentaries.

Breslauer's camera showed people walking confusedly to the trains carrying luggage, and stepping into train cars, waving to people standing nearby. It includes an unforgettable image of a terrified young Sinti girl wearing a headscarf, who has since been identified as Settela Steinbach, peering out from a gap between the nearly closed doors of a cattle car. Settela, along with her mother, two brothers, and a sister, also died in the gas chambers of Auschwitz. The camera follows a large contraption that looks like a wheelbarrow, bringing sixty-one-year old invalid Frouwke Kroon to the train. She was killed three days later in Auschwitz.

In 2021, the Dutch media archive, Sound and Vision, completed a restoration of the footage Breslauer shot in 1944, adding some recently discovered footage to the original, and setting the film to the correct speed (so people walk at a normal pace, rather than that jaunty old-fashioned movement we're used to in historical moving pictures).

Broersma and researcher Gerard Rossing took the initiative in the meantime to investigate everything they could find out about the film, and their research led to a number of new identifications. They were able to discover the identities of two toddlers filmed through the windows of a carriage bound for Bergen-Belsen:[4] Three-year-old Marc Degen, and his one-year-old sister, Stella Degen, were deported in that train, along with their cousin, Marcus Simon Degen, who would soon turn four, and his parents. Miraculously, all three children survived the war.[5]

In Breslauer's footage, we observe hundreds of other people, with their last remaining possessions in sacks thrown over their shoulders, clamoring into open compartments. An unidentified old woman tries to cover her face, as she sits on the train floor, amid straw and baggage. Gemmeker stands outside, with a group of other SS men in their intimidating uniforms and high boots; when he gives the sign, his officers press the massive iron cranks on the train doors, locking these passengers into the dark, stifling prison of the cabins.

Shooting ended abruptly, for unknown reasons. Breslauer, his wife, and three children were put on a train to Theresienstadt in September 1944, and later ended up in Auschwitz, where his wife and two sons were gassed. Rudolf died in an unknown location in February 1945; only his daughter, who was fourteen to sixteen years old in Westerbork, survived.

Breslauer's moving-picture images of the camp conveyed more than what Gemmeker had asked for. The footage is a permanent record of the unfolding genocide. When viewed alongside written accounts of Westerbork experiences, such as the diaries of inmates Mirjam Levie and Philip Mechanicus, we can no longer see this camp as a mere transit station, or "gathering place" on Dutch soil. It was, quite clearly, a way station to death.

10

"UNTIL AT LAST THE TRUCK WAS FULL"

July 1942–December 1942

ELISABETH VAN LOHUIZEN, GENERAL STORE OWNER, EPE

FRIDAY, JULY 10, 1942—Our thoughts are consumed by the fate of the Jews, especially in Amsterdam. They say that 1,000 apartments in the city must be evacuated before July 15, and of course this rule applies only to Jewish homes. If the husband is under forty, he and his family are ordered to appear at the station at 1:30 in the morning, bringing everything, including children and babies. There, they are forced into train carriages, in which they must stand, packed together. They're told to bring enough food for three days.

It seems the plan is to send them to Poland, but what happens to them there—we'll have to see. There are heart-rending scenes. It is all so dehumanizing that it's impossible to think of these practices as Christian. Why, oh why, do they bring such tremendous suffering to this group of God's children? Sometimes you see no sense in it; they can't be blamed for the war. A wave of hate has washed through our country again. There will be indescribable suffering. . . .

Miek is coming home tomorrow, and she may have more news about people who are able to get away and escape death. Houses in Amsterdam on the Stadionkade* and Donaurstraat have already been emptied out. It seems that area [of Zuid] is also not safe. They are also evacuating homes in IJmuiden. What's next? It feels like we're living on a volcano.

This afternoon, we collected a family (a wife and three children) from the train station and took them to three families on different farms. The husband left for England on April 22, 1940, and the wife lived through the bombardments; her nervous system was shot. Her face was like a mask when I saw her for the first time at the train station. When I took her out to the farm and she looked around at the bucolic surroundings, some life came back into her face. It made me realize how quiet things are in our village, and how little the local people have experienced so far.

SATURDAY, JULY 11, 1942—German Jewish families are being sent to Drenthe.† The pretty girls go to Berlin, and the rest . . . Here, there is increasing chaos and shortages of everything. Hardly any vegetables, little fruit, not to mention so many other items. We are not allowed to hand out ration cards for children's shoes.

MONDAY, JULY 13, 1942—Again today, many men (you don't hear anything about women yet) were arrested as hostages. The news traveled from village to village like wildfire. We don't know any names yet, on day one, or how many. They may be doing this for fear of riots against the mass deportations of entire Jewish families to Poland. Everybody is full of outrage, but what can we do? Several people are trying to find ways to hide Jews. Someone showed up at G & S's‡ house

---

* Stadionkade is near the Olympic Stadium.
† To Camp Westerbork.
‡ Ger and Siny

this morning, and another arrived this afternoon at half past four. The first one had an identity card without a J stamp.[*] The second was a woman, and she didn't have anything.

Luckily, I was able to find a good hideout for one of them; the other is, for now, staying with Ger and Siny. We have so many guests at our house these days, it's difficult to take someone in here. The regulations forbid them to even enter the homes of Christians, so that makes it dangerous to hide them. But their lives are just as valuable as ours; we must help, and not be afraid.

DOUWE BAKKER,
POLICE DIVISION CHIEF,
AMSTERDAM

TUESDAY, JULY 14, 1942—Heard grenades going off around 2 a.m. not far from here; then airplanes overhead. It's cloudy and drizzling.

Something is happening; no railway strike, fortunately, but apparently Jews from age 18 to 40 are being hauled off the streets. When I went into the city this morning I saw Green Police patrols and small transports of Jews, men as well as women. Our unit is also being called to duty, I hear. Apparently the Jews aren't showing up when they're given summonses, so they have to be fetched. There was a group rounded up in the Oosterpark and I saw another transport of about sixty Jews on the Amstel.[†] In the afternoon, I went with Tilly to the Cineac movie theater to see the war news. . . . When we got out later, it was raining softly, but then the weather cleared and it became pleasantly warmer. In the evening, more disturbances.

---

[*] This was probably a falsified ID; it seems that both of these people are Jewish.
[†] On July 14, 1942, more than 400 Jews were rounded up in Amsterdam and transported to Mauthausen.

ELISABETH VAN LOHUIZEN,
GENERAL STORE OWNER, EPE

WEDNESDAY, JULY 15, 1942—Yesterday some acquaintances of ours went to Amsterdam, and saw riots there. Hunted Jewish people leapt out of windows or jumped into the canals. Several were shot dead in the street. In front of the SS headquarters on the Euterpestraat, there was a line of arrested Jews, who were forced to stand against the wall all day. School children of fourteen years old and older are just taken. And the fact that we free Dutch citizens can do nothing is hard and bitter. Now the Jews aren't allowed to use a telephone, and they are not allowed out of their homes after 8 o'clock. So they can't communicate with the rest of the world from 8 p.m. until 6 a.m. What happens if someone becomes sick?

THURSDAY, JULY 16, 1942—We were required to sign a document saying that no Jew can use the telephone [at our store]. We signed, but we remain free, and we will do whatever we want to do. The first transport of Jews has left Amsterdam already. What will become of those poor souls? The letter that they receive contains an order to arrive at the train station at half past one in the morning. For the time being this applies to Amsterdam residents. They have to bring two blankets, four bed sheets, two sets of underwear, work shoes and clothing and foodstuffs for three days. They aren't allowed to bring valuable documents or jewelry. If they do all this, they "have a right" to transport by train.

It is beyond comprehension, all of this. Such a transport must be horrible, and everybody knows that nobody comes back alive. They're sending whole families, even babies. What comes next? Quite wisely, the paper does not report anything about that. Still, it's an honest paper, so you have to believe their reports. I wonder about how the NSB-ers feel now. The Jewish question was not a Dutch issue. When will the misery for these poor wretches end? People are working hard to hide Jews everywhere; the more we can keep out of their clutches the better.

INGE JANSEN,
HOUSEWIFE, THE HAGUE

WEDNESDAY, JULY 15, 1942—Adriaan finally began his job for the first time today. It's so very quiet at home without his singing in the morning. He has a great deal of paperwork to grapple with, and he finds that very boring. There are also many employees in all the different divisions, it's just dizzying. On Friday, we will have a little dinner with the Mayor at Ans' house. Very sweet of Ans to allow our parents to join. Unexpectedly, Bets van Dieren* was in the city and so I had a very lovely lunch and chat with her at 't Goude Hoofd. Adriaan complained that he feels as if he's in jail at the office, because it is so boring, he says he also can't talk to anyone there. Surely, the boredom won't last for long!

DOUWE BAKKER,
POLICE DIVISION CHIEF,
AMSTERDAM

SATURDAY, AUGUST 22, 1942—The night quiet: the weather pretty good, dry. This morning, we discovered 180,000 pamphlets in a printing plant at 22 Kromme Waal and confiscated them. They were supposed to distribute this Orange† propaganda on August 31. Yesterday

---

* The wife of NSB leader E. van Dieren.
† Orange, for the House of Orange, the Dutch Royal Family.

afternoon, I arrested a man for listening to the English Radio Oranje channel and a shopkeeper of the photo shop Lux on the Rudolph Hartplein[*] for stocking the *Vrij Nederland*.[†] I also found two firearms that were hidden in a secret niche in a wall, behind a coat rack. He's in serious trouble.

Elisabeth van Lohuizen, general store owner, Epe

TUESDAY, SEPTEMBER 1, 1942—We received an upsetting message from Rotterdam this morning. A friend of Miek's housemate, Frits, phoned to say that Frits and the other housemate[‡] had been caught. He was supposed to come here Tuesday, but on Monday afternoon, detectives showed up at their house. Of course, Frits denied that anyone else was in the house other than he and Miek, but apparently they knew everything. What will happen now? There are severe penalties for hiding Jews. The other man will most certainly end up in Mauthausen. We are also very anxious about Miek. In the meantime, the K. family from Apeldoorn arrived here, and we took them to another location this evening. We hope to be able to rent a house to accommodate them.

FRIDAY, SEPTEMBER 4, 1942—Homes of Epe Jews who have gone into hiding were at first sealed, but now they are being emptied. The police have been ordered to do it. It's rumored that they send all the possessions to Germany for the bombed cities, with the inscription, "Liebesgaben."[§] Fortunate are those who have already gotten rid of

---

[*] This arrest at the Lux photo shop will become central to Douwe Bakker's post-war criminal trial.

[†] A resistance newspaper.

[‡] "The other housemate" is a Jewish person that they were hiding.

[§] Gifts of love.

their best and most valuable goods. In what kind of state will people find their homes if they manage to come back alive? Life now is like a nightmare. We knew that they would treat the Jews horribly, but we had no inkling that it would be like this. Their motto is, "No More Jews in the Netherlands." . . . The peoples' resistance is weakening. My weight has dropped to 104 pounds.

SATURDAY, SEPTEMBER 6, 1942—Aalt van Vemde,[*] who was heavily involved in the black market, and who also sheltered Jews, has been arrested. He was warned and he did have a chance to make them all disappear, but he waited too long and it happened the next day. The Jews were taken to another location. We leased the house, Larikshof,[†] until May, and the Scholten family will go there as soon as possible. God grant that things go well. You want so badly to help people. Every life is worth it.

SUNDAY, SEPTEMBER 7, 1942—I took the Kahn family to their temporary home tonight. Scholten was a bit nervous. Thea will arrive tomorrow and then Fietje de Vries comes in the evening. I hope that they will be able to remain there peacefully until this misery is over.

SATURDAY, SEPTEMBER 12, 1942—Tomorrow Dick and I will go to Rotterdam to collect Miek's clothing and linens. For safety's sake, she took unlimited sick leave . . . because they're technically vacating the house by October 1, but they have paid rent up to December 1. It is the safest thing to do. We just don't know what's going to happen; at least everything will be here.

SUNDAY, SEPTEMBER 13, 1942—Everything from the Rotterdam apartment is here again, except the furniture. Frits' replacement says

---

[*] Misspelled in the original, Aalt van Vemde, from Epe, helped Jews and other resistance fighters to go into hiding. He also took part in local and regional armed resistance.

[†] Larkishof was the name of a house nearby, most likely a second home owned by someone who rented it out for summer guests.

that Miek has not been named in the charges and will not be interrogated. It was a terrifying moment. She'll never forget the expressions on the faces of her two friends as they were taken away in the
police van. In spite of all that, we continue to help. Today, another
one[*] came from Amsterdam. We'll keep her here for a few days, then
she will have to move on. The list grows steadily. How can we help
them all?

MIRJAM LEVIE, 25,
A SECRETARY FOR THE JEWISH
COUNCIL, AMSTERDAM

TUESDAY, SEPTEMBER 15, 1942[†]—Our doorbell rang at around midnight. This time it really was the police, with a list with our names
on it. I had answered the door, but not before I had told Bobby[‡] to
hide and smoothed her bed. We were told to get dressed and to come
along. I asked if Grandmother could stay at home. This was allowed.
Then I said that Mother should stay at home as well, or there would
be nobody to look after Grandmother. They did not agree to this at
first, but later they did, providing Father and I—remember, Bobby had
hidden—were ready in five minutes. We wanted nothing better than
to leave as quickly as possible, because the later you arrived at Adama
van Scheltemaplein[§]—which is where you were taken—the smaller
your chance of being released. And I was "overjoyed" that only the
two of us had to go, because the fewer people that need releasing, the

---

[*] Another Jewish person seeking a hiding place.
[†] This diary entry was written later, on February 1, 1943, but it describes in retrospect the
    events of September 15, 1942.
[‡] Bobby is her sister.
[§] This square in the Apollobuurt in Amsterdam Zuid was the location of the *Zentralstelle*,
    where Jews who had received a call-up were ordered to present themselves in the early
    months.

easier. And I really wouldn't have known how to get Mother ready; she was paralyzed with fear.

I had to get dressed in the presence of the two policemen. Meanwhile, they were joined by somebody higher up, who searched the whole house and even shone a torch on Bobby who was hiding in the attic, but didn't see her. I forgot to tell you that the policemen asked: "How many people are in this family?" I said: "Five: Grandmother, parents and two daughters. My sister has an evening permit and is at work."

Luckily I hadn't kept quiet about Bobby—this was deliberate, because her bed is in our room and during a search they would have seen two wardrobes, etc.—for one of the policemen said: "The young lady is telling the truth. I've been here before, and I've seen the family in its entirety." I hadn't recognized him, but he was one of the policemen who had come to take away the Boassons. [The officers] were fairly decent, although one of them slipped a bottle of wine into his pocket, looked in all the cupboards and asked if we had been hoarding food. I replied: "We have no money for that." When he took the bottle of wine, I said: "That's for ritual purposes." And believe it or not, he gave it back.

As soon as I knew that only Father and I had to go, I went to call the *Expo*.* The line was constantly busy. Then I called my boss and told him what had happened. So you see how fortunate we were to still have a telephone. Later, our good fortune would prove to be even greater than we realized at the time. The policeman who took us to the "Houtmarkt"—the current name of J.D. Meijerplein†—was very friendly. He had come around completely, and said: "You're certain to be released, and then we'll drop by." He said it was a shame I was already [engaged]. He had seen my ring. He was definitely flirting with me.

---

* The Expositur, or the department of the Jewish Council that worked as a liaison with the *Zentralstelle*.
† The German occupiers removed all "Jewish" street names and gave them new names.

When we got to the car—we were to be transported in a truck—we were handed over. And then all hell broke loose. The scenes inside that truck were indescribable. People in terrible panic were shouting, sobbing, screaming. The policemen continued to pick up more people and we heard doors being kicked in. Sick, elderly people, in nothing but pajamas and a coat, were literally dragged out of their homes and thrown into the truck like a bunch of rags. You see, the truck had a very high footboard and the elderly people couldn't get in without assistance. So the policemen escorting the truck would pick them up and literally throw them in. All this in the pitch-dark. The drawbridge between Weesperstraat and J.D. Meijerplein was up and had to be lowered every time the truck needed to cross. We drove back and forth, until at last the truck was full.

By then it was half past one, and I was desperate, because I'd given up hope that anything could be done on our behalf now that it was so late. But once we arrived at Adama van Scheltemaplein, I revived. It appeared that the worst was over. Our case had been passed on and dealt with, despite our absence, and we were free. As I stepped out of the truck, I said to Father: "Hold on tight, or we'll lose each other." It was like a film or a bad dream. We walked across the courtyard in the dark. On either side were soldiers with rifles. To the left and right, behind the soldiers, was the transport, ready to depart.

As I stepped out of the vehicle, I heard Sluzker[*] say: "Is Mirjam Levie in this group?" Then I knew that everything was all right. We weren't ushered into the room where the others were taken, but were allowed to join the line of people who had been released. We stood for half an hour. Of course, we were very happy, but the sight of the others in our truck having to join the transport group was dreadful. Max was there too, as were many acquaintances, and they all came to chat with us. I'll never be able to explain how I felt.

---

[*] Edwin Sluzker, head of the Expositur.

Having stood for half an hour, we filed out to Jan van Eijckstraat, to a school where we were to spend the night, because of course we weren't allowed out in the street until six in the morning. But Mr. Blüth, who lives opposite the school, came to fetch us. In Mr. Blüth's kitchen, we cried a little and afterward—it was half-past two—we made ourselves comfortable in the living room, together with Mr. and Mrs. Blüth and Sluzker, who also spent the night there. Max had already called Mother and we called her again at half-past two, which meant that she hadn't been in suspense any longer than us. I went to bed at half-past three. Father stayed up and went home at six o'clock. I slept until ten, went home and then later on to the office. Still, I felt tired and drowsy that day.

That night, at half-past twelve, the doorbell rang again. I went to the front door, because I'm always the first one out of bed. Bobby hid again. The same policemen had come to check if we had been released. At half-past midnight! What do you make of this lack of sensitivity? And these were actually the decent ones. You should know that the previous night, as we were walking to J.D. Meijerplein, I had said, when they told us that they'd come and enquire after us: "Then you'll get a glass of wine." They had come for that, I could tell right away. And if we hadn't been released, they would have looted the place. For example, I had this fine hand-cranked flashlight, and the previous evening one of the policemen had taken it from me and given me his instead, which was actually rather decent of him.

Well, three of them turned up and flirted a little with me. They thought I had a good figure for horse-riding, would you believe it. I was in just the mood for that. I'm ashamed to say that I actually gave them a glass of wine in a bid to stay on friendly terms with them, because they told me they patrol our neighborhood. And sure enough, a few days later the doorbell rang at ten o'clock. A call-up for Grandmother for the *Arbeitseinsatz*.* But while they were still downstairs,

* Labor duty.

they said they weren't going to take her. It was purely a social call, and they talked nicely, among other topics, about English radio. We didn't say much, naturally.

MEIJER EMMERIK, 47,
DIAMOND CUTTER, AMSTERDAM

CIRCA SEPTEMBER 21, 1942[*]—On the great Day of Atonement, such a holy day for us Jews, hundreds of people had to wait in line to get a stamp, which took all day and all night. Maxie,[†] who was seriously ill at this time, lay in the Maria Pavilion,[‡] which was actually forbidden, because, thanks to the Krauts, said Jews can no longer be treated anywhere but a Jewish hospital. The same was true at the sanatorium, because Maxie was a sanatorium patient, but by order of the Germans, a child under the age of one could also not be treated there. As a result, we were terribly worried about the child, partly because I didn't trust Jewish hospitals, knowing they could be emptied out at any moment. The Krauts had already started to drag Jews from their homes after 8 p.m., mostly at night, forcing people into the street in every sort of weather, taking people of every age, from the infants to the elderly.

Even those who until now were protected by their Sperre were hauled away. Sick or not sick, everyone was taken, small children rousted from their sleep, and carried away in the middle of the night. Could anyone express in writing the great sorrow that has befallen us Jews?

Sam's[§] parents, two of my brothers and their wives and children,

---

[*] This diary entry was written later, in 1943, as part of Meijer's summary of events prior to going into hiding.
[†] One of his two toddler grandsons.
[‡] A hospital ward.
[§] Sam is his son-in-law, married to Lena.

my sister and her husband, were dragged from their homes. My oldest brother had his teeth knocked out on the Adama van Scheltemaplein, because his hat didn't come off his head quickly enough. His grandfather of 84 years old, who lived with him and can no longer walk well, was grabbed by two of these bandits and flung into a car. . . .

At least I decided not to surrender voluntarily. If the worst came to the worst, I resolved to go into hiding. Sam, however, refused to do this, preferring to go to Poland, which meant that Lena, and perhaps the kids, would have to go too. This worried me deeply; my wife wouldn't go into hiding without our daughter.

When the time came for Vogeltje[*] to report, I managed to convince her to stay back, and I sent her an address in Amersfoort that I had gotten from one of my brothers, who recommended it and said it was trustworthy. The man was working for an illegal organization, and I had made an arrangement with him that in an emergency, my wife and I could go into hiding at his house. When Vogeltje was called up, I had [the man] come to my office, and I asked him if he would be willing to take Vogeltje instead of us, because she was in immediate danger. He and his wife, who was with him, both said they would take her and that I could come later as well, because they had plenty of room. As Vogeltje no longer received any [ration] coupons, I agreed with him that I would pay them 50 guilders a week for her, and I paid an advance of 600 guilders, and Vogeltje left for Amersfoort on September 15, 1942, to stay with Tuinhof. That was the name of the man in Amersfoort. Later it turned out that that man was unfortunately very unreliable (but I'll come back to this later). On October 14, I was hospitalized for a serious problem, and my wife stayed with Lena during that time. Two weeks later, on October 30, my wife and Lena visited me in the hospital and told me that Sam had been taken from his home by the police two days earlier.

---

[*] Vogeltje, also named Fietje in the diary, is his wife. Vogeltje means "little bird," or "Birdie."

Elisabeth van Lohuizen,
general store owner, Epe

SUNDAY, SEPTEMBER 20, 1942—Miss de Hond[*] has been with us for a week already, and we don't have a house for her yet. I've noticed that she is becoming more relaxed. We have decided to allow a couple with a child to come as well.

THURSDAY, SEPTEMBER 24, 1942—We rented another cottage, Idwo, and expect guests there soon. There is so much demand for help.

FRIDAY, SEPTEMBER 25, 1942—In addition to Leni van den Burg we've had another guest, Mr. Rotschild, who's been with us for a few weeks already. He will move into Idwo with his wife now. Since she is Christian, she can take the lead of the household.[†] He is a rare books dealer and a very sensitive and distinguished person. He has traveled a great deal and visited many castles and cloisters to collect antique books. He's also very musical. He has been playing the cello since he was eight years old, and he knows many famous musicians.

SATURDAY, SEPTEMBER 26, 1942—House #2[‡] will receive its first residents today. The couple with child arrived from Amsterdam already, at 10 o'clock. Mother left here on a trip at 12 o'clock. We had a full, mixed table with five Jews, and Irmi, Annelies Ehrlich, and of course, us. We get to meet so many people this way. We plan to rent out the Blauwvoet, but we have no news about it yet. We hope to hear soon. People are waiting for a spot. The terror continues in Amsterdam. A Jew who fled was shot dead in the street, and his body lay there for several hours before it was taken away. They probably left it there as

---

[*] A young Jewish teacher.
[†] A non-Jew served as the "face" of the house, who could deal with Dutch and German authorities, if necessary.
[‡] Idwo.

an example. On the Roelof Hartplein, a Christian who made a remark against the SS was beaten to death. They're dragging Jews from their homes. Irmi heard that Haitians in Amsterdam are also being interned, including women and children.

MONDAY, SEPTEMBER 28, 1942— . . . It is so strange, but the house is like a beehive. There are always more people coming.

WEDNESDAY, SEPTEMBER 30, 1942—We received two more ladies tonight. One has a doctorate in biology, who is studying to become a pharmacist. Her sister is a biologist. These educated ladies make for illustrious company. Mrs. Rotschild also arrived, so the house is again full of people. Friday night they will all move into Idwo. Those who have been at House #2, as we call Idwo, will move to House #3, Blauwvoet, tomorrow. There is so much to organize. We have such a large group of guests in the evening (six now), and always wonderful conversation. One cannot comprehend why these people are being persecuted.

SATURDAY, OCTOBER 3, 1942—Today is our thirtieth wedding anniversary. We kept it very quiet, but we still received flowers, including some from those we are helping. We don't like parties, and also, maybe, we had a premonition of what was going to happen tonight. Again, there has been widespread persecution of the Jews, not only in Amsterdam and Rotterdam, but also in Zwolle, Meppel, Deventer, Zutphen, Arnhem and Apeldoorn. Women and children hauled out of their homes, taken to schools at night, and deported in the morning. Everybody is so nauseated about it. In Amsterdam it continued until 5 o'clock in the morning. At the same time, whole labor camps have been emptied. Hitler said in his speech that the Jews want to destroy the Aryans, so instead they destroy the Jews. There's nothing you can do about it, except try to help them. As a Christian, you feel such guilt toward those people, and that you must help. We work as carefully as we possibly can, we don't say anything about it to anyone, but we try to help everyone.

This afternoon, we received a call from Wenum. Another is coming. She appears to be a 67-year-old lady named Mrs. Heymans, and she is the mother of the famous pilot,[*] who flew to the Indies and back. She's a lovely, courageous lady, very religious, the first one we've had who keeps kosher. We can only keep her with us for two days, and then she goes to House #2. She would like to stay here, but that cannot be done.

SUNDAY, OCTOBER 4, 1942—Today, the pastor gave a grave sermon about loving your neighbor. I certainly don't hate the others, but it is impossible for me to love those who embrace this regime. The sorrow they bring to everyone is so infinitely great that I cannot extend love to them. Would Christ really ask that of us? I do not believe so. We have been very lucky with our guests. They are such nice, well-educated people. Ger and Siny were here the whole day with baby Marja. It was a fine dinner with a very nice bottle of wine from a guest in House #1. Another new guest arrived today.

MONDAY, OCTOBER 12, 1942—We got another house. This is House #4, and it is already occupied. We will try to lease another one as well; there is still an enormous demand.

MONDAY, OCTOBER 19, 1942—I was too busy for a few days to write. I went to Amsterdam on Saturday and Sunday. I had to deliver some messages on behalf of several people, and I tried to obtain funds for some of our visitors who are completely penniless. Many Jews are still walking around the city, of course mainly in the Jewish Quarter. They look so awfully sad. There is not much in the future for these miserable souls. The way they've been treated is indescribable. Now people as old as 90 are being hauled away. I heard about an 88-year old woman in Rotterdam who was dragged out of her bed at four in the morning, and

---

[*] Justus Heymans was a Dutch pilot.

made to sit for 28 hours on a chair in a warehouse. Luckily, she had an Aryan daughter-in-law who was able to free her. It's impossible to understand how they come up with these regulations. If you start to think about it seriously, it's as if you can't breathe anymore.

SATURDAY, OCTOBER 24, 1942—Luckily we have good sources who informed us that tomorrow they will start searching farm houses around here for rye and also for Jews. God grant us that nobody will be betrayed, and all Jews we have in our care will be safe. Oh, when shall we be free again, and when will these people be able to walk around freely once more? It can be so oppressive. I'm not concerned for myself, but for all these people.

You get the feeling that something is in the air; everyone seems to be excitedly anticipating change; many believe it will be coming in November. I doubt that it will come so soon. Even if we suffer terrible cold and hunger this winter, I would accept it to be rid of this constant terror. You have to always check behind you, be vigilant because betrayal can come from anywhere. We aren't used to that. We used to be able to share our opinions freely, to protest when protest was needed, and now we are paralyzed.

Ger is coming—maybe he has something to tell us at this late hour; if it is good news, we won't have to suffer through such anxiety.

It remains the same, the police will perform so-called house searches tomorrow, ask about Jews but find nothing. It has been organized so wonderfully well, if it were up to them they would not find a single Jew. And it should not happen. I would rather be taken along myself, than that one Jew will be caught. . . .

In house #1 there are seven; in #2 there are six; in house #3 there are six; in house #4, two; and with us here another two. They all have to be saved.

Tomorrow is my birthday. This is no time to celebrate, but one shouldn't let a day like that go unnoticed. Miek has been asked to preach the youth sermon.

MONDAY, OCTOBER 26, 1942—Had a busy day yesterday, with many visitors, received many bouquets of flowers. From house #1, I received a book, from house #2, a cake. At house #3 they did not know it was my birthday, and they felt bad about it. I received a wonderful book about Dutch landscapes from our temporary houseguests. They wrote a wonderful poem to go with it. I wonder sometimes; these people put me on such a pedestal—won't I fall off of it?

Miek's sermon was very good. We created a hiding place behind the wall of our clothes closet for our temporary houseguests to flee to, if necessary. You never know what may happen. Today there was a very nervous mood all over. Nobody knows when those folks are coming to search the village and surroundings. The houses have been informed and everybody remains inside, and I hope that they will remain calm.

Ger was here at 10 o'clock. Police are doing a so-called search, but not really. They come to the door and ask, "Are there any Jews here?" When someone says, No, they leave. We have another guest, a brother of Jo Juda,[*] a quiet boy. We hope to sleep well; it's been so emotional.

MEIJER EMMERIK, DIAMOND CUTTER, AMSTERDAM

IN LATE OCTOBER,[†] I arranged that Maxie would be admitted the Nederlands Israëlitisch Ziekenhuis,[‡] because he had grown worse at the Maria-Paviljoen, and would get specialist treatment at the N.I.Z. After that, I immediately got in touch with a lawyer, Mr. Kastein from the Keizersgracht, who did everything he could to find out where Sam[§] had been taken, but it all proved useless.

---

[*] Jo Juda was a famous Dutch Jewish violinist who was among a group of Jewish intellectuals arrested early in the war, in July 1940. Jo had two brothers, Arnold and Charles. It's not clear which one this is.

[†] This entry was written later.

[‡] The Nederlands Israëlitisch Ziekenhuis (Dutch Israelite Hospital) in Amsterdam.

[§] His son-in-law.

ELISABETH VAN LOHUIZEN,
GENERAL STORE OWNER, EPE

MONDAY, NOVEMBER 2, 1942—We have leased Duiveland for another six months for 100 guilders a month. The whole group from Blauwvoet will go there on Thursday. Little Idwo, where we planned to send the bothersome ladies from Idwo, is not habitable, so now they will have to go to Blauwvoet. I heard more stories from Amsterdam yesterday. A twelve-week-old baby lay in its cradle in an empty house; later, he was taken from there. Mothers (Jewish) are forced to leave their children behind as foundlings. On Saturday, Wim Leesink, who is an acquaintance of Miek, Frits, and Bram, was here to speak with me. He asked if we could hide Bram's parents. Miek will go to Amsterdam tomorrow to organize everything. You want to stop all the time, but when they ask, you cannot refuse. . . . We now have five houses and many residents.

SUNDAY, NOVEMBER 22, 1942—After moving some people around, there's now a good mood in the houses. We have had Jewish people in our own home for the last three months, too, the most recent were here for five and a half weeks. Tomorrow another one is coming.

This week *Het Parool** came again. I have great respect for those men who continue to put out this paper in these times. . . . In this issue was an important article that I will copy here:

"While we know that the Jews are being removed from their houses, and their property is plundered, and they often suffer a horrible treatment, the following article appeared in the *Hamburger Fremdenblatt* dated July 24:

It is reported from Amsterdam that Dutch citizens act like beasts toward the Jews. As a result the Jews approached the

---

* A resistance newspaper.

German Wehrmacht, requesting that they protect them. The Wehrmacht has, in spite of their eternal enmity, taken the Jews under their protection and transported them at their own request to Germany, where they will be able to perform their trades safely. In a show of gratitude for this assistance, the Jews have made the contents of their homes and jewelry available to homeless families in Germany, who have been made homeless by English pilots."

No comment required.

MEIJER EMMERIK, DIAMOND CUTTER, AMSTERDAM

ON NOVEMBER 21,[*] Lena received a letter from Sam[†] from Camp Amersfoort dated November 5, from which we ascertained that he'd been detained from October 28 to November 2 and then, without any questioning, sent to Camp Amersfoort. We all felt so desperate; how was such a thing possible?

What made it worse was that this camp is the most notorious for sadism. I immediately informed my lawyer of these facts but he said that, in that case, there was absolutely nothing he could do for him. He said I have to wait until he is released. Should he be sent to Camp Westerbork, the camp from which they send everyone to Poland, then another attempt could be made to help him. . . .

I decided to make some inquiries to find out whether anything could actually be done to get him released. That was how I learned that I might be able to get him freed in exchange for industrial diamonds. . . . Only the Germans are capable of thinking up such a

---

[*] This entry was written later.
[†] Her husband.

scheme. I don't blame anyone for attempting to save their lives in this way, but I certainly didn't want to do it. Then I spoke to Lena and shared what I had learned. I told her that I'd been informed that Sam could be saved in this way, but that it wasn't a sure thing. I also shared my point of view. She insisted that if this was possible, that I must; she was willing to do whatever it took to get Sam released.

INGE JANSEN,
HOUSEWIFE, THE HAGUE

MONDAY DECEMBER 14, 1942—Adriaan has managed to arrange for the requisition of the house at Handelstraat 17 for us, and I'm so very happy about it! The Hochberg case is also currently being addressed by the S.D. and there is a good chance that the young Jewish boy, David,* will rescind his claim on the property. What a relief all that will be!

ELISABETH VAN LOHUIZEN,
GENERAL STORE OWNER, EPE

SUNDAY, DECEMBER 6, 1942—Oh, I just wish that we were free already, so that the Jews would not feel hunted like animals. In the big cities, most of the Jews are now gone. Where to and how? You dare not really think about what has happened, otherwise you just can't really live anymore. It is a kind of horrifying, crazy nightmare or a horror novel. Today, the military police came to search a house where Jews were hidden, according to rumors. For a while, we felt extremely

---

* The house was "requisitioned" from a Jewish person, who she identified as David, but may have been someone else.

anxious for all our people. Late last night, another couple came to #4; we can now only accommodate a few more. At #1 are seven Jews; at #2, eight; at #3, five; at #4 six adults and a child; at #5, nine and a child. That is 35 total; it is a great responsibility.

FRIDAY, DECEMBER 25, CHRISTMAS DAY, 1942—I was in Emst this morning, where Miek gave a wonderful sermon. She is so much calmer in her speaking and less dependent on the paper. After the Amen, I sang, "Honor to God." There is a peculiar charm in hearing your own child preach like that.

The weather was cold, foggy but until now, rather mild. Yesterday we received flowers from house #4 and #5 as well as from Ad, Irma and Leni. Today I got a beautiful book from Marte and Hans and a rug from the Van Gelders. Fietje de Vries went to Ger and Siny these last three days; we invited Fietje de Jong and Leni for dinner. Decorated the rooms, a red tablecloth for the table, and candles. You could really tell how much they enjoyed that. I felt again that we have made the right choice to act as we have and to support people as we do.

Henk stayed with us this week, and he tried to warn me, to encourage me to stop. I do not agree with him. Talking does not help; you have to do something, if you really want to be of some help to all of the people in hiding. We will be careful, but we will continue.

11

"IF ONLY THERE WERE MORE PLACES FOR THESE POOR PEOPLE"

Elisabeth van Lohuizen

The first 100 to 150 pages of Elisabeth van Lohuizen's 900-page diary, written in six notebooks of varying sizes, contain a lot of material that would be of great interest to a historian of wartime economics. In tiny penmanship that rarely bleeds across the lines, she describes almost daily the incremental adjustments she and her family business were forced to make due to war rationing. As the owner of a general store in the center of town, she had to be particularly conscious of constantly changing prices of staples, shoes, winter clothes, and the shortages of vegetables and meat.

"Butter, fat and margarine on ration coupons," she noted, for example, in July 1940. "The sale of flour, rice, pudding, macaroni, vermicelli etc. forbidden for a week. Butter 250 gr. per person per 14 days and another 250-gr. fat in that period." In October, she predicted that the winter would be particularly harsh because "everything but everything" was on the ration list. "Eggs also rationed, 1 per week, prices prescribed, highest 8 cent. A prohibition on the sale of pulses for 14 days, so for the time being no beans."

The contents of her diary take a sudden and remarkable turn in the summer of 1942, when Elisabeth, known to her friends as Bets, starts to write about "visitors and guests" from Amsterdam. Her first few references are oblique, but within a few days it becomes entirely clear that she is hiding Jews.

It was around this time that she, a local school headmaster, Derk Hendriks, and a local postman, Tiemen Jonker, decided to help as many people as they possibly could to escape Nazi deportations. Their small resistance organization would later get a name, *Het Drieman-*

schap, or The Triad. Elisabeth van Lohuizen, Hendriks, and Jonker were the three founders of the group, but in fact The Triad relied on a fairly large network of family members and friends—who would end up saving the lives of scores of people.

The first time Elisabeth mentioned aiding a visitor in her diary was on March 5, 1942. "For a week, we've had an 8-year-old boy from Rotterdam staying with us," she wrote, "at the request of Miek," her daughter. It's unclear from the diary whether the child was Jewish or an orphan of the bombings, a child who had been placed because his parents were in the resistance or one who had an entirely different story.

Elisabeth wrote that it was "bitterly cold" that week, with icy rain. She noted cold shortages, Indonesia's capitulation, and military planes roaring overhead—but apart from noting the boy's arrival, she recorded nothing else about him. Throughout the first months of her involvement with the resistance, Elisabeth put very little into writing, understandably. So the moments when she mentions "a visitor" jump off the page like a spark.

"We collected a family (a wife and two children) from the train station and took them to three families on different farms," she wrote on July 10, 1942, but did not specify if these were Jewish guests. Three days later—the same week the first Westerbork transports to Auschwitz departed—she observed that "several people are hiding Jews," without mentioning doing so herself. Then she recorded that "someone has arrived" at Ger and Siny's house and specified that the person didn't have a "J" in their identity card. This "J" is the only clue. Was the "J" absent because the person had falsified papers? Or because she wasn't Jewish?

What we do know for sure is that a fifteen-year-old boy named Lou van Beets, "with a very dark Jewish appearance" but dyed blond hair, showed up in Epe in July. A local farmer named Proper took him in temporarily, allowing him to stay in his empty vacation house in the woods.

The boy had run from Amsterdam when both of his parents had

been deported. Proper didn't think the boy would be safe with him for long, since holiday-goers would soon be arriving in nearby cottages. So he asked Rev. Willem Frederik Hendrik Ter Braak, pastor of the local Reformed Church, what to do. Ter Braak suggested he reach out to Derk Hendriks, the headmaster who'd recently retired and moved to a quiet spot in the woods.

Els Hendriks, Derk's daughter, remembered that night, and later wrote about it in an unpublished memoir. "When he arrived that evening in our home he was extremely upset," she recalled. "All fear, tensions and uncertainty had overcome him completely. At first we let him talk, relate what his family had experienced, how unsafe, uncertain and abandoned he felt." It was the first time that she and her family grasped the situation fully, she wrote. "We appreciated it so much more that our house stood at a quiet spot, surrounded by tall wood walls and garden doors facing away from the road."[1]

The "visitors" kept arriving in the town, most likely because it was in a secluded location with lots of surrounding forests, but also, perhaps, because word had got out in resistance circles that there were helpers in Epe.

By August, Het Driemanschap was preparing for more guests. "There is a lot of work to be done," she wrote. "If only there were more places for those poor people."

Het Driemanschap leased its first house, Larikshof, in September. "A very roomy villa in the center of fir woods that have grown so tall that one cannot even see the house from the public sand road," wrote Els Hendriks. Eight people moved in. The Van Lohuizens took people into their own home near Pelzer Park, while they tried to find a second house to lease. That would be Idwo. By October, they'd leased a third, Blauwvoet, "a wooden summer residence."[2]

Hiding didn't suit everyone, it turned out. Gerhard Badrian, a thirty-five-year-old German Jewish man, for example, found that after a short time staying with Ger and Siny he became far too antsy. "He couldn't find his feet with us," Ger would later recall. "He was a fine, sensitive fellow. He read a lot, but he was clearly uncomfortable. After a week he told us that going into hiding wasn't for him. He felt that those who were hiding him would be taking too great a risk because he was so restless. If he wanted to take his own risks, it was better that he was part of the resistance."[3]

Badrian remained an important contact for Het Driemanschap. He went on to work for the Paper Identification Center, an illegal printing operation that produced false identity cards and ration coupons. Elisabeth used a pseudonym for him in her diary, referring to him as "Bernard," the name he also used on his false identity card: Bernard van Essen.[4]

In addition to supplying many Jews with false papers, Badrian somehow got his hands on an SS uniform, which allowed him to infiltrate Nazi events dressed as one of them. With his flawless German and blond hair, he could easily impersonate a German guard. In this way, he quietly liberated Jews from prison trucks. He also participated in armed resistance activities, until he was killed in a barrage of bullets during a police raid of the Records Center in June 1944. He and others had attempted to destroy the registration cards that had helped the occupier send so many to their deaths.[5]

THE MEMBERS OF Het Driemanschap were all affiliated with the Liberal Dutch Reformed Church, Ter Braak's congregation, and they were also all members of a left-liberal political party, the Liberal Democratic Union. Elisabeth served as a deacon at the church and leader of the women's group. She was also a member of Church and Peace, formed in 1924 to advocate universal disarmament and nonviolence. And she was involved in the larger women's movement. She'd helped organize a Women's Peace March that was to take place on May 18, 1940, and noted in her diary a feeling of "bitter irony" that it came too late—eight days after the Nazi invasion.

Elisabeth van Lohuizen cut an unlikely figure for a resistance fighter. With short gray hair and round tortoiseshell spectacles, she appeared serious and sober as a Catholic schoolmarm. The Van

Lohuizen family had owned a general store in town on the Beekstraat since 1743. It advertised itself as a seller of "Colonial goods and other foodstuffs," which meant it carried a surprising array of products, from spices and sambal from Indonesia, coffee, tea, "sauerkraut in bottles," cough syrup, cameras, and sponges.

Elisabeth and her husband, Derk Jan (Dick), still ran it as a family business, and in addition to selling groceries in the main shop, a small adjacent building offered liquor and wines, and their son, Gerrit Sander (Ger), a pharmacist and optician, ran the little attached drugstore. As such, the Van Lohuizen general store was a magnet for nearly all the 6,500 people who lived in town, and some 9,000 more who lived in the larger municipality. Their work also connected them to suppliers of all kinds of goods, a network of businesses across the country—links that proved useful for their resistance work.[6]

Although Elisabeth was in charge, Dick, Ger, and Siny also became the key players in the resistance work, as did both of Derk Hendriks' daughters, Reina and Els. As a student, before the war, Ger had spent a year studying in Brunswick, Germany. The year Hitler came to power, he'd witnessed a Nazi book burning there, which had made a "great impression" on him. He'd experienced first-hand how citizens' rights were curtailed under the Reich's new regime, and he brought that information back home to Epe.

A few years later, he became engaged to Siny (Klazina Jentje Becker) from Meppel; she was on the board of an association called Unity Through Democracy,* which fought the advance of both the NSB party and the Communists, and he became a member in Epe.[7]

"We were anti-German because their regulations were aimed at *people*," Ger said after the war. "Against individual people, against groups of people, against Jews, gypsies, and homosexuals. We were opposed to that, to the oppression and injustice that was directed against individuals. It was not out of some kind of 'patriotism.' That word has no meaning to me."[8]

---

* *Eenheid Door Democratie.*

Ger was one of the few non-Jewish Dutch people who wore a yellow star on May 3 in solidarity with Jews. "I thought it was important to oppose the Krauts in public," he explained later.

Het Driemanschap found the moral rudder for their resistance activities in their church. Reverend Ter Braak[9] must have been an extraordinary pastor; in his weekly sermons, as Elisabeth would often record in her diary, he preached powerfully about aiding those in need; for some in his congregation those messages resonated with meaning that was very specific to the times.

His pulpit was the Grote Kerk, the largest church in Epe, dating to the twelfth century, with an imposing tower hovering over the city's main square. Inside, its spare, unadorned Protestant style calls attention to the lovely white high-vaulted ceiling, and its red-and-gold organ embellished with angels, standing on red marble plinths. Its cherished set of church bells in the massive spire date to the thirteenth century and alert the entire county to the time, every quarter of an hour, as well as the moment, on Sunday, to head to church.

In 1938, when the Dutch government closed its doors to German Jewish refugees, Pastor Ter Braak penned a letter on behalf of his church council, beseeching the Dutch government to take its "duty of charity" in line with Christ's attitude of "generous hospitality," urging it to "do everything possible by opening its borders to provide refuge to the afflicted Jewish people."[10]

Pastor Ter Braak continued preaching Christian charity and service throughout the war, and it is clear from Elisabeth's and Els' accounts that he provided both spiritual and material support to Het Driemanschap.[11]

As with many small Dutch towns in the pre-war period, Epe had only a tiny Jewish population. "There were only a few Jewish families, but we knew all of them," wrote Els, "because they had lived in the village for a long time. Two Jewish butchers, one of whom also had a café next door. . . . Also a family [named] Frank; both the father and his son Simon were cattle dealers, but did not own cattle themselves. [. . .] Next a family Gosshcalk, who had a small export butchery, which was run by father and son. All these people had always taken part fully in all the activities of the village and were well-liked compatriots. Mother Stern was also still around, but she was already rather old."[12]

Els wrote that she never remembered any discrimination against the Jews in the village before the German invasion. Even when many locals became NSB members in the 1930s, she recalled, she could not "remember any noticeable hostilities."

"I never heard my parents speak with negative words about Jews," she wrote. "And also not about people who had other ideas, the orthodox Protestants who were in the majority in Epe and surroundings, nor about the Catholics in Epe. According to them, everyone had a right to live according to their own convictions, as long as those ideas were not harmful to others in the community."[13]

When forced to register in 1941, thirty-eight residents of Epe qualified as "fully Jewish," about half of whom considered themselves to be religious Jews. Perhaps ironically, the unofficial number of Jewish residents of the area likely rose during the war, as Het Driemanschap took in Jewish people fleeing roundups elsewhere, and as deportations intensified.

Epe was forested, agrarian, and full of summer homes that were vacant for much of the year. It was also full of hotels, guest houses, and smaller back-cottages that locals rented for extra income. For the resistance, barns and other farm buildings could store both people and weapons; those in hiding could procure food grown locally, rather than trying to scrape together ration coupons.[14]

"People could hide in all kinds of remote places," said local historian Willem Veldkamp, who counted at least ten resistance organizations based in Epe that either provided aid to Jews or participated in the armed resistance. They were led by "several powerful characters," he said. "Many of them were left-oriented, which is quite remarkable for a Veluwe village. All kinds of associations, including political parties and trade unions, played an important role, but other forces, such as ecclesiastical leaders, ensured that people worked together and trusted one another."[15]

Their efforts were substantial and their success rate was high. Veldkamp found that 76 percent of the thirty-eight Jewish inhabitants of Epe survived the war—a far better survival rate than in the vast majority of Dutch towns, or the average for the nation.[16]

12

"THE TIME HAD COME TO GO INTO HIDING"

Meijer Emmerik with his daughter, Lena, around 1920

There is a unique Dutch word for going into hiding: *onderduiken*. A literal translation would be "to dive under water," derived from the word *duiken*, to dive. More loosely, it means "to disappear from public life." I find the Dutch noun form of this word, *onderduiker*, far less clumsy than the equivalent English phrase, "person in hiding."

About 15 percent of the Jewish population became *onderduikers* at some point in the war. The decision to hide was determined by many factors, as diary writers make clear. Parents with small children and the elderly had to consider practicalities: babies were apt to cry and older people might have health issues that would be difficult to address in hiding. Dutch identity cards, which had been designed with great precision, were hard to forge, and fakes were easily identified.

By far the most important factor was: Who would take you in? Was there someone you trusted enough to hide your family, to provide you with all your basic necessities for months, possibly years? Those who sought assistance had to know people outside the Jewish community; poor families and observant Jews rarely did.

Onderduikers who relied on strangers also risked being defrauded, abused, or betrayed. Some hosts and helpers demanded exorbitant sums of money. Could one trust such people, and could you afford to pay?

Even those who implicitly understood that hiding was the best option often could not bring themselves to do it. "They lacked energy, contacts, money, played down the dangers of deportation and exaggerated those of going underground," wrote Dutch historian Jacques Presser. "They were frightened, terribly frightened; they were unsure of their own strength, they wanted to remain with their families, they did not want to depend on others, or endanger them."[1]

MEIJER EMMERIK TRIED several courses of action before he decided to go into hiding. He'd read in the newspaper that "essential" workers in the diamond industry could apply for something called a "120,000 Sperre," which would allow them to defer "labor service." The 120,000 was the last in a series of numbered Sperre (10,000 to 120,000) that were available for purchase with precious stones, precious metals, gold, or hard foreign currency. In other words, Jews could buy their freedom for approximately 20,000 guilders per person at first, and later, 30,000 guilders (about $7,500 at the time).[2]

In July 1942, 545 diamond workers submitted applications for the 120,000 Sperre. Including wives and children, these stamps would temporarily bar 1,230 people from deportation.[3] The Germans would have received quite a diamond haul, worth at minimum 10.9 million guilders (or $4 million), and potentially up to 24.6 million guilders (or $7.7 million).*

The Amsterdam diamond industry had relied on Jewish workers since around 1600, when Sephardic Jews from Spain and Portugal emigrated north to escape the Inquisition. Although they were welcome to live in Amsterdam, Jews were restricted from most professional trade guilds, and without guild membership, one could not work. Cutting and polishing diamonds were crafts that had no guilds, so many Jews entered the industry, and by the early twentieth century it was largely a Jewish industry, employing more than 1,000 Jewish workers in Amsterdam alone.[4]

These jobs were, contrary to stereotype, not all well-paid; cutters and polishers usually earned lower-working-class wages. It may seem unusual that they were considered "essential" to the war effort, but

---

* By my calculation; it is hard to know how many children under the age of fifteen, included gratis, were in this group.

there was justification for this as far as the Nazis were concerned: SS Reichsführer Heinrich Himmler planned to establish a German-run diamond industry in the Netherlands, and he intended to force the Jewish experts to train Aryans in the trade.

To be kept in Amsterdam for this purpose, however, the diamond industry workers would have to pay. Emmerik understood that the price was 30,000 guilders in *addition* to a "top quality diamond." The German in charge of the transaction also required a 10 percent commission.

Emmerik recognized it as a trick. He knew at least one Jewish diamond merchant who'd handed over "beautiful, pure cut diamonds" in exchange for a Sperre, and was deported anyway. He was, of course, wise to be wary. Although some people did manage to delay their summonses by purchasing the 120,000 Sperre, to keep a stamp, one had to keep paying and often with more diamonds.

The scam provided some people with a false sense of security. One diamond merchant's wife, Josephina Lewijt, said in post-war testimony that, although the family had been offered eleven hiding places, her husband felt sure that the diamond bribes would protect them.

"They needed diamond workers," she said. "They needed him. Like they needed me to work in the salt mines later on. They needed people to work for them, because they practically owned everything during the war."[5]

Eventually, the Sperre became too expensive for many people. Most diamond industry workers were deported to Westerbork by the end of the summer of 1943. On September 29, 1943, the last holders of the 120,000 stamp were picked up in a raid and sent to Bergen-Belsen, where most were killed before the end of the year.[6] Fewer than 100 Jewish diamond industry workers survived the war.[7]

"We always thought, quite wrongly of course, that we were safe more or less, because my father still worked in the factory at the Achtergracht, didn't he?" said one child of a diamond worker in his post-war testimony. "And as long as that was the case, we thought maybe in our naïveté that that would go on forever. Then we were safe. But yes, well, that turned out not to be true."

Meijer grasped the danger in February 1943, when he saw a lot of 120,000 Sperre holders rounded up. For him, it was obvious: "The time had come to go into hiding."

Emmerik moved into various hiding situations over the next ten months until he finally settled, at the end of the year, in the southern province of Limburg. His protector there, who he calls "Miss Tini," was Albertina Maria van de Bilt, a member of a student resistance organization, Utrecht Children's Committee. It helped hide Jewish children, mostly in homes in north and central Limburg, including her own home.

Van de Bilt would save the lives of 114 children,[8] including Meijer Emmerik's grandsons. When little Loetje moved to a hiding place in September 1942, Meijer worried, "This will be his fifth address before his second birthday." Albertina helped Meijer secure a more permanent hiding place for Loetje, and also for little Maxie, who had tuberculosis, and needed constant care. "It has turned out that this woman is a true saint, who has saved our lives," Meijer wrote in his diary. "She is the kind of which only one in 10,000 is born, and who cannot be bought with money."

MEIJER WAS ONE of the lucky ones. By the beginning of 1943, at least 12,000 and perhaps as many as 28,000 Jewish people had managed to avert their call-ups by going into hiding—and more than half would be caught. This dismayed the National Socialists, who did not want a single Jew to escape. It turned out that many of the ordinary Dutch police tasked with making sure that Jewish people showed up for their deportations, were lax. Sybren Tulp, facing this reality, decided to train a new cadre of younger policemen who would show more enthusiasm.

New recruits were sent to a special training camp in Schalkhaar, not far from Deventer, a Nazi bootcamp known as the Police Training

Battalion. There, starting in 1941, about 2,500 young policemen were prepared for the work of Jew-hunting and deportation coordination; anti-Semitic propaganda was also central to their training.

These fanatical *"Schalkhaarders,"* as they were nicknamed, were then returned to Amsterdam and The Hague where they lived in barracks, and were at the ready as a kind of riot police, to work alongside police departments. The first group of trained Schalkhaarders, wearing black uniforms and helmets and carrying carbines, marched in closed formation through the streets of Amsterdam on March 4, 1942. They were quickly nicknamed "the Black Tulips."

"They themselves said proudly that they were 'hunting for Jews,'" said Guus Meershoek. "You can see them like football hooligans who had that kind of camaraderie, brutality, and misbehavior."[9]

Tulp also tried to motivate all Dutch police officers to hunt for Jews by offering "bonuses" for each Jew who was arrested. The bonus started out at 5 guilders "per head" and was later raised to 7.50 guilders, and ultimately to 40 guilders per person. This fee applied whether they captured an adult, an old lady, or a newborn. The fee was doubled if the captured Jew was a *"Straffälle"* or a "criminal case"—which was frequently the case, because a criminal offense included minor offenses such as not wearing the Jewish star or not showing up for a call-up notice.

In September 1942, SS police leader in the Netherlands, Hanns Albin Rauter, praised the work of these men, saying, "The hundreds of new Dutch police officers are doing an excellent job on the Jewish question, arresting hundreds of Jews day and night."[10] A month later, Sybren Tulp took ill and suddenly died,[11] and the regular police forces were relieved of the job of enforcing anti-Jewish measures; the Schalkhaarders took over the job entirely.[12]

The activity of "Jew hunting" emerged first in Poland in the 1930s, according to Christopher R. Browning's groundbreaking book, *Ordinary Men: Reserve Police Battalion 101 and the Final Solution in Poland.* Jews who had escaped mass shootings, systematic deportations, and ghetto liquidation were chased into forests, bunkers, and other hiding places by devoted groups of soldiers. In occupied Poland during this period, any Jew found outside the borders of the ghetto could be summarily executed on the spot.

"No one could be left in any doubt that not a single Jew was to remain alive in the battalion's security zone," wrote Browning. "In official jargon, the battalion made forest patrols for 'suspects.' As the surviving Jews were to be tracked down and shot down like animals, however, the men of Reserve Police Battalion 101 unofficially dubbed this phase of the Final Solution as the *Judenjacht,* or the Jew hunt."[13]

"*Jodenjacht,*" the same word in Dutch, was the title of a landmark study of the "enthusiastic role of the Dutch police" in hunting Jews, by Dutch historian Ad van Liempt and Jan H. Kompagnie, first published in 2011. Van Liempt's 2002 *Kopgeld* (Head Money) focused on a mercenary group of private Dutch citizens, the *Henneicke Colonne,* who worked as Jewish bounty hunters during the later stages of the occupation.

The Colonne, or column, was named after its leader, Willem Henneicke, a wayward thirty-something, who'd married for the third time on the day of the German invasion. He'd apprenticed as a carpenter, but became a warehouseman, then a taxi driver and a vacuum cleaner salesman. Once he joined the Sicherheitsdienst, however, he had steady employment and legitimacy with the occupying regime.[14] In the first half of the war, he cleared out Jewish homes after families had been deported. Then in March 1943, he was tapped to lead the Jew hunting forces, a substantial promotion, which made him the leader of a large team.[15]

"About eighty percent of the Jews in hiding in the Netherlands were arrested by these 50 or so people," Van Liempt told me. "It was very lucrative work. That 7.50 guilders at the time would be about 40 euros ($40) now. But you couldn't buy much because of the rationing. What you could buy was drinks and women. They drank a lot. For normal people it was almost impossible to get liquor, but they also drank to quiet their consciences."[16]

In addition to the bonuses, the employees of the Henneicke received "a very attractive salary," wrote Van Liempt. One member of the Jewish Council recalled, "Everything about their lifestyle suggested they were rolling in money."[17]

And they actually were. One police officer testified after the war that he'd witnessed the "Henneicke paying out sums varying from 300 to 450 guilders per person," somewhere around $2,000 to $3,500 in today's money, which he said were "much higher than their salaries," which they took home as well.[18]

After the war, many of the Jew hunters were interrogated, and Van Liempt studied their statements. "My conclusion was that the first motivation with the Colonne Henneicke group was money and the second was anti-Semitism," he told me in an interview. "When I did the same study for the police, it was the opposite. The main motivation with the police that hunted Jews was anti-Semitism, and then it was money."

The ultimate "head count" from the Colonne Henneicke amounted to 8,370 Jewish men, women, and children, an even greater "success rate" than that achieved by the Dutch police in Amsterdam, 6,000 Jews.[19] These two organizations together arrested 14,370 Jewish *onderduikers*. There were also others, such as the Green Police, who regularly chased Jews, and a force known as the Voluntary Auxiliary Police, organized by Rauter in May 1942, made up of Dutch Nazis and W.A. thugs.

"Almost solely concerned with the pursuit of Jews, they rapidly gained a reputation for brutality and illegality," wrote Bob Moore. Scattered across the Netherlands, each with specific knowledge of regional topography, they became invaluable to the Jew hunt, because they had "no moral qualms about what they were doing."[20]

The success of these units depended on help from informants and tipsters. Often these were neighbors, former friends, and relatives of the hunted. "In 1943, Amsterdam was crawling with squealers and snitches, and much of the time bonuses were not even necessary," wrote Van Liempt. "A Dutch Jew had no one he could trust; you could be betrayed by anyone."[21]

Israeli Dutch historian Pinchas Bar-Efrat examined informant testimony in post-war trials of police informants. "The principal motive
for denouncing Jews and handing them over to the Nazis was greed,"
he concluded. "Many also denounced the Jews in order to 'buy' their
freedom after they themselves had been arrested by the Germans."[22]

Bar-Efrat noted, by contrast, that it was different from the situation in Germany, where informers were more often driven by ideological motives than the hope of personal gain. From the trials he
examined, he found that 17 percent of Dutch informers were NSB
members, which, he notes, "exceeds their share in the population."[23]

One Dutch man who betrayed forty-three Jews and six non-Jews
to the Sicherheitsdienst said at trial that he "couldn't stand" Jews, so
it was perfectly natural that he earned 750 guilders for "denunciation
services." Another man accepted an advance of 10,000 guilders from
a group of Jewish people trying to escape to Britain, before turning
them over to the Sicherheitsdienst. He repeated this betrayal with four
other Jewish people attempting to flee to Switzerland.[24]

There were so-called "apartment traps": People might offer a hiding place to a fugitive Jewish family, often for a fee, and instead turn
them over to the S.D. In this way, they would earn money twice: from
the Jews and from the bounty. Then they'd just take in a new group of
Jews, and repeat the process, until word got around and they couldn't
run the scam anymore.

Sometimes it wasn't a scam. The non-Jews hiding Jews just became frustrated with their guests or had quarrels and turned them in
rather than telling them to leave. Often, Jewish people paid for their
hiding places, and when their money ran out, the people offering hiding denounced them to the police. Sometimes Jewish people asked
neighbors to take their valuables for safekeeping when they went into
hiding. Rather than risk the chance that they would return and claim
their possessions, the neighbors informed on them.

Van Liempt found examples of extraordinarily petty reasons why
people would snitch: There was a malevolent sister-in-law who turned
in a woman after a "dispute over a radio," and a building concierge

who used his "earnings" from informing for liquor. But betrayals could also be unintentional. One sixteen-year-old girl, who worked as a maid, accidentally mentioned a hiding address in passing, when some police officers were standing nearby.

There were some Jews who betrayed other Jews. The most famous was Ans van Dijk, who purchased her safety during wartime by giving up the addresses of 145 Jews in hiding; she was executed by firing squad in 1948. She was the only Jewish person convicted of such a betrayal, out of 15,000 known collaborators tried after the war.

Most of the other Jewish people who betrayed others to save themselves or family members ended up in concentration camps. One Jewish woman, Ms. V., gave up eighty names to the Henneicke in March 1943 in return for the promise of freedom. Less than a month later, she was murdered in Sobibor. "Her sacrifice, eighty useful tips, was not enough to save her life," wrote Van Liempt.[25]

Those who genuinely wanted to save Jewish lives had to overcome the combined cunning of the Nazi overseers, local police forces, privateer Jew hunters, and all the willing informants. Bounties became increasingly appealing to non-Jews as food and supplies became scarce and black-market prices for basic staples rose precipitously.

In rare cases, people who'd offered help to Jewish people found that as the war continued, and supplies became scarcer, they could no longer help, and they sometimes just asked them to find another place to hide. "The number of concealers who denounced Jews because they feared getting caught was probably small," wrote Bar-Efrat.[26]

Those caught aiding Jews were often sent to punishment camps, such as Vught, Amersfoort, and sometimes Dachau. They were often tortured or punished in ways that, while not always fatal, took an enormous physical and emotional toll, often for the rest of their lives. Those who genuinely and selflessly offered safe haven under progressively dire circumstances found such work increasingly treacherous as the occupation, and the Jew hunt, grew more hostile.

13

"THE WORST YEAR FOR ALL JEWRY"

January 1943–June 1943

MEIJER EMMERIK,
DIAMOND CUTTER, AMSTERDAM

JANUARY 1943[*]—And so it became 1943, the worst year for all Jewry, and for me personally. One of my brothers, a patient at the Zonnestraal Sanatorium,[†] sent me a letter saying that the Jews might be cleared out of the sanatorium at any moment, and I advised him to go into hiding. My other brother, who worked as a nurse, was also in danger, so I advised him, too, to go into hiding.

One evil day a few Germans arrived at the stock exchange and said that all diamonds that were registered with the state, and were our property, should be handed in that very same day, and that they would save them for us. I don't know how many millions of guilders' worth of diamonds were turned in that day, but I do know that many people were immediately made penniless.

---

[*] This entry was written in September 1943.
[†] A tuberculosis hospital originally established for diamond cutters in Hilversum.

Because of me, we have lost all these goods. My lawyer visited his contact, a Jewish man called Engelsman, to press for Sam's[*] urgent release, but every time he told my lawyer a different story.

The Krauts had gathered up all the Jews who had been sent to work camps on a particular Friday evening, right after being released from work duty, without warning and without giving them any food. They had put them on a transport to Westerbork, from where they would be deported to Poland. The day after, they took these men's wives and children and put them on transports as well. On February 11, many diamond industry workers were hauled from their homes. The special Sperre stamps, for which they had paid a great deal of money, were declared invalid. All of these people were taken to a camp in Vught in North Brabant, from where, later, a large group were then deported to Poland. . . .

We planned that I would go to [Tuinhof] on Saturday, February 13. Lena, who wanted to wait for Sam to come back, decided to take Loetje and go to Sam's sister (Jo), who is in a mixed marriage. And so on Feb. 13, we left for Amersfoort, and Lena and Loetje went to Jo's. It was a Saturday, and when we arrived in Amersfoort that Saturday evening, Vogeltje was overjoyed to see us. A German Jewish couple, the Wolfs, were also staying there, so in total they had five Jews hiding with them. . . . We had arranged that Agnes would come once a week to keep us up to date about Lena and the children. After having spent just over a week there, Agnes came and told us, to our great alarm, that the Krauts had emptied the Jewish hospital. Nothing had happened to Maxie, because Lena had heard about it, and immediately went to see them. Together, they drove there and took him out.

Maxie was with them for the time being, but Agnes said her husband and son, Bob, were opposed to him staying there. She'd tried to connect with a nurse in Haarlem, but without success. There we

---

[*]   Sam is Meijer's son-in-law, Lena's husband, who, last they heard, was in Camp Amersfoort.

were, completely powerless in Amersfoort, while Lena and the children were in danger in Amsterdam. It is perhaps understandable that my nerves got the better of me. Before she left again for Amsterdam, Agnes promised to do everything she could for Lena. . . . She returned some days later to let us know that her husband had finally agreed that Maxie could stay with them. . . . I arranged to pay them 40 guilders a week as compensation, as well as any extra costs associated with his care. That's how our minds were put at rest as far as this was concerned, and I am pleased to report, seven months later, that Maxie has stayed in their care, and Lena and I cannot be grateful enough to Agnes for this, as she literally plucked the child from the jaws of death.

INGE JANSEN, HOUSEWIFE, THE HAGUE

SATURDAY, JANUARY 2, 1943—At an ungodly hour, in the pitch dark, we left hastily and just managed to catch the train with Madam Op ten Noort and Juul.* Smooth ride, first through torrential rains, and then with magnificent sunlight into the center of Amsterdam. Adriaan went with the luggage immediately to Amstel Station, and I went to the house, where Alex and most of the furniture had already arrived. It looked so terrible that I just started crying. Everything was so dirty and miserable that I didn't know where to begin.

SUNDAY, JANUARY 3, 1943—Went to the house many times. We have a blissful bathroom and wonderful beds in the hotel. Beyond that, I find it boring, expensive and dark. The breakfast is nice in the dining area with a beautiful view over the water.

---

* NSVO co-founder Julia Op ten Noort and her mother.

ELISABETH VAN LOHUIZEN,
GENERAL STORE OWNER, EPE

SATURDAY, JANUARY 23, 1943—Today we heard tragic news. The Jewish sanatorium, Apeldoornsche Bosch, was cleared out. Along with the mentally ill, there were several people with nervous conditions who had taken refuge at the hospital. Those [Jews] who were still in Apeldoorn were also brought over there. Yesterday,* all of them were driven to the train station in trucks and loaded into cattle cars, forty cars in all.

There were terrible scenes; the screams were heart-rending. One wagon was full of children; the poor dear ones had to stand. Jews from Westerbork were forced to assist with the transport, German soldiers behind them with pistols. It is so horrifying what they do to these poor people. There are no words to describe it; but no one in Apeldoorn will ever forget it. The lady who works at the kiosk was so upset that she closed the shop. A conductor who drove the train from Bentheim said that he'd seen urine running out of the wagons. Those who "volunteered" to help were told that they would get a note to exempt them from being "gassed."

SUNDAY, JANUARY 24, 1943—I went to Apeldoorn today. What happened at the Apeldoornsche Bosch made a deep impression on the people there. The director of the center committed suicide. They say that severely ill patients were given injections.† They've never experienced such a terrible thing. How can human brains even conceive of it? And they call themselves the "new order."

---

* On January 23, 1,300 people, patients, and staff were rounded up at the Apeldoornsche Bosch. None of them survived.

† They were given injections of poison, and died immediately.

MIRJAM LEVIE,
SECRETARY, AMSTERDAM

WEDNESDAY, APRIL 14, 1943—Do you remember that winter evening, a Saturday evening, when we went shopping together on Kalverstraat? We went to Hoying, where we bought those lovely fruit knives. I'm sure you remember how happy we were then and how wonderful it was to buy things for our home together. I remember how much I enjoyed it, what everything looked like. The weather was mild, all the shop windows were beautifully lit and each shop window was a work of art in itself. When we came out of the shop, the street was one big, surging mass, and everything was bright and gay. And turning onto Dam Square, which was so spacious and so beautiful, and seeing the illuminated windows of De Bijenkorf[*] and the cafés crammed with people, it all felt so cozy. And Muntplein, with its cars and trams going to and fro and flashing neon signs, and Reguliersbreestraat packed with people! You know how much I enjoyed it all.

I have drawn you this picture to tell you what the city looks like now. Kalverstraat is a sea of shutters. Even in the daytime only some of them are removed; most of them are nailed shut. Shop windows all display the same wares. Wooden brooches, for example, are sold by lingerie shops, furniture shops, department stores—in a word, by everybody—because there's nothing else to sell. Goldsmiths have shut up shop, so the windows are boarded up and the doors are locked, also boarded up. Bensdorp is closed. Focke and Meltzer, that beautiful china and ceramics shop, is also closed, while the shops that remain open have almost nothing in their windows. And of course it's dead quiet in the evening, with all the shops closed and the windows boarded up, even on Saturday evening. Muntplein is so quiet now that there's no more police. . . .

---

[*] A high-end department store, similar to Bloomingdale's.

And now the Jewish Quarter, e.g., Breestraat. It's dead quiet, because a large part of the population has been taken away. Many of the houses have been ransacked. They're emptied by a company called Puls[*] and we refer to it as "pulsed by the Dutch pilfering corporation." Until they're emptied, the doors are sealed with gummed tape, the windows boarded up, and the black-out curtains are usually down because people are taken away in the evening and therefore don't have a chance to draw the curtains. A scene of utter poverty and despair, which you can't picture unless you have seen it with your own eyes. And on, say, Tugelaweg, windows have been smashed and shutters broken by "ordinary" burglars, who beat the Huns at their own game. Rumor has it that there's an organization of professional burglars who ransack the homes, and if the inhabitants return after the war they will receive their possessions back, provided they pay a storage fee. *Si non è vero . . .* [†] The city looks like a battlefield. The whole city does, wherever houses have been emptied. During the day, you see the big removal vans all over the city. These vans dump their contents into Rhine barges moored along the Amstel. Somebody told me he had found a volume of Levy's dictionary on the embankment at Weesperzijde. It must have fallen out of the van, missing the barge.

ELISABETH VAN LOHUIZEN, GENERAL STORE OWNER, EPE

TUESDAY, APRIL 20, 1943—Had a great scare this morning. Van Essen came to tell us that there was no response at the Blauwvoet.[‡] Dick

---

[*] The Puls company was a removal company that emptied out property from the houses of Jews who had been sent to Westerbork or Vught. Abraham Puls himself was a Dutch Nazi.

[†] *Si non è vero è bene trovare* is Italian for "Even if it isn't true, it's a good idea."

[‡] House #3.

went there with him and they went inside. The house was a big mess and all eight adults and the nine-year old boys were gone. Nobody knows how it could have happened; even the police didn't know and, in the neighborhood, no one had heard anything. I have been to see Jonker* already; Hendriks is not home.

Irma, Karel and Nancy had to move out. They packed everything at #2 once we let them know about it. I went over there quickly. Oma, Leni and Marius will go to Wenum and on from there. It is a disaster; we have to wait calmly, to the extent that anyone can be calm. We don't know what the consequences will be, for them, or for us. Was it a betrayal by someone in the NSB? The fact that we know nothing makes it so much harder. In the coming few days, we won't sleep at home; Mies will take us in, while mother stays at home. For the time being, Irma and Ad will temporarily stay with Van Dijk, Karel to Dinah, and Nancy will go to Van Leeuwen. Our quiet, peaceful life is suddenly changed, they said. We'd had such a good period.

FRIDAY, APRIL 23, 1943—Ger came here late last night; I could tell right away that something was wrong. . . . He said that Nancy has to leave again, and Hendriks has to go in hiding as well, because apparently his name was mentioned. . . .

At that point, we had to make the most difficult decision we'd made in years: To flee and desert the work. I considered the choice so cowardly. It was Good Friday but I couldn't go to church or the Lord's Supper. Everything felt so dark and difficult. Dick felt right away that we must go and our children also encouraged us to leave. . . . I shed bitter tears, but we did decide to go. We are both exhausted and depleted; we really needed rest. The last eight months have been so tense. Tonight, we will go to Vierhouten.

SUNDAY, APRIL 25, 1943—It is Easter Sunday. How different from what we had imagined. We can't go to church, so we took a walk in

---

* Tiemen Jonker, one of the three members of Het Driemanschap.

the woods, though the weather is bad. I had not thought it would be so difficult for me. I am so tired, through and through.

MONDAY, APRIL 26, 1943—Ger came this afternoon. He's been working constantly to place people, but he says it's incredibly difficult. He was quite despondent—it is such a big job! Carla, Nancy, Do, will all have to leave. The farm has to be vacated within fourteen days; what do we do with all the people at #5? It's seeming more and more grim. K. gave Ger addresses for the children. It is so rotten to put him in charge of everything. Mr. van B. wants to take over house #2, and we can place three people there. How suddenly everything can change! Perhaps it is good for us to experience this. Everything went so smoothly for a while, as if we were running an inn.

THURSDAY, MAY 13, 1943—We're back in Epe. So glad to once again be in our own surroundings. The first night we slept at our children's place. During the evening, they told us everything, how things had been organized. Exhausting. We are still so far from having places for everyone, and yet everything has to be arranged before June 1. We'll have to jump right back into it.

MIRJAM LEVIE, SECRETARY, AMSTERDAM

SUNDAY, MAY 23, 1943—I went home at eleven, where I said goodbye to Mother who was going into hospital. As soon as she and Father had gone and I was by myself in the house, I cried my eyes out because I knew the game was up, and because I was so upset that the J.C.* had once again lent itself to this barbarity instead of saying:

---

* Jewish Council.

Enough is enough, go hang. It reminds me of the following sick, but very telling, "joke": Asscher and Cohen are sent for by the Huns and they are told that the Jews will be gassed, whereupon the Professor's first question is: "Will you supply the gas or should we?" Such was our predicament.

I slept until two, then went back to the office. There I had to strike all the bigwigs' friends and family off the (interim) call-up list. How about that? In a word, I was given a list of their cronies and had to check whether they would be called up and, if so, I had to strike them off the list. I almost wept with fury and indignation, but there was nothing I could do. Home at half-past six, back at eight.

INGE JANSEN,
HOUSEWIFE, AMSTERDAM

FRIDAY, MAY 28, 1943—Drank tea this evening at home of Mr. Hermans, previous owner of our house (who liquidated the Jewish property). He has a nice wife, rather mundane, of bourgeois descent; they live in a lovely apartment on Apollolaan. There, we met an ophthalmologist, Oltmans, and his wife; he gentlemanly, she rich. He quit the board of the Artsenkamer* when there was all that fuss about the strike. Hermans was a favored member of the SS.

SUNDAY, MAY 30, 1943—Unexpectedly, Dr. Reuter† called and stopped by this morning for coffee. He is such a pleasant man and no longer shy. In the afternoon, went to visit the Verweys. Mrs. Verwey, I think, found it very difficult to have two NSB-ers in her house. Her oldest son didn't sign up, and since he left she hasn't heard from him

---

* A Nazi medical association, organized by the Germans.
† Chief of the Public Health Department.

for more than three weeks. Maybe it is good for some of these students to be put to work in Germany; that way they will find, to their surprise, that their notions are wrong.

MONDAY MAY 31, 1943—Had a lot of pain in my leg, so I lay down for about an hour on the large chair on the balcony, in the sun, and then at about three-thirty I went to my German lesson. After that, relaxed at home, as Adriaan had SS duty.

14

"THE MAN WHO GOES ABOUT WITH HIS NOTEBOOK"

Philip Mechanicus

*A*lgemeen *Handelsblad* journalist and foreign desk editor Philip Mechanicus arrived at Camp Westerbork on November 7, 1942, weighing eighty pounds and with fingers on both of his hands broken.

He'd come on a transport from Camp Amersfoort, a *Politzei Durchlager,* police transit camp run by the SS, which handled political prisoners, members of the resistance, Jehovah's Witnesses, and other "dangerous" figures arrested by the Sicherheitsdienst.

The men on Mechanicus' transport were in terrible shape. An orderly who worked in Westerbork's camp hospital, Ernest Frank, took notes as almost all had to be admitted immediately for medical treatment of injuries and malnutrition.

"We received a group of human wrecks," he wrote. "They were so completely weary, physically and mentally, that it was almost as if they weren't people anymore. Without exception, they had such animalistic fear in their eyes that one did not dare to ask what they'd endured. . . . They startle at the sight of a uniform, and shrink from every question."

This particular group of internees was so bad the whole group got a nickname: the "moaning transport."[1] Ernest Frank took special note of one particular member of the group. "Among these victims is the *Handelsblad*'s foreign correspondent, Mr. Mechanicus," he wrote. "I lift this man, who weighs barely 80 pounds, like a feather into a separate bed in a separate room, where he will receive special care."[2]

It is not entirely clear what had happened to Mechanicus at Camp Amersfoort, where he'd spent just two weeks, because there is no record of any writing or correspondence. Almost no mention of his time in Amersfoort was made in his later diaries, either, except when he remarked on the poor condition of his hands. He must have somehow conveyed something of his treatment to his daughters and his ex-wife, Annie Jonkman, because she knew that at Amersfoort he'd been "badly abused."

His good friend, Johanna Heinsius, wrote later that she suspected the guards had stood on Mechanicus' hands until the metacarpals were crushed. Heinsius guessed that they'd chosen this method of abuse because he was a famous journalist, and his hands were the tools of his trade.[3]

At Westerbork, Mechanicus had a separate room for a week so that he could heal and also perhaps as a form of quarantine, and then he was transferred to the hospital barracks. He would spend the next nine months there, recovering and attempting, by various means, to avoid being placed in the camp's general population, because as a hospital patient he was barred (at least for a time) from deportation.

Mechanicus arrived at the camp with an "S" stamped into his identity card, meaning that he was *Strafgeval,* a punishment case. This status would normally have meant that he'd have been processed through Westerbork within a day or two, and transferred to one of the death camps. But Mechanicus managed to make friends with several doctors, who, although they were Jewish, had a small amount of power within the camp to defer deportations. One of them, Fritz Spanier, somehow eventually also managed to get the "S" removed from Mechanicus' ID.[4]

Mechanicus' name appeared on a transport list to Auschwitz at least five times that first November alone, but each time someone stepped in to prevent him from being moved. In this way, he was able to remain in Westerbork for an almost inexplicably long seventeen months. During that time, he produced what is widely recognized as one of the most important eyewitness accounts of the camp in operation.

"How grateful we must be to him for not wanting to be anything more than the man who goes about with his notebook, noting down events from day to day," wrote Jacques Presser after the war. "In fact, [he was] a war correspondent setting down his record while his life was constantly in danger, although he hardly ever seemed to realize it."[5]

The first diary entry that survives from Mechanicus' life in Westerbork was dated Friday, May 28, 1943, in a journal labelled #3. This indicates that he'd written two earlier volumes before that spring, but these have been lost. It's hard to know how long it took his hands to heal enough so that he could write. Somehow, however, he began writing in student cahiers that he'd procured from the Westerbork camp school.

Once he started, he didn't stop. From his first entry to his last, on February 28, 1944, there were only twenty-eight days on which he did not write in his journal. Sometimes, he jotted down no more than a few lines, but most of the time, his entries were voluble, often as long as four pages of handwritten text.

Mechanicus treated writing as his priority and as a moral duty; not a pastime, but an assignment. As he put it in one of his first entries, he felt like "an unofficial reporter of a shipwreck," who wasn't brought here against his will, but, "took the trip voluntarily to do my work." He tried to describe the shipwreck as an objective observer, as if he weren't about to drown along with all the other voyagers.

His "voice" as a narrator is removed, and he tried, as historian Bettine Siertsema put it, to "keep himself as much as possible out of the picture." But the work had an impact on his personal experience. "Writing also acts as a distraction, and as a means of counteracting the numbness," Siertsema wrote, because becoming numb to the horrors of his situation, and to what was happening around him, was a constant threat.[6]

He was diligent in his reporting duties, and approached them with professional rigor, too. "He developed informants, sources, the way journalists do when they are covering a country or a crisis," Broersma said. "He had a feeling that his diaries would be important after the war. I even have the feeling he wanted to stay in Westerbork as long as he could to keep doing this job."[7]

The fact that Mechanicus was so prolific under such conditions was also remarkable. In the 1980s and '90s, Broersma interviewed surviving journalists who'd found it nearly impossible to focus on writing while imprisoned, "because there was only one priority at Westerbork, which was to eat and stay alive." They were impressed with Mechanicus' resolve to "work" no matter what the circumstances.

Mechanicus moved out of the hospital barracks in the summer of 1943, presumably too healthy to justify his spot in a bed there any longer, but by that point he'd found other means of averting transport. Critical to his fate was the camp's chief administrator, a German Jewish *Ordedienst* officer named Kurt Schlesinger, who had been interned as a refugee at Westerbork since February 1940 and had been placed in a position to oversee the camp. In other words, he was "a Jew in charge of Jews," as some inmates nicknamed him, or, "King of the Jews."

If it was this friendship—if one could call it that—with Schlesinger that prevented his transport, Mechanicus was not entirely convinced of his security, and he was simultaneously working other angles. As he was in a so-called "dissolved mixed marriage" to a non-Jewish woman, Annie Jonkman, and he had a technically "non-Jewish daughter" from that union, Ruth, he had applied for Calmeyer status, which could potentially downgrade his Jewish status. He also paid to be added to the Weinreb List, another type of protection that turned out to be an entirely fictitious escape scheme. Finally, he negotiated with various camp officials to be sent to one of the "better" camps, Bergen-Belsen or Theresienstadt. These dilatory tactics worked as long as they worked, until they didn't.

PHILIP MECHANICUS WAS born in 1889 in the heart of the Jewish Quarter on the Lange Houtstraat to Elias Mechanicus and Sarah Gobes. Philip was the eldest, and he had seven younger brothers, but three died at a very young age. Father Elias, sometimes described as

---

* The *Ordedienst* (OD), or Order Service, was a group of mostly German Jews who had been appointed by the Germans to maintain order in the camp.

a "clothing maker," was in practice more of a rag-seller, and mother Sarah may have been a yarn or ribbon hawker. They lived in near-abject poverty, wrote Broersma, on a street that was "a hollowed-out honeycomb of gray, dilapidated houses." Elias was also an alcoholic and perhaps something of a brute; Sarah threw him out just around the time that Philip finished primary school, and Philip, as the eldest, became the "man of the house."[8]

At age twelve, his school headmaster helped land Philip his first job at a socialist newspaper, *Het Volk* (The People). Even though he was a mere child, he quickly rose through the newspaper's ranks, becoming first a fact-checker and later a reporter, and by seventeen a member of the paper's editorial board.[9] His colleagues and bosses encouraged him to keep up his studies, and he attended classes organized by the Social Democratic Workers' Party at night.

When he turned eighteen, Philip was called up for service in the Dutch military, and spent a year in the 3rd Battalion, 2nd Company of the 7th Regimental Infantry, and afterward he secured himself a contract with the *Sumatra Post* in Medan, in the Dutch East Indies (as Indonesia was called at the time) as a fact-checker-editor. While there, he married a young Jewish woman, Esther Wessel, whom he'd met through the Social Democratic Workers' Party evening lessons. Esther was still living in Amsterdam when they got married in 1913, through a solicitor's permit, and he was abroad. Together, they had two daughters, Rita Julie, born in 1918, in Indonesia, and Julia (Juul) Serah Mechanicus, two years later, when the family had returned home to Holland.

This was the first of his two marriages; Esther and Philip divorced in 1922, and three years later, he married Annie Jonkman, with whom he had a third daughter, Ruth. This marriage also didn't last long; the couple divorced in 1929.[10] There would be other women in Mechanicus' life as well, including Jo Heinsius, whom he met while vacationing in Switzerland with his two oldest girls.

"Lots of ladies were in love with my grandfather," Elisabeth Oets, Juul's daughter, told me. "I guess you could call him a womanizer. Maybe they had an affair, I don't know." Broersma disagreed. "Philip certainly didn't have a relationship with Jo Heinsius," he told me. "They were just very good friends." His girlfriend before the war was concert pianist Olga Moskowsky-Elias, who was later deported to Sobibor and killed there in 1943. While at Westerbork, Mechanicus also had a romance with a fellow journalist, Annemarie van den Bergh-Riess, a German foreign correspondent who'd worked in Paris before the war.

In 1919, when he returned to the Netherlands from Indonesia, Mechanicus got his first job at the *Algemeen Handelsblad,* where he remained for the next twenty-one years. He was fired in 1941, along with other Jewish journalists across the country.

"Immediately after the occupation he learned that his presence on the newspaper was not tolerated by the Germans," wrote Presser. "He remained an employee at home for a while, writing anecdotal stories under the pseudonym Père Celjénets, until the newspaper's management dismissed him in a formal letter."

Broersma explained that the "anecdotal" pieces he wrote for the *Handelsblad* were sometimes about zoo animals or other quirky topics, but they always contained not-so-hidden political messages and observations. This work, too, came to an end in 1941, after the Nazi crackdowns on resisters became vicious; the paper decided it was unwilling to take any risks in secretly employing Jewish writers.

Meanwhile, Mechanicus had arranged to send his two older daughters, Juul and Rita, both in their twenties by this time, into hiding with Heinsius.[11] Recognizing the imminent Nazi threat to Jews, Heinsius, who was Christian, had told Mechanicus that if he ever needed any help, he should call on her. She owned a storefront pharmacy in Nijmegen, a town near the German border, and lived in the apartments upstairs. She welcomed Juul and Rita to live with her there in her attic space, and provided them with everything they needed, so they could stay completely out of sight. The building, as it happened, was right across the street from the city's Green Police headquarters, but the girls managed to survive there undetected.[12]

Ruth, meanwhile, who was still a teenager during the occupation, was protected from deportation because she had a non-Jewish mother, and she was categorized as Aryan. She was safe to go on with her life unmolested, but chose instead to join the resistance, working for the underground newspaper *Het Parool*.

In late September 1942, Philip Mechanicus was arrested in Amsterdam for failure to wear the Star of David. Presser wrote in 1964 that he'd been riding on the back platform of a tram, and, most likely, a fellow passenger had betrayed his identity to the police.[13] Broersma found evidence that he was in fact arrested a few days earlier than Presser had reported, on Van Woustraat, a wide avenue in an area known as De Pijp, possibly on his way to catch a tram.[14]

"He was very stubborn and he refused to wear the star," Oets told me, taking a risk that might have gotten him arrested at any time, after the requirement went into effect in early May. "That was his attitude every day. This just happened to be his fateful day."[15]

After his arrest, he was jailed for a month in a detention center on the Amstelveenseweg, in the south of Amsterdam, before he was sent to Camp Amersfoort at the end of October.

MECHANICUS' JOURNALS TESTIFY to the profound suffering experienced at transit camp Westerbork, in spite of the fact that inmates were not usually physically harmed there in ways they were victimized in other Dutch camps.

His work goes beyond testimonial reportage, and moves to the level of sociological analysis. He provides his readers of the future— and it seems clear that he was writing not with a single reader in mind but rather a large public—with insight into social and class divisions within the camp. He explores the different responses to persecution among religious and secular Jews—he categorizes himself among the "nonbelievers"—the power dynamics between the newly arrived Dutch Jews and German Jewish refugees who'd been long interned on Drenthe soil. He provides us with their camp nickname, *Alte-Kamp-Insassen,* German for "old camp inmates," used as a slur because the

German Jews had become so integrated into the governing structure of the camp that they were sometimes considered akin to Nazis.

He described with acuity the cruel admixture of the tedium of camp life with the terror of the impending transports. Rarely using the pronoun "I," he still managed to draw readers into his own psyche, and into the specific torment of his personal predicament.

In the autumn of 1943, he saw an opportunity to escape, for example, and debated the matter in his journal; his thoughts inevitably went to the possibility of capture, and he was reminded, with horror, of his time at Camp Amersfoort. "I got to know the executioners there," he wrote. "That's enough, more than enough for a lifetime." After weighing these options, he resolved, instead, that it was better to face the Russian roulette of Westerbork transports, than to end up at another Dutch camp.[16]

Around the time that Mechanicus's diary began, a major shift had occurred in the national mood concerning the German occupation. In February 1943, the Russian army defeated the Germans in the Battle of Stalingrad, which turned the tide of World War II in favor of Allied forces. For the first time, many Dutch people started to realize that the Germans had not won the war—and Colijn's prediction that they'd remain under the thumb of the Reich until the year 2000 probably would not materialize.

Then in April and May 1943, Dutch workers mounted another large industrial general strike, mostly in the eastern part of the Netherlands, and various small resistance movements finally galvanized into a meaningful force of counteraction.

It all began when German authorities announced on April 29 that all Dutch enlisted men who'd battled invading Germans in May 1940 would be shipped to the "Fatherland" to work in factories there. Outrage erupted that day in the province of Gelderland, where workers at the Stork Machinery Factory in Hengelo were the first to walk out, and two iron foundries in Vaassen were among those that followed suit. These two factories, Industrie, with about 600 employees and

Vulcanus, with about 400, supplied raw materials to Stork, and contact between their workers explains their quick synergy.

Other factory and farmworkers followed, with dairy farms in the Northern Veluwe refusing to supply factories with their milk, until about 200,000 people across the eastern Netherlands were participating. This largest Dutch general strike of the war period lasted for six days from April 29 to May 3, 1943. Generalkommissar Rauter then instituted martial law and the occupier commenced reprisals: at least 100 people were summarily executed, and some German soldiers took it upon themselves to shoot people dead in the streets.[17]

But these retaliatory actions only served to strengthen the workers' resolve. The Gelderland-based National Organization for Aid to People in Hiding,* known simply as "the L.O.," became a central link between smaller resistance groups, and the Dutch resistance began to coordinate all kinds of acts of defiance against the occupiers. These efforts came largely too late for the Netherlands' Jews. In May 1943, the Nazis were getting ready for their final push, to remove the last group of "privileged Jews" from Amsterdam.

A THIRTY-EIGHT-PAGE "GUIDEBOOK to the Jewish Council," a brochure of the organization's departments, staff members, and addresses issued in March 1943, included no fewer than fifty offices throughout Amsterdam, including chairmen's headquarters at Nieuwe Keizersgracht 58, Expositur headquarters at three locations on the Jan van Eyckstraat, and the *Het Joodsche Weekblad* newspaper offices at three more addresses on the Jodenbreestraat.

"M. Levie" was listed as secretary to R. H. Eitje, General Manager of Work Permits for the department for non-Dutch Jews, located at Waterlooplein 119–121.[18]

Although the Council had grown into a massive organization by

---

* Landelijke Organisatie Voor Hulp Aan Onderduikers.

that time, described as a "state within a state,"[*] or "the Jewish government," charged with addressing all the concerns of tens of thousands of people, by May 1943, so many people had already been deported that its *raison d'etre* seemed to have evaporated. This was completely in line with Aus der Fünten's removal scheme: after giving some "privileged" Jews a false sense of security, he could now withdraw it.

On Friday, May 21, 1943, Aus der Fünten told the Jewish Council that 7,000 of its members would have to report for "work in Germany." In other words, 7,000 of the 17,500 Sperre that had been issued to Council employees were suddenly invalidated. It was up to the Council itself to decide who no longer deserved this protection, and the organization was given four days to choose, because the workers would have to report on May 25.[19] This was the first time that the Council had been explicitly ordered to make a list of Jews for deportation, rather than a list of those to be protected.

Mirjam Levie ran home to her family's apartment when she first got the news, sobbing, because she couldn't stand the idea that the Council had not stood up in defiance of the order. "I was so upset that the JC had once again lent itself to this barbarity instead of saying: Enough is enough, go hang," she wrote.

She described at length the chaotic madness that ensued over the wrenching next few days at Council offices. Her boss, Eitje, was one of those charged with the order's implementation, so Mirjam's job the following evening was to collate the call-up list with cards from the index of registration cards, while a team of Council accountants, "did nothing but count and count, but the figures just didn't add up," she wrote. "They remained well below 7,000."

Her team of coworkers "was beside itself with rage. Of course we kept coming across the names of good friends, colleagues, sometimes even relatives, brothers and sisters and even parents and children! The mood became more and more charged until one of the men (a former theater director and impresario) burst into tears and shouted that he

---

[*] By Presser.

refused to go on. At that point we all chucked it in and one of us went to tell the Professor that we couldn't possibly do this insane and barbarous work."

Mirjam described how many team members joined the renegade group in Cohen's office, while one brave soul spoke and "everybody was crying and barely capable of voicing their objections." Cohen, who was also in tears, she wrote, responded by arguing, "If we fail to do this, terrible things will happen."

The Germans, she wrote in her diary, had warned Cohen that, "the repercussions would be unimaginable."

"If the terrible things you keep speaking of will happen anyway," Mirjam replied, "then why do this nauseating work instead of lying in the sun and gathering our strength for Poland?"

Many other members of the Council nodded in agreement. "The Professor looked around at all the sobbing men—I was the only woman—and said, 'Please don't make things difficult for us, the call-ups *have* to be dispatched.'"[20]

Several Council staff refused to go on and walked out. Some of the organization's leaders stayed and continued to count, others stayed but refused to participate. When Mirjam returned to the office once again the next morning, Eitje asked her to cancel as many of the call-ups as possible. She learned that many of the names on the list were "undeliverable"—meaning that some call-ups had been issued to people who had already been deported or had gone into hiding.

Ultimately, there were not enough names on the list—they had not reached 7,000, and not enough people showed up for the May 25 call. This enraged the Nazis, who retaliated with a random sweep the following day, picking up 3,300 Jews. Willy Lages was still dissatisfied with that result, less than half of the number Aus der Fünten had demanded.

Lages secretly planned the next Razzia for a few weeks later, on June 20. Starting at 3:30 a.m. that Sunday morning, cars with loudspeakers drove through the Jewish sections of Amsterdam Zuid and the Transvaalbuurt in Amsterdam Oost, ordering the Jews to report at assembly points. Anyone who didn't come voluntarily was forcibly torn from their home. More than 5,500 Jewish people were rounded up that day—among them, Mirjam Levie.

"This is it, I thought to myself," she wrote. "What I've been dreading so much is actually happening now."

It was a blisteringly hot day, but families left their homes wearing their winter coats, laden with baggage and blankets, assuming they would need these for the colder months of "labor service." Dutch Nazi propaganda photographer, Herman Heukels from Zwolle, arrived at Olympiaplein, a famous Olympic sports plaza in Zuid, to capture images of the roundup, planning to sell his pictures to *Storm*, an official paper of the Dutch SS.* These would be some of the final portraits ever taken of most of the adults, children, and the elderly, who would be deported that day. Among those Heukels captured in his photo series, was Jewish Council co-chairman David Cohen, engaged in a conversation with two other men.

The other co-chair, Abraham Asscher, who had biked over to Zuid to check on his daughter, who lived on Apollolaan, and to try and prevent what deportations he could, also ended up in the Olympiaplein as an arrestee. Asked repeatedly to show his ID, he finally told one officer that he'd had enough, and received a bloody nose for his insubordination. Asscher fought back, throwing the Green to the ground. The other police tackled him and brought him to the square, where Aus der Fünten settled on punishing him with house arrest for one night. Neither chairman of the Council was deported that day.[21]

In Heukels' photo series, Dutch police or SS officials who organized the roundup are left outside of the frame. The only images of anyone in uniform are those of Jewish *Ordedienst* men from Westerbork, who'd been forced there, probably at gunpoint as in other raids, to facilitate the process.[22]

While these photos are some of the most valuable visual evidence historians have of that day's massive Razzia, they reflect none of

---

* The image on the cover of this book.

the threat posed by the occupier, or the terror experienced by the victims.

Diaries fill in the emotional experience for both victims and bystanders, such as that of Cornelis Komen, a traveling salesman for an English asbestos company, who witnessed the raid out of the windows of an Amsterdam tram. He and his children were going on a trip out of town to pick cherries. "The last Jews are being rounded up," he wrote in his diary. "Herded together and taken away like cattle. From hearth and home to foreign parts." He also added, "They may not be a pleasant people, but they're still human beings."

The raid attracted rare American media attention to the plight of the Dutch Jews. "Netherlands Jews Ousted by Nazis," was the headline of a *New York Times* article printed on June 23, 1943, with the lede: "All Jews in Amsterdam have been deported by the Germans to Poland, thus completing the removal of the entire Jewish population of the Netherlands."[23]

The article of no more than 200 words on page 8 of the paper reflected the catastrophic nature of the June 20 sweep: it certainly left the impression that the entire Jewish population of the Netherlands had been deported.

In fact, the article was just a little premature. Some stragglers from the Jewish Council still resided in the city through the summer, until September 29, 1943. On that day of the festival of Rosh Hashanah, Jewish New Year, the Nazis officially dissolved the Jewish Council, and all the remaining staff members, including Asscher and Cohen, were among the last 10,000 Jewish people in the Netherlands to be deported to Westerbork as well. By then, the country was considered by the Germans to be "Judenrein"—Jew free.

15

"LIKE JOB ON THE DUNGHEAP"

May 1943–August 1943

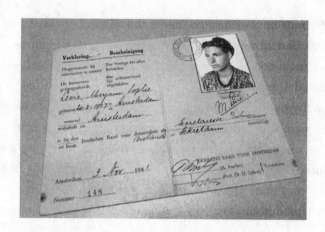

Identity card of Mirjam Levie during the war

Philip Mechanicus, 54, Journalist, Westerbork Transit Camp, Drenthe

SATURDAY, MAY 29, 1943—I have the feeling that I am an unofficial reporter covering a shipwreck. We sit together in a cyclone, feeling the ship leaking, slowly sinking. Yet, we're still trying to reach a harbor, though it seems far away. Gradually, I have developed the notion that I wasn't brought here by my persecutors, but that I took the trip voluntarily to do my work. I'm busy all day long, without a second's boredom, and sometimes I feel as if I have too little time. Duty is duty; work ennobles. I write a great deal of the day, sometimes beginning early in the morning at five-thirty, sometimes I'm still busy until the evenings after bedtime, summarizing my impressions or experiences of the day.

I play chess a few times a day, read the papers attentively, speak with various people, with doctors, nurses, and other patients. I visit the camp in the afternoon hours, and smoke my pipe. What more does a man need to spend his time in this Gypsy camp?

Chief Rabbi Dasberg* was sent back to Amsterdam today. One of my friends also received a letter from his wife, dated Wednesday afternoon, in which she writes that since Sunday she has been imprisoned in the Jewish Council building on Nieuwe Keizersgracht in

---

* Simon Dasberg was deputy rabbi of Amsterdam at the time.

Amsterdam. The children had been left to their own devices all that time. Last night, a transport of about 450 people arrived from Amsterdam. The commander has decreed that, during working hours, Jews are no longer allowed to go for a walk on the middle path of the main street, the Boulevard de Misères,* and must only tread along the sides, and very quickly at that. Today, the commander was riding his bicycle and kicked a Jew in his backside, while he was loading a train, saying that as the man had his back turned toward him, he didn't show the proper respect. That's not such an easy thing to do.

SUNDAY, MAY 30, 1943—The Jews here in Westerbork are like Job on the dungheap. All they possess are a single set of clothes, a suit and some undergarments to cover their meager limbs during the day, and at night a blanket; one pair of shoes, a cap, a knife, spoon and fork, and a cup. The pious Jews still maintain their faith in God, just like Job did, and testify every Friday night and Saturday to their devotion to the Almighty. The non-pious, who are strong, have faith in their own mental fortitude, and bow their heads to the religious traditions of their campmates.

The devout do not ask to know the grounds on which they suffer this fate, their debasement. They accept it and carry it as undeniable and unavoidable, in the unshakable conviction that their God will help them through this, just as he helped their forefathers through trials of a similar nature. A steadfast faith in God is the foundation of their attitude.

The thinking Jew, who does not possess this faith, poses the question: Why have I been placed in this humiliating, degrading situation? There must be more profound reasoning for which he has been stricken; the simple fact that he is a Jew does not satisfy him as the cause of his misery, his dispossession, his isolation, his exile. That is too simplistic, too conceited, there is no life lesson in it, no

---

* Boulevard of Misery, a camp nickname for the main thoroughfare that ran through the camp.

incentive to undergo any moral, mental or social reflection. He asks himself: Am I personally at fault, or must I atone for the blame someone else brought upon himself? He is willing to acknowledge his guilt hands down, even if it is not evident to him what he has done. He admits that he may have been overly proud or unjust or unwitting. He is, according to the Karmic principle of communal guilt, prepared to share in the penance of others. He is willing to take his exile as a period of atonement, abasement, cleansing. But atonement for what purpose?

Should people leave this to Mystery, Godliness, Providence or question it instead? How many times in history has the Jew already been cast into perdition and forced to chasten himself? It began with his expulsion from Egypt, it continued with his captivity and bondage in Babylon, his brutal diaspora across the globe, his banishment from Spain, his torture in Eastern Europe. His fate may not yet have been as trying and his future may not yet have been as perilous as now. Is he forced to atone forever? Is this the kind of atonement that he will have to continuously endure? Is this the means of atonement for the survival of peoples and civilizations, which have been radically destroyed or have perished? Atonement would then amount to a kind of natural selection, eradication of the weak and survival of the strong, to a spiritual hardening, the will to live, perseverance to the limit.

The majority of the Jews here have a strong will to survive. They believe that, unless they are killed, or unless the war lasts a long time, they will make it through. They are vital, and, materialistic as they are, hold on to life so tightly that they will use every ounce of bodily strength and their willpower to survive and try to live as long as possible. Their powerful mental attitude in the concentration camps testifies to this: there are many casualties, but most have demonstrated a strong willpower that has brought them through very severe hardships and has toughened them for what lies ahead.

In Westerbork, we have seen badly injured Jews brought in from concentration camps Amersfoort, Ommen,[*] and Ellecom.[†] They were so mentally and physically exhausted that people here were surprised that they endured the torture of staying in these camps for months. It is certain that, in general, the strong—the mentally strong—are the ones who managed to endure the attempts to crush their mental and physical health. The psychologically weak have lost the fight and lost their lives. One may assume that the many persecutions the Jews have endured throughout history have hardened them and produced tough types. Still, this latest trial demands something else of the Jew, and requires something beyond the urge and the will to save their skin.

TUESDAY, JUNE 1, 1943—Quiet morning. Drizzling. Not the usual homicidal Tuesday morning procession. In total, four people from my room were selected for the transport out of thirty from the hospital barracks. A young doctor discreetly informed them at around six in the morning. No dramatic scenes. Still, the transport for today totals three thousand people.[‡]

A question: Why so few sick people this time? Rumor has it that they want to keep the doctors and nurses on staff as long as possible, because they plan to turn this camp into a German military hospital. It doesn't sound very likely. More plausible is that Dr. Spanier,[§] who has gained favor with the commander, has something to do with it.

The transports continue to arouse revulsion. They are carried out, actually, in animal wagons intended for horses. The deportees no longer lie on straw, but have to find a spot on the bare floor, between their own bags of food and their luggage. They are shoved in with the sick who, until last week, had been given a mattress. The OD picks

---

[*] Erika work camp near Ommen housed prisoners convicted of violating the 1939 Rationing Act.

[†] In the village of Ellecom, the Avegoor country estate was used as a Dutch SS training camp. Jewish slave laborers were forced to build a sports complex there.

[‡] A transport to Sobibor death camp of 3,006 people.

[§] Dr. Fritz Spanier, the German Jewish Chief of the Medical Service at Westerbork.

them up in front of the barracks at seven o'clock in the morning, and then takes them to the trains in rows of three, along the Boulevard des Misères in the middle of the camp.

The train is a long mangy snake consisting of old, filthy wagons, that divides the camp in two. The Boulevard: a desolate road lined by OD men, who ward off spectators. The exiles have a single bag for bread strapped over their shoulder that hangs over the hip, as well as a rolled-up blanket attached to the other shoulder by a rope and dangling on the back. Shabby emigres who own nothing more than what they carry. Men, silent, with long faces; women, often sobbing. The elderly stumbling under the burden of their belongings, across the bumpy road, filled with mud puddles. The sick on stretchers carried by the OD.

On the platform, the commander stands with his entourage, the Green Police, and Dr. Spanier, the chief physician,[*] in plain gray or pitch-black civilian clothing, bare-headed. Next to him is Schlesinger, head of registry: britches and wellies, miserable face, straw-colored hair under a flat cap. Beside the train are doctors, standing by in case the sick need help. The exiles who must board the train are sent through the barriers and are surrounded by OD men (to prevent them from fleeing), who count them, to make sure they correspond to the barracks list, and then they go straight into the train. Whoever hesitates, or stalls, is helped on; sometimes propelled, sometimes pushed, sometimes beaten, sometimes punched, sometimes kicked—as often by the Green Police as by the OD. . . .

Men and women, the old and young, children and babies, the healthy and the sick, are all stowed together in one and the same wagon. Healthy men and women thrown in with people who require constant nursing care, who have lost control of bodily functions; the lame, the deaf, gastric patients, the mentally handicapped, the demented. Everyone pressed together on the bare floors, in between and on top of their luggage. A barrel—a single, small barrel—in the corner

---

[*] It was very likely Dr. Spanier who "protected" Mechanicus at the camp for a long time.

of the wagon, is where *devant tout le monde*[*] they must relieve themselves; a barrel that is too small for such a large group of people. On the side, there is a bag of sand, to grab and throw over it. In another corner, there is a water bottle with a tap to quench their thirst.

As they boarded the train, agents of Lippmann, Rosenthal & Co.[†] follow the exiles closely, harassing them with jabs and strong-arming to turn over their last worldly goods, bank notes, fountain pens and watches. Anyone who hasn't already given their possessions away in the barracks, or given them to others for safe-keeping, now tries to throw them off the train. After the train has pulled out, the Jewish Gestapo, who are used during transports as spies, scavenge the tracks like hyenas for money or bank notes left behind.

Once the quotas are filled and the wagons are full, the doors are shut. With a hand gesture, the commander gives the signal for departure. Usually around eleven o'clock, the whistle shrieks, chilling all in the camp to the bone. The mangy snake, with its belly full, shuffles away. Schlesinger and his entourage jump on the footboards of the moving train to catch a ride. Otherwise, they will have to walk back—the things they do to prevent wear and tear on the soles of their shoes. Satisfied, the commander strolls away; Dr. Spanier wanders back to his office, hands on his back, head bent in worry. When he says anything about the transport, people in the camp make a gagging sound. Three thousand and fifty people departed today.

INGE JANSEN, HOUSEWIFE, AMSTERDAM

FRIDAY, JUNE 4, 1943—I went with Adriaan, looking very smart and handsome in his SS uniform, to the Colonial Institute this afternoon.

---

[*] In front of the whole world.
[†] A formerly trusted Jewish bank that the Germans Aryanized and turned into a looting bank.

Its auditorium is a very beautiful gothic hall, and it was full of people. We saw a film about the life of Friedrich Schiller,[*] which was very nice and beautiful. I spoke with Dien van Kleef and her sister, both NSB. They run three bookstores together. In the afternoon, I rested as much as possible.

SATURDAY, JUNE 5, 1943—This morning Krista van Dijk[†] stopped by and brought me to see Jessy Tulp,[‡] who had an umbrella that I had loaned her. They were both constantly complaining about "all the people who must go away." I am quite down-to-earth, I think. I'm always cheerful, really. Perhaps the misery just passes right by me because I hardly speak to anyone. It's possible that tomorrow we're going to the Championship Tournament between Feyenoord and ADO in the Olympic Stadium. Karel Lotsy[§] promised to save me seats!

SUNDAY, JUNE 6, 1943—It was very bad weather so we stayed cozy at home in the morning, had an early dinner and walked to the Olympic Stadium, where it turned out that we had wonderful seats in the grandstand. Along with the very nice match, which ADO won over Feyenoord, 3–1, we also got to see athletics and a handball match. It was nice to be in the Stadium again.

MONDAY, JUNE 7, 1943—Adriaan had a discussion on June 2, before the second meeting with Van Ravenswaay, Croin, and Eggink from the Artsenkamer. He later heard from Van Ravenswaay that Mussert does indeed want to go to Hitler to discuss the whole situation again and to appoint a group of people, including Adriaan. Then they can't blame him that the NSB has no competent members.

---

[*] The German dramatist and poet.
[†] This is a pseudonym.
[‡] Amsterdam Chief Constable Sybren Tulp's wife.
[§] Chairman of the Dutch Football Association, who was accused of collaboration after the war.

I skipped my German class today. I just didn't feel like sitting on the hard wooden benches, and went to buy groceries instead.

PHILIP MECHANICUS, JOURNALIST, WESTERBORK

THURSDAY, JUNE 10, 1943—Around the camp, just behind the barbed wire, there is a majestic field of purple lupins in full bloom. It is a refreshing sight to the eyes of thousands of battered men, women and children who walk the barren streets between the lifeless barracks; a glimpse of nature for those who peer out the fogged windows of the filthy laundry sheds.

Between the lupines, there are guard towers every hundred meters or so, where military police with grim-looking helmets on their coarse heads and armed with frightful carbines keep watch, ready to shoot anyone who tries to escape. Along the barbed wire, more military police, also with their carbines slung over their shoulders, are patrolling the fences. The lupines are also under strict surveillance: anyone who is not allowed out of the camp to work should not think of picking one of the pretty lupines. Nevertheless, the camp is teeming with lupines. There are bouquets on the rough wood tables in the resident barracks, they are in old tin cans on the windowsills. They add a little color, beauty and fragrance to the dirty beds that are crammed together, to the stench of unwashed clothes and sweaty bodies. Toward evening, when the young men and women return to the camp from the heathland, dusty and sweaty, marching apace, aware of their vigor and unquenchable thirst for life, they carry bunches of lupines, which they picked as a reward for their hard day's work.

SATURDAY, JUNE 12, 1943—An estimated three hundred people who are in mixed marriages and their children were summoned to the

Registry Office again this morning. Gemmeker gave them a choice: they can either be sterilized and sent back to Amsterdam, without a star and with a distinctive type of J, or risk being sent to Poland, to succumb to inhumane labor. They must make their decision by Monday.

History has an ironic twist. When the Germans initiated their measures of exclusion against the Jews in our country, many Jews who were married to Aryans dissolved their bonds (sometimes temporarily) to protect their families, and to save their property. Until last year, the Germans respected mixed marriages, and even those that had been dissolved where children were involved, not tearing them apart, and exempted from deportation any Jews married to Gentiles. Those who had separated from their Aryan spouse often regretted their decision.

What the Germans had given with one hand, they took away with the other. First, they threw the *dissolved* mixed marriages out the window; then they tore apart mixed marriages with no children (except those with church affiliations or baptized before January 1, 1941) and now they're forcing those in mixed marriages with kids to undergo sterilization, if they want to avoid the hell in Poland. Those who dissolved their marriages to save their families should no longer feel any regret, unless they would prefer sterilization to avoid going to Poland. For men whose married life has ended due to impotence, the choice the Germans pose is not especially difficult. But for men in the prime of their lives it is horrifying. They are in the clutches of a Moloch* that never releases its prey.

Westerbork has become a bee park. Yesterday, a swarm of bees including its queen flew into the camp and was collected in a butter barrel. Apparently, the bees have nothing against living among Jews.

THURSDAY, JUNE 17, 1943—The child mortality rate here is alarming. This week, two children from the same family died, a four-year-old child and a two-year-old, while the mother is pregnant with her third child. The family came through Vught. The death rate at this moment

---

* A thorny devil out of the book of Leviticus.

is fifteen children a week. Here's an example of how sick children are treated: A child who had a middle ear infection was sent in an open bus to the Academic Medical Center in Groningen, alone without his mother or father, or any other escort. His ear was punctured[*] and immediately after the operation he was sent back on the bus to Westerbork, where his father picked him up at the camp gates. The child was continuously sick for six months, suffering from flu, angina, etc. Middle ear infections, throat infections, organ and other kinds of infections are very common here. The climate here is bad, raw, and there's a lot of dust.

MIRJAM LEVIE,
SECRETARY, AMSTERDAM

IT WAS A mad rush, but by Shabbat, June 19,[†] I was all done: Curtains washed, cupboards stocked, floors waxed. Everything was ship shape, even if I say so myself. I had slaved away, because I wanted it to look good for Mother. That day I had an "open house." I invited your father and Els, Eitje,[‡] Jo Pronk (Bobby's boyfriend, who had been a great help. He is very handy and did all kinds of odd jobs for me) and Aunt Phine, ordered delicious fondant, baked proper biscuits with butter that I bought on the black market (cheap at 10 guilders for half a pound) and also bought a cake, a real butter cake, on the black market.

I forgot to tell you that on that Thursday we had been forced to hand in our bicycles. A new list had been submitted, and a number would be engraved on our bicycles. I would have it back by Monday. That week, the Professor[§] had been told that as of Monday (i.e. June 21),

---

[*] Most likely this means that he had an operation called a myringotomy, in which a small incision is made to the eardrum to allow fluid to drain.

[†] This entry is dated July 7, 1943, but it describes the events of June 19 and 20.

[‡] Eitje is her boss at the Jewish Council.

[§] Cohen, presumably.

some measures favorable for the Jews were to come into effect, which prompted me to say to Eitje: We are bound to receive some bad tidings now. When the Huns* say "favorable," it really means "unfavorable."

My "open house" was a great success. Everybody stayed a long time and inspected the house from top to bottom. I even had some proper lemonade; everything was just perfect. Eitje also brought me half a real butter cake. Extremely kind. At six o'clock, I ate with the Dunners, in Den Texstraat, and got back home at ten. Little did I know that, for the time being, this was to be my last night in Amsterdam. For how long? That remains to be seen. As it happens, I slept badly that night (not unlike King Ahasuerus), but when I turned in, I did think to myself: how wonderfully soft and warm.

The following morning, at the crack of dawn, I heard the roar of a loudspeaker outside. I couldn't believe my ears. On a Sunday, and after all the reassurances we'd had! Perhaps it's something else, I thought, but then I told myself: You know what this means, it's over. Then suddenly I thought: Mother! All alone in hospital. So I got out of bed, this time I did get washed and dressed, put on stockings (despite the heat), smart shoes and a beautiful silk dress as well as an elegant tailored coat and a nice handbag, because I wanted to impress the Huns. I wanted to get through.

From the balcony I understood what was happening. The Jews were being rounded up, of course! So off I went, without breakfast. I was in two minds about what to do. You see, the Professor once told us that in an emergency, he would have us picked up. I was now living in Pretoriusstraat and the two other secretaries in Ingogostraat, so the three of us lived quite close to one another. But then I thought: Perhaps there's no time to lose. So off I went.

Everything had been cordoned off again, and as I made my way, I learned that it was the same story in Zuid. At Nieuwe Weesperpoortbrug I tried my luck with the Green Police, who had cordoned off the place. No luck whatsoever! Not even with my "most charming smile."

---

* A common nickname for the German occupier, like Krauts.

I retraced my steps to try at the Amstel Brewery. Along the way, a Jew asked me: "shall we try together?" The soldier who had spoken to us told us to go to the Colonial Institute for an *Ausweis*.* I have no intention of putting my head in the lion's mouth, I thought to myself (that is where the Green Police were based), but my companion said: "You've got nothing to lose; you'll be rounded up anyway. At this early hour, they may still issue one."

I let myself be persuaded, and headed for the Colonial Institute. But on my way there, I was stopped by a Green who asked me where I was going, and when I told him I wanted to go back home to fetch my luggage, he grabbed me by the arm and took me to . . . the Colonial Institute. I was hopeful at first. We received a polite welcome, and were asked to hand in our exemption papers and identity cards. My exemption paper happens to be rather good, with a low number (the same as with cars), an old date and the personal signatures of Professor Cohen and Asscher, instead of the later stamp. We had to stand facing the wall (there were four people already). But as more and more time passed, and more and more people came in, and we still didn't receive any further information, I thought to myself: It's over, I backed the wrong horse, better not dwell on it, it can't be helped. It was mainly hospital staff coming in. Later I learned that they had telephoned Dr. Kroonenberg, the director of the NIZ,† and had been advised to go to the Colonial Institute, where they would be given an *Ausweis*.

Despite the fix we were in, I couldn't help but laugh at the sight of us, standing there, staring at the wall. One woman needed the lavatory and stood there moaning: "I really need to go!" And then one of those fellows would bark: *"Wenn Sie nicht schweigen gebrauche ich mein Schutzwaffe,"‡* or something to that effect. If somebody else had told me this, I would have thought: How awful. But now I didn't think it was awful at all, only insane, that these men would fly into a rage whenever you as much as turned your head.

---

* A special identity card, in this case, a permit to stay in Amsterdam.
† The Jewish hospital.
‡ If you don't keep quiet, I'll use my weapon.

Around eleven o'clock—we had been standing for approximately three-and-a-half hours—we went outside. I forgot to tell you that meanwhile hundreds of Green Police, who had been called in from outside, were filing into the building. One of them had jumped off the train too early, and was carried in dead on a stretcher. Too bad it was just the one. I briefly harbored hopes that we would be taken to the theater,[*] but no. We were taken to Polderweg in trucks. This is the area, not far from Muiderpoort station, where those with call-ups had had to report. For a moment I thought we would be boarding the train straight away, but we were taken to a sandy area enclosed by a wooden fence. . . .

It would take too long to tell you everything in detail. It was all fairly easy-going. Rennig served as our lavatory attendant, and we took turns going to the lavatory in a hut housing the Dutch military police. I seized the opportunity to telephone Eitje. The military police were really very decent. Heilbut, one of the heads of the Expositur, showed up, but wasn't allowed to enter the enclosure. Later on, Mrs. Sluzker arrived, followed by Sluzker with Aus der Fünten.

Everybody's hopes were up. But to no avail. Sluzker had no say. I even went up to Aus der Fünten (I had nothing to lose) and showed him my papers, but he said: "*Spielt keine Rolle,*"[†] and to Herz he said: "*Es wird nur noch auskwartiert.*"[‡]

We were herded to the station. This is it, I thought to myself; what I've been dreading so much is actually happening now. . . . At the station, the wagons were waiting. Goods wagons, cattle trucks rather: "8 *chevaux,*" 8 horses, it said in French on the wall of my wagon. . . .

Many were in tears, naturally, while others just sat there staring. Children were wailing, there was screaming and shouting, but also some jolly greetings, such as "You here as well?" from spirited youngsters. I found a fairly acceptable wagon that wasn't quite as jam-packed as the others because it had all the bigwigs. We also had a decent Black Police-

---

[*] Hollandse Schouwburg.
[†] "It doesn't matter."
[‡] "She'll be deported anyway."

man* (every wagon was escorted by a member of the Black Police), who kept the connecting doors open to give us (and himself) a little fresh air.

The transport from Central Amsterdam had consisted of passenger trains deporting 2,800 people. This transport, however, was made up of cattle trucks deporting 2,400 people. The train left at three, and was extremely slow because, of course, the engine had trouble pulling this long train. The pregnant women suffered most. There was one in our wagon, and considering the special care these women require and seeing them trodden on, jostled and thrown about, and thinking how this will affect these women, you realized just how low we had sunk. The train stopped hardly anywhere, only in Zwolle, where the station staff treated us very well and filled our canteens with water. As I mentioned before, I didn't have anything with me, but everybody shared with me. The journey went well, and at around nine o'clock we arrived in Westerbork.

I forgot to tell you that in Amsterdam the people were standing on the roofs of their houses, with binoculars, watching us go. A fine spectacle indeed! And while we were sitting there on the floor of that sluggish train, passing the beautiful forests and places such as Bussum and Hilversum, where we used to spend our holidays in such completely different circumstances, I did feel a bit sorry for myself. But I kept thinking: Don't dwell on it, just wait and see what happens next. Others went through all this a year ago.

DOUWE BAKKER,
POLICE DIVISION CHIEF,
AMSTERDAM

SUNDAY, JUNE 20, 1943—I went out this morning at 8:15 a.m. to get strawberries from Reitema. The German Green Police have posted

---

* While German police wore green uniforms, Dutch police wore black uniforms, so they were often referred to as either "Green Police" or "Black Police."

sentries on the bridge across the Ringvaart leading to the Linnae-usstraat, and they will not let anyone through. I'm allowed to drive on, however. It appears that the entire eastern part of the city, up to the Celebesstraat and all the way south to the Amstelveenseweg, as well as the bridges across the Buiten-Singelgracht have been closed off. No one is allowed in or out without a special pass from the S.D. Cars with loudspeakers pass by telling the Jews to prepare for today's departure. Many will be processed.

At Reitema I got the strawberries, cherries and tomatoes and then I drove back. I don't have much trouble passing except at the last post on the Berlagebrug. The guard there objects. But by coincidence, Lages is there, and he immediately allows me to pass.

CORNELIS KOMEN,
SALESMAN, AMSTERDAM

SUNDAY, JUNE 20, 1943—Many people on the train don't even know what's going on in Amsterdam. The last Jews are being rounded up. Herded together and taken away like cattle. From hearth and home to foreign parts. First, they're taken to Vught, then they're transported to Poland—oh, the misery these people must be going through. Separated from their wives and children. They may not be a pleasant people, but they're still human beings. How can the Good God allow this?

But we're on our way to Tiel. The train is packed, and in Utrecht another bunch piles in. But people are in a good mood, because everyone's getting out today, to eat or buy cherries. In Geldermalsen we change trains to Tiel. Even more crowded. The carriages are bursting at the seams. But we're getting there, and Van Dien is waiting for us. How peaceful it is, this small provincial town. When we arrive, there's breakfast on the table. As always, this is such a lovely surprise to us. Smoke-dried beef and rusks.

Afterward, we have some coffee, and then we're off to the cherry orchard. We need to walk three quarters of an hour. It's beautiful in the Betuwe. We're surrounded by nothing but rustling wheat fields, interspersed with beautiful orchards. Apples here, pears over there, and sometimes plum or cherry trees. One even more beautiful than the other. Then we reach Farmer Kerdijk. Van Dien immediately orders a box of 7.5 kilos of cherries.

We sit ourselves down and start to eat. The box is empty in less than half an hour, but then we're fed up with cherries. That's the problem; if you have too much of something, it soon starts to pall. We run a race. Van Dien loses to me. Wim beats Bert. The Willinks are the champions. Then we do some boxing. And then the boys try to wrestle Van Dien down to the ground. Not a chance. He breaks into a sweat. It's lovely getting tired this way. How wonderful life is.

While in Amsterdam, the Jews are herded together like cattle. Carrying their bundles on their backs. Their blankets. They packed their things days in advance. Still, how hard their departure must have been. Parting from their familiar living rooms, their friends and acquaintances. While we are eating cherries, one basket after another. Lazing around. How lovely this place is.

PHILIP MECHANICUS, JOURNALIST, WESTERBORK

SUNDAY, JUNE 20, 1943—Tonight, at the end of a gorgeous summer day, the latest wave of Jews washed in here from Amsterdam. In the scorching sun, two thousand men, women and children, rode into the camp in cattle cars. Today it was boiling hot in the barracks. In the sick barracks, the patients lay half-naked on top of their covers; the children shirtless. Whoever was "relieved of duty" sought some solace on an empty bit of heath just inside the fence on the East side of the camp. This piece of heath has been turned into a kind of dune landscape.

Heaps of sand, unearthed to build a canal, has created hills along the barbed wire that border the terrain.

On the camp side, just behind the barracks, there is a flourishing forest of oak coppice, still thin and spindly. This imitation landscape would be ideal if not for the piles of dirty, stinky half-burst open mattresses right in the middle. In this marred landscape people find relief from the heat of the camp. Paired-up men and women, boys and girls sat between the bushes, against the embankments of the dunes, with the view over the heath to the other side of the canal, with their backs toward the barbed wire fences. It appears that they exchange sweet words and intimacies, unencumbered and unaware of the impending tragedy . . . Couples strolled along the canal as along a beach, their attention focused on any lofty word spoken in the spirit of love. Their bodies are bronzed by the sun. Everything that happens is respectable and virtuous, as they are in the clear view of the armed military police in the watch towers.

While people manage to forget their personal tragedies for a moment, consciously or unconsciously, and engage in amorous chitchat in the sun, a new tragedy is unfolding: Others, torn from their foundations, robbed of their property, destitute, degraded and humiliated, arrive in animal wagons. It is a familiar scene and people have witnessed it before, time and again. A seemingly endless chaotic procession of evacuees, like nomadic gypsies. Men, women and children, loaded down with all the baggage they can manage to carry. The tragedy has been accepted; it has lost its original grandeur, its coarseness. It no longer seems shocking.

The first waves to wash in here were strong young men and women who had prepared themselves excellently for this mysterious adventure. They'd marched from Hooghalen, and a shock went through the camp, initially out of admiration, and then from pity and horror, for this brave, resolute vanguard of Jews. After that came mixed groups of proletariat and paupers, with their many children, in shabby clothes, carrying meager belongings. A pitiful procession from Hooghalen, bedraggled and miserable, forced chaotically into the camp with a lot of ruckus. Everyone felt compassion and deep pity for these battered souls, who had lived their whole lives at the edge of existence, and now, plundered, had been delivered into the storm. Wave upon wave of these proletariats and paupers washed up here, again and again the very picture of misery, poverty and dearth. Sometimes, without even a moment's pause, they were sent on, often as scruffy as they came, sometimes with a few rags hastily collected from others, directly to Poland.

The third of October was the pinnacle, still marked with the blackest coal. Ten thousand souls were stowed here at one time, including the men from the various work camps, with their wives and children who had been rounded up in the most diabolical and terrifying round-up ever. The road from Hooghalen to Westerbork moaned from the misery of the Jews, from the harshness and shamelessness of their persecutors. A sea of despondent, beaten people, including children—and still more children—the throng jostling and stumbling into one another. Inside the camp, there was a shortage of beds. Overcrowded in the barracks, thousands of men and women slept outside, under the open sky, on the assembly grounds. The largest group is still always the proletariat from the heavily populated neighborhoods of the cities. Gradually, this great mass of humanity was transported to the East.

After that came the old people from the convalescent homes, and the seriously ill from the hospitals across the country. The first transports came with the train just to Hooghalen, from there, those who could came by foot, hobbling and heaving toward Westerbork; the rest came by ambulance. A macabre march of the crippled, blind and frail old men and women shuffling into the camp, guided by members of the security service. It was heart-breaking to witness, and tragic to look on, helpless and powerless, as those who have lived such long lives were treated this way.

Later, they extended the train tracks right into the heart of the camp.* These elderly, uprooted people died like rats in the camp. Their remains were burned in the crematorium, like nothing more than rags. After that, the prisoners from camp Vught arrived. Literally stripped to their undergarments, men, women and children were transported in animal wagons, and they were often covered in lice. First, men and women entered the camp together; later, they were ruthlessly separated and were alone. That was a separate tragedy in the general tragedy. This was followed by a massive deportation to Poland in muddy animal wagons—forty, fifty, sixty people to each car, stuffed in among the luggage and close to the latrine bucket.

Now we are almost at the end. The Jews who had managed to stay in Amsterdam arrived in consecutive transports of about 2,000 people to each train—also in livestock trains. They were the last remnants of the proletariat and the petty bourgeoisie, and among them a great number of intellectuals.

The arrival of today's transports didn't create the tragic impression of previous transports, because the people were for the most part well-dressed and healthy looking, supplied with good blankets and provisions, which made them seem as if they were well-traveled people arriving for a vacation. The few sick ones were barely noticed as they were carried to the hospital barracks on stretchers. The public here didn't react as if it was a tragic moment in a tragic time. They were mostly excited to see friends, family members or acquaintances among the new arrivals, as if running into them at a seaside holiday retreat. The sound was also not hushed sorrow and pity for our fellow brothers and sisters arriving at a prison, a place of calamity. Instead, there were jovial cries of recognition and greeting. One enthusiastic resident even called it Westerbork-le-Bain.†

---

* See previous note; the Westerbork train line was completed in December 1942.
† "The beaches of Westerbork."

DOUWE BAKKER,
POLICE DIVISION CHIEF,
AMSTERDAM

MONDAY, JUNE 21, 1943—The longest day of the year's weather forecast: The night was quiet, dark and rainy weather; bright spells during the day, quite pleasant in the evening. However, the weather remains unsettled. I went back on duty today, because it's no fun having time off. . . . Yesterday, about 15,000 Jews were rounded up and sent to Vught.* They estimate there are still about 15,000 to 20,000 Jews here in the city.

INGE JANSEN,
HOUSEWIFE, AMSTERDAM

MONDAY JUNE 28, 1943—Schmidt† is dead. Probably suicide, on a mission to Paris he felt sick and fell out of an open train window, according to the improbable story in the paper. What changes will this lead to in our country? My first thought is that Mussert must certainly resign, as the mood at headquarters must be at its lowest point. Now that it appears that Hitler does not want to receive Mussert and, moreover, he had to turn to the SS Reichsführer‡ for difficulties. Schmidt probably could not bear the shame of his failed policies. At the same time, I find it so very tragic, because the man undeniably had capabilities.

---

* He's misinformed; the total is estimated at around 5,500 and mostly they went to Westerbork.

† Franz Schmidt was the SS official (see Emmerik diary) who promised to exterminate all the Jews in the Netherlands within a year. A supporter of Mussert, he was often in conflict with Rauter. It is not clear whether he committed suicide or was killed.

‡ That is, Himmler.

I had to stand for an hour in line to get peas, a half a pound of berries with accompanying sauerkraut. Frau Maess came for tea this evening, a resolute little woman, brought beautiful carnations with her.* In the afternoon, Ans and Betty were here with gladiolas, a brooch and stationary and cards, and it was really very enjoyable. Etty talked about some kind of dreadful phosphorous fluid that they put into small bottles attached to balloons and it makes the most unquenchable fires.

PHILIP MECHANICUS,
JOURNALIST, WESTERBORK

THURSDAY, JULY 1, 1943—The first half of the year has passed. Strange. I didn't choose to be here, and I have no purpose other than to wait, to wait. Yet, at least half a year has flown by. Every day I ask myself, as everyone else does: how much longer? Waiting is an art. I don't have any choice but to wait, but still it requires some talent. To practice patience is actually a kind of grace. It asks fearlessness for what's in store. Whoever has the courage to look life in the eyes must also have the courage to face death. Contempt for death clashes with the will to live. One can only die once. Everyone in Europe is at the front or could be called up at any moment. So that makes everyone reckon with death. That's what makes life bearable, and what makes people strong in the most difficult of times. Space and time have dissolved. One lives against a backdrop of nothingness. If he falls, he falls, and if he manages to continue with his life, he will be stronger in the future. This waiting period is a time of moral education and maturation, of coming to the insight that life is a destiny beyond one's control, that one has been given life on loan, and must calmly give it back when it is reclaimed from us.

---

* It's her birthday again.

SUNDAY, JULY 4, 1943—The announcement of the transport list is approaching again, and it shivers through our souls. There is whispering again from everywhere, all around. It has become known that this time two hundred patients from the hospital barracks will be deported and that for every patient that will be deported, three nurses will go. Last time, four hundred patients were required, but only 257 were sent. The writer of this diary has received unofficial information that this time he is on the transport list. Highly unpleasant news. Just yesterday I received news from Amsterdam that I might be put on the Puttkammer list, and consequently get a red stamp.[*] For me it's a flip of a coin. Today is O.'s[†] birthday. This afternoon I played chess with Dr. Bloch, who I thought I would easily beat, but in fact I lost. That bothered me.

MONDAY, JULY 5, 1943—Last night, a child cried all night for his mother and father. The other patients cursed and complained. His high, childlike voice penetrated the nocturnal silence. The child has been crying for his parents every night, all week, and every night, patients have been yelling and complaining. The child also cries for his parents during the day, but then his voice gets lost because of the general din of the adult patients. The child arouses no pity; everyone is already too preoccupied with their own quiet concerns. . . .

Today, the Jewish Council was liquidated.[‡] This morning some of its members, sixty with families, were sent back to Amsterdam. Another sixty, who have stayed behind, have been granted a red Z stamp, which gives them the same status as our "Alte-Kamp-Insassen" who have already been at the camp for four and a half years. . . . It is, in fact, a demonic obeisance to the representatives of the regime that Jews have been used to capture other Jews, to deliver Jews, and to police Jews. . . .

---

[*] The Puttkammer list was one of the "protective lists" that supposedly prevented one from being deported, but later it turned out that it was a fraud and extortion scheme.

[†] He may be referring to concert pianist Olga Moskowsky-Elias, his girlfriend before the war, but her birthday was actually July 2.

[‡] He seems to have gotten the date wrong.

Those Jews have abetted their tormentors with the ghastly services, primarily out of desperation to get a stamp to secure their own safety, to save their own lives. . . .

Now, those who have been selected return home to an empty, dead city, in which unrest and fear lingers like a heavy fog. But the anxiety will remain, because at any moment there could be another round-up, and they could be deported again. And do they still have a home to return to? Hasn't it been looted or confiscated in the meantime? Where will they live if they don't have a home anymore? Most likely they will end up in the new ghetto, the Transvaalbuurt,* which might soon be cut off from the rest of the city. They'll live there in bleak isolation, despite their coveted stamp. Meanwhile, their counterparts in Westerbork live with a certain freedom, and experience joy, albeit behind barbed wire, enjoy the view of the wide-open heath and sky.

TUESDAY, JULY 6, 1943—Weeping women. Cleaning women sobbing against their broomsticks, women gazing out open windows, bathed in tears. This morning their brothers, sisters, fathers and mothers, left on the transport.† Men can't hold back or swallow their tears. The train screeches and the venomous snake begins to scrape along. Two train cars full of S-cases.‡ I myself have passed through the eye of the needle. This morning at four o'clock I was informed that my name was removed from the list. People congratulated me left and right; everyone around me shook my hands. I graciously accepted their expressions of sympathy, but inwardly, I felt agony. Everywhere, other men are roused from their beds to prepare themselves for the dark transport. For those who were forced to depart, my congratulations must have felt like a slap in the face.

---

* As mentioned in Mirjam's diary, the Nazis moved the Jewish ghetto to the East of Amsterdam in a neighborhood called the Transvaalbuurt, relocating the remaining residents of the old Jewish quarter there.

† The transport from Westerbork to Sobibor on July 6, 1943, included 2,417 people. The camp was one of the Nazi "killing centers." According to USHMM, some 167,000 Jews were murdered there; only 58 survived.

‡ *Strafgevallen*, or criminal cases.

INGE JANSEN,
HOUSEWIFE, AMSTERDAM

THURSDAY, JULY 8, 1943—I ran around quite a bit because the cleaning lady didn't show up, and this evening Frau Reuter[*] came to visit with Hildburg and Gero. She is a cheerful woman, but I could tell immediately that she is used to everyone conforming to her needs. The English have landed in Sicily, and there is heavy fighting; hopefully [the Germans] can last.

FRIDAY, JULY 9, 1943—Dinner at the Amstel Hotel to make the acquaintance of Obergruppenführer Grothe, the replacement at the Ziekenfondsen for Conti.[†] He is a very pleasant man. Adriaan was extremely satisfied with their later discussion, after they brought us home. Hopefully they can finally make progress. They will have revenge!

SATURDAY, JULY 17, 1943—All day there were air raid sirens, making us very nervous. On the other side of the IJ, a lot of working-class neighborhoods were affected, including a church and a large oil tanker. Quite a few dead and wounded, unfortunately.

Dr. Reuter reported some news in the evening, a lot of wild stories going round. The Hermans and the Roskams came for tea. She's a German doctor; he's important—a publisher, very rich but luckily very simple and an SS man. He says he must get used to the military nature of the SS; I never heard Adriaan complain about such a thing. According to Fritz, the aviator, a lot of fighter planes have been sent to Sicily for a Grosz Angriff;[‡] it is dangerous to say something like that.

---

[*] Wife of Dr. F. Reuter, chief of the Public Health Department.
[†] Leonardo Conti, a Swiss-German physician and SS-Obergruppenführer; tried at Nuremberg after the war for his leading role in the Nazi euthanasia program, he hanged himself in his cell.
[‡] Major offensive.

Jessy's dog, Tipsy, had to be put out of its misery, and I feel really sorry for her.

PHILIP MECHANICUS, JOURNALIST, WESTERBORK

SATURDAY, JULY 24, 1943—There's a story going around the camp that I'm writing a novel about Westerbork, with the permission of the Oberstrumführer, and that every day I have to read him a chapter. Yesterday, it was unofficially announced that there would be no more transports, none from Westerbork to the East and none from Amsterdam to Westerbork. Today, like a thunderclap in clear skies—although the skies here are never clear; because a dark cloud is always hanging over us—came the news that a train was on its way from Amsterdam.

Yesterday there was a rumor making the rounds that there were still Jews in the Hollandsche Schouwburg, and this evening around 6 p.m., a transport arrived with 450 Jews. For the most part, they were members of the Expositur,[*] but also (with few exceptions) the group of sixty Jews from the Jewish Council who'd been sent back to Amsterdam last week with a protective stamp for good behavior. A bit of bitter irony: some of the Jews among them had returned to Amsterdam with all their possessions, pots and pans, peas and beans, packed and sacked; they had left Westerbork as misers. This time they were only carrying a single backpack and a blanket. The man was unshaven and his wife was disheveled. You could overhear people saying things like, "It couldn't have happened to nicer people . . ." and "If only he had used up his money," and that sort of thing. Malicious pleasure. The Führer's servants play cat and mouse with the Jews. They chase them from one corner to another, relishing their fear and their gradual exhaustion.

---

[*] A division of the Jewish council that processed exemptions, or Sperre.

SUNDAY, JULY 25, 1943—A decree from Dr. Pick, chief of the quarantine department: since flies transmit infection, every resident of the camp is required to catch fifty flies a day and deliver them in a piece of paper to the quarantine station. The cart before the horse. They forget the heaps of garbage near the camp and the filthy, open toilets, where the flies thrive and which are the source of contamination. People have hung up flypaper in one of the barracks, which catch hundreds of thousands. Flypaper is extremely scarce.

THURSDAY, JULY 29, 1943—Today, I escorted my brother to the *marechausee* barracks. He is married to an Aryan. For nine weeks, he has been hospitalized for his multiple sclerosis. As with so many of the patients with chronic illnesses here, his health has rapidly declined due to the lack of proper medicine, but more from the terrible conditions here and the lack of attentive nursing care. His legs resist and he can barely walk without help.

I could easily have escaped. With two OD members, who transported my brother, and without the military police noticing, I went in the truck that took my brother to the train in Assen. For one split second I felt the temptation, but I resisted it. Under no circumstances did I want to endanger my brother or cause him any difficulty. But above all, the thought shot through my mind: it's not worth it anymore, the war will soon be over. It is a curious sensation to be so close to freedom and then to reject it. Like a man turning away from a beautiful woman.

And still, this freedom is a relative victory. Whoever survives Westerbork, dodging the transports, can do more with his positive captivity than those Jews in Amsterdam who live in relative freedom or those who have gone into hiding, and sit between four walls, living every minute in fear of being arrested. Our imprisonment is the barbed wire and the imposed discipline of the barracks, but apart from that, with a little imagination and humor and some love of nature, men can shape their own world, and in this way, man can forget the imprisonment of his physical body. One can equally forget physical captivity through work, as long as it is not too excessive (and it isn't in Westerbork), and then spend his free time outside, enjoying the expansive skies, the moorlands, and the birds. The skies here are so priceless, the heather has many colors, the sunsets are exquisite, and there are great flocks of seagulls. . . . I could stand for hours watching the seagulls, a true symbol of freedom. They leave the earth whenever they want, sailing freely on the wind, rising and falling, sometime in unison, sometimes erratically, like a succession of disconnected thoughts, but they are always graceful. Watching them, while my body can be trapped inside this barbed wire, my mind is free and unbound.

16

"SHE JUST HAD A VERY LARGE HEART"

Elisabeth van Lohuizen's family members Dick, Siny, and Ger

My nine-year-old daughter, Sonia, was in the back seat of the rental car with our labradoodle, Coco. She was using Google Maps on my phone to navigate our trip to Epe. When she told me to take the next right, I hesitated before signaling, because it looked more like a hiking path than a road. But I knew that the place we were staying was a small cottage in the middle of the woods, so I pressed my foot into the rental's clutch and followed her instructions.

We drove for about ten minutes down a dirt path surrounded by high fir trees, and I became increasingly panicked that we had made a mistake. This must be a horse trail, I thought, and at any moment some equestrian will appear and berate me. When we came to a fork, Sonia told me I had to turn left—which was even more perplexing. This road seemed to be bike path. Was I to drive up onto the pavement, not wide enough for all four wheels, or continue on the dirt road—or just turn around?

I stopped the car and called the Airbnb host, a woman named Patricia who'd informed me that she might not be home when we arrived. Just in case, she'd given me a code to the lock box on the cottage. Thankfully, she picked up. "I think we may be a bit lost," I said.

"Where are you?" was the natural next question. I looked around for landmarks. Nothing but tall trees to the left, tall trees to the right, tall trees to the front and back. There was a little sign that read, "Verboden Toegang" or "entry forbidden." Before I tried to answer her question, she said, "Wait, I think I see you."

It turned out we were just yards from the gate to her property. Searching the woods, I could now see a woman with short brown hair standing in front of a large white gate, waving at us warmly. She hauled the gate open and ushered us in. I drove into a gravel parking lot behind a large slate-colored barn next to a stately mansion.

Our residence for the coming three days would be behind the mansion, "De Koepel," a single-room circular shed with a thatched roof, that had once been used as a "tea house." It was painted dark green, with shutters on the windows and doors that closed it up like a box.

Inside, it was modestly furnished with two twin beds, a small wood table, a stone kitchen sink, and a tabletop gas burner. No bathroom. For our needs and our ablutions, we'd use the outhouse, to which Patricia guided us, along a dirt path under a thicket of tangled bushes. The outhouse was another little shed, with a sink, shower and flush toilet, situated just next to a lily pond brimming with gurgling frogs.

The setting was bucolic and restful. Yet I didn't let out a sigh, now that we'd arrived at our holiday haven. In fact, from the moment we had stepped out of our car, I had the certain, eerie feeling, that we'd arrived in a wood haunted by *onderduikers*.

THE IDEA OF this trip was to see, with my own eyes, the places where Elisabeth van Lohuizen and her resistance group had lived and worked. I also wanted to get a sense of the unique physical attributes of this part of the Veluwe national forest region, and the small city of Epe, to understand what had made it possible for some people to find refuge here. We'd be meeting a local historian, Willem Veldkamp, who would give us a tour of Het Driemanschap landmarks from Elisabeth's diary.

Geography, or the fact that the Netherlands is largely flat and lacking large forests, has frequently been named as a factor that made it nearly impossible for Dutch Jews to flee the Nazis or to hide without being discovered. Historian Raul Hilberg, in *The Destruction of the European Jews,* began his section on Holland arguing that the "thoroughness" of the decimation here was, in part, a function of its "peculiar geography."

"The Netherlands were bounded on the east by the Reich, on the south by occupied Belgium, and on the west and north by the open sea," he wrote. "It was as though the Dutch Jews had already been placed in a natural trap."[1]

Only about 1,800 to 2,700 people managed to flee the country during the war, across the sea to England or overland to unoccupied countries such as Spain or Switzerland, according to historian Peter Romijn.[2] Bob Moore, in his 1997 *Victims & Survivors,* wrote that geography and topography "undoubtedly made it difficult to find hiding places and rendered almost every community reasonably accessible."[3]

In 2004, two Dutch doctoral students, Marnix Croes and Peter Tammes, attempted to parse this out. Were there certain places where it was easier to survive and other areas where there was greater danger of discovery? While the fact remains that only about a quarter of the entire Jewish population survived the war, there were many regional differences—survival rates varied by locale.[4]

The highest survival rates, for example, were in the southern provinces, such as the coastal province of Zeeland (56 percent), and the two southernmost provinces of Limburg (49 percent), and North Brabant (48 percent), near the Belgian border. Provinces in the north fared worse: in the province of Drenthe—where Westerbork was located—20 percent of the Jewish population survived, and 22 percent in neighboring Groningen province. But proximity to Westerbork wasn't the decisive factor, because the rates of survival were also wildly uneven in adjacent provinces, and sometimes higher in provinces far away.

Exploring this data prompted Croes and Tammes to wonder if scholars may have been asking the wrong question. Instead of, "Why did so few Jews survive in the Netherlands?" they suggested, "What factors influenced the chances of survival?"[5]

They concluded that the main determinant of *onderduiker* survival was, as they put it, "the ferocious hunt for Jews"—not only the avidity of the local hunters, but their success rate.[6]

The city of Epe, and the nearby town of Tongeren, where most of the Van Lohuizen "guests" were hidden, are located in the province Gelderland, where some 6,600 officially registered as Jewish in 1941; by war's end, about 2,500 of them were still alive, or 38 percent, which was about 15 percentage points higher than the national average. In addition to those who resided here before the war, the region attracted many more Jews fleeing larger cities, who'd also survived here in hiding.

From a purely geographical perspective, it seemed like a relatively good place to hide. About half of its 2,000 square miles of land is made up of forests, and it also has the country's highest land masses. While much of the Dutch "lowlands" are below sea level (−5 or −10 feet below), Gelderland has hilly regions that rise to more than 350 feet above.

On the other hand, Gelderland is adjacent to Germany, and in some areas more pro-German, since many local inhabitants had German ancestry, business relations, or friends right across the border. During the war, it was teeming with Germans, who had training camps in the region. Several local hotels—including one next door to the Larikshof—served as a popular R&R locale for NSB-ers.

Nevertheless, the Veluwe received thousands of *onderduikers*, who hid "in small attic rooms, under the rafters, behind bookcases, in haystacks, in chicken coops, or simply in huts in the woods," wrote local historian Aart Visser. "Many risked their lives to support them." Alongside Het Driemanschap, Visser counted at least a dozen other resistance groups in the region, which hid people, for example, in a sanatorium, a chapel, and a whole village of underground huts known as *Pas-op Camp* (Watch Out Camp) or *Het Verscholen Dorp* (The Hidden Town), in the woods between Nunspeet and Vierhouten.[7]

"WE HAVE A very personal connection," read one of the comments next to a *New York Times* article I published about the NIOD diaries in April 2020. Elisabeth van Lohuizen and her family, the reader explained, "played instrumental roles in saving the lives of each of my

parents as well as other members of my mother's immediate family."
It was signed, "Dolf, in Waterloo, Ontario."

I was eager to contact Dolf, but because the identity of *Times* comment writers is private, all I had to go on was a Google search for "Dolf
in Waterloo, Ontario," which led exactly nowhere. I put that quest to
the side, while I delved into Elisabeth's 900-page diary, in addition to
hundreds of her letters and postcards, all in Dutch. At some point, I
happened to be rereading the summary in her NIOD folder and noted
a sentence I'd somehow overlooked: "An English-language translation
of this diary (made by Mr. Vomberg) is available on CD-rom."

CD-ROM? I quickly shot an email over to René Pottkamp, coordinator of the Adopt-a-Diary program, asking if, by any chance, he
knew of this translation of the diary on CD-ROM, and if, by chance,
he had a CD-ROM player?

To my total amazement, the answer to both questions was yes.
Within a week, I had the fully translated text of the diary in my hands.
That saved me a great deal of time, and I was grateful to its author. But
who was this "Mr. Vomberg?" The opening note on the translation
gave me one more clue: it was signed by "J. Vomberg, Ontario." Ontario? Why was that ringing a bell?

Could J. Vomberg still be out there? The only result I found for
him online, unfortunately, was an obituary, dated 2013. I figured my
search would end there, but I read the brief notice: "Loving father of
Dolf (Heather), Elisabeth (Gary Shapiro) and Emanuel 'Mac' (Janice).
Beloved 'Opa' of Marni (Kris), Aaron, Paul, Joshua, Ephraim, Naham
and Lauren. Great 'Opa' of Alex."

Wait. . . . Dolf? How common could that name be in Ontario?
With a few more clicks I'd found a business owned by Dolf Vomberg
and sent an email to an office address. A day later I received an email
in return: "Thank you for reaching out. You have indeed reached the
Dolf Vomberg who commented on the article."

He continued, "Indeed both our parents, our maternal grandmother, and a great aunt and uncle were assisted by 'The Group' in
Tongeren," he wrote. "We consider the Van Lohuizens, Kuijlenburgs

and Hendriks families our family, and have maintained contact with their descendants."

Bingo.

Dolf referred me to his sister, Elisabeth Vomberg Shapiro, who he said was the keeper of all the relevant family documents and "knows everything." I reached her in Minneapolis, where she currently lives with her family. She asked me to call her Lis. We soon arranged an interview by video chat, and she showed me the items her father had brought with him to Canada from Holland.

"My dad saved everything that he possibly could from the war, including a unique toilet paper wrapper that they were given at the end of the war because it had an interesting cover," she told me during our first interview. "Everything was relegated to a filing cabinet in our sun room behind the sewing supplies."

Their parents rarely talked about the war, she said, but this was mostly her mother's decision. "When my mom went out, I'd say to him, 'Papa, show me what's in that cabinet.' So he'd take some things out and put them on the kitchen table and explain."

Shapiro said that her entire early family lore was tied up with The Triad in Epe, which her family refers to as, simply, The Group. She said that she considers its members as part of her family, because they'd saved the lives of so many of her relatives. Els Hendriks, she told me, maintained contact with the family and attended Lis' wedding. She lived to be 100 years old and had no children of her own, but considered those she helped as part of her extended family as well.

Jozef Vomberg, Lis' father, was born in 1923 in Zutphen, a small town about an hour's drive from the German border, where his parents ran a dry goods business. There was a direct train line from Germany to Zutphen, and many German Jewish refugees traveled that line to escape Nazi Germany when they still could in the 1930s. Members of the local Jewish synagogue, including Jozef's father, came to their aid.

His father "had permission from the station master to go on to the platform without buying a platform ticket for a nickel, to see if he could assist anybody, in whatever way assistance was needed," Jozef

Vomberg recalled in a videotaped testimony for the USC Shoah Foundation in 1997. "Many a time, we had people at home at night or over the weekend."[8]

When asked what he, as a teenager, had learned from these visitors, Jozef answered, "Everything. They were telling about how the Jews were treated in Germany, how they were maltreated. The bad things that went on. How they were picked up, how they were being forced into labor camps in those days, how windows were being smashed, how life was being restricted for them. The whole *spiel*."[9]

He also vividly remembered his parents discussing whether they should flee to either the United States or South Africa, but ultimately they concluded, "'That can't happen here. That won't happen here.' On top of it, they felt obligated to my grandmother, who still lived with us, and my paternal grandmother who was still alive. And, 'We have a good business here, a well-established old business. How, at our age, can we go, can we start somewhere else from scratch, from nothing?' So we didn't immigrate. We didn't apply."[10]

Nevertheless, his father prepared in his own way for a potential German invasion, joining the Civilian Home Guard and signing up Jozef, too, in its junior division. "We had weapon training, bayonet fighting—I could still do it if needed," Jozef said. "My dad happened to be on guard duty the night the German army invaded. At six o'clock in the morning, the German army stood at our front door. The bridge across our river blew. The German army commandeered sleeping places all over town, and we had German people staying in our house, too."[11]

Jozef was seventeen, and life began to change rapidly. He could no longer study, he had to wear a star on his clothes, his neighbors stopped speaking with him in the street, his synagogue activities were banned. He could not even use the public library to get books.

After the Germans ordered his parents to close their business and transfer the inventory to a competitor, the company's assets were deposited in the German-run looting bank. "We never saw a penny," said Vomberg. "Even after the war, we got paid only a fraction." Conditions became increasingly dire. The family discussions were all about, "'How will we survive? How will we survive without the business?' Day in day out," he said.[12]

Thanks to a network of Jewish and non-Jewish friends in the area, the family received extra food, "eggs, bread, homemade butter, cereal grains, vegetables," and one farmer brought the family live chickens, because Kosher slaughter was no longer allowed.

In August 1942, a local policeman came to warn the family that they would be arrested later that day. Jozef's father had prearranged with a member of the resistance that his son could work for a while on a farm in the nearby town of Hellendoorn. When they received the warning, Jozef's father begged him to leave as quickly as possible; he jumped on his bike, tearing off his Jewish star, and pedaled as fast as he could.[13]

Jozef spent two months as a farmhand, but one night, he biked back to Zutphen and found no one home: his parents and sister had gone into hiding. A local lawyer, a family friend, housed him for a few weeks, and put him in touch with The Triad in Epe, which took him in. He arrived at his new hiding place, on a country estate called Duiveland, in November 1942.

The estate was large, he said, and there was a bed for everyone; Jozef shared a room with another student. "We were all supplied with ration coupons for food, and the organization looked after us fantastically," he said. "Money was no object. If someone had, he could pay what he had for his upkeep, but if someone didn't have, it made absolutely no difference. Even after the war, nobody asked for money or any other form of recognition. They helped to help."[14]

Elisabeth van Lohuizen mentioned Duiveland in her diary for the first time on October 27, 1942, when her family had too many guests for the four houses they'd already rented. "We might take that one too," she wrote. Within a week, she noted, "We have leased Duiveland for six months for 100 guilders a month. The whole group from Blauwvoet will go there Thursday." In her diary, she refers to it as House #5.

At the center of the Duiveland estate was a large redbrick bunga-low with a massive thatched roof. It was surrounded by both trimmed and wild hedges, and encircled by enormous birches and firs. Jozef remembered joining eighteen people who were already in hiding there. It was well concealed by the verdurous woods, and secondary hiding places were set up as well. The residents sawed a trapdoor into the living room floor and dug a long tunnel to the side of a hill near a lake. There, they built an underground shelter, stocking it with supplies.

"We had a terrific thing going," he said. "It was a nervous time. It was a very tight and tense time. But yet, looking back, it was a good time. You learned a lot."[15]

In both his testimony and in a memoir he wrote after the war, Jozef notes the names and professions of all those who lived in Duiveland. A Berlin lawyer and his mother, a professional cellist, a saleswoman and accountant from Amsterdam, a businessman who had worked for years in Indonesia, and a dockworker who had served in the Spanish Civil War. "Imagine the political discussions!"[16] As a teen, he found it to be a fascinating mix of personalities, and he said he absorbed so many different philosophical perspectives from these intelligent house-mates, that he could have "earned a PhD."

He also enjoyed freedom to walk in the woods, a rare luxury for people in hiding; there was physical labor, too, like chopping trees for firewood and hauling water. "Regularly a fisherman came to bring us fish caught in the Zuiderzee, and also a baker," he wrote in his mem-oir. "Mr. Olthof brought rye bread every now [and again]; we had to be careful for that. We placed traps and twice caught a rabbit to eat. There were foxes, owl and other wildlife around. We also constructed a primitive warning system to alert us of possible approaching Ger-man raiders. Charles Juda had his cello with him and played many a concert. Mr. Kuijlenburg also came a few times to play the violin with him."[17]

This separate peace was shattered in late April 1943, when The Triad had a scare at another property. "Van Essen came to tell us that there was no response at the Blauwvoet," wrote Elisabeth in her diary.* "Dick went there with him and he went inside. The house was a big mess and all eight adults and the nine-year-old boys were gone."†

Three days later, they found out that Hendriks' "name was mentioned." They quickly had to reorganize the houses, and decided that House #5, Duiveland, was also no longer safe. The day after, it was cleared of its residents, the police indeed arrived, and searched the house, finding no one.

"The saleslady and I were placed with a family, Arend Proper, a baker, who was very Calvinistic, but got nowhere with us in his attempts to try to convert us," wrote Jozef. The others dispersed. One day, Dick was arrested while Razzias were conducted across the village.

"Mr. Proper got scared and preferred not to keep us any longer," Jozef wrote. "I had been given an emergency address for just such an occasion to go to and on a pitch-dark rainy night after curfew walked to the farmhouse of the Van Essens. He . . . brought us to a construction shed built in the center of a young tree plantation, situated within the [German] military training camp, Oldebroek. We were there about one week and could hear the German army exercising daily."[18]

After that harrowing experience, Jozef and others were transferred to Larikshof, The Triad's House #1, where he was placed with a dozen others. Like Duiveland, this new hiding place was a quaintly charming country villa with a thatched roof, shrouded by tall fir trees and verdant shrubs, submerged in a forested grove, accessible only by a dirt path. It had four bedrooms and a large attic, whose entrance was a pull-down ladder, and the dining room and library, with its large fireplace, were converted into bedrooms so that the house fit about twenty people.

The bucolic backyard, large enough for the *onderduikers* to find

---

* House #3.
† Among those caught there were Salomon Wijler (murdered November, 30, 1943, in Dorohucza), Pauline Wijler-Vomberg (murdered May 14, 1943, in Sobibor), and Natan Vomberg, who at age eight was heroically rescued by the resistance and survived the war in hiding.

respite from the chaos of a shared home, provided an additional escape route. They also built a large shelter in the woods. It had "wooden walls, and for an entrance door, we had the front of an old stove, and a ladder going down."[19]

But the house was situated in a treacherous location: Right alongside the entry path was a road leading to Oldebroek. Also, a local hotel, not five minutes walking distance from Larikshof, served as NSB regional headquarters.

"We lived in that house as ghosts," Jozef said.[20]

AMONG HIS HOUSEMATES at Larikshof was an older, diabetic woman, Amalia Wijler-Bamberg, who needed daily insulin injections. The Triad supplied the medication, and Jozef administered it. Amalia and her teenage daughter, Bettje Wijler, or Bep, had escaped their hometown of Lochem in 1942 just before a Razzia, thanks to a tip from a local nurse.* She'd instructed Bep to make her way by bus to Epe, where Derk Hendriks met her at the station, and took her to the home of the new Tongeren school headmaster, G. Kuijlenburg. She lived there in "open hiding" working as a maid and au pair for the family with young children, using false papers supplied by Het Driemanschap.

One day, Bep was leaning out of the window of the two-story country home, beating duvet covers. She took notice of a young man who had come around to dig up the Kuijlenburgs' rock garden, which the family planned to convert it into a vegetable patch. Bep told Lis the story so many times in the years since, that Lis had committed it to memory. When Bep saw Jozef, "this handsome guy who was two years older than her, and her heart boomed out of her chest," Lis said. "She thought to herself: 'If anyone makes it out of this war, *let it be him, let it be him, let it be him.'*"[21]

---

* Bep's father, Adolf Wijler, had already died in 1935; Bep's older brother, Samuel, was in hiding. He was later captured and arrested. He died in Auschwitz at age twenty-four on January 25, 1944.

Not long after this encounter, however, Larikshof was discovered. When NSB members showed up at the door, almost all of the women and children were out walking in the woods, and got away. But four of the men, including Jozef, were arrested. They were taken "in a commandeered horse-drawn farm cart to Zwolle," he remembered, and interrogated in a high school with at least 100 other men. "We had to admit to being Jewish and were brought to the local prison."[*] They were put on a train to Rolde railway station, and from there forced to march nineteen miles to Westerbork.

Jozef arrived in October 1944, just after the last transport to the death camps had already left. At first, he was put to work chopping wood, and later sent to the machine shop to sharpen saws; he wore out the last days of the war working as an orderly in the camp hospital.

"One day we noticed the German SS-ers were very nervous," he wrote. "We were ordered to assist them loading boxes into their vehicles, preparing wood for their gas converters on their cars (we urinated on the wood to sabotage it), and they left that night.

"German infantry had taken over guard at the camp and told everyone who dared to talk to them: 'Leave if you want to.' We heard rumbling guns, saw parachutists diving from planes and realized what was happening."[22]

Jozef Vomberg was among the last 750 residents still housed in Camp Westerbork when it was liberated on April 14, 1945. He returned to Zutphen to find that his parents and siblings had all survived in hiding. The windows had been blown out of their home by bombings, and the roof was partially caved in, but it was still standing. All things considered, he felt, "in pretty good shape for those days."

ON OUR VISIT to Epe, Sonia, Coco, and I quickly discovered that it was not so much of a city as a bustling little town. After our first night

---

[*] Vomberg unpublished memoir; Jozef's name on his fake ID was Henk Kamphuis—a man he met by chance fifty years later at the farmer's market in St. Catharines, Ontario.

in the "tea house," we set out early the next morning to meet Willem Veldkamp, a local historian and history teacher, in the town center, a kind of open-air shopping mall, with a surprising number of clothing shops, shoe discount stores, and terrace cafés. As we'd arrived early for our meeting, we did a tour, and about an hour later plopped down beside the imposing Grote Kerk with lots of shopping bags. Willem laughed when he saw us and remarked that we'd obviously discovered Epe's famous retail culture.

My expectation was that we'd spend about an hour with Willem, but he knew every single spot that had relevance for Het Drieman- schap and wanted to show us all of them. We visited the former lo- cation of the Van Lohuizen family store (closed in 1973), the Grote Kerk, where Ter Braak had preached his resistance gospel, as well as Larikshof, and the Tongeren school, where Hendriks had once been headmaster. He also took us to the former Town Hall building, now an upscale restaurant, where we could stand on the balcony where Elisabeth van Lohuizen had stood with the town's mayor on Libera- tion Day in 1945. We also visited Elisabeth's and Dick's side-by-side burial plots on the Epe graveyard, marked by a single white cross.

It struck me that Willem related to these places as hallowed ground, markers of a proud local history of resistance, one he could teach his students without shame. I asked him how he made sense of Van Lohuizen's drive to save as many people as she could. Did he feel she was a product of her environment, or just a really rare individual?

"Anyone reading Bets van Lohuizen's diary will be impressed by this versatile and principled woman," he wrote to me later. "She knew doubts and struggles, but above all she had one great goal in mind: to help her fellow human beings and fight against injustice." He added, "She just had a very large heart."

When I spoke to Lis, she also emphasized the very special nature of the relationship between the The Triad and their "guests."

"My father always said, 'I was very lucky,'" she said. "'They did what they did not for money, not to convert us, not to get some of our possessions, not for sexual favors.' They did it because they were truly altruistic human beings."

Jozef and Bep reunited and married in 1949, in Zutphen, where two of their children, Dolf and Lis were born. Four years later, concerned about the Cold War, they applied for visas to move to either America or Canada. Since Canada approved them first, they moved there. A year later, Amalia joined them. Their third child, Emanuel (Mac), was born in Montreal. Three years later, they settled in St. Catharines, where they lived out the rest of their lives in peace.

Bep was ninety-five years old, and "doing very well," in a Jewish independent-living residence in Toronto. "She's a great model for us," said Lis.

I asked Lis to request an interview on my behalf, but her mother declined. I wondered if her daughter could persuade her, at the very least, to tell the love story about that day in Tongeren with the duvets and the vegetable garden. Elisabeth tried. She wrote me by email a few days later. "When I asked about how she saw him through her window, she replied, '*Och kind, dat is zo lang geleden!*[*] Why would anyone be interested in us?'"

I'd asked, I supposed, because it was poignant. That place, in that moment, had ignited a flame, a hope, and an incantation: "Let it be him. Let it be him." Bep's wish had been granted, and over one generation, and then another, it become a new genealogy, a new family line.

---

[*] (Oh, my child, that was so long ago!)

17

"THE TENSION IS SOMETIMES TOO MUCH TO BEAR"

September 1943–December 1943

ELISABETH VAN LOHUIZEN, GENERAL STORE OWNER, EPE

FRIDAY, SEPTEMBER 2, 1943—Today was an awful day. I was headed to the village at 10 o'clock, when Van Essen stopped me and told me that two men had gone into Ger's, while three others stood outside. First I went right home to put things away, and then I went back to the village. I sat with Dick and Siny and they told me what had happened. It was five Sicherheitsdienst men, who had apparently behaved very roughly. They accused Ger of delivering ration cards and food to Jews, and they said Ger and Gert-Jan had to accompany them to Tongeren. Where will they go, do we need to warn anyone, do we need to go after them, what could be the matter? What will happen? All kinds of things went through our minds. Hendriks went to look around in Tongeren. We had to just wait, and do nothing. It was miserable. Oh, I imagined all kinds of things.

Miek, who went to inquire on my behalf, returned at 2 o'clock. De Haye has been caught, she said.[*] They are being taken to the village. Oh, this misery again. The people in the house were arrested. That sentence will stay in my mind forever: "De Haye has been caught." . . . Could we have done something to better protect them?

Later, Dick arrived with Kuijlenburg, who'd raced to Epe to tell us. He was deathly pale and very depressed. He'd been looking after these people for such a long time. Six young people caught. At around 3 o'clock, they passed by on the road that leads to the barracks. Ger was with them, as well, which was a horrible sight. Thank God I did not see them. Later there was a house search of their place. They searched all over, I had taken away the ration coupons they had there, so that, thank God, they did not find anything. In the hallway they smashed all the photographs of members of the Royal Family. They first stepped on them to shatter the glass, and then ripped the photos apart.

We visited Ger in the evening at the barracks. Dick brought him lunch in the afternoon, and in the evening, he and Siny brought dinner. How did it leak out, who betrayed us, what happens now? Poor boy; will he have to pay for our actions? He was brave but a bit depressed; it was all too much for him. They said that he will have to go with them, to be confronted with that Jew, and that he would be back in a week. The transport will leave tomorrow at 7 a.m., and the Jews will be in chains. Ger was allowed to sleep in the officer's guest room. This morning, they had ordered him to remove his glasses and then they beat him around his head; they also kicked him in his knees. Ger didn't tell me this himself; I heard it from Dick. These brutes will get their comeuppance later; nobody does this with impunity. We will have to see to that. Ger will be strong in the coming days, but this will

---

[*] De Haye is an area of the Tongeren nature reserve known as "the moor." When she says "De Haye" has been caught, she means that the people who were hiding in that area were captured.

be difficult for all of us. The last thing Ger said before we left was, "Mother, please be careful."

SATURDAY, SEPTEMBER 3, 1943—Ger is gone. We all heard the whistling of the train, but none of us had the courage to go to it. How miserable that trip will be for all of them—and what awaits them? This morning Siny was extremely nervous, I myself was calm. There is so much to do. We had to get everyone out of House #1, and I managed to place them all elsewhere. One old gentleman is in Tongeren; one is in the village; the couple went to a family, and the other eight have to stay for now in a "shed," uncomfortably close to the Germans in Oldebroek. Van Essen will arrange their food; they'll have to sleep on the ground. None of them wanted to remain at House #1, not even Dien. . . . Everyone in the village commiserates with us greatly.

SUNDAY, SEPTEMBER 4, 1943—I've been very nervous today. This morning, I received an anonymous letter advising us to stop all our work and not to allow meetings to take place at our house. What should we do? Jan and M. came in the afternoon. They were upset that we can't go on using our place, and they also needed money. We decided to do it elsewhere.

TUESDAY, SEPTEMBER 6, 1943—Still no word from Ger. It seems certain that we'll have to wait another week. All the while you're thinking, how he will fare there? He'll be hungry, of course, and here our life continues as normal. Siny is holding up very well. We were aware of the consequences, but I would have preferred if they'd taken me. Probably more Razzias tonight. What can you do? You are very worried, but you cannot send old people into the woods. . . . How much longer will this go on? The tension is sometimes too much to bear.

Meijer Emmerik,
diamond cutter, Amsterdam

I'D ARRANGED IT so that my wife and Lena could take turns visiting the boys on their second birthday, September 7.[*] . . . I will never forget how happy my wife was that night to know that she would finally see Maxie after months of separation. Lena and I stayed at Robert's that night. Meanwhile, a few days earlier, the Speel family from Hilversum had come to pick up Loetje. . . . This will be his fifth address before his second birthday. Marie came to me that same day to say that Ten Kate had probably found a new address for her and also for Lena, and they would know for sure that evening or the next day. In the afternoon, Agnes' husband came to say that he was working on another address for us, as well, and that my wife could stay with them. He was also present during Loetje's departure. And because I didn't want to endanger my dear friend Robert any longer than strictly necessary, I decided to look for something new. I spoke to a man on the Fahrenheitsingel named Baas, who turned out to be willing to temporarily let us use his house. I took some things home and planned to discuss it amongst ourselves.

When I got to the Berlagebrug, Robert's wife came running towards me very upset, and said that the SS police had arrested Maxie and my wife at the Van der Meulen's home. What I felt at that moment is impossible to put on paper, but the fact that I haven't already gone mad is still hard to believe. I don't know how I got to Robert's, but there I learned that we had been betrayed, and that my wife had confessed everything, and was taken away at once.[†] Maxie will be moved in the afternoon to the SS office in Amstellaan. [Robert's wife] was told not to leave her house, but she quickly biked over to warn us.

Later I realized that before she came to see us, she went to Annie's on

---

[*]   This entry is from Meijer Emmerik's summary of his first diary; page 24, section 47.

[†]   Vogeltje Worms-Emmerik and Max were picked up by two members of the Colonne Henneicke, wrote Ad van Liempt in *Kopgeld: Nederlandse Premiejagers Op Zoek Naar Joden, 1943* (Amsterdam: Balans Publishers, 2002), 65–66.

Hasebroekstraat, and that in the meantime, we could have been arrested ten times already. At 2 p.m. she had her cleaning lady take Maxie to Amstellaan. As a grandfather, it is incomprehensible that someone who has taken care of a sick child for seven months can let their maid hand him over to such criminals. Of course, I know that they faced threats if the child was not delivered, but I would never, ever have done that to a child.

So here I was, my wife, who I was married to for 26 years, and my two-year-old ill grandson, taken from me in a single stroke, and in such hands. Lena gave me a great deal of support, but it was her son and her mother who'd been taken away. Later it occurred to me that Staal, who had been informed about our misery by Agnes, must have informed on us. This woman must have been a secret Gestapo agent, and it became clear to me that this must be how Vogeltje had been betrayed. We were in an absolutely life-threatening situation, so we had to act decisively, since I expected a raid of Robert's house at any moment.

I left Robert's house immediately, and the two of us went to the home of my boss, who lived near Jo.* I forbade Jo and Karel to tell anyone where we were, and I asked Karel† to go to the creche on the Middellaan‡ to check if Maxie had already arrived there, because little children were always taken there before they were deported. I knew that there would be very slim chance to get him out of there. Jo thought it was necessary for Karel to eat something first, even though every minute was precious, and this was her brother's son.

When Karel returned, he said that Maxie hadn't been brought there yet, but he thought it could happen at any moment. I immediately understood that my wife was hopelessly lost, but I wanted to save Maxie at any cost.

Lena and I spent the night at my boss' house, a night that I will never forget. Early the next morning I went to the creche without a

---

* Sam's sister.
† Karel was not Jewish; Jo was in a mixed marriage so she was, at this point, theoretically safe from deportation.
‡ The Plantage Middenlaan day care center, across from the Hollandse Schouwburg theater, was where all Jewish children were taken before they would be deported.

star on my coat, knowing that my wife had been transferred to the Hollandsche Schouwburg. Robert went to check on my wife, because it was better that I not do this myself. I was told at the creche that Maxie hadn't yet arrived there, so I had to go back empty handed. I was back at my boss' house when a woman came in to speak to my boss. This woman, who I refer to in my diary as Miss Tini, turned out to be a member of an illegal Catholic organization. She had already taken two children from my boss to safety, and she had come to tell her herself that she would be picked up the next day, Friday, to be taken to safety elsewhere. We explained our situation to her, and she promised to provide us with help and support. As I write this, it has turned out that this woman is a true heroine, who has saved our lives, including Maxie's. She is the kind of which only one in 10,000 is born, and who cannot be bought with money.

MIRJAM LEVIE, SECRETARY, WESTERBORK

MONDAY, SEPTEMBER 6, 1943—My darling, it's "Monday before transport" and this afternoon everybody has time off to pack. The mood here is indescribable. What happened is that last Friday the commandant informed the *Dienstleiter*[*] that the camp will be dissolved around November first. Four transports are earmarked for Auschwitz, and the Obersturmführer announced that people from other camps would also be going to Auschwitz. One transport to Theresienstadt, one to Vittel. The one to Theresienstadt in cattle-trucks, too. Barneveld to Theresienstadt. Vught to be dissolved, too. In other words . . . the liquidation of the remnants of Dutch Jewry. A consequence of Himmler's decision to clear Western Europe of Jews. And now the news that beats everything else: The remainder of the Palestine

---

[*] German for "service leader," a Nazi party rank.

NIOD researcher Rene Kok introduced the author to the institute's diary archive in 2019. It is held within a former bank vault in the basement of the NIOD in Amsterdam. The entire wall of camel-colored boxes contains World War II diaries written by Dutch civilians—more than 2,100 in total.

The author and her daughter, Sonia, try to open the archive's door.

An exterior image of the NIOD Institute for War, Holocaust, and Genocide Studies on the Herengracht in Amsterdam's historic Canal District.

Amsterdam police officer Douwe Bakker wrote about 3,300 pages in eighteen notebooks. His earlier diaries were smaller; his later ones larger.

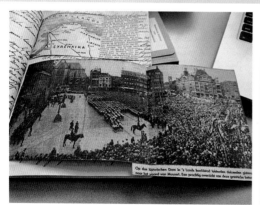

In addition to keeping notes on his daily life, Bakker clipped images from newspapers and inserted them into his diaries, so it also served as a scrapbook of the fascist movement. *Above:* Mussert's rally on Dam Square in Amsterdam. *Right:* Seyss-Inquart's Nazi gathering in front of the Rijksmuseum in Amsterdam.

Ina Steur, who worked as an office clerk for the Werkspoor factory in Amsterdam during the war, kept her diary in a single black notebook. She kept it in her drawer until she discovered that her younger brothers and sisters would take it out and read it aloud when she wasn't there. After that, she hid it under a hatch in the living-room floor.

Ina in her later years, with her daughter, Anneke Dijkman, who had her NIOD diary published in Dutch.

Dutch Nazi socialite Inge Jansen kept her diary in a single hardcover blank book known as a *gendeboek* or "memory album." She wrote infrequently and haphazardly, and her entries were not in chronological order.

Journalist and *Algemeen Handelsblad* foreign desk editor Philip Mechanicus kept a diary during the seventeen months he was imprisoned at Westerbork transit camp in Drenthe. The first volume that survived the war is labeled #3, so it seems we're missing the first two. The rest were smuggled back to Amsterdam to his non-Jewish ex-wife, Annie Jonkman, who delivered them to NIOD after the war.

Diamond industry worker Meijer Emmerik lost his first diary when he fled Amsterdam, so he started a new one while in hiding somewhere near Beringe in the southern province of Limburg. He wrote by hand on loose pages, first completing a summary of his previous diary and then writing of his experiences in hiding. At right, Rebecca Emmerik, who translated his diary.

Mirjam Levie, a secretary for the Amsterdam Jewish Council, at first wrote letters to her fiancé Leo Bolle on loose pages, which she typed up herself. Later, when she understood that it had become a kind of diary, she wrote in small notebooks, which she managed to smuggle out of Bergen-Belsen concentration camp. It is preserved at NIOD along with her identity card. Below, Mirjam Bolle telling stories at her home in Jerusalem in 2022.

Epe general store owner Elisabeth van Lohuizen kept her diary of her resistance work in notebooks of different sizes and shapes, as well as on loose pages. She wrote more than nine hundred pages from the beginning of the war until after liberation.

Left: Engagement portrait of Jozef Vomberg and Betje Wijler. *Right:* resting place of Elisabeth and Derk Jan (Dick) van Lohuizen.

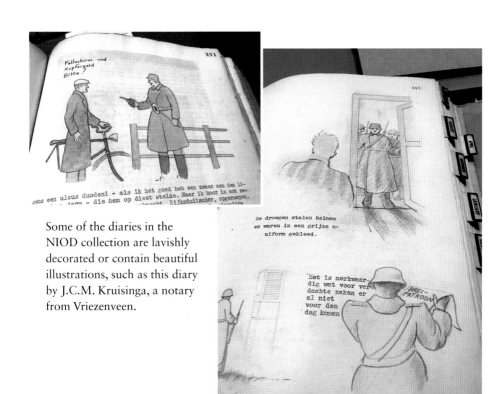

Some of the diaries in the NIOD collection are lavishly decorated or contain beautiful illustrations, such as this diary by J.C.M. Kruisinga, a notary from Vriezenveen.

Below left, an anonymous Dutch Nazi created a diary with Hitler on the cover; inside, he drew sheet music, musical notes, and lyrics to a German Nazi marching song.

Below: the "tea house" Airbnb the author rented in the Veluwe Forest near Tongeren and Epe.

A memorial sculpture at Camp Westerbork in Drenthe, used as a transit camp in World War II. Some 107,000 Jews and more than 200 Roma and Sinti people were deported from the camp to concentration camps in "the East." Only about 5,000 returned after the war.

Right: the author with Rebecca Emmerik, looking at the wall of Emmeriks in Daniel Libeskind's National Holocaust Names Monument in Amsterdam, March 2022.

List (approximately 300 people with the right papers) is going, along with the baptized, Ecuadorians, Paraguayans and what have you, to "*Mitteldeutschland*."* Where exactly remains uncertain.

My darling, I don't have the peace of mind to tell you how I feel, because everybody is watching me, curious about all this writing. Today is writing day and you're allowed to write only two postcards or one letter. I've already written my postcards, so this letter doesn't make sense to them.

A funny incident. A Polish Jew went to the registry, where his official documents are kept, to have a look at his papers. "What kind of papers do you have?" "Paraguay." They searched and searched . . . but no trace of Paraguay. The entire registry was turned upside-down. At long last they found his papers . . . they were Ecuador papers! The man had actually forgotten what nationality he had [bought].†

MONDAY, SEPTEMBER 13, 1943—My dearest, I really ought to write you a letter when all around me is dead quiet, so I can concentrate and gather my thoughts, but this is impossible in the barracks. Since hearing of my departure, I set out to write to you a hundred times and even thought of phrases to express my feelings, but meanwhile I'm feeling completely different again. As I've been telling you over and over again, one moment you bear up quite well and the next it's all too much.

On Shabbat morning I received a letter from my boss, which I'll treasure. I went to pieces, because at that moment I had a very clear vision of what it really means to go away, into the unknown, not knowing whether you'll be hit by a bomb or, when the Germans are facing defeat, be destroyed some other way. And yet I still believe that we'll hold out the short while it will take. But afterward . . . how much time will pass before their lordships will have decided our fate?

And regardless of whether you're interned in Central Germany—they say the Palestine people are going there—or whether you'll be put

---

* Central Germany.
† A number of countries, including Ecuador and Paraguay, sold passports to Jews who had the financial means.

in the *Auschwitzreservaat,*[*] when the war is over it will take months to get out again. It means I'll have to wait even longer to be reunited with you. And when I think that the war may be over a week after we have gone . . . And much more importantly: When I'm gone and the war is over and I manage to get hold of a postage stamp to inform you of my whereabouts, I still have every hope that you can get me out. But Father and Mother! . . .

I'm writing relatively calmly now, because this morning I learnt that the Palestine List has a few weeks' reprieve. And although I know perfectly well that such rumors and announcements are meaningless, I cling to them, because a few weeks can make all the difference.

PHILIP MECHANICUS, JOURNALIST, WESTERBORK

TUESDAY, SEPTEMBER 14, 1943—(Five o'clock in the morning)—Today, my judgment was pronounced, without any warning. The commander himself drew up the latest list, without any opportunity for my protector to intervene. I accept this judgment with great composure, in the firm belief that I will see my family and friends again. Heartfelt thanks to my friends, including those in Westerbork, who have taken care to keep me well and healthy. I take wonderful memories of them with me. Strength to all of you. Until I see you again. PHILIP MECHANICUS

(LATER THE SAME DAY; IN THE EVENING)—My sentence was not carried out, for the time being. With the help of some friends, I had neatly packed up all my things: two blankets in a sheet tied up with string, a backpack full of clothing, a bag with preserves, one bag with fresh foods, a box of apples and pears, and some tea in a canteen. For

---

[*] The "Auschwitz Reservation."

a long trip. I had written my final farewells to my family and friends on a postcard that indicated my change of address. Under "New Address," a dash, I had written: "I don't know." This is what I had agreed to do. I had taken leave of all my friends and acquaintances in the barrack, shaking twenty, thirty hands. One roommate, who was temporarily assigned as a porter, took my bags to the train using a pushcart, with the exception of my bag of food, which I slung over my shoulder.

Every couple of steps along the way to the train, another handshake. Then I transferred everything to a wheelbarrow and, not according to custom, stood on the platform, waiting for the men from the former Jewish Council or the Antragstelle,[*] to see if I could present my case to Schlesinger.[†] Schlesinger had assured me that I wouldn't be put on the transport. But the commander had made up the list indiscriminately: there was a shortage of human material and whoever didn't possess a valid stamp or wasn't selected for the Thousand List,[‡] had to go. That's how the Grand Inquisitor had wanted it. Several well-known figures at the camp, who have practically taken root here, were also put on the list. While I stood waiting, they passed by, and we shook each others' hands. First came the former members of the Jewish Council. "We have worked on it the whole night. We are going to continue trying."

"I intend to escape; I don't want to go in these animal cars."

"I wouldn't do it without preparation. The legal way is best. It will be okay. Let's see, car 48."

After ten minutes, Dr. Ottenstein from the Antragstelle, a good-looking, bespectacled, wry, withered figure wearing a straw-yellow jacket, says, "Wait here a moment. I'll be right back."

Ten minutes later he returned with Schlesinger, who was dressed in a black doublet, leather britches and jackboots. A look of under-

---

[*] This was an organization within the camp that helped people get various exemption stamps.

[†] Schlesinger is the German Jewish camp leader, "King of the Jews," who was Mechanicus' main protector in the camp.

[‡] The commander was required to send 1,000 people on the transport; perhaps also a cynical joke about the various "lists."

standing. He stuffs a note into my hand, with the assignment to follow an orderly to the registration bureau. In addition to my name, the note reads: *Reason: By order of the Obersturmführer*, with the stamp: Lagerkommandantur, and Schlesinger's signature, a snaking line. . . .

Life is a lottery. Here, a lottery with no prizes. And why should I be sent away sooner than strictly necessary? . . . And what is going to happen now? Next week or the following week, exactly the same game, again awakened in the middle of the night in the blinding light, to hear the toneless voice of the Inquisitor: Mechanicus, Philip? . . .

But why do I stay? Why don't I try to flee? Escaping is a risk. Everywhere around the camp are the eyes of the Inquisitor's servants, who, if they catch sight of you, will hunt you down and bring you back as a twice-marked man, this time to the penal barracks. I got to know those torturers in Camp Amersfoort. That is enough, more than enough, for a lifetime. And still the thought haunts me: how can I get out of here? At night, I make detailed plans for my escape. Not that Poland or somewhere else frightens me, not that I am afraid of death, which will eventually come. But I don't want to be a slave, I don't want to be tormented or tortured. I don't want to be in the clutches of my enemy. That is my right, which I continue to pursue. The transport has left: a thousand people.

THURSDAY, SEPTEMBER 16, 1943—Last night I went to the revue again.[*] Chock full. . . . The reactions of the audience were mixed. They had great admiration for the performances, they laughed at the jokes and enjoyed the text and melody of the songs about the camp, as well as the master of ceremonies, Ehrlich.[†] Yet, the majority of the audience was hesitant and was not really ready to let go. Singer Camilla Spira[‡] invited us to sing along with the chorus of some catchy

---

[*] This appears to be the second performance of the Westerbork Revue, which premiered on September 5, 1943. An attempt to make life a little more bearable for the inmates of the camp, it featured some of the Netherlands' most talented performers.

[†] Max Ehrlich, a German Jewish theater artist who founded and directed the Westerbork Revue, a cabaret troupe that put on six productions at the camp during its eighteen months of existence.

[‡] A famous German actress, who starred in silent and sound films, and in the theater.

songs, but only a few of the younger people joined in. The older generation remained quiet; they can't unwind from all the suffering they endure on a daily basis. They also held back their applause, while the younger generation rose on occasion and burst out clapping. Many of the older generation justified themselves, saying they should not have gone, but they want to be able to talk about everything that goes on at Westerbork. They deceive themselves. They don't really want to miss the revue; it's their only outlet. They have nothing else at Westerbork.

There are those who refuse to attend the revue. The German Jews say the contrast between the "fun" and tragedy of the transports is too painful; the Dutch Jews because they cannot enjoy themselves while their family members . . . are suffering an unknown fate, deprived of all pleasures, in Poland. But the young leap at the chance to get tickets, which cost only ten cents. People have never seen anything so good for such a low price, and they probably won't ever again. Still, a fog of melancholy, of grief, hangs over the whole revue. The performers joke and flirt onstage, but offstage they have their anguish to bear. One wants to weep over the lot of the afflicted, but feels compelled to live with the living.

MEIJER EMMERIK, DIAMOND CUTTER, BERINGE

FRIDAY, SEPTEMBER 17, 1943—The next day, Saturday, Miss Tini came back to tell me that she had visited the crèche, where she had spoken to Dr. Süskind,* who was a good friend of hers, and she thought that she could probably get Maxie out of there soon. She promised to keep helping me, too. I wept with joy, because I trusted this woman instantly and blindly. Also, I was finally convinced that Lena and Marie were going to be safe.

---

* Walter Suskind was a member of the Jewish Council's Expositur, who worked in the resistance and helped many children to escape into hiding.

SATURDAY, SEPTEMBER 18, 1943—Today I spent almost the whole day in my room.

SUNDAY, SEPTEMBER 19, 1943—Everyone has gone to church; Sundays are celebrated very piously here in this region. There are also quite a few visitors who come to the farm on Sundays, so I'm forced to stay in my room. I sleep a lot during the day, but on the other hand, I sometimes hardly sleep a wink at night.

MONDAY, SEPTEMBER 20, 1943—Every Monday, a seamstress from Venlo comes here to sew, and I have to stay in my room until 5:30 p.m. in the evening. Since the first day I got here I have not been able to sit calmly for a single moment because of the many flies. This is difficult to get used to for someone who comes from the city. With every bite of food that you bring to your mouth, there are flies on your spoon or fork. My plate is black with flies. I have never seen so many flies in my whole life. Today, I'm going to get a screen for my window, and I'll try to make my room free of flies. Today, I donated 500 guilders to the church in Beringe for a new organ.

THURSDAY, SEPTEMBER 23, 1943—This morning, Miss Tini came by to tell me that my wife was put on a transport to Westerbork on September 17.

PHILIP MECHANICUS, JOURNALIST, WESTERBORK

MONDAY, SEPTEMBER 27, 1943—Today, it's exactly a year since I left home. I tell myself that time has flown by, but I know that is not the case. If I look back, so much has happened in this year that the time can't have flown by. I know that every period of this year—my time in jail, my stay in the concentration camp Amersfoort, my various visits to the hospital barracks—has lasted a long time in my memory, sometimes endlessly long. And still that time has gone by as if in a film, a ghastly, yet captivating film. This is how it appears to me, now that it is all behind me. I have not seen the film as a spectator in an easy chair, but as an actor, who grits his teeth while performing his role. . . .

In November, when I left Amersfoort concentration camp, I thought: maybe I will be lucky enough to stay in Westerbork. . . . In December of last year I thought: will I make it to January? And in January: will I make it to February? And so on. And now it is almost October. I can make it to October. But November? In any case, be that as it may, I have gained a year. Those with whom I was in jail and those with whom I was in Amersfoort and who arrived here at the same time I did were mostly sent on to Poland, sometimes after less than two days' rest and just a bandage on their wounds. How did they fare, those fellows? . . . I have never received word from any of these exiles again and neither has anyone else, as far as I know. . . . A year of isolation, physical torment and mental torture has passed. What does the second year have in store?

DOUWE BAKKER,
VICE SQUAD CHIEF, AMSTERDAM

FRIDAY, OCTOBER 1, 1943—Quiet night, beautiful, mild weather. . . . This morning, Posthuma* informed me that the newly reorganized criminal investigation department is expected to be up and running within a few weeks. Modderman will become the Chief of Inspectorate II D., Vice Police. He didn't know what would happen to me, since

---

* Jacobus Ligtle Posthuma was a chief inspector in the police department. As part of the reorganization, he would become deputy of the Criminal Investigation Service in January 1944.

I had still not been assigned to the department. I had to ask the [chief] if he had anything else for me. I will thank him for that. I'm considering writing a personal note to the Chief of Staff of the Directorate General. It is against the rules, but I dare to risk it.

FRIDAY, OCTOBER 8, 1943—The night quiet; nice weather, clear and sunny. Van Geelkerken* spoke at a meeting at the Concertgebouw on Wednesday. Addressing the murder-terror perpetrated against us by our political opponents, he said, among other things, that the NSB is armed. For every comrade that is killed, at least three of our opponents will fall. That's a pretty bold statement. Three Anti's† were murdered in Meppel, last week. Now everyone thinks that it was the NSB's response to other attacks. Maybe so. An eye for eye, a tooth for a tooth, blood for blood.

The sugar situation in our country has suddenly become dire. Due to supply chain issues, we might only receive a half our ration this month. Luckily, we have stocked up on quite a bit of sweetener: Agnes bought a barrel a while ago, and I've been saving up the sugar that I get at the office every morning. We're allowed two lumps each.

In the evening, I attended a meeting of the brigade of the Germanic SS from Amsterdam Oost in the Standaardkwartier at Koningslaan 12. I ran into my neighbor from across the street, comrade Verhagen, who is also the "brigade leader." Leader Slot discussed the propaganda action. Comrade Hylkema is our section leader. By the time the talk ended, it was already 10 p.m., and I had to walk home, which was not easy. So I didn't arrive home until 11:30 p.m. I heard from comrade Slot that the under-guard of the State Police, P. van Dijk of Heemstede, was shot by Jews. He went to catch a Jew hiding in a haystack, and when he got inside that mountain, he was fatally shot. Instead of one, there were about 60 Jews inside the haystack. We seized 35 of

---

* NSB leader Van Geelkerken. His speech is mentioned in Arnhemsche Courant, "Van Geelkerken over de Bewapening der Beweging"—"Zoo noodig zal men inderdaad bemerken, dat het wapens zijn," Arnhem, October 8, 1943, 2.
† His word for resisters, short for "Anti-Duitsers" or anti-Germans.

them. The farmer who had given them the opportunity is now also a fugitive.

WEDNESDAY, OCTOBER 13, 1943—Peaceful night, thick fog all day. I'm on duty again today, but at 10 a.m. I have to appear as a witness before the Civil Servants Court chaired by Rev. Hazelhoff Roelfzema in the case of Stavast and Voûte. Stavast was to be punished with 21 days 2 hours penal service for improper treatment of an arrestee on May 30 at the Inlichtingendienst Office.[*] Staff from that time, along with Voordewind and Posthuma and the accused, were all summoned. The Rechtsfront assigned comrade Dufour as his defender. I believe that Stavast has a good chance of winning this case.

In the afternoon I went to the office. The furniture has already been moved. The decorations in the room are in a class of their own. The bookcase has not yet been moved, but it should be in the next few days. I will then be in room 203, on the other side of the Elandsgracht again.

SATURDAY, OCTOBER 16, 1943—The night was quiet; nice weather but very cold. Today I'm on duty again, as far as it can be considered "duty." It's the last day of my command of the Vice Squad or Inspectorate II D. All our materials have been transferred to room 203, including the beautiful bookcase, which is the last remnant of the Nieuwe Doelenstraat bureau. In the afternoon, Feldmeijer, the leader of the German SS in the Netherlands, spoke at Bellevue. His subject was "Justice first." The hall was crowded.

MONDAY, OCTOBER 18, 1943—The night quiet; rainy, but it cleared up later; mild weather.

I'm without work today. I said goodbye to the Vice Squad staff and moved into my new room. But I'm certainly not bored. I have my own work to do. The other Inspectorate and section chiefs will start work

---

[*] Bakker was also implicated in this case, as discussed at length in his post-war trial records.

here at headquarters today also. Modderman is not here yet, because he is ill. They say it's his heart. I think he wants to retire and get his discharge. . . .

Captain Hans Dieter Frank,[*] who earned the Knight's Cross as one the most famous night fighters, has fallen. Polizeiführer Rauter has issued an order that stipulates that all National Socialist policemen, and other officers, must be protected when they are away from home, on or off duty, practically any time when they are out of the house. It's a nice idea, but almost impossible to implement and rather unpleasant. I have been in discussions with Posthuma about the order, but for the time being we do not see any way of implementing it.

Mussert and Rauter spoke at the swearing in of a new batch of 600 Dutch Landstorm[†] recruits. They announced that an armed force of National Socialists would be formed. These would be SS and W.A. men, led by SS Standartenführer Feldmeijer and W.A. Commander Zondervan. They will be divided into country and city guard units, and they will act to protect National Socialists against terrorists, and also to protect the food supply. These forces will be armed with rifles and they will have the authority to stop anyone on public streets.

PHILIP MECHANICUS, JOURNALIST, WESTERBORK

SATURDAY, OCTOBER 30, 1943—My lust for writing has been tempered lately. The daily battle against the disgust for society, against the cacophony, against the banality, against the vulgarity, uses up much of my energy. Through writing, I have so far found a distraction that can sometimes help me forget these troubles. Also through playing chess. But lately I lack the motivation to take any notes. Am I

---

[*] German Luftwaffe military aviator.
[†] This was a unit of the Waffen-SS.

just tired of observing the camp, or have I become indifferent to what takes place among the people here, just like others who have stayed here for a long time? Certainly, life here blunts the senses. Everyone must try to resist the dullness in order to make anything of their lives. That takes energy. . . .

I'm one of the few people in the camp who has no official job, but I'm not at all ashamed of that. After all, the majority of the work here is done to assist the German Wehrmacht. And therefore I feel no calling. For me, it seems more important to record the daily goings on here for those in the future who will want to have a picture of what happened here. That's why I have a duty to continue writing.

Elisabeth van Lohuizen,
general store owner, Epe

THURSDAY, NOVEMBER 25, 1943[*]—At 6.30 a.m., all of a sudden, we heard footsteps and talking around the house. I heard somebody say, "Van Wielink."[†] I knew immediately that it was police. Loud ringing of the bell. Dick went to the window. "Police, open up." While they continued ringing, Dick went downstairs. *"Anziehen und sie gehen sofort mit!"* (Dress and come along without delay!) Suddenly, the house was full of police, searching everything. They saw a half a bottle of cognac in the cellar and said, "Must be for the Tommies."[‡] Hermien's suitcase was in the hallway. They asked whose it was. I said, "Mine." I started to go downstairs to make tea. Siny had come in with them. It seems that ten men had arrived at her place at 5:45 a.m., searched

---

[*] These diary entries were actually written in the middle of December. Elisabeth notes in her diary: "A lot happened between November 24 and today. So much that I will never forget. Although I wasn't able to keep notes during that period, I'm going to try to write it down as it happened each day, since it's nicer that way."

[†] Elisabeth's maiden name was Van Wielink, and Elisabeth sometimes went by Van Lohuizen-Van Wielink.

[‡] German nickname for British soldiers.

the house, and began an interrogation. Obviously they were looking for Ger. When Siny mentioned Dick's name, she was told to dress and show them the way to our house.

. . . They were awful fellows. We had dressed; Siny had poured tea, prepared some sandwiches. I packed some clothes and toiletries for Dick, as if we were going to stay with friends. We were quiet. Dick was very pale—he is always so scared—but it all went so fast that we didn't quite realize what was happening.

The detectives left, and some Germans remained, who were reasonable. We had to go to the police van, parked near the church. I can still see the three of us walking through the cold morning, not knowing what awaited us, and that miserable feeling, knowing that Siny would be alone after we left. . . . She was brave, said goodbye to us at the police van, promised to look after things, and then went home alone. . . . When we got to the prison, men and women were separated immediately. I watched Dick move away from me in his row. That was miserable. I just wanted to run after him.

We were registered, everything was taken away—money, documents—and then we were searched and after that placed in the cell. Later, Mrs. Bik and Lien Overbosch came into the cell, so we were three in a one-person cell. One got the bed, two on the floor; I being the older one, in the bed. The bed was hard, but that did not matter. We got three slices of dry bread and very weak coffee, but we couldn't eat. I was completely calm but still could not fall asleep. Much had happened, too much to think of it all. Had we not been careful enough? Why was Dick taken? Would Ger suffer more because of us? All kind of ideas. I tried to think through what they might ask me and how I should reply. Why had they picked us up? Was it because we were helping Jews, or because of the evenings with Jan and Maureen? Although they didn't do much to actors anymore. Or was it the parcels to Vught?

FRIDAY, NOVEMBER 26, 1943—The next morning, we learned the rules of the prison: haul water inside, take the barrel outside, ventilate, and so forth. My thoughts were with Dick and in Epe the whole time. I was continuously thinking about poor Siny, now that all three of us are gone.

SATURDAY, NOVEMBER 27, 1943—It was a large room, where there were twelve of us. Large windows, a table, and everything neatly organized. Everyone introduced themselves and very soon we soon felt at home, like we were no longer in prison. We were treated to pancakes because on Friday a suitcase full of goodies was sent for Mrs. Jacques Rutgers. When we asked, how did you smuggle that in here, the answer was: through the front door. We read, played games, did some needlework, and learned about how things worked: how the interrogations went; what they always asked, and so forth. We received useful information. A lot of Reformed people there. . . . We were allowed to write one letter. The food was rather good and the old timers made a spread out of raw vegetables that was delicious on bread.

Nel Molenaar lit the stove in the morning. That evening we received our beds, 12 mattresses on the floor, with covers for each of us. We had to move things around to make space for the beds. . . . It was very primitive but we had a telephone in the room and in the evening we received a phone call bidding us good night. In the cell the lights went out at 7 o'clock, but here we were allowed to keep the lights on until half past 9. . . . We had a silent hour from 1 p.m. to 2:30 p.m.; no talking allowed. Also on Sunday mornings for one and a half hours. We read a lot, knitted, played cards, etc. A fantastic amount of wool clothing came out of that time. Our days passed quietly, those who were there for a long time already advised us in preparation for our interrogations: what we should say, believe, and not believe.

I had no interrogation the first week, and everybody considered that unfortunate, since my case could not move forward. I thought often of Dick how he would fare on the other side. Miek and Riet came to bring all kind of things. I was able to darn a lot, including socks for Dick, which they passed along to him. Several men from Epe were at the end of our hall, but the voice I wanted to hear was not among them. I did inquire if they knew anything about him, but they didn't.

SUNDAY, DECEMBER 5, 1943—We celebrated St. Nicholas[*] with chocolate milk and *speculaas* cookies. It was so pleasant, we forgot about the prison.

MONDAY, DECEMBER 6, 1943—Suddenly, the telephone rings. We are informed that Mrs. Jacques Rutgers will have the first interrogation, a short while later, Jeanne Uytenboogaart from Epe, and right after that San Bik and then me. We had to rush. Those gents were always in a hurry. I had not had breakfast, so they quickly prepared something for all of us; we would not be back before one o'clock. We went downstairs, where there were already a lot of men—but alas no Dick—and a couple of snarling S.D. men.

They took us in a moving van to the Utrechtseweg. We were told that anyone who tries to flee will be shot dead. The group was varied, but quite cheerful. Placed again in a women's cell. Mrs. Jacques Rutgers was called rather quickly; she was here about a friend of hers who had gone in hiding. Next Jeanne. Then finally I was called. A Dutch detective, A. Hoekstra, was in charge of my interrogation. He acted very kind hearted, but was as mean as the Germans. He started out by saying that they already knew everything because they had Boogert, who had admitted to everything. If you tell the truth, they said, you'll be home again tonight. The mailman and the cobbler have also already confessed. I did not know yet where this was headed.

First, he asked all kinds of formal questions, then suddenly he wanted to know if I knew the Teahouse Schaveren, and the Rinkerhof. He said he didn't quite understand, but then retrieved notes that had been written about Cor, a Jewish boy. Then I knew what it was all about. He [Cor] had said father and son Van Lohuizen were in charge

---

[*] The Dutch celebrate the arrival of St. Nicholas, or SinterKlaas (similar to Santa Claus), on December 5 every year.

of distribution of ration coupons. Mrs. Lohuizen delivered them. I kept denying everything, right and left, until I had to sign my name.

I, who am unable to tell a lie, told one lie after another, but when the moment came to sign, I got scared. I said, "I delivered one letter there once." He asked, "Did you know what was in it?" I said, "No." He said, "Sign!" He brought me away, saying he would do his best for me. Out in the hall, I saw San Bik. All four of us were technically free, but they took me to a cell again. I was very calm, and I had a feeling that they could not do anything to me, as if I was protected, or as if many good thoughts were going out to me.

MONDAY, DECEMBER 13, 1943—I was summoned again by telephone for another interrogation. Just like the first time, I was calm, but for a moment I clasped my hands together, and prayed that I would not betray anyone. In the van, someone told me that he had seen my husband. He was ready to go to his interrogation, when it turned out that they'd called for me. Once again put in a cell, then I had to wait in the hall. Witt came out neatly dressed, and I had to go with him. I felt uneasy for a while. He pulled out the big guns right away: "You lied to us, etcetera." I said, "No, I admitted that I was there." He asked, "How did you dare do that while your son is in Vught? You did so just to oppose us." "No, I only helped people." He took out some papers and started to type. I thought that will be my judgment. But then he said, "*Bitte Frau van Lohuizen* (Please Mrs. Van Lohuizen) you are free, but do not interfere anymore." The typist let me out. There I was, a free person again, walking through the streets of Arnhem.

. . . I could barely get to the station. I had a terribly sore back from a fall in the slippery courtyard. . . . But once I got there, I called Epe. Siny could not believe it. On the ride back to Epe, I met so many people I knew, who congratulated me. In Apeldoorn, Miek and Riet met me at the train, very happy. It became too much for me for a moment when I saw little Marja. I felt the urge to cry away all the tension, but I kept a grip on myself. Siny was extremely happy and immediately treated me to a wonderful meal. My thoughts were with Dick; I just wanted him to be free. In the evening, I visited Riet Roelands, then took a wonderful bath and went to bed.

WEDNESDAY, DECEMBER 15, 1943—I'm staying in our old house with Siny. She prepared our old bedroom (now their room) for me, with the fire burning. If anyone asks, she will say that I am away. I do not feel like talking with anyone until I have some news about Dick. Siny and I have the same problems now. We do not have to say anything to be able to understand one another.

THURSDAY, DECEMBER 16, 1943—At 5 o'clock I was downstairs when Betje H. came to tell me that her fiancé, Jan Leenhouts, had been sent to Vught along with some other prisoners. Dick's name was not included. Half an hour later, B. Bruynen also came by, and he had the complete list. Now it is certain; Dick has also been sent to Vught. In that case, at least Ger will see his father. I should have been the one to go, not him, but women count for less when they have their men. Maybe it's better this way; at least I can help Siny when baby comes, and look after the business and the household. For a while, we were very depressed, you have to process it. Then Siny said, we will prepare a parcel for Papa at once, and you have to write to him; we have to do something! We will certainly not be defeated; we have known that this could happen. I just hope Dick can persevere. Will Ger come home for Christmas?

FRIDAY, DECEMBER 17, 1943—I received a very short note from Dick, a sign of life:[*]

Mrs. v. Lohuizen, Epe

We all are on the way to Vught.

D

---

[*] The note is pasted into her diary.

MEIJER EMMERIK,
DIAMOND CUTTER, BERINGE

WEDNESDAY, DECEMBER 15, 1943—Today it is quite cold again. I'm downstairs in the farmhouse, where all the doors are closed. Every time someone comes in, I run upstairs. . . . Miss Tini came and told me that she had bad news for me. Dr. Verberne from Panningen tested my sputum and found that it is positive.* Now the doctor is of the opinion that I should not stay here at the farm, because there are four children here. I was very upset, because I have finally found myself among people who I can really trust, and who are extremely good to me. I discussed this with Miss Tini.

We agreed that when the farmer would come to get me I would tell him everything and let him make the decision about whether I must go or if I can stay. But then if I do stay, I must separate all my things and keep myself completely apart from the children. When the farmer did come to collect me at 10 a.m., we did just that, and he had so much empathy that he began to cry. He said that nothing would be too much for them and that if I wanted to stay I could stay. They would bring me more milk and eggs and anything I needed, and I should let them know anything else that I require. I was moved to tears, and even Miss Tini became emotional. She will discuss the matter with Dr. Verberne and will let him know that I can stay where I am. As long as I live, I will never forget the kindnesses of these good, simple people.

THURSDAY, DECEMBER 16, 1943—This morning I wrote a letter that, given the current circumstances, will have to serve as my last will and testament. I have deposited it here, in case anything happens to me. The farmer will have to give it to Lena, and if that isn't possible, it must be handed over to Robert. The people here are exceptionally good to me; I really couldn't receive any better care.

---

* For tuberculosis.

SATURDAY, DECEMBER 18, 1943—This morning Miss Tini brought me a letter from Robert in which he said that he has heard nothing from Van der Meulen.[*] He told me that from now on, only one package weighing two kilos can be sent to Westerbork each month. For people who only have one child with them, this is less than two ounces of food per week, and less of course if there are more children under their care. His opinion is that there will be no more transports to Poland. There are indeed so bitterly few Jews left behind that the Krauts probably think it is no longer worth the effort to transport them.

MONDAY, DECEMBER 20, 1943—Because the seamstress is here today, I went to see Mr. Simons, and there I met Lena. She told me that she has to leave her hiding place for two days, because the people she's staying with are going away for two days. These people don't care at all about their person in hiding; they only care about her money. Hopefully Miss Tini can find a place for her somewhere else. I stayed with her until 5 p.m. and I'll go back tomorrow. While there, I saw an illegal newspaper called *"Ons Volk,"*[†] from December 1943, part of which I'm pasting into the diary here. It reports on the fate of our prisoners of war and the fate of the remaining Jews in Vught.[‡]

TUESDAY, DECEMBER 21, 1943—I went back to Mr. Simons' house today until five o'clock and have agreed with him that Lena can stay with him until Miss Tini finds something else for her. In any case, she won't have to return to her old address because those people are incredibly disappointing. I met another gentleman there who said he listened to the English radio station yesterday, which reported that the Krauts were now transporting the Jews who are in Poland in animal wagons. They are gassed in these wagons and then they are brought to

---

[*] The family that was caring for Maxie.
[†] A resistance paper. The newspaper clipping seems to have been lost.
[‡] Concentration camp Vught.

the border of Ukraine where their bodies are thrown into large lime-stone pits. When I heard this, my first thought was: maybe it is better than to be forced into hard labor without decent clothing, at some clothing factory and probably under constant assault. But how long will this misery last? I have begun to despair of every hope.

18

"THE DIARY BECOMES A WORLD"

A page from Douwe Bakker's diary

D ouwe Bakker wrote on every available page of Volume #18 of his diary, including the unlined inside cardboard leaf of the book's marbleized back cover. Numbered #3292, it is the final page of his last extant journal, dated Sunday, October 24, 1943.

Was this the last journal that Bakker kept? Or did he start another that was lost? Were there many more volumes that he destroyed before they were discovered? It's impossible for me to know. What is known is that eighteen volumes of his nearly 3,300-page diary were discovered by criminal prosecutors in 1946,[*] and entered into evidence in his post-war collaboration trials. Afterward, they were transferred to NIOD.

The first entry in Bakker's initial volume, labeled "Kronyck," (chronicles), was dated January 3, 1938. His primary goal seemed to be to record the progress of National Socialism, and Hitler's advance through Europe, rather than to explore his intimate thoughts and feelings. Bakker's diaries were not merely made up of words, either; he filled them with newspaper clippings, maps indicating the Reich's military interventions across Europe, and anti-Semitic posters and flyers.

Flipping through his pages, one finds images of Nazi land and sea battles, multiple portraits of Hitler, and photos of Nazi rallies: Mussert's NSB rally on Dam Square, for example, Heinrich Himmler's visit to The Hague, and a large SS military parade outside the Rijksmuseum on Museumplein.

These were sometimes sourced from Dutch-language Nazi propa-

---

[*] Meershoek said they were discovered in a safe deposit box, but I was unable to confirm this.

ganda papers, which included the leading homegrown NSB daily, *Het Nationale Dagblad*, the weekly *Volk en Vaderland*, and *Storm*, a self-described "radical battle magazine" published weekly by the Dutch SS. Often, his clippings came from *De Telegraaf*, one of the mainstream Dutch papers that continued to operate under the occupying regime.[1] As historian René Vos has demonstrated, such papers served as a "collaborationist press" during the war.[2] *De Telegraaf* regularly filled column inches, for example, with translated articles from the German news agency *Deutsches Nachrichtingsbüro*, which was run and controlled "with an iron fist" by Joseph Goebbels' propaganda ministry.[3]

Almost every day, Bakker wrote a few paragraphs of "German War News Report," usually parroting Nazi propaganda papers; often he included a second "report" on military news about Axis powers Italy and Japan.

My guess is that there were more Bakker diaries that have been lost. By late 1943, he had developed a very robust habit of accounting for his daily activities—the weather, the war news, police actions in Amsterdam, his personal reflections—so it seems unlikely that he would have concluded his diary without summary remarks, and without signing off. But are there clues in his final pages as to why he might have stopped?

Bakker's last entry was about a largely uneventful day: He planned to visit a "comrade" to pick up a kilo of apples and four corn husks that Agnes would pound into cornmeal. He noted that seven "murderers, saboteurs and spies" had been sentenced to execution. While attending a football match at Ajax Stadium, he heard air raid sirens at precisely 16:37. Schiphol was attacked, he reported, and a dozen enemy planes flew overhead.

The ink has faded to gray on the final page of Bakker's diary, but he completed his thought: "Everything indicates that the enemy will not be long in coming here. Our fighting forces are ready at the border and waiting for the attack."

Could he have stopped writing because the Allies were making headway? If Bakker understood that the tide of the war had turned, he may have decided that keeping a diary was no longer wise, or he may have made a greater effort to hide his later volumes—perhaps he hid them so well that they were lost forever.

In late October, Bakker's work life might have been upsetting him, too. His job with the Vice Squad came to an end on October 18, and while the entire police force was undergoing a reorganization[*] he was not given a specific role in the new structure. He was also not fired. He was given his own room, #203, in a building on the Elandsgracht, but no specific instructions on what to do there. Although he claimed in his diary "I have enough of my own work to do," he was clearly at loose ends.

Within the space of a month, he penned a letter to SS Hauptsturm-führer Alfons Brendel[†] requesting a new assignment. It was strictly against department rules to go over the heads of one's direct commanders, but Bakker said he was willing to take the risk. The letter was essentially a curriculum vitae, outlining Bakker's police career achievements, NSB affiliations, and political allegiances, and ended with a declaration of his loyalty to the Nazi cause. He described himself as, "a strong proponent of the Greater Germanic idea [who] unconditionally recognizes the Führer, Adolf Hitler, as the leader of the coming Greater Germanic People's Community."

The letter landed on the desk of Lieutenant Colonel Henri Arend van Hilten, an NSB member, who, like Bakker, was part of a small cadre of twenty-one NSB policemen who'd been interned for suspected treason during the 1940 invasion. Like Bakker, Van Hilten had subsequently risen through police ranks to become president of the Amsterdam department on December 1, 1943. After less than two weeks on the job, he'd placed Bakker in a new post, as Chief of the Bureau of Social Police, a department he would lead for the next eleven months.[4]

The Social Police, according to Van Hilten, were first tasked with

---

[*]   One of at least four that would happen throughout the war.
[†]   Former commander of Nazi "hell camp" Ellecom.

arresting illegal ration card traders, but later focused on arresting "loitering" young Dutch people to send to labor duty in the Netherlands and Germany. Bakker was perfectly suited for such work, Van Hilten would testify, because he had "no objections of conscience," in working on behalf of the occupier. "Otherwise, I believe he would have presented them to me," he said.[5]

After D-Day on June 6, 1944, when 155,000 American, British, and Canadian troops landed on the beaches of Normandy, France, the whole landscape of the war shifted. The Allies had finally broken through the Western Front, and the Nazi military began to retreat in earnest. Many Dutch NSB members and other pro-German collaborators in the Netherlands tried to cover their tracks and change their traitorous behavior. Some even became involved in resistance activities in the last year of the war, hoping that this would serve them in good stead if they were ever accused of previous war crimes. Thousands of Germans, NSB members, and pro-German Dutch also began to flee the Netherlands.

Bakker wasn't among those who evinced shame or guilt about his participation, however. He remained chief of the Bureau of Social Police until October 30, 1944, and thereafter stayed on duty in the Amsterdam police force until Liberation. Five days later, on May 10, 1945, he was arrested at the Heineken Brewery in Amsterdam, and subsequently taken into police custody.[6]

"NOTORIOUS POLICE INSPECTOR on Trial," was the headline of a very brief news summary in the *Nieuwe Dag* newspaper in August 1946, one of the first to announce Bakker's criminal indictment. The item said the trial would focus on his role as "part of the S.D. in Nieuwe Doelenstraat in Amsterdam, where he interrogated numerous people who listened to English radio broadcasts, printed or distributed illegal literature, or insulted the German Reich or Hitler in some way."[7]

A more extensive article in the *Volkskrant* a couple of days later ran with the headline, "The S.D.'s Stupid Accomplice," presenting

Bakker as a buffoonish sycophant to the occupying regime. *De Waar-heid* newspaper ran a very different kind of headline, "He believed it was his duty: Inspector Bakker tells judges." It focused on Bakker's defensive strategy: he would claim to be "just following orders."

This was the first trial for collaboration Bakker would face, out of several that would last through 1948. It was held in the Bijzondere Ge-rechtshof, the Special Court of Amsterdam, a new judicial body set up hastily in the war's aftermath to prosecute accused collaborators. The case against him had been assembled by two police detectives from the Political Investigation Department, also established immediately after the war, to root out wrongdoers. In the autumn of 1945, two Amster-dam police detectives[*] interrogated several figures who'd worked with Bakker at the Inlichtingendienst, including Willy Lages, who was by then in jail, and Kurt Döring, Lages' S.D. middleman.

Lages testified that Bakker was the chief of the department, and described how their relationship had soured over time. He explained that he'd eventually shuttered the Investigations department, largely due to Bakker's insubordination. Döring corroborated Lages' account. "The Bakker Department did not work to the liking of the S.D.," he stated in his testimony. "It repeatedly destroyed important cases for the S.D. by intervening too early." He added that Bakker had "repeat-edly pushed for the release of prisoners," and, perhaps attempting to aid in Bakker's defense, added, "Some even regarded [Bakker] as a friend to the Jews."

Lages told the court, according to various newspapers, that Bak-ker had "screwed up many a fine case."

When Bakker appeared in court, one newspaper reporter de-scribed him as "a completely broken man, incessantly wringing his hands," who answered questions put to him, "timidly, humbly." Bak-ker claimed he was an insignificant player in the investigative unit—adding to the impression that he was no more than an obsequious and incompetent fool.

---

[*] Gerardus Clement and Frans Badenhuizen.

The prosecutor, M.H. Gelinck, concluded that Bakker "hadn't been of much use to the Germans." Based on Döring's testimony,[8] it seemed even possible that Bakker had inadvertently sabotaged some of the Sicherheitsdienst's cases. Using this reasoning, he told the court that he would not seek the maximum criminal penalty that was possible for collaboration. Instead, he requested a sentence of twenty years.[9] Two weeks later, the court returned with a verdict: Bakker would go to prison for seven years, minus the time he'd already served in pretrial detention.[10]

A year later, however, Bakker was back in court. He was facing a second indictment for collaborating with the enemy while chief inspector of the Documentation Service, and chief of the Social Police under Van Hilten. A new police investigator—Gerrit Bakker, no relation—was assigned to the case, and he conducted many more interviews, and went digging for more evidence to convict Bakker.

The witnesses in this trial included at least a dozen former S.D., NSB, and Rechtsfront police agents, again including Willy Lages and Döring, as well as Van Hilten and Bakker's subordinates, Nicolaas Jonker and Hendrik van den Berg, who provided detailed accounts of Bakker's callousness and brutality toward suspects in his custody.

These "once passionate people-hunters," wrote a *Volkskrant* journalist, now sat on the court benches like a "tamed herd," meekly following the course of events.[11]

Several linked testimonies focused on abusive treatment of a single detainee, Emanuel A. Stellingwerff, a fifty-nine-year-old man who'd been hauled into Bakker's Documentation Service in May 1943 when his wife was accused of selling illegal ration coupons. His wife, Stellingwerff testified, had been subsequently deported to Poland; it is not clear from the files if she was Jewish.[12] One of Bakker's agents, named Stavast, had forced a stick into Stellingwerff's trouser leg—a form of police torture—and had also beat him so badly that his cries and shouts were heard throughout the police department.

Another policeman who'd witnessed the events confirmed that Bakker's agent had abused Stellingwerff, and that Bakker had "come into the room and seen what was happening, but did nothing to stop it," the agent testified.

"In my opinion, Chief Bakker should have acted decisively at this point and ordered Stavast decisively to stop this way of interrogation," the agent continued. "Chief Bakker, however, did not do so as far as I can remember. He retired to his room, after which Stavast continued the assault on the detainee."[13]

In May 1947, just as the second trial was coming to a close, newspapers reported that "new facts had come to light." The "new facts" were contained in a monumental piece of newly discovered evidence: eighteen volumes of Douwe Bakker's diaries.

"Douwe Bakker Noted His Crimes in His Diary," was *Het Parool*'s headline.[14]

The *Volkskrant* included extensive quotes from the sections of Bakker's diary that Gelinck chose to highlight for the court: "In his diary one finds passages such as: 'they'll have to set up large concentration camps' and 'the sons of plutocrats should also go to Germany to work.'"

Gelinck asserted, based on these declarations, that, "Bakker was an unspeakably bad influence on the police corps." Furthermore, he stated, "Bakker led a vicious regime and often fueled the betrayal against fellow citizens."

He cited Bakker's journals repeatedly. "Once more, from his diary: 'Arrested 42 communists, a bit of tidying up.' 'Ten Jews collected; a rather poor result.'"

On May 16, just three days before the trial concluded, Bakker tried to explain why he'd kept his diary and what it meant to him, in an interrogation conducted by Gerrit Bakker. He started by simply confirming that the books were his own: "The eighteen-volume diary that you are showing me was personally written by me," he said. "All the events I have described in this diary were written down by me, either immediately or shortly after the events occurred, and therefore they are correct. But I certainly can't remember what I wrote in it."

He went on to disavow the sentiments the journals contained. "I recognize that some passages in my diary are very fanatical and give the impression that I was a fanatic. Yet I readily declare that my words were more fanatical than my deeds."[15]

This extraordinary attestation, suggesting that Bakker had exaggerated or else misrepresented his motivations and beliefs in his own diary, would become central to his defensive strategy. "Despite the mentality which indeed appears from my diary," he testified, "I am in my heart an opponent of violence and I hereby expressly declare that I have never harmed anyone personally, nor have I ever promoted any harm that was caused by others." He added, "I know this may sound unnatural after writing such a diary and yet I cannot explain otherwise."

Bakker also denied supporting anti-Jewish measures. "In practice, I was certainly not an anti-Semite," he abjured. "This may be apparent from the fact that in 1943 my wife still had a Jewish female manicurist, who still regularly came to my home and with whom I often conversed. I have never complained to my wife about her presence."[16] (It was not clear from his testimony whether this Jewish service provider, about whom he "never complained," was still alive.)

Bakker also mentioned that he had "often counseled and assisted Jews who were in violation of the Jewish ordinances." He told the investigator that he could provide names and addresses for such individuals, although he couldn't quite remember them at that moment. Finally, he added that there were many more facts he could cite that would demonstrate that "I was not as fierce as my diary might indicate."

Bakker's effort to disavow the pro-Nazi sentiments expressed in his diary is a transparent defensive strategy, but it does raise an important question: To what extent were his daily entries an expression of his "true" feelings and political beliefs? And to what degree was he fictionalizing in his journals?

Williams College professor Alexandra Garbarini, who has written extensively on Jewish wartime diaries, cautions that it's not always appropriate to equate a person with the "persona," or even alter ego, that they create of themselves in their diary.

"There's this notion that a diary is a place where someone is most comfortable and is truest to themselves, rather than a place where people perform in a different way than they do when interacting with people," she said. "It doesn't necessarily mean that that's an authentic reflection of a person's activities in life."[17]

It is certainly possible that Bakker used his diary as repository for his most fanatical ideas, a zone where he could express them freely, without censure. "A diary can be a space for a certain kind of unloading, or it can be space where a person gives play to certain outbursts," said Garbarini.

Bakker wrote in his diary so often, and with so much fervor over such a long period, that it's possible, she suggested, that he created a whole secondary identity for himself in his journals. "This extremely dedicated type of diarist is quite rare," said Garbarini. "He's among the people for whom the world of his diary is an important one. For people like this, the diary becomes a world in which the diarist lives."[18]

Contrary to the prosecutor's assessment, I found that Bakker came off as *less* radical in his diaries than he was portrayed by others in court. While Lages characterized Bakker as power hungry and independent, in his diary he frequently comes across across as obsequious, hoping for the attention of his superiors. The tone of his commendations for his agents, when they succeeded in capturing resisters, too, is much more boastful than the language that he employed in his journals.

In attempting to understand how Bakker crafted his "diary identity," it's important to understand who he was writing his diary for, or to. At his trial, he explained, "I wrote this book in order to record, for posterity, the events that took place during war, which made a deep impression on me." He labeled some of his volumes, "Chronicles," which suggests an intention to keep a record, and a scrapbook of his times. That may explain why his tone is generally measured, reportorial. The outbursts that the prosecutor quoted about plutocrats, communists, and Jews, are in fact somewhat rare in his journal pages.

THE VERY NOTION of granting collaborators and perpetrators an audience for their personal narratives may also seem, to many people, to be repellant at its core. At the very least, there's either an emotional or a philosophical awkwardness built into the act of listening to the stories of those who participated in Nazi crimes. How much can we trust such people to tell the truth, or even to provide information that is not tainted by their moral turpitude?

Because we tend to endow the act of witnessing with moral authority, it can seem "highly problematic and even conceptually contradictory to attribute the capacity of bearing witness to perpetrators, regardless of whether they were torturers or desktop murderers," wrote philosopher Sibylle Schmidt.[19]

She argued, however, that we must attempt to understand the motivations and intentions of those engaged in genocide and political violence, because valuable insights can be gained from their stories. They are, she wrote, "valid forms of testimony" as long as we approach them with caution and reflection.[20]

Hitler's fallen elite repeatedly testified at the Nuremberg Trials in 1945 and 1946 and subsequent criminal proceedings, that they were mostly cogs in the National Socialist machinery, "just following orders"—a phrase that is now known simply as "the Nuremberg defense." Hitler's close confidant Wilhelm Keitel, head of the German Armed Forces High Command, for example, described himself at trial as the Reich's literal appliance, an object without human will, "a piece of office equipment, proud to be used by others," especially the Führer.[21] Accused Nazis repeatedly denied their own agency, and frequently attempted to shed their wartime identities.

In her legendary account of the Adolf Eichmann trial in Israel, Hannah Arendt was struck by the ordinariness of that leading Nazi perpetrator, defined as the architect of the Holocaust. Since then, the notion of the "banality of evil" has been extended to most perpetrators of mass violence—but perhaps it has been over-extended. She analyzed Eichmann not as a perpetrator, but as a defendant on trial, denuded of his Nazi uniform, his military medals, and his sense of ideological purpose. Eichmann at trial, as legal scholars Thijs B. Bouwknegt and Adina-Loredana Nistor have demonstrated, was no longer Eichmann the Nazi leader. Nor do other perpetrator and collaborator criminal testimonies provide historians with a particularly useful framework for grasping a culprit's motivations and beliefs, they argued.

"The proceedings do not and cannot forensically reveal what the perpetrators were thinking or feeling when they were committing their crimes," they observed. "Rather, we are witnesses to how *defendants* of international crimes rationalize and deal with their actions by speaking 'legalese'—the only language used in a court of law."[22]

Bouwknegt and Nistor argued that those Nazi criminals who faced trial had one identity in wartime, and another when they were on the witness stand. It would be fruitless to expect them to reflect accurately on their former Nazi identities, or to explain or admit criminal behaviors, in the courtroom context.

To interpret what perpetrators say, one needs to account for the complex social, psychological, philosophical, and judicial dynamics at play in their testimonies. Any interrogatory exchange must take into account the multiple reasons a perpetrator might have for offering their story, and how they might reinterpret the past, falsify elements, or lie all the way through.

Newspaper reporters described Bakker in his second trial as sitting in the courtroom with his head bowed, his face wan, his hands trembling. When he spoke, he stammered, claiming that he himself couldn't understand what he'd written. "I must have been hypnotized," he said.[23]

No longer regarded as a bumbling buffoon, Bakker was painted by Gelinck as "a fanatical NSB-er, a fierce Jew-hater and an obsequious servant of the Krauts. Someone who despises both religion and royalty."[24]

The court concluded that Bakker had provided "support and encouragement to lower-ranking officials in their treacherous work." And as department chief, "He did not intervene when his subordinates mistreated suspects, and even if he didn't promote such behavior, he at least tolerated it."[25] But the deciding factor, one newspaper wrote, was the revelation provided exclusively by the diary: that he'd collaborated with the occupier in "his heart and soul."

The verdict was delivered in June. An additional eight years was tacked on to Bakker's prison sentence, so now he had fifteen. Gelinck immediately requested a new hearing, demanding the death penalty in an appeals court known as Cassation Court. Police Commissioner Hendrik Voordewind, head of the Investigation Department in Amsterdam, supported the request, testifying that Bakker's mild sentence had "aroused great indignation in the Amsterdam corps."

"During the reign of terror, it was all too well established how this thug had chased the resistance, killed the resistance members, either directly or indirectly," Voordewind testified. As a result, "There was a general belief in the Amsterdam police corps . . . that Douwe Bakker would not escape the death penalty." He added, "I can't say anything good about this man. He did everything in his power to serve the cause of the Krauts."[26]

On January 5, 1948, the Cassation Court revised Bakker's sentence. This time, he was given life in prison.

EVER SINCE I began reading Bakker's diary, I looked for clues about his family members or descendants. In his diary, he frequently mentions Agnes, his wife, and his daughter, Tilly (born in 1926), and, less often, his son, Bob (born in 1929; died in 1974), whom he describes as "an invalid." Agnes died in 1962. I thought Tilly might still be alive, if quite elderly, because I couldn't find a record of her death, but I also found no evidence of any of her descendants.

One afternoon, I found myself on a web page[27] that described Bakker's brief involvement in a police force in Zwolle. Beneath it, in the Comments was a note by Marije Essink. "He was the husband of my grandfather's older half-sister," she'd written.

I located Marije easily through social media, in the region of Groningen; her LinkedIn profile described her as "Researcher, Translator, Editor, Available for you!"

Marije turned out to be exactly as accessible as her profile had promised, and responded promptly to my inquiry. She explained that she'd stumbled on to information about Bakker, who had married into her family, while exploring her family's genealogical history. Because he was not a blood relative, she said she felt dispassionate about his story, but extremely curious. She'd charted out family connections, dug into newspaper archives, and even reached out to Bakker's daughter, Tilly, about ten years prior. She sent Tilly her genealogical summary, but Tilly "wasn't too happy about it," Marije said. "She asked me not to talk about that so much."

Marije wasn't sure if Tilly was still alive; when they'd had contact, she was already an octogenarian. She mentioned that she knew that one of Bakker's granddaughters lived in the south of the country and another in Amsterdam, but they'd never had any contact. With these tips I could locate them on the internet. I emailed each of them, requesting interviews. They responded jointly, declining politely, and requesting that I keep their names anonymous.

"The convictions of my grandfather during WWII were not known to us until we were adults," read their letter, which they gave me permission to quote: "It did not play a part in our upbringing, my parents never talked about it. He died when we were young children and we do not have any special recollection of him." They added that they were told little about Bakker, other than that he was a policeman during the war, and went to jail, "and that he had 'some sympathy' for the wrong side. That's all they ever told us." They also asked me not to contact Tilly, though they confirmed that, at that time, she was still alive.

I asked Essink if she knew how others in the family had felt about Bakker.

"What I understood from the rest of the family was that he was considered a kind of 'black sheep,'" she told me. "None of them had much to do with him."

Unfortunately, these relatives did not want to, or could not, provide me with much insight into the intergenerational impact of his collaboration. I didn't find it surprising that his granddaughters did not want to talk—many relatives of NSB members have shut out the wartime past, either because there was so much silence around it that they knew little of what occurred, or because they felt shame or guilt.

In the Netherlands since the war, people like Bakker have usually been called *"fout in de oorlog,"* which in Dutch simply means "wrong in the war." Legally speaking, the Special Court of Cassation in 1948 charged and sentenced him with "deliberately giving aid to the enemy in a time of war," a crime akin to treason.[28] It's not terribly surprising that his descendants wanted to distance themselves from his actions, his ideology, and his deeds. Unfortunately for us, however, the family history here leads to a dead end.

IN A LANDMARK 1993 book, *Perpetrators Victims Bystanders: The Jewish Catastrophe, 1933–1945,* Raul Hilberg laid out a three-pronged typology for witnesses of genocide that is still frequently used today. Perpetrators such as those within the Dutch police department were part of a "widespread bureaucracy, and each man could feel that his contribution was a small part of an immense undertaking." These types of functionaries were aware that "process of destruction was deliberate, and that once he had stepped into this maelstrom, his deed would be indelible."[29]

Christopher R. Browning, who explored the role of the "ordinary perpetrator" in his pioneering book *Ordinary Men: Reserve Police Battalion 101 and the Final Solution in Poland,* used the term "desk murderers" for collaborating Nazi functionaries in occupied territories. Because the "bureaucratic nature of their participation" involved "tiny steps," often performed "in a routine manner," he wrote, they could feel a separation from the inevitable consequences of their participation. Because their work was "segmented, routinized, and depersonalized," such functionaries could do their work, he found, "without confronting the reality of mass murder."[30]

In 2004, Browning tried to develop new critical tools to unpack all of Adolf Eichmann's various documented testimonies—thirty-two court sessions in Jerusalem in 1961, plus more than 500 pages of handwritten memoirs. Browning recalled how his colleagues ridiculed him for trying to find truth in, "a useless conglomeration of faulty memories on one hand and calculated lies for legal defense and self-justification on the other."[31] But Browning felt he might be able to "sift nuggets of useful information from the mass of mendacious sludge."

He ultimately found a few nuggets that he felt were "not only possible but also, I would argue, quite probable" in all of Eichmann's accounts—eight events in 1941 and 1942 that clarified his thought process and decision-making around the Final Solution. He concluded that historians could still retrieve useful information from such "tainted" sources, and should continue to scour "even highly problematic evidence."[32]

Many perpetrator studies specialists have attempted to unpack former Nazis' emotional or psychological states, based on their testimony or personal documents collected in the post-war era. Often they found that perpetrators had created mental barriers toward their deeds that were often articulated as: I didn't know, I couldn't have known, and even, that wasn't really me.

Katharina von Kellenbach, for example, studied letters between prison chaplains, and imprisoned Nazis and their wives and children. "Almost without exception," she found, "they were unable to openly admit culpable wrongdoing. They could not bring themselves to articulate remorse and were devoid of contrition." Their testimonies often used the "same cold logic and dispassionate indifference toward victims" that had made it impossible for them to feel compassion and empathy for the victims in the first place. Strikingly, they were also unable to feel responsible for their behavior. "They were driven by an obsessive need to minimize moral agency," she wrote, "and they strenuously avoided specific memories of doing harm."[33]

In her book, *Reckonings,* British historian Mary Fulbrook pioneered much new ground on this subject. She broke down what she called perpetrator's "self-distancing strategies" into two categories:

The first was the "geographic strategy" of claiming one didn't know because the atrocity had happened elsewhere. A police officer helping to round up Jews in Amsterdam, for example, could claim that he wasn't part of the death camp system, because the camps were far off in "the East."

Fulbrook found that this moral defense could be taken to absurd extremes. She recounted the story of Marianne B., a schoolteacher in Oświęcem, the town where the Auschwitz death camp was located, who educated the children of SS officers working at the camp. Marianne B. wrote in her post-war memoir that she "didn't know" about the genocide taking place right next door, because she could not "see" what was going on inside the camp. However, she mentioned that the desks in her classroom were frequently covered in a very fine dust that blew over from the large chimneys that hovered over the town.

"It lay like cigar ash in beautiful white-gray flakes of a quite curious structure on the black wood of my desk," she wrote.

Marianne B. asked the landlady, "What on earth might that be?" After leaning out the window, the landlady answered, "They are burning there again in the crematorium. So that is human ashes. We have had that already many times!"

The schoolteacher recalled being "shocked and deeply shaken," but still confused. "A proof of mass murder it was not," Marianne B. decided, in spite of all evidence to the contrary. "After all, every big camp had to have a crematorium—even so, I will never forget these curiously beautiful, sad flakes of ash."[34]

Her classroom must have had a fine patina of human remains for the entire year and a half she worked there, from September 1943 until Auschwitz was liberated in January 1945. Yet, Marianne B. chose to assert that she could "not have known" what was happening, and she rejected the implication of complicity because she didn't "see" any murders taking place.

Other perpetrators, collaborators, or implicated witnesses chose a less literal form of self-distancing to justify their involvement in, or acceptance of, mass murder. They essentially divided themselves in two: there was the person who "acted" in the past, and then there was the person that they "really" were in the present. This "authentic self," Fulbrook explained, could be differentiated from the person who committed the heinous acts. "The person who acted or behaved in certain ways was not the 'real me.' The 'real' self is the moral inner self," she wrote. "The outwardly visible self that acted was prompted by external considerations over which it had little or no control."[35]

To be able to live with themselves, perpetrators and collaborators had to construct the identity of a "'good self' persisting across time despite changing circumstances."[36] This moral inner core could still exist, regardless of their violent, cruel, or homicidal acts.

Because of these incredibly complex psychological mechanisms that allowed perpetrators to distance themselves from moral blame, it becomes much more challenging for us to understand their self-narratives in the post-war era. A person who is accused of wrongdoing has what we might call "an inner core of goodness" that they're fighting desperately to maintain. Their testimonies, often a conglomeration of defense strategies, should be viewed like a portrait in a fun-house mirror. They may contain elements of reality, but there are multiple types of distortion that are reflected back, too.

HOW DO WE read Douwe Bakker's post-war testimonies, then? And how can we compare his diary entries to his post-war statements during his interrogations?

Bakker argued in court that he was a "fanatic with words but not deeds," and that his diary didn't represent his authentic self. He claimed that, contrary to his own written journals, he was not anti-Semitic and he was "never violent." When he looked back on his former self, he concluded that he "must have been hypnotized." These are all self-distancing strategies, and whether they are "legalese" or psychologically motivated, it's difficult to determine.

Prosecutor Gelinck, certainly regarded the voluminous diary as a reflection of Bakker's wartime beliefs and feelings. But it might be more accurate to call it a fabrication of his wartime identity, a slightly fictionalized version of his true perpetrator self. If in reality he was a subordinate to Lages and Tulp, in his diary he was a leader of his own department. In the real world, he was an unpopular commander of a hated unit of NSB renegades. In his diary, he was a loyalist in "the movement," a "comrade" in the struggle for the New Order. In his diary he could see himself as a valued documentarian, a prince in the Reich's kingdom.

Weeks after Bakker was arrested in 1945, police investigators from his old department asked him how he could've placed himself in the service of the enemy, acting as a traitor to his own country.

"I declare that in my opinion after the capitulation of 1940 there was no longer a state of war between the Netherlands and Germany," he responded. "Now that the occupation of the Netherlands had become a fact, it was in the interest of the Dutch population to cooperate with it. I was also convinced of a German victory and that we would continue to work together with Germany after the war."

By his own testimony, Bakker was just living history forward. He thought, as the industrialists and the civil servants did, and as all the others who went along did as well, that the outcome of the war had been decided once the occupation had begun. Bakker's diary, in this light, can be seen as a 3,300-page construction of a world in which he assumed that he already lived.

After his conviction, Bakker was imprisoned in Leeuwarden, Breda, and Hoorn.[37] In June 1958, once he had spent nearly ten years in prison, Queen Juliana, as part of a broader national effort to demonstrate compassion for wartime collaborators, commuted Bakker's sentence to twenty years, minus the time he had already spent incarcerated.[38] He was freed immediately.

Douwe Bakker died on May 28, 1972. He was eighty years old.

19

"THE LAST OF THE MOHICANS"

January 1944–August 1944

MEIJER EMMERIK, DIAMOND CUTTER, BERINGE

MONDAY, JANUARY 10, 1944—I went to bed last night at nine and stayed in bed this morning until nine, without a single minute's sleep. I just can't get over losing my wife. Though the people here are good to me, I feel very lonely. When I go visit Mr. Simons every now and again, a five-minute bike ride, that's all I see of the outdoors. Otherwise, I'm only in the house day after day, week after week, month after month, moving from one chair to another. Sometimes I lie in bed the whole day. Such inactivity can drive you mad.

As of February 13, I'll have lived this way for a whole year. I can't let go of the feeling lately that if change doesn't come soon, I won't make it to the end of the war. The only thing that gives me the strength to keep going is caring for Lena and the children, who will still need me very much. I haven't seen Loetje since the beginning of September, or Maxie since the beginning of August 1943. I don't want to consult a doctor because I'm afraid they'll admit me to the hospital. I can only hope that this breakdown will be fleeting.

TUESDAY, JANUARY 11, 1944—During the day I often sit in the living room, where their children often are. There are four now and a fifth is on the way.* The oldest child in the house is five years old, a little boy, who when strangers come, often comes to me and says, "Uncle" (that's what the kids here call me), "crawl under the table." Every time he says that, in his Limburg accent, I go into a fit of laughter. You see, I can still laugh.

PHILIP MECHANICUS, JOURNALIST, WESTERBORK

TUESDAY, JANUARY 18, 1944—With the regularity of a clock, the train departed once again this morning, but this time it was of course entirely different from the transports to Auschwitz, and also different from the exodus of the *Austausch*† Jews a week ago. This already seems to have happened months ago, so much has transpired in between. This time, there was a train of third-class passenger wagons with baggage wagons used for the sick, and animal wagons for the provisions.

The travelers could reserve their seats beforehand, especially those from the special Alte Kamp–Insassen . . . and could even deposit their luggage the night before. The infirm received cots with mattresses that had been specially produced for them. For the first time since the transport to the East, no Sperre was required at the barracks during the transport, so that those who stayed behind were able to accom-

---

* These are most likely children that Albertina was helping to hide.
† "Exchange" Jews, or Jews who can be used as "trading material" for German POWs.

pany their friends up to the OD cordon around the train, and there, as on a platform, even wave goodbye to those leaving. A kind of luxury train to Theresienstadt.

The word Theresienstadt already had a kind of magnetizing influence on the spirit, like Wernigerode,[*] or the Isle of Wight, or Capri. There is a fantastic story going around that it is so humane there that there are no barbed-wire fences, and people can live in little cottages and move freely about the grounds of an old fortified town. Some of the young people wanted very much to see a fortified town. And isn't it in Czechoslovakia, friendly territory after all?

How gullible people are, how naïve, so willing to believe that the grass will be greener somewhere else. People had to resist the impulse to try to join the transport, which had the appearance of a pleasant excursion. In the last year, people had become so accustomed to see the deportations in cattle cars that to see a normal train with passenger cars seemed to them like Mercy from Heaven. Or at least, they could see in it some kind of humanity, arousing gratitude, and regard the journey as a pleasure cruise. Had Fraulein Slöttke[†] herself not said this was a unique trip, "nothing like it will come again?" Had the Jewish leaders of the camp not said, Theresienstadt was the best that anyone could hope for? Weren't there also letters from men and women who'd been there for months, who had declared that they were healthy and doing fine?

So the train went off carrying men and women with heavy hearts that they were leaving their friends and Dutch soil, but who took comfort in the notion that they were going to a place where they would be free of the scourge of war, the cruelty of the concentration camp or the harshness of the slave driver playing boss in Poland. A luxury trip with some sightseeing. Even if it takes a little longer. On the side of the locomotive, painted in lovely cursive script in large white lettering,

---

[*] Wernigerode was a holiday destination in Germany.
[†] Gertrud Slöttke was a German secretary who made up the deportation lists at Westerbork.

were the words, *"Erst Siegen, dann reisen,"** and on the other side, *"Räder rollen für den Sieg."*[†]

Fancy! Hitler wants to exterminate the Jews. He has said so more than once. But he picks up Jews with proper trains to take them to a privileged place in Europe: Theresienstadt. He exterminates them in classes, just like an undertaker places the dead into the ground in classes. Those who go to Poland depart in cattle cars; those who go to Celle[‡] travel in passenger trains and are served refreshments along the way; those who go to Theresienstadt ride in passenger trains and are served only bread. . . . Hitler plays the undertaker and takes off his hat to those Jews who, in life, had achieved an elevated position.

TUESDAY, JANUARY 25, 1944—The storm was wrathful last night. It raged with clenched fists against the ramshackle, unprotected barracks on this barren patch of heath. It is so hard to believe that they weren't torn to splinters and the roofs flung off. During this wicked storm and pouring rain, a transport of another one thousand people departed for Auschwitz.[§] Again in cattle cars. The largest group, five hundred and ninety people, came from the S-barracks. The rest were young men from the Aliyah,[¶] old men from the hospital, and thirty-one little, nameless children from the orphanage, whose parents are either in hiding or have already been sent to Poland. Among these children, a ten-year-old boy with a fever of 39.9 degrees[**]—in other words, just one tenth of a degree too low to qualify him for the happy category of "untransportables."

A tidying up of the criminal and unwanted cases, who put a strain on the camp budget. Still, as ever, no one has any idea what happens to those Jews who are deported to Poland. They curse the National

---

* German for "First succeed, then travel."
† German for "Wheels roll for victory."
‡ Bergen-Belsen, a camp near the town of Celle in Germany.
§ The transport of January 25, 1944, included 949 people.
¶ Those who wanted to emigrate to Palestine.
** 103.8 degrees F, or just .2 degrees below 104 degrees F, a high fever that would disqualify him from deportation.

Socialists and try to find ways to express their feelings of disdain, disgust, contempt, and hate, but no one can find the appropriate words. People are powerless, they pile one word on another but end up with a sound of disgust: Bah!

"When, when will the war be over? When will the misery of these weekly transports end?" the women lament. "The war is going well, but every week there's another transport," the men scoff at those who believe that the war will end soon with an Allied victory. The winter progresses and the fear is that if there is no decisive battle this winter, the war will last through the summer and there will not be a single Jew left on Dutch soil. Hope and fear alternate: Where are we going, what is our lot, what does our future bring?

MEIJER EMMERIK,
DIAMOND CUTTER, BERINGE

MONDAY, JANUARY 31, 1944—I was with Mr. Simons until six this evening. Lena is looking well. I got ahold of an illegal newspaper from January 1944, containing a speech by the Queen, in which she confirmed that Hitler had unfortunately succeeded in exterminating all the Jews from the Netherlands.

PHILIP MECHANICUS,
JOURNALIST, WESTERBORK

TUESDAY, FEBRUARY 1, 1944—The transport has gone,[*] and we have the feeling as if our family has gotten smaller, as if our family has become poorer, that we have lost our good, our best friends who we had

---

[*] A transport of 908 people to Bergen-Belsen.

so wished to save, but had no power to help. We have the feeling that we are the last of the Mohicans, and we are waiting for our verdict, and that verdict will not be long in coming. We were not sentimental when we said goodbye, as at no other farewell, since we have that Dutch sobriety from our land and our language. But the tears well up in our throats, just as with every leave-taking, adding to the sea of misery and stirring up all our feelings of pity and revulsion that well up from our hearts.

MONDAY, FEBRUARY 7, 1944—Today marks the sixteenth month of my stay in the camp. I've had enough of it, more than enough. I know that men should check their pride, and judge their fellow man with gentleness and mercy, but I find myself on a fast track to misanthropy. I felt that it was a sin, and I didn't want to confess it to others, but at an unguarded moment I shared these feelings with another, most decent man, and he eagerly responded: I too have become a misanthrope here. And I never was before."

He had apparently been waiting for a moment to confess it as well. Just as I had. There are others who are becoming misanthropic, or have become so already. A mass of human beings, forced to live together under terrible conditions, is the most hideous, loathsome thing imaginable. It is a scandalization of human life, when the chaotic, immoral impulses of twenty, a hundred, or a thousand humans come together in a small space, and it is repulsive. Plain selfishness seeks its own way in all things great and small, without consideration or courtesy.

TUESDAY, FEBRUARY 8, 1944—Every week, I have the same sensation. Although I am not fated for the regular transports, at least not until now, I am never fully assured that no mistake has been made that will pull me into the maelstrom. I have the feeling that I stand above icy waters on a high diving board, with my feet on the edge, and that I, along with the rest of the camp residents, am waiting for the command: Jump! I am teetering on the outermost edge of the trembling plank, and see many others next to me also teetering, with anxious faces, many in agony. Only when the command is given will I know if I must plunge into the ice-cold water or if I can wait for another week. A week passes quickly. Others turn away too but still with thoughts of those who are in those waters, floundering about in distress, their limbs numb, wrestling with death. . . .

Most of the people who are still here were going about with a pass-partout in their wallets for Bath Celle or Bath Theresienstadt, and it was often a heavy disappointment that they must go to Auschwitz instead. As if people on a pleasure cruise bound for Madeira went off course, hit an iceberg, and fell into the water. People had not intended this, hadn't dreamed of it. Auschwitz was for the proletariat, the poor, those without money for a pleasure cruise, not for the rich, who had money to spend, or for the mighty, who could rely on their connections to vouch for them, and secure a place on the cruise.

Schlesinger* has been arrested by a military police officer. He didn't take off his hat when required to do so, and for that reason received a reprimand. This officer, like most of the Germans, doesn't like the German Jews, who kick Dutch Jews onto the trains, and he was pleased to teach their boss a lesson. Schlesinger was indeed belittled, and stood there stuttering and stammering while the officer was gloating.

Gradually, the Dutch Jews have become the majority in the camp. The Alte Kamp–Insassen number only about sixty. These days only Dutch Jews arrive at the camp, mostly found in hiding . . . With one more transport to Theresienstadt, the old guard of Kamp-Insassen will have disappeared.

WEDNESDAY, FEBRUARY 9, 1944—The transport of the sick from the hospital to the train yesterday defies description. The nurses had

---

* Mechanicus' protector at the camp.

to begin dressing the patients as early as two in the morning. The OD men brought an open cart with horses, and shoved the patients on their beds into it, as if pushing coffins into a hearse. Meanwhile, sleet fell out of the dark skies, covering the winter morning with mist. The patients were driven, bumping and jostling, to the livestock wagons, where they had to wait under the open skies to be loaded.

Children with scarlet fever and diphtheria were carried crying to the snake. Parentless children from the orphanage. Perhaps the beastliest transport of all the transports that have ever gone. One can become numbed to the spectacle because of its frequency, coarseness and brutality, but this transport capped all in terms of insensitivity to the sick. Before the train had even left the station, one patient had already died. They added an empty train car, reserved for those who would die along the way.

In the past, people fearing transport fled to the hospital; yesterday, people were seen to flee the hospital in fear of the transport. The doctors gave the word: Get out as soon as you can! Today about eighty patients have left the hospital. Barracks 81 and 82 have been cleared out. Barracks 1 to 6 still remain. Now the hospital staff suddenly greatly outnumbers the patients—more than eight hundred for less than five hundred sick people. They expect to be dismissed in droves.

Meanwhile the love for Celle and Theresienstadt is growing. Many who had tried to avoid such transports in the past now say, if Celle comes up again, I'm going. If there's a chance to go to Theresienstadt, I'm going. I will not take the risk that I will be sent to Auschwitz in cattle cars. Out of fear for the greater evil, men choose the lesser.

Some people hope that the long-awaited invasion will somehow intervene. Rumor has it that proclamations have already been posted in both North Holland and South Holland* stating what people should do during the imminent invasion. This is refuted. It's also said that a decree has been issued here that residents of the camp must prepare

---

* Two of the largest Dutch provinces.

themselves to march within two hours after the order is given. This is also refuted. People are most afraid that if the Netherlands is invaded, we will be forced to walk across the German border. And so one is tossed back and forth here, not knowing what to wish for; not knowing what to do, or not to do.

MEIJER EMMERIK,
DIAMOND CUTTER, BERINGE

WEDNESDAY, FEBRUARY 9, 1944—This evening, visitors came already at half past six, forcing me to retreat to my room, so that I was in bed today for almost 20 out of the 24 hours, since staying in the room without being in bed is impossible. Because I spend so much time in bed, the short walk to Mr. Simons' house, just ten minutes from here, has become a great ordeal. My body has become weak because of the continuous sitting and lying in bed. I'm of the opinion that the farmer could at least limit his visitors in the evening somewhat. Maybe by finding an excuse or other to keep the visitors away, and I expressed as much to the farmer this morning. I pointed it out to him because I believe I may not last if we can't do it differently. He immediately agreed that I was right, but he said he had not thought about that, and expressed regret for his failure, and promised not to do so anymore, unless there was some extremely good reason.

INGE JANSEN,
HOUSEWIFE, AMSTERDAM

THURSDAY, FEBRUARY 10, 1944—Adriaan took a tin of cookies to the office. Unpleasant birthday because of his illness, but we did get a lot of mail.

MONDAY, FEBRUARY 14, 1944—Mrs. Haefs came to drink tea here today; she issued a warning about Adriaan's disease, which rather shocked me. She was not at all comforting. It is already difficult enough!

PHILIP MECHANICUS, JOURNALIST, WESTERBORK

WEDNESDAY, FEBRUARY 16, 1944—I got a newspaper today for the first time since they lifted the mail blockade. The camp is enlivened: newspapers are passed around. People discuss the progress of the war based on reported facts, and the names of battle sites on the front. But they are dissatisfied because they feel the war is proceeding too slowly, the Russians aren't moving quickly enough. On the Italian front, the British can't advance, and with all the setbacks, the invasion won't come. And the transports continue with the regularity of a clock.

There are only 4,700 Jews in the camp and it seems that unless the war is over soon, the camp will be emptied and the rest of the Jews here will be sent to the East. We have expanded our hopes again *nolens volens** and would be satisfied if only the war would end this year, before the winter. The optimists count on mid-June. The newspapers are a blessing, even if they provide little salvation to impatient souls. They deliver us from our spiritual isolation. It seems unbelievable that the Germans should give us this privilege and then, after taking it away from us, return it to us again. Incomprehensible even for these thugs, who portray us as criminals so that they can exterminate us and set up England and America for war.

---

* Against our better judgment.

INGE JANSEN,
HOUSEWIFE, AMSTERDAM

TUESDAY, FEBRUARY 22, 1944—Unfortunately, Adriaan has a second lung infection.

TUESDAY, FEBRUARY 29, 1944—Adriaan was examined for the third time. He has absolutely no pain anymore, but he is critically ill. They think it's pleurisy.

FRIDAY, MARCH 17, 1944—Adriaan was taken away on a stretcher, attended by a kind nurse who had cared for him once before. This tragic moment was such a contrast to the day: the crocuses were blooming on the Leidseplein.

I was allowed to come along. They have set up a private room for Adriaan in the internal medicine department. Everyone there is very nice to him. Adriaan looked so serious, like he'd never return. He said that he would either be home very soon or that the radiation will take a long time.

SATURDAY, MARCH 18, 1944—When I got up this morning, I felt nauseated, and I was exhausted. I just can't believe it. I had a crying fit in the middle of the night at 3 a.m. I had a premonition that Adriaan will not come home to me. I received a few hopeful responses when I called the hospital at 9 a.m., but at 10:15 a.m. the nurse called to say he had great difficulty breathing. I could not get a car or a taxi. I called Krista and she immediately came to look after the house. I took the bicycle and went as fast as possible, trying to avoid the traffic.

When I arrived, Dr. Drukker told me that Adriaan has sarcoma, and that he could not be saved. When I went in to see him, he had just received a second injection, and he looked very happy to see me. I went and secured the bike and stayed there with him. Wil Brunet came, and also Dr. Reuter, who was very sweet to me. I ate there, only leaving him from 12:30 p.m. until 2:30 p.m. When I came back, I thought he looked very poorly. I gave him a little drink, and we gave one another a long kiss. When Mien came in, Adriaan's head fell to one side. Heart attack, surely. Luckily, he didn't suffer much.

I went home, stopping by the Van Kleefjes, who could call various people for me and let them know. I just can't understand.

MONDAY, MARCH 20, 1944—Met with Beijland B.L. of the SS to discuss everything for the death announcement and the funeral.

WEDNESDAY, MARCH 22, 1944—Funeral at 2:30 p.m. at the Nieuwe Ooster Cemetery. Beautiful flowers and wreaths. Dr. Schroeder came on behalf of the Rijkscommissioner, but not Mussert. . . . I didn't actually see anyone; it was like a bad dream. Bets Keers[*] stayed faithfully beside me the whole time.

---

[*] Elisabeth Keers-Laseur, one of the founders of the NSB's women's organization, the National Socialist Women's Organization (NSVO).

"A JOURNALIST IN HEART AND SOUL"

Group portrait at work camp Vledder, near Westerbork,
including Philip Mechanicus (front left)

Philip Mechanicus' last notebook, logged at NIOD as #15, was only half-filled when he stopped writing on February 28, 1944. His entry of that day began, "Everyone here steals, and no one feels the least bit of shame about it or blames anyone else."

The rest of the entry is a cynical assessment of human nature under conditions of scarcity, in which even those from the highest ranks of society are reduced to thievery. "The old norms of decency have faded or disappeared," he wrote. "In this regard, society is certainly rotten: the human type is no good. Everyone here is a robber on a small or large scale, but without being a criminal."

His critique was harsh but there was compassion in it; these petty crimes were motivated by hunger and food shortages that clearly plagued the camp. Boys raided the canteen in the morning, trying to snatch a few potatoes or an onion. They robbed pieces of coal for the fading stove. Their mothers were horrified by this behavior, Mechanicus wrote, and yet faced a quandary: "Discouraging means: a chronic shortage; encourage, and they stimulate a bad element, which could do them harm later, when they return to normal society."

It was evident from Mechanicus' final entries that circumstances had dramatically deteriorated at Westerbork. Food rations were insufficient, and inmates were desperate. "For weeks on end we have been eating cabbage of all varieties, accompanied by unpeeled potatoes, peat potatoes, very occasionally interspersed with barley soup," he wrote on February 27. "Small portions." Camp inmates formed long lines at the small shop that sold necessities like toilet paper and buttons. Only a few thousand people were still left at the camp.

After months of transports departing for only one of two camps, Sobibor or Auschwitz, two new destinations were: Theresienstadt and Bergen-Belsen, known to camp inmates as "Celle," for the town where it was located.

"Exchange material," people like Mirjam Levie, who might be swapped for Germans in Palestine, were destined for Bergen-Belsen, where they would be housed in slightly better conditions than other prisoners. Theresienstadt was rumored to be an ancient Czech fortress where inmates were allowed to roam freely. These were misconceptions. By 1944, both these camps were nearly as fatal as the "extermination" centers, because of the spread of diseases such as diphtheria, polio, and typhus.

Mechanicus spent his final weeks at Westerbork wrangling to be sent to either one of these two camps, and trying to get his girlfriend at the time, Annemarie, on one of these lists as well. He was aware of the system and the symbolism of the trains. "Meanwhile the love for Celle and Theresienstadt is growing," he wrote on February 9. "Many who had tried to avoid such transports in the past now say, if Celle comes up again, I'm going. If there's a chance to go to Theresienstadt, I'm going. I will not take the risk that I will be sent to Auschwitz in cattle cars. Out of fear for the greater evil, men choose the lesser."

After months of waiting on the edge of the cliff, Mechanicus finally got the news: he was on the list for Bergen-Belsen. From February 28 until his departure date, March 15, 1944, he wrote nothing in his diary.

He did, however, post a letter to Ruth. It was dated March 8, and it was brief, informing her that he was on his way to "Celle, near Hannover," where he would "await Calmeyer's decision," and he hoped that his case would be delayed as long as possible. "Many greetings to all friends, especially Mom. Bye, Dad."[1]

The following day, he sent another, somewhat more optimistic letter to both Ruth and Annie, announcing that there were clear signs of spring at the camp:

"The birds twitter and sing again; the crested larks hop across the terrain in search of food. The fields are still brown, but a spring mist shimmers upon it whenever the sun shines." He added that he was "often filled with a feeling of great gratitude," that he could still "feel their hearts beating" through their missives. As the world around him became increasingly "bare" he wrote, "I appreciate that I can still maintain contact with you."

He signed off, "Bye, until the next time! Paps."[2]

JUST 210 PEOPLE were placed on the March 15 transport to Bergen-Belsen, the smallest group of passengers to depart Westerbork on any train yet. Its passengers were mostly "special cases," including ninety-five holders of Calmeyer stamps—people whose categorization as "Jewish" was still a matter of administrative debate—as well as Palestine exchange certificate holders, and some people with dual citizenship.[3]

Although Mechanicus no longer kept a journal, among the passengers on the same transport were two other diarists, Renata Laqueur and Louis Tas, coincidentally, whose works would later be published.[*] They both described the trip to Bergen-Belsen in some detail.

The passengers were required to embark at 8 a.m., and Laqueur described the overall mood as "not too sad," because they had received a third-class passenger car with windows and seats, rather than cattle cars—a fact that made them feel optimistic. "We travelers, and many of those who stayed behind, expected a lot of good from Bergen-Belsen camp."[4] Louis Tas expressed a similar sentiment, writing, "Taking all the circumstances into account, it looked reasonably promising."[5]

The journey took a day and a half. "We were huddled together between luggage and clothes," wrote Laqueur. The train halted several times, sometimes standing still for hours. At one point bread was passed into the train cars, but sausage and jam also intended for the prisoners had already been eaten by the guards.[6]

---

[*] The Louis Tas diary was published under the name Loden Vogel.

At Celle station, the inmates were allowed to disembark, but they had to walk three miles to the camp. It was raining lightly when they arrived, as Tas noted in his diary.

"A gray drizzle made the sight of the gray-green barracks with their small windows, with shutters held in place by sticks, and barbed wire and watchtowers visible from all around, very frightening," Tas wrote. "When the barrier closed behind us, everyone, including my mother and I, who glanced at one another, thought: we are trapped and will never get out. The repugnant scent of rutabaga filled the air. The few Jews we saw seemed already marked by death, even though they'd only arrived one month before us."[7]

Tas described conditions as "not so bad" because prisoners were allowed to retain their own clothes and some belongings. Their heads were not shaved, and although men and women were separated into different barracks, they could visit one another for a few hours a day. For the first six weeks after arrival, the entire transport from Westerbork was placed in quarantine, as there was already an epidemic of polio at the camp. They were fed relatively well and didn't have to work at first.[8]

They were even allowed to organize a cabaret night, with poetry readings, performances, and short comedy routines, in which Mechanicus participated, giving a reading. The revue took place in early April, and Laqueur wrote in her diary that she felt she could survive if the war continued like this. But conditions quickly became dire. By the end of the month, she noted, "we were starving." The group left quarantine and was divided among the barracks, and their lives took another turn for the worse.

"Thursday out of quarantine," Tas wrote on April 25. "It's a shit camp. There is a high risk of dying here." He described the faces of the inmates as "leaden, yellow or green," and their bodies as skeletal. "There are two to six deaths each day, and since there are 3,000 people here that's a 20 percent mortality rate every six months, if it doesn't increase further."[9]

Slave labor was twelve hours a day, beginning with a 6 a.m. roll call, and a fifteen-minute lunch break, at which they were usually served kohlrabi soup, "no protein and mainly water," as Tas described it. He was on shoe-duty, a job that involved stripping the leather from used boots for other purposes. Tas was fairly certain that Mechanicus had the same assignment, but they did not interact until later that summer.

It is clear from Tas' diary that he admired Mechanicus. "I was very proud when Mechanicus told me how someone found only the two of us 'out of place' here," he wrote. "No greater compliment exists here."

Very little is known about the rest of Mechanicus' time at Bergen-Belsen. His final postcard sent to Ruth arrived in Amsterdam in April 1944, and was, unaccountably, written in German: "I'm healthy again after an infection. Lots of sunny days in April, colder now. Parcel receipt is allowed; please send sweets, cheese, smoking tobacco. Ask Vosje and Ben. Please write me a few lines. Greetings to all, Paps."[10]

After that, his pen went silent.

In October, Bergen-Belsen camp administrators announced that a "special" transport would be leaving soon, for which they were seeking volunteers. No more information was offered about its destination or what made it unusual. Rumors spread that volunteers might be part of a Palestinian exchange; many felt that, at least, it was an opportunity to trade up to a better camp. Mechanicus took the gamble.

The train, however, arrived on the morning of October 9, 1944, at the gates of Auschwitz. Three days later, all 120 passengers were taken to a "shooting room" with soundproof walls, where they were reportedly murdered at once.[11] Philip Mechanicus was fifty-five years old.

ALL THREE OF Mechanicus' daughters survived the war. Juul and Rita emerged from hiding in 1945, as did their mother, Esther Prins-Wessel. Ruth had been arrested, at the very end of the war, for resistance work and imprisoned briefly in the same house of detention on the Amstelveenseweg where her father had been jailed three years prior, but she was ultimately released. They all returned to Amsterdam, anxiously awaiting news from Philip.

A report of his death was a long time coming. The *Algemeen Handelsblad* printed the news one year later, only after all the facts had been verified by an eyewitness: "The suspicion that our colleague Philip Mechanicus would not return to us has been confirmed," it stated. A column-long obituary described his work from his first job at *Het Volk* in Indonesia, to his final position at the *Handelsblad,* and characterized him as "a journalist in heart and soul."

"The war would put an end to his career," the article concluded. "He became the victim of the Nazi practices that he had so often fought with his pen. In him, the *Handelsblad* has lost an outstanding employee."[12]

Seen in another way, however, the war did not put an end to Philip Mechanicus' career; he continued to work, as if "on assignment," for as long as he possibly could, even while a prisoner. And his career, as it turned out, did not end in Auschwitz, either.

Once the war was over, Anne Jonkman learned of RIOD's campaign to collect wartime diaries, and she brought her ex-husband's thirteen Westerbork journals to the Institute, handing them over in person to Loe de Jong. The diary was photocopied and added to the collection as #391. In its archival summary and review, most likely written by the discerning Sjenitzer-van Leening, it won great praise, as "Outstanding," and, "carefully and precisely written, the work of a gifted and seasoned author."[13]

De Jong was concerned about the fragility of the originals, and he warned Annie that "the ink is fading." He and Presser urged her to find a publisher. Although Annie was at first hesitant, Presser connected her with a start-up publishing house, Polak & Van Gennep, and she agreed.[14]

In Dépôt was published in 1964, with an introduction by Presser. It was one of the very first camp diaries to be released to a general audience after the war.

Completely unlike the other Jewish war journal that was already a worldwide sensation, Anne Frank's diary of her time in hiding, it was nowhere near as successful. It was too bleak, perhaps, and lacked the universal appeal of Frank's youthful voice. It was also less well-read than the wartime diary of fellow Westerbork inmate, Etty Hillesum. However, historians such as Abel Herzberg, Jacques Presser, Bob Moore, and Ad van Liempt found it to be an invaluable source. There is no other diary that describes life at Westerbork in more minute detail. It was reprinted several times and translated into English as *Waiting for Death* by Irene Gibbons, published for the first time in 1968, but it soon went out of print.[15] The Dutch version was reprinted in 1978, 1985, and 1989.

Today very few people, apart from Dutch war historians, are familiar with Mechanicus' writing. Maybe its publication was premature; maybe, as a Holocaust document, it was too upsetting, analytical, and cynical, for a general readership. Or perhaps it just described a horrifying reality that the public wasn't yet ready to face: a description of an earthly purgatory, and a very personal hell.

WHEN JUUL'S DAUGHTER, Elisabeth Oets, was a child and asked about her grandfather she was told only that he had "died in the war." Oets had assumed this meant that he'd been a soldier killed in battle, and she didn't ask more questions, sensing that the conversation was closed.

In the post-war period, Juul had married a non-Jewish man and kept her own Jewish identity to herself. She also decided not to raise her own children as Jewish, still fearful of the potential repercussions. The only Jewish cultural habit that Elisabeth picked up in her family home was eating matzoh with butter and sugar on Easter—a fact she still finds amusing.* At about age fourteen, however, she took an interest in her Jewish heritage, and bought herself a necklace with the Star of David.

"I showed it to my mother, and she was alarmed," Elisabeth re-

---

* These springtime religious holidays usually come around the same time; in Dutch the word for Easter is "Pasen."

called. "She asked me not to wear it, saying I should not let people know that I was Jewish. It influenced my life in a big way. I never felt free about telling people that I was Jewish after that. That lasted until my mother died."

Once her mother was gone, Elisabeth became depressed about this feeling of disconnection; she wanted to understand more about her family history. She'd known about her grandfather's diaries, which had been published before she was born, and she'd read them when she'd turned eighteen. "But they didn't make a big impression on me then," she confessed. "It was as if I had to keep a kind of distance from it, to try and protect myself."

Around 2012, however, she was talking to a friend and musical collaborator, a pianist whose father had emigrated to the Netherlands from China. They each had intense, complicated, and somewhat traumatic family stories to share. Her friend encouraged her to tell the story to a women's group they both attended, and Elisabeth decided this would be a good way to start to engage with other people about her family history.

She prepared a hybrid musical and narrative performance, with Power Point slides, which incorporated songs composed by a Jewish inmate of Theresienstadt, Ilse Weber. The first time she presented it to her women's group, she was astonished by the response. "It was stunning; half of the women were crying," she said. "They all said to me, you have to go on with this and bring it to other theaters and to other people."

So Oets developed the short piece into a longer musical performance, "Philip Mechanicus, *wachten op transport*,"[*] which she has performed at various synagogues and other venues across the Netherlands since 2015. "It really freed me," she said, "because all the reactions were so positive and so moving, and I only ever received really good energy around it. I also found some extended family members, and that was very nice, you know?"

---

[*] Waiting for Transport.

She was especially pleased to discover that non-Jewish people could appreciate the material, and that no one attacked her for presenting herself as Jewish. "At that time, I realized, why am I afraid?" she told me. "I realized that there are people who are anti-Semites, but I thought why do I want to be afraid of them. I don't want to, it's too much of a burden."

Oets thinks a lot about her grandfather now, and even though she never met him, she feels an intimate connection through his writings, which she continues to perform. To her, Mechanicus found a way to cope with life under terrifying circumstances. He returned to what he knew, journalism, and used it to liberate his mind.

"It was his *metier*," said Oets. "He had to write to observe what happened. I also think it was a way for him to cope with the terrible days at Westerbork. It was a means of survival."

PART III

TOWARD
LIBERATION

MAY 1944–MAY 1945

21

"I REALLY SHOULDN'T MISS THE VIEW"

May 1944–July 1944

ELISABETH VAN LOHUIZEN,
GENERAL STORE OWNER, EPE

SATURDAY, MAY 6, 1944—I'm sure that we will remember this day for years to come, especially when we come to the Stationsstraat. This afternoon at half past four, while walking there with little Marja, suddenly, I saw Ger. He was one of the first travelers to come out of the station. I could not believe my eyes. It seemed like a ghostly apparition. I just had never imagined he'd arrive like this. It was as if my heart stopped. But it was him, indeed. Baby Marja, of course, did not recognize him.

We went home in a hurry, and didn't accept visitors. By chance, Siny looked up through the window as we were approaching, and when Ger waved, she ran outside. The two of them were just so immensely grateful. I left them alone for a little while, taking Marja with me, so they could have some time together. But suddenly I felt as if the world was caving in on me and I became very tense, like I'd had a bad scare. When I told Mother, I broke down in tears. I had not thought it would affect me so much. Eight months away! He looks well, heavier and tan. Dick also is well, but he's had a more difficult time. When will I have him back home again? Nobody left the children be; everybody came charging in, giving flowers. The house soon became a flower shop. He doesn't tell us much yet about what happened.

WEDNESDAY, MAY 10, 1944—Today is Ger's 30th birthday. We had not dared imagine that we'd be celebrating together at home. It's also the fourth anniversary of the war. The Queen spoke on the radio this afternoon. The end should come soon.

MONDAY, JUNE 5, 1944—I received a letter from Dick today. He is very curious to know what Ger's homecoming was like. He said that two weeks ago, on May 21, he signed the *Schutzhaft*.[*] Ger says that as a result, he could be home within six weeks. We shall hope. We hear that Wim Houwink[†] was probably sent on. When we send him a letter it comes back with a note that says, "wait for forwarding address." All of them have gone to Dachau.

TUESDAY, JUNE 6, 1944—Herman came over early this morning. I knew that he had news. Those who live within 20 miles of the coast have been advised to evacuate. Official notices will follow. At around noon, everyone was talking about the invasion of Normandy. They say it involved some 11,000 planes, 4,000 ships, gliders, etcetera. People were also talking about Calais and Dunkirk. Could June 6 be the beginning of our liberation, and thus, a <u>great day</u>[‡] for our country and the history books? People call out to one another in the streets. Everyone is talking about it. They are warning that major cities, rail-

---

[*] *Schutzhaft* was the Reich's term for the arrest and imprisonment of political prisoners, without a court decision. Schutzhaft could not be challenged in court and there was no judicial protection against ill-treatment during this imprisonment.

[†] Willem Houwink, another member of the resistance, survived Dachau, and later became a renowned economics professor in the United States.

[‡] Underlined in diary.

ways and large intersections could be bombed, but we will get advance notice.

Minister Gerbrandy has demanded calm, and no sabotage. Resisters know what to do. Oh, how I wish that Dick was already home, but we'll wait patiently. Ger went to Zwolle for an examination; the after-effects of Vught have made themselves felt on his brain. They say he must rest. The doctor told him to lie completely flat for two full weeks. He's not even supposed to read for the first week, and after that he can use a small pillow. After five or six weeks he can get up again. He dreads it; we just hope this will help him. Siny is anemic. I'm exhausted, but I still need to call the insurance company. I must do it before Dick gets home.

WEDNESDAY, JUNE 7, 1944—Today was wonderfully relaxed. Almost no news, and no planes flying overhead. It is cold again and very rainy. Someone who was released from Vught came to tell us that four men from Epe were sent to Germany as part of a large transport. Namely, Vosselman Bosch, Scholten, Jonker and Bruynes. Wim Houwink was also sent on. We don't know yet about Leenhouts. Thankfully, not Dick. Siny and I are once again so incredibly thankful that Ger is already home. The Germans are mostly gone, the Landwacht[*] are leaving the Hotel Jachtlust. First, they claimed the hotel Zomerlust, then the Witte Raaf.[†] Twenty guests from the Witte Raaf must leave within 24 hours. The German forces will be stationed at Jachtlust.

THURSDAY, JUNE 15, 1944—Another significant day in our lives. Unexpectedly, Dick came home from Vught tonight. I couldn't believe it; I can't even describe how I felt that moment I saw him for the first time. I was in such a rush to get all the insurance work finished by June 15. I had a meeting today in Arnhem. . . . When people asked me when he would come back, I said, "If he's home by August, I'll be

---

[*] The armed forces of the NSB.
[†] All local hotels.

happy," but each day I hoped he'd be home. I thought, if he's arriving on the same train as my son, he'll be there now. So, I went to the train station, but he was not there. Ger said, Mother, wait two more weeks. Then I went home, feeling exhausted, planning to go straight to bed. I puttered around for a little but then I heard male voices. For a second, I thought it was the police, but then I heard the door of the patio opening and saw Dick standing there with Willem Holkeboer[*] behind him. He had, in fact, come home on the 9:30 p.m. train. It was wonderful to be together again. Siny came at once, as well as Pastor Ter Braak, Vos and Jonker. A stranger had informed Pastor Ter Braak and Siny. Dick was jubilant to sit in a soft chair and drink coffee with milk, after seven months on hard benches. Mother went home with Siny, to give us two time together alone. There was also so much to tell one another.

Dick said that the first two months had been incredibly difficult, and Ger seemed to be afraid he wouldn't make it. He had the flu and a fever of 40 degrees for three days. But the six weeks in the sick ward did him good. . . . He did all kinds of labor after that, digging, picking metal apart, and working in the post office. He had to sign some kind of paperwork that said he wouldn't reveal what happens there, but he'll probably share it with us anyway. . . . Dick also said that he feels no regret for what we've done, and that he would do it again. He looks well, only his eyes look tired. It is so hard to believe that we were separated for seven months. His prisoner number was 8474.

FRIDAY, JUNE 16, 1944—We talked a lot more last night. We are so thankful that everything turned out okay. We had so many visitors today, but they were very spread out across the day; lots of flowers from many people. Dick is enjoying freedom, our house, the garden and everything. We ate in the village and saw our children. Marja is now calling Ger "Pappie," at last. Dick still cannot believe that he is out of Vught; he shares a lot more of his experiences now. With the

---

[*] Another member of the resistance.

war things are progressing, but it feels like that's all just a backdrop at the moment.

MONDAY, JUNE 19, 1944—Dick says that he still feels like he's still completely in Vught. We will keep him away from all business until September so that he can rest. The whole experience has made a huge impact on him and now he can rest, which means he can relax, and he is sleeping a lot. We are so incredibly grateful that we have him back, and we are to be envied.

MIRJAM LEVIE, SECRETARY, LEAVING BERGEN-BELSEN

FRIDAY, JUNE 30, 1944—I'm on the train, and I still can't take it all in. I ought to look out of the window, since we're passing through a glorious landscape, but I want to tell you what happened. Briefly, in telegram style, because I really shouldn't miss this view. Besides, I do hope to see you in a few weeks, perhaps even a few days!

Yesterday, June 29th, emerging freshly washed out of the washroom at a quarter-past five, I saw Lübke (a Green) in front of Barracks 15 and people jumping for joy. I realized: We're leaving. Didn't stop to think, but acted. Ran off with towel under my arm, said goodbye to friends, realizing that there wouldn't be time later. Terrain cordoned off. From half-past six in the morning until half-past seven in the evening, four Greens went through every individual item of luggage. We left the barracks at approximately half-past one (we = the women). Crossed the main road, *Leibesvisitation** in garage. Didn't amount to much. Our luggage had to be left in the barracks.

The men's turn at half-past seven. Saw the luggage taken away on carts. At three o'clock in the morning we marched off, the sick and

---

* Strip search.

the elderly in trucks. The moment the barriers were raised is one I'll never forget. It was still night (three o'clock), and I had a bit of a cry in the dark. (I wasn't the only one, I think.) At five o'clock, after an extremely tiring walk, we arrived at Bergen station. Luggage a mess. Managed to retrieve a few things. At seven o'clock sharp, the train pulled out. Old second-class carriages, seven to a compartment next to open corridors, lavatories, in a word, everything we hadn't had for years. An armrest! Velvet seats! Nothing special in and of itself (e.g., no water, no sleeping facilities, the seven of us slept packed together *à la sardine*), but our standards have changed. The sight of shops, views of the countryside without barbed wire.

Our journey: magnificent doesn't do it justice. Through the Thuringian Forest, Hildesheim, Northeim, Göttingen. Mountains, densely forested and with a wide, sloping valley running through them. Sometimes with villages, sometimes with just a few houses. And with orchards. Every conceivable shade and shape of green, the bright yellow of corn, the red of poppies, the pink of clover. And now, the river Main, with a broad valley and the mountains, curving around the valley in a protective embrace.

The train winds its way through, revealing new vistas all the time, so wide and peaceful and lovely that I really ought to write about them, but instead I keep looking outside. Until now there has been little to remind us of the war, except this: No men, and those you see are in uniform (mostly SS), and female workers at the stations. In fact: very few people and no cattle in the fields. Notices at the railway stations: DIE RÄDER ROLLEN UNS ZUM SIEG, UNNÖTIG REISEN VERLÄNGERT DEN KRIEG.* On the train: VORSICHT BEI GESPRÄCHEN, FEIND HÖRT MIT.† That's all.

Würzburg. The people seem to know there's something special about us. At every station, people are leaning out of their windows to see the *Sonderzug*.‡ We are also given water and sometimes warm

---

* "The wheels roll us to victory. Unnecessary travel prolongs the war."
† "Caution while speaking, the enemy is listening."
‡ Special train.

milk and warm water for the Hartog babies. Our transport guards are fairly decent. One in civilian clothes (wearing gloves for fear of contamination), two in uniform. But I still can't quite comprehend it; I can't quite take it in. It's all too sudden. Nuremberg. Not bombed very often, but fairly battered looking. Dead, dead quiet in the streets, six people at a giant station. Our guard, in addition to the man in civilian clothes, consists of two Greens who, after each station, walk up and down the length of the train (I almost wrote barracks), counting. As if we'd run away. We're precious, you know.

SUNDAY, JULY 2, 1944—What we are experiencing is really worth recording in a diary. And it's only now, now that we're returning to a more or less normal society and we're slowly embracing the feeling that we've been saved, that we realize just how low we had sunk. Slowly, for we have such fear of disappointment that we dare not let ourselves go. Let me continue my story. The camp had given us: One *Kuch*,[*] half a pound of margarine per person and a tin of delicious, rich liver pâté to share among five people. But my stomach had grown so unaccustomed to food that yesterday, when we had to get off the train, I felt dead nauseous. We arrived in Vienna (at half-past seven, I believe), where we were met by about five Greens. We got off, put our luggage on the platform and waited.

But because I wasn't feeling well, I returned to the train and lay on the bench. *"Sie fahren als allerletzte,"*[†] the Green said kindly. *"Und bleiben Sie nicht in der Sonne liegen. Sorgen Sie dafür, dass das Fräulein im Auto sitzen kann,"*[‡] he said to the group leader. Treated like a human being! We're not used to it anymore. Really not. In a truck to the *Obdachlosenheim*.[§] A colossal building, stone staircases, large bright dormitories. Beds, not on top of and right next to one another, but separate, with clean, white sheets. A washroom with basins and

---

[*]   German rye bread.
[†]   "You will travel fast."
[‡]   "Please stay out of the sun and see to it that this young lady gets to sit in the car."
[§]   Homeless shelter.

hot and cold running water. And this is relief for the homeless. Normally, we would have said: Looks quite decent. Bare, of course. It was a palace to us. My hands hadn't been properly clean in months. A shower when we arrived. Food.

Curried rice and a mug of soup. All plates, spoons, etc., belonged to the *Heim*. We all received a meal ticket, which is punched. As well as a ration of bread. And the people, the staff, extremely friendly. Last night, Taubes delivered a speech, saying that, thank God, the conversations about thick or thin food are now a thing of the past. And he's right. We're learning to laugh again, are kinder to one another—in a word, we're becoming human again!

We're continuing our journey today and will shortly, at the request of the Turkish government, be inoculated. Last night the transport from Vittel, which is to be exchanged with us, arrived.[*] They were tremendously spoiled, private rooms, a park, only the best. And in sharp contrast, a transport of Hungarians arrived yesterday evening, which is just now leaving for Poland. Enough.

More on the train, I think. We're escorted by a commission: One man from the *Auswärtige Amt,* one man from the *Polizeipräsidium*[†] and one man from the Swiss Consulate. Thursday in Constantinople!!![‡]

LATER THE SAME DAY—In Hungary now, in a Mitropa[§] train, second-class. Just ate in a *Speisewagen*!!![¶] Stars of David off. Finding it difficult to write. Just taking notes. Forgot that in Nuremberg we saw the Halle where Hitler gives his speeches. I never thought I would see this place. In Vienna—soldiers. In Hungary—*puszta.*[**] A pity we are traveling through all these cities without seeing them. Budapest—suburbs

---

[*] In Vienna, sixty-one Jews from the Vittel camp joined the group of Jews to be exchanged from Bergen-Belsen.
[†] Police headquarters.
[‡] Istanbul.
[§] From the word *Mitteleuropa*, Central Europe: The company that provided restaurant and sleeping cars for different trains passing through the expanses of Europe.
[¶] Restaurant car.
[**] Hungarian plain.

in ruins. Three huge fires. We're in Újvidék* now (border of Romania and Hungary). Original route was via Belgrade, but too dangerous.

Yugoslavia after all. Indescribable. Traveling hundreds of meters above the Danube. Trees up to their tops in the water. Meadows in the middle of the river. On the other side, villages and small towns built against the rocks. Poor, poor, poor. Sheep with shepherds and a dog. Small horses. Women with yokes and two round baskets. All barefoot. Men stripped to the waist. We're waiting in front of a tunnel, are about to set off again, I believe.

It is now a quarter-past eleven. The train has come to a halt. Bombardment. Columns of smoke wafting toward us. Have the tracks been hit? Half-past one: We're still stuck and, taking advantage of the situation, I carry on writing. Until Vienna we were treated well, i.e., we had comfortable seats and enough provisions. We had no water, but the journey was generally quite pleasant. From Vienna onward it's all show, because this train will take us into Turkey.

THURSDAY, JULY 6, 1944—We are living a fairy tale. At the moment, we're on a boat, sailing on the Bosporus. Beautiful houses, too exquisite for words, and the water a shade of blue I never thought I would see. This is one big adventure. A newspaper. Parcels containing: Chocolate! Hazelnuts! Cheese! Egg! Fruit! Cigarettes! But there are downsides as well. We are *schnorrers*,† beggars. We're put on a boat, isolated from everybody else, and must live off charity. And we've acquired the mentality of *schnorrers*, i.e., we've learnt to beg and get everything for nothing. Perhaps we'll break this habit soon. And to think that we used to be the people who gave, rather than received, charity. Still, it's a fairy tale.

FRIDAY, JULY 7, 1944—The Golden Horn. Mosques, the sultan's palace, donkeys laden with baskets, beautiful round-bodied pitchers with narrow necks.

---

* Novi sad.
† A Yiddish word.

Lovely boats and sailing ships, but most impressive of all: the blue, blue water. We'll be on our way again tonight. And we're coming closer and closer to you. We now have a magnificent train, incredibly stylish and beautiful. Father and Mother have a sleeping compartment, quite extraordinary. And yesterday evening we dined with the lights on! The mountains with thousands of illuminated windows, the full moon. All equally beautiful and divine. Veiled women. Graveyards with rough stones. Rocks, wadis. Everything we see here is biblical. Traveling along the edge of the desert. Primitive villages, camels.

SATURDAY, JULY 8, 1944—In Adana now. At the station a plaque of Roosevelt and Churchill, who met here. We're riding through boiling hot tunnels.

SUNDAY, JULY 9, 1944—Aleppo. Breakfast, washing and showering in a tent camp erected by the British soldiers who have escorted us from Turkey. People are sleeping on the roofs.

MONDAY, JULY 10, 1944—Hama, Homs, Tripoli. Desert wind, tent villages, humid heat, snow-capped mountains. Beirut, Mediterranean. Ras el-Nakura (Rosh Hanikra).

PALESTINE!!!!!

22

"ALL THE TRIVIAL THINGS"

A crowd gathers in front of the Jewish Council's
main building at Nieuwe Keizersgracht 58 in Amsterdam.

Mirjam Bolle had reached the grand old age of 105 in April 2022, when I finally met her in person at her home in Israel. The day was sweltering, and Sonia and I had taken a taxi from Yits'hak Navon train station to her home, in a leafy district known as Talbiyeh, not far from the Israeli Knesset. The hilly streets of white stone houses were bathed in light, and a lovely scent of blooming flowers filled the air.

Mirjam came to the door herself, without the help of an attendant or a walker or any other means of support, and we were surprised to discover that she lived alone in a charming, spacious house, rather than some form of nursing home. She welcomed us into her living room, where the coffee table was arrayed with cookies and chocolates, offering us coffee and lemonade.

For about two years already, Mirjam and I had been corresponding by email, and I'd interviewed her over the phone as well, but I had been unable to visit her because of the COVID-19 lockdowns and travel restrictions to Israel. Our conversations were halting, conducted in a mixture of Dutch and English, and I had assumed that their bumpy nature had been a combination of translational errors and the usual memory hiccups associated with old age. But once we got to speaking in her living room—this time entirely in Dutch—I understood that I had misread the problem: her mind and her memories were totally clear. The only real trouble had been long-distance communication.

I could say that I liked Mirjam immediately, but it's more accurate to say I'd liked her already. Reading and rereading her letters to Leo, I'd become enamored with the buoyancy of her youthful prose, and the obvious chutzpah that animated her narratives. Reading transcripts of her interviews, watching her appearances on Dutch TV, and hearing anecdotes about her from NIOD researchers who'd met her before, had given me the illusion that I already knew her, a bit. No matter how many times I read her pages describing how she'd been whisked away from Bergen-Belsen, traveled through a decimated Europe and arrived in Palestine, I still cheered with her and wept every time.

Sonia and I were visiting Israel just a few days before the country's annual Holocaust Memorial commemoration, and Mirjam's schedule was rather full. "I have another interview later this afternoon," she told me. "And one tomorrow as well."

I commented that she was very much in demand.

"Yes, there aren't so many of us left anymore," she said. I asked how many survivors were still alive from her Bergen-Belsen exchange group.

"Just two," she said. One of them, she explained, had a mixed-up memory, and the other suffered from a disease that made it hard for her to speak. She was pleased to be able to tell her story, she said, as long as it didn't require her to walk long distances. "That's not really possible for me anymore," she confessed.

The first time I interviewed her in 2020, when she was a youthful 103, I decided that, rather than begin with talking about the Holocaust, I'd ask her about the moments of her life she looked back on with happiness and pleasure.

"Our wedding in *Kvutzat Yavne*," she replied. "The births of our three healthy children. My husband's promotion ceremony at the University of Amsterdam; his nomination as principal of the Maaleh High School in Jerusalem. The day our son got his wings as a pilot in the Israel Air Force." She trailed off. "I'm sure that I've forgotten some."

It had been a long time since Mirjam Bolle had been Mirjam Levie. The war had been five years of her twenties, she told me, and so much had happened then, but also, so much had happened *since* then. Although she'd gone to heroic lengths to preserve her letters and her notebooks, Mirjam said she didn't think about them again for decades once she'd arrived in Palestine.

"There were so many things to think about other than these letters," she explained. "There was the siege of Jerusalem. There wasn't enough food and we had issues with hunger. There was the curfew imposed by the British. There was every conceivable kind of problem. When the war was over, we had three kids to raise. My husband got work and I got work. I wanted to start a new life, and I didn't want to read the letters anymore." It was interesting, she mused, that people still wanted to know so much about the war.

CITRUS GROVES WERE the first thing the passengers on Mirjam's train would see as they passed the Palestine frontier station, through the coastal city of Nahariyya, on their way into Haifa. Lots of little white houses appeared between lush trees. Then, seemingly out of nowhere, shouts: "Shalom, Shalom!" The ancient greeting from dozens of well-wishers waiting for them at the railway crossing. As the train slowed to a crawl, the inhabitants attempted to hand food and drinks in through the windows.[1]

"There was enormous excitement," Mirjam said. "All kinds of small cars and trucks drove alongside the train, and the people were throwing grapes and chocolates and all kinds of goodies through the windows. Everyone was crying, how could it be otherwise? Something incredible!"[2]

Another passenger on the transport, Helmuth Mainz, had similar memories. "Many of us can no longer hold back our tears," he wrote, shortly after arrival. "We are deeply moved by the overwhelming warmth with which we are welcomed. At every road, house or factory, as the journey continues, these heartfelt calls are repeated; we feel that we are welcome here!"[3]

That miraculous, unfathomable train, not meant for livestock or goods but for actual human beings, stocked with nourishing food, had catapulted them to safety. It contained two hundred and twenty-two *AuschtauschJuden,* or "exchange Jews," who had been put on an emigration list by Jews in Palestine. It was nicknamed "Transport 222," but in fact there were more Jews from other camps who had also been allowed to depart on this "ten-day journey through burning Europe," as another survivor, Ya'acov Yannay, put it,[4] to an embattled territory in the Middle East.

The German train traveled through cities under bombardment, and as it was not marked as a Red Cross or another type of special transport, it could easily have become an Allied target. A few times, bombs fell nearby, but miraculously never hit. News of the arriving transport had been on the front pages of all the Palestinian newspapers, however, and everyone in the country had seen lists of those who were expected to arrive. Mirjam's name, strangely, was not on the list.

Arriving in an ancient city on the edge of the Mediterranean Sea, and facing the bewildering new reality, Mirjam recalled, "I felt euphoric, I couldn't believe that we were saved," she told me. Yet, she added, there was "an undertone of sorrow for those we'd left behind."

Many on board would not learn the particulars of their exchange until the 1980s. They had been swapped for an equal number of German Templars, members of a German Protestant sect that had established their own colonies in several parts of Palestine in the 1860s. Many of the Templars were Nazi sympathizers, and British authorities had been holding them in Mandate Palestine since the outbreak of war. The Nazis wanted them *Heim ins Reich,* "at home in the empire," and were willing to exchange one Templar for each Palestinian Jew in the camps. However, the Germans couldn't locate enough Palestinian Jews to make an equal exchange, because so many had already been murdered. A Dutch organization in Palestine, led by a Dutch couple from Jerusalem, Mirjam de Leeuw and Leib de Leeuw, proposed they send Dutch Zionists and rabbis whose relatives already lived in Palestine. At first, the British, who at that time took an anti-Zionist stance, rejected the proposal. But ultimately, they conceded.

Transport 222 was greeted by these wary British officials, the De Leeuws, and Moshe Shapiro, a member of the Jewish Agency. Apart from these few ambassadors, however, only soldiers were allowed to get close to the train in Haifa. The British suspected that some of the newcomers might be German spies, and they were wary of infectious diseases that survivors might be bringing from the camps. Rather than let the refugees enter the population, they were immediately placed on buses and driven down the coast to Atlit Detention Camp.

"There are moving scenes of reunion between the few who were allowed into the station and some of the arrivals," Mainz recalled. "Then we enter the buses. From all directions we are overwhelmed with refreshments, sweets and cigarettes."

When the caravan of busses began to depart, there were more shouts of "Shalom! Shalom" coming from everywhere. "We are met with rejoicing as if we are conquerors returning from battle. In our transport we sit almost in silence, we cannot really grasp that we have now actually arrived."[5]

Just before Mirjam's bus reached Atlit, it came to a stop. A man stood at the curb, weeping uncontrollably, as she recalled. He asked if he could help anyone, if anyone needed money. "We didn't need money, we were all just high, so to speak," said Mirjam. "But when he asked if he could do anything for any of us, I said, 'Yes, I don't know if my fiancé knows that I have arrived; and maybe you can let him know.' 'Who is your fiancé then?' he asked. 'He is Menachem Bolle, Kibbutz Jawne, at such and such address.' He replied, 'Oh, I know him because my daughter is also at Jawne. I'll write to him immediately.'"

I asked Mirjam how she'd felt being sent to a detention camp, with barbed wire and watchtowers, as men were separated from women for delousing, and others removed from the group and taken to the hospital, or for interrogation.

"Of course, I was a bit afraid," Mirjam told me. "But Atlit was totally different. We had clean beds; we had showers, the food was sufficient, and I stayed there for only three days. The officials were proper, if not very friendly. I had to answer two or three questions and then they apparently believed that I was not a spy."

Mirjam's medical exam found her relatively healthy, she said, but she was suffering from edema—a condition that causes swelling in the limbs—possibly the result of prolonged protein deficiency. "Most people were terribly thin, like skeletons," she told me. "But I wasn't. I had very bloated arms. I was fat, but sickly."

When she was released and walked to the gate, there he stood, dressed in khakis, looking just as she remembered him: her beloved fiancé, Leo. The weeping man had kept his word.

Rediscovering one another again after a separation of six years might have been difficult, Mirjam knew. "We both had realized that we had lived in two different worlds and that it was possible that our feelings had changed," she wrote to me in an email. "But that didn't happen. The moment we embraced, we fell in love as before."[6]

Later, she encountered a woman who'd witnessed their reunion. As she described it, Mirjam said: "They embraced, they embraced, they embraced."

DURING THE WAR, contact between Jews in the Netherlands and Palestine was not allowed, "not by post, not by plane, not by ship, not by telephone," Mirjam told me. "The only communication possible was through the Red Cross. We were allowed once in three months to write 25 words on a Red Cross form, that was censured and reached the destination after two months approximately." In these briefest of notes, little could be communicated. "It was forbidden to write about the war, about politics, etcetera."

During the year and a half that she wrote letters that she couldn't send, her reasons for writing changed. "When I began writing the letters I did it because I wanted to tell Leo after the war what had happened in the Netherlands," she told me, "but I continued because I saw that it became a kind of diary."

When she was in Westerbork in 1943, she brought the letters with her, but immediately realized that this was not safe, so she asked a colleague from the Jewish Council, who was still allowed to travel back and forth to Amsterdam, to smuggle them to her father's former secretary at the Netherlands-Asia Trading Company. She had stuffed them into a "swimming bag," a small tote with a cloth exterior that was intended to hold wet bathing suits and swimming caps. The secretary hid the swimming bag in the company's vast warehouse on the Hoogte Kadijk in Amsterdam's Eastern Docklands, along with other Levie family property. That's where they remained until the end of the war.

"Most of our property was stolen from there," Mirjam mentioned. Luckily, however, "no one had much interest in a woman's swimming bag."

Mirjam continued to write her diary/letters in Bergen-Belsen, but from then on in notebooks. "I'm vain enough to believe that this diary may be found hundreds of years from now and serve as an important source of information," she wrote one freezing January night at the camp, after a dinner of turnips and potatoes.

"That's why I included all the trivial things, because they may provide an outsider with a more vivid picture. After all, I'm so caught up in this that I can't put myself in the shoes of a person who isn't going through this himself and therefore knows nothing about it. Perhaps one day our children will read it."

Was it hope that she could pass these writings on to her children that gave Mirjam the gumption to smuggle the notebooks out, I asked? She laughed. "That was really stupid of me," she answered, "because if they had noticed, I wouldn't be sitting here today."

Before getting on the train in Celle, all members of Transport 222 had to pass through a series of SS security checks; all baggage was meticulously surveilled.

"The contents are examined piece-by-piece by SS people for any written notes, letters, notebooks," noted Mainz. "On the floor behind the tables there are mountains of paper. They leave us no mementos of our dead."[7]

Mirjam wrapped her notebooks in a shirt and threw them over the barbed wire. Her bag was searched, nothing discovered, and she managed to pick up the "satchel" before getting on the train.

ONCE THEY'D REUNITED, Leo Bolle took Mirjam with him to Jawne, a religious kibbutz in the coastal plain just east of Ashdod. They married there six weeks later. Together they would have three children, Chananya, Ilana, and Rinna. Mirjam's parents settled in Cholon, near Tel Aviv. In the end, they became, as they had planned before the war, Zionist pioneers in the formation of the state of Israel, and lived what she described as "quite a normal life."

They returned to the Netherlands for the first time more than a dozen years after the war. In 1958, Leo took a job as an emissary of the Jewish Agency, bringing the entire family with him to Amsterdam for two years, while he also worked as a senior lecturer at the Nederlandsch Israëlietisch Seminarium, a day school.

"We had a pleasant time in Holland, but we were overjoyed to return to Israel in 1960," Mirjam said. After that, they decided to visit briefly once a year, but it never felt like home. "I remember Amsterdam as I left it in 1943," she explained. "Not as the town of my happy youth."

The family faced tragedies in Israel. Their oldest son, Chananya, became an Air Force pilot, and he was killed in the 1967 Six-Day War. Their daughter, Ilana, grew up to be a private in the military, and died in 1970, when her Jeep rode over a Syrian mine in the Golan Heights. Leo died in 1992 of heart failure.

Six decades passed between the moment Mirjam stuffed her bundle of letters into her swimming bag and the moment anyone would read them. On Holocaust Remembrance Day in 2002, her sister, Bobby (who in Israel changed her name to Shifra Ron), lived at a kibbutz. One day, she was telling the children there about the Passover Seder her family had managed to hold at Bergen-Belsen during World War II.

Mirjam thought Bobby's story was incorrect. As she'd remembered it, they had celebrated Purim (the commemoration of an averted Jewish massacre in ancient Persia) not Passover (the festival of liberation from Egyptian slavery). The two sisters argued about the recollection, until Mirjam realized she could fact-check. She dug out the swimming bag and notebook, which another family member had managed to retrieve from the storage facility, and the matter was settled: Bobby, as it turned out, was right. It *was* Passover, not Purim.

Bobby, however, was fascinated to learn that Mirjam still had her war diary. She borrowed the entire entry about Passover and translated it into Hebrew to read to the kibbutz children. The children were transfixed by the material and asked Bobby to translate more excerpts. Bobby took up the task with the help of her own granddaughter, Adva Ben-Shahar; Mirjam's daughter, Rinna, reviewed and edited the text.

Before the Hebrew translation was even finished, however, scholars in Amsterdam who had read the diary at NIOD contacted her to ask if they could publish her diary as well. Mirjam agreed, and the Dutch version of her *Letters* was first released in 2005 as *Ik zal je beschrijven hoe een dag er hier uitziet: dagboekbrieven uit Amsterdam, Westerbork en Bergen-Belsen.* Rinna was the only one of her three children who was still alive to read the published version. Yad Vashem published the English translation by Laura Vroomen as *Letters Never Sent* in 2014. It has so far been translated into six additional languages.

MIRJAM BOLLE IS, almost without a doubt, the last surviving staff member and the only living documentarian of the Joodse Raad, the Amsterdam Jewish Council. Yad Vashem historian Dan Michman, in the introduction to *Letters,* wrote that Mirjam's unique contribution to wartime literature is her insider's perspective on the Council, which has been the focus of frequent controversies since the war.

"Mirjam knew more about the unfolding events than the other tens of thousands of Jews in Amsterdam," he wrote. "The letters are the work of someone who knew more than others—and definitely understood more."[8]

Established by Böhmcker's command in 1941, the Jewish Council had been forced into an untenable position as an intermediary between the Reich and the entire Jewish population of the Netherlands.

In the summer of 1942, this insufferable predicament became a horror show, as the Nazis demanded that the Council help facilitate deportations to "labor camps in Germany." While outwardly attempting to accede to German demands, the Council "shifted its priorities to preventing deportations and keeping its people inside the country."[9] It was rarely successful in these efforts and was accused of trying to preserve an ever-smaller cadre of upper-class, professional, and highly educated Jews, while allowing German Jewish refugees and members of the Jewish proletariat to be scooped up and herded away.

Because the Netherlands lost nearly three-quarters of its Jewish population during the war, Amsterdam's Council has sometimes been charged with greater failure than other Councils in countries where more Jews survived.[10] Could it have done more to rebel, resist, or simply warn its community? To what extent can the Council be blamed for the extraordinary loss of Jewish life in Holland?

Such questions have been posed repeatedly over the years, even while the occupation was underway, as several diaries reveal.

One of the most common misconceptions about the Council, emphasized NIOD researcher Laurien Vastenhout, who specializes in Jewish Council history,[11] is that it made up the lists of Jews to be deported. It did not, she said, and in fact, it did precisely the opposite: The Council attempted to protect as many people as possible from deportation. Its strategy, directed by co-chairman David Cohen, was nonconfrontational; he hoped to win concessions through cooperation.[12]

The occupying forces allowed the Council to make choices about who they could "save," a burden which became "desperate and corruptive," turning Jewish people against one another. This was part of a Nazi divide-and-conquer strategy, which shifted the blame away from Nazi leaders, as well as from the Dutch administration and Dutch population, onto the Jews themselves.[13]

Its aims were transparent to some people from the early days of its implementation. The former president of the Supreme Court of the Netherlands, Lodewijk Visser, who'd been dismissed from the high court because he was a Jew,* warned the Council not to do anything the Germans asked. He penned a letter to David Cohen in November 1941, arguing that it was the Council's duty not "to appease" the occupier, but "to put spokes in their wheels."[14] Occupation officials banned Visser from all his own Jewish community work; in 1942, he was threatened with deportation to a concentration camp if he did not stop; he died a few days later.

Meanwhile, no Dutch government intervention on behalf of the Jewish community came from the exiled national leaders in London, nor were there any instructions from Dutch civil administration officials at home in the Netherlands.

The Nazis had effectively cut the Jewish community off from the state, rendering all 140,000 Dutch Jews and some 20,000 German-Jewish émigrés stateless. This system of communal isolation and enforced self-governance was far from unique in the domains of the Reich. Establishing a small group of Jewish leaders to oversee Jewish communities became the *modus operandi* in all Eastern European occupied territories starting in 1939, as YIVO archivist Isaiah Trunk explored in his landmark 1972 book, *Judenrat*.[15] Similar Western European representative organizations were established in France, Belgium, and the Netherlands in 1941. Vastenhout found they followed a similar pattern, with minor variations depending upon their governing states.[16]

Whether appointed as "ghetto administrators" in Warsaw and Łódź, or as directors of large national Councils in Paris and Brussels, these organizations were forced to take responsibility for housing, feeding, advising, and communicating with often enormous, and increasingly marginalized populations. As Vastenhout found, they frequently had to respond to ad-hoc German regulations on the spot with little opportunity to plan or make thoughtful decisions.[17]

Trunk's six-year-long investigation of such bodies found that Coun-

---

* And chairman of the Jewish Coordination Committee, an organization set up to aid Jews during the occupation, but which was dissolved by the Nazis in October 1941.

cils across Eastern Europe tried many and various tactics to resist, forestall, or avert the German's murderous intentions. Yet, it is clear that Jewish Councils faced excruciating moral dilemmas on a daily, sometimes hourly, basis.

Believing that they had a measure of power early in the war, Councils in Eastern Europe issued petitions to seek relief from small acts of persecution, such as random arrest of Jewish men on the street, seizures of property, desecration of synagogues and holy scrolls, and regulations that prevented artisans from acquiring raw materials for their crafts.

Petitions rarely worked, but often, bribing officials did. "Because of the widespread corruption of the German occupation apparatus, bribery was one of the most common means of 'softening the hearts' of Nazi bureaucrats and of their helpers among the natives," wrote Trunk.[18]

When "relocations" or "resettlement programs" started later, Councils would try to mediate the release of deportees by cobbling together as many valuables as possible. "Sacks of gold, jewelry, and diamonds were given over by Council members," in Częstochowa in 1942. "Yet the deceived, doomed Jews were all put into cattle cars and sent to Treblinka."[19]

In Będzin in 1943, "Scores of crates with silver candlesticks, candelabras, spice boxes, Hanukkah lamps, and other valuables were delivered to the Gestapo by the Jewish Council. Three months later the Będzin Ghetto was liquidated."[20]

Ultimately, it became clear, wrote Trunk, that such Council interventions, premised on the notion that rescue was still a genuine possibility, did nothing more than serve the elaborate Nazi spoliation scheme.

In the early days of the war, Trunk wrote, most Jewish Councils shared the belief that the Germans would not kill those who proved crucial to their success. They often promoted employment in German industry as a possible mode of rescue, and frantically sought work opportunities for as many Jews as possible. There were even towns such as Łódź, Chełm, Skałat, and Zamość in Poland, where Jewish Councils established "productive ghettos" on their own initiative, to keep the residents there safe.[*]

Once the National Socialist genocidal machinery was in place, Councils faced "the most excruciating moral predicament encountered by a representative body in history," Trunk wrote, realizing that they could not save everyone.[21] For many Council members who survived, these decisions became a source of lifelong misery.

Jacob Gens, for example, was ordered to "reduce by half" the population of the Oszmiana ghetto, which had about 4,000 residents at the time. The Germans told him plainly that those expelled would be shot. Gens informed the Council, which began to negotiate with the Nazis, and they managed to drive the number down to 406, by selecting only elderly people who they said, "would die off anyway in the winter."[22]

"I don't know whether everybody will understand this and defend it," Gens said, but the attitude was, "rescue what you can, do not consider your own good name or what you must live through."

Such desperate dilemmas caused Council members great moral agony. Some committed suicide under the weight of the pressure; those who refused to cooperate were frequently killed and replaced with more compliant individuals.

Urging constituents to flee was sometimes the best option. The Jewish Council in the Dutch city of Enschede, for example, counseled local Jews to go into hiding, leading to higher rates of survival in that region. Some Eastern European Councils organized escape attempts into local forests, Michman said, and the next day the forest was surrounded, and everyone was killed. "It was a good, rebellious idea but the result was a disaster."

After analyzing the various outcomes of different choices, Trunk concluded that their decisions ultimately had "no substantial influence" on the survival outcomes.[23]

---

[*] Such councils may have underestimated the Nazis' determination to exterminate all of European Jewry, but it has been shown that, to at least a small degree, those Jews who did participate in the war economy were more likely to survive.

NEVERTHELESS, IN THE immediate aftermath of the war, Jewish Councils throughout Europe were charged with collaboration. Several provisional judicial bodies, known as Jewish Honor Courts or Courts of Honor, were established as early as 1945 in Displaced Persons camps in Germany and Italy to try those Jews who others felt had collaborated, such as Kapos, Jewish ghetto policemen, and members of Jewish Councils. More than forty trials were held.

In Poland, members of Jewish Councils faced a People's Court, *Sady Spoleczne,* established by the Central Committee of the Jews, offering such cohorts the opportunity to "rehabilitate" themselves.[24] Honor Courts in Western Europe, such as the *jury d'honneur* in France, which tried leaders of its Jewish Council between 1944 and 1947, similarly attempted to "restore internal cohesion to the Jewish community."[25] In spite of these efforts to reset or reconcile, historian Léon Poliakov wrote in 1954 that, "an indelible shame would seem to stick to these organs of collaboration." That was the general consensus in the post-war period, according to Polish historian Piotr Wróbel.[26]

Loe de Jong in 1977 called the question of Jewish collaboration "without a doubt the most difficult, most intricate, and most painful element of the entire theme of the Holocaust."[27] And by 1997, Wróbel concluded, "This aspect of the Holocaust is still far from settled."[28] Michman, interviewed in 2021, took the milder view that this form of victim-blaming was the inevitable consequence of the divisions imposed on the Jewish community by the occupying forces.

"As often happens, your anger and misery turns towards the person or authority that is behind what's happening to you," he said. "That's why, among Dutch Jews, the staff of the Joodse Raad were nicknamed the Joodse *verraad,* or the 'Jewish treason.'"

In 1945, Cohen and Asscher, who had both survived concentration camps, faced both government prosecution and indictment by a Jewish Honor Court in Amsterdam. This semi-judicial body of peers, which ultimately handled twenty-six cases, was organized, "to evaluate the acts of persons who during the time of German oppression have behaved in a way that is irreconcilable with most elementary principles of solidarity, which . . . could have been expected of all Jews."

Gertrud van Tijn-Cohn, who'd worked for Cohen and had been saved on Transport 222, accused Cohen of "selecting lower-class Jews for deportation instead of Jews from his own social class," charges that were later echoed by another Dutch survivor in Palestine, Salomon de Wolff, as well as a non-Jewish member of the Dutch resistance, Laura Mazirel.[29]

Cohen stood before the court in the early months of 1947. He and his lawyer argued that he had tried to act in the best interest of the community and had misjudged the murderous Nazi program. Asscher refused to attend the trial. The court ruled that both men were guilty of helping the German occupier "blackmail" the Jewish community into obedience, reiterating Nazi threats, and drafting Sperre lists. Their punishment would be excommunication, and exclusion from any future leadership positions.

Asscher and Cohen suffered a second blow when they were arrested on November 6, 1947, facing charges of collaboration at a Special Court in Amsterdam. Even among their critics, there was a feeling that the state had no place judging these two Jewish men. De Wolff, who had previously accused Cohen, wrote an opinion piece in the resistance newspaper De Vlam (The Flame), saying that to brand the two Jewish Council leaders as war criminals in the context of Nazi terror would be an injustice.[30]

Public protests ensued, and Abel Herzberg stood as their lawyer and defender in the community, but even though an indictment was formulated, the case was never brought to court. Asscher died in May 1950 as "a broken man," according to friends. He wasn't buried in the Jewish cemetery—some scholars say this was his choice, others say he was barred from burial there—and instead in a public graveyard.

Cohen, suffering a "severe collapse" in 1956, consented to dictate his memories of the war years to De Jong's secretary at the Institute, and granted Jacques Presser rights to use them for his research. In 1982, "under obscure circumstances" the magazine Nieuw Israëlie-

tisch Weekblad obtained a transcription and published his account for the first time in serialized form.[31] A few decades later, the entire 141-page manuscript was edited and published in a book by NIOD researcher Erik Somers.

One morning at NIOD, I met with Somers and asked him if working on Cohen's memoir had left him with a sympathetic feeling for the former co-chairman's perspective. He thought about the question for a while before he answered.

"I think that David Cohen was really naïve," he said. "That's for sure. On the other hand, he had a wrong belief, and I can follow his logic, in a way, that the war wouldn't last so long. When the Germans started invading Russia, most people were convinced that was the end, because it was impossible for Hitler to win a war on two fronts."

He added, "He tried to find ways to cooperate in one way or another with the German authorities because, he felt, if you shut the door, the Germans would do it on their own and they would be more brutal and more efficient in achieving their policies. He had the wrong understanding of the situation, and he was certainly used."

During a 1977 conference, Loe de Jong pointed out that the Councils were not the only institutional bodies in Europe that failed to adequately resist. Most people in occupied countries, he asserted, "obeyed the Germans." The Jewish Council, he said, like most other Dutch organizations, went along with the idea that cooperation was the safest and wisest strategy.[32]

Many of the moral reckonings faced by the Councils were predicated on the notion that they might have known or could have known or did know about the death camps and the gas chambers.

NIOD researcher Vastenhout said about 50 to 75 percent of the organizational records from the Amsterdam Council were preserved from its two-year existence. She has read much of it, but not all. I asked her if she'd ever come across any evidence that indicated that members of the Jewish Council, either the chairman, board members, or staffers, had been informed by anyone—the SS itself, or some rogue Germans or Dutch officials—about mass murders in the East?

"No, I never found a document like that," she said. Although such rumors were circulating, she added, there was "No smoking gun. The Germans weren't that stupid to cause that kind of unrest."

Michman confirmed that no existing scholarship indicates that any Council members in Amsterdam were informed by Germans of "the Final Solution." Mirjam Bolle also did not think the Council members had, or withheld, such information. "I don't think that the chairman knew more than he told the community," she said.

After a lifetime of reflection on the matter, Mirjam Bolle told me that she now feels the post-war criticisms of the Council were "too harsh."

Her perspective is that most people did the best they could under horrific circumstances. "I don't know if someone else would have done it better," she said. "I don't believe that the outcome would have been any different."

She added, "After the war, sometimes I have been asked if I was not ashamed to have worked for the Jewish Council. The answer is: by no means."

23

"THE SILENCE IS ALMOST MURDEROUS"

September 1944–December 1944

MEIJER EMMERIK,
DIAMOND CUTTER, VENLO

SUNDAY, SEPTEMBER 3, 1944[*]—Us Jews have received news that we had greatly feared. I heard a report from Paul Winterton,[†] an English correspondent on the Russian Front who witnessed the Russian attacks in Lublin, which went so incredibly quickly that they didn't even have the chance to save anything. It has become clear that the Germans, who at first murdered Jews at random, have now used their famous German organizational talent to set up a system to do it, and have created huge buildings for the purpose—which they've made the Jews build themselves. There were large gas chambers, incinerators and long stone tables in these buildings, which were used as follows: Large groups (i.e., the Jews)

---

[*] This entry was written from a hospital in Venlo, but it's not entirely clear why he has been hospitalized.

[†] A British war correspondent on the Russian front visited concentration camp Majdanek, which had been liberated by the Red Army.

must line up, and then they must take off their shoes and undress, and once they are all neatly registered, they must hand over all their gold rings to the administrators, and then they are brought into the gas chambers. Afterward, the corpses are placed on the stone tables and the gold teeth or their molars are pulled out of their mouths, and after that all the bodies are taken to incinerators and the ashes are used as fertilizer in the fields.

Paul Winterton reported that the complete lists [of names] and 800,000 pairs of shoes, plus those buildings, fell into the hands of the Russians. . . . The size of ovens of that nature had the capacity to burn 3,000 Jews a day. . . . He concluded his report by declaring that not only the perpetrators of these crimes, but also those who knew about them and kept their mouths shut, can no longer claim to be called human, and will receive their deserved punishment. I should also mention that the shoes that were found belonged to both infants and adults.

This afternoon the rector came to visit me again for a while. Theelen also came to see us and brought us all some delicious things to eat. Although it wasn't necessary for him to say, he said we could always come to him, while he arranged for the doctor to come to Kessels. This evening there were air raid sirens twice in a row, the second time the airport here was bombed. I didn't go to the bomb shelter this time, because I wanted to see it, a dismal but fantastic sight, the white phosphorus bombs came down by the hundreds.

MONDAY, SEPTEMBER 4, 1944—There was no air raid here last night and I slept quite well. It is half past one in the afternoon as I write this, and a raid alarm is going off while I am on my way to the bomb shelter. I hear from various sources that the Americans have crossed the Dutch border. The doctor confirms this, and he adds that they have already liberated Maastricht. It's unbelievable how fast all of this is happening, almost too good to be true. The people here are all firmly convinced that we will be liberated this week. God grant it! The air-raid siren lasted one hour, but no bombing here.

At 4 p.m. the doctor came back and advised us to leave today or tomorrow, if possible. I had agreed that the three of us would leave tomorrow. But then suddenly it turned out that all men and boys, regardless of age, were being taken from their homes and picked up from the street, and all put to work at the airport. The doctor feared that they would also come and remove the patients from the hospital, so he showed me a good hiding place. Of course, I can't leave under these circumstances. The whole day, I was on the lookout, but nothing further happened. I received a letter from Robert, in which he shared that he plans to visit me on Saturday, September 9. I don't think there will be any chance to travel now, because of the tremendous tension here these days. In any case, I discouraged him from coming.

TUESDAY, SEPTEMBER 5, 1944—Nothing special happened here last night, but there is such terrible nervous tension. We have been in the bomb shelter for hours, without air raid sirens. A lot of Germans are leaving the region, and I expect they will continue to go. They're retreating to Germany. Tonight, the Germans set fire to buildings at the airport.

INA STEUR,
FACTORY OFFICE CLERK,
AMSTERDAM

TUESDAY, SEPTEMBER 5, 1944—Now at last, there is progress! Tilburg, Den Bosch, and early this morning, Dordrecht. The next minute you hear that Rotterdam has fallen. By golly, they are approaching! . . .

Today I'm watching the exodus of the German sweeties and darlings. They pick up the devil and his old sister and drive them away in trucks, luxury automobiles and cars from the Red Cross with the wounded inside, with busses full of German women and NSB wives. Everyone. And everyone is leaving Amsterdam. A blissful tidying up. Suddenly, we hear airplanes. We dive away, under the assumption that they're snipers for the troops. We think that the English troops are approaching. Because according to "people" we should be expecting this at any moment. Alas, it is nothing other than shooting coming from the backs of departing trucks.

A train should ride off, full to the brim with NSB members who find it safer to run to (for the moment) a safer haven: Germany. Those lazy bums want to avoid their punishment, but that won't go smoothly.

At three o'clock we see the glint of an English airplane high in the sky. Just when the airplane flies over the train you hear gunshots and then the train doesn't move anymore. Four train cars burst into flames and there are about thirty-five dead and a hundred wounded. And then you hear nothing more. The silence is almost murderous. The transmitter silent, the radio silent, people quiet. No one says anything and no one knows anything. It is terrible. . . . How the people blather anyway! In any case, this knowledge breaks the tension a bit.

All the bicycles and cargo bikes that have been left behind are picked up. Public transit has come to a standstill. If this is going to last a long time, people will starve (or, indeed, there will be starvation). We won't be able to get potatoes very quickly anymore, just like we already can't get meat or milk. Things are going to get a lot worse. Gas is already being rationed and the use of it is limited. During the day we have gas from six thirty until eight thirty, and then again from eleven until one. And also, from four-thirty until six-thirty. Everything is just horrible.

MEIJER EMMERIK,
DIAMOND CUTTER, VENLO

WEDNESDAY, SEPTEMBER 6, 1944—Although there were still no more air raid sirens, the patients have been in the bomb shelter all night, until 5 a.m. I lay down on my bed with all my clothes on at 1 a.m. and slept for a few hours that way. During the day, there was an air raid here again and the patients had to go back to the bomb shelter, again until 6 a.m. I'm in my room. Everything that had been rumored here—namely that Maastricht, Breda, Tilburg and Dordrecht had fallen, and that they were on their way to Rotterdam—turns out to be untrue. I myself now doubt whether the Allies are at the Dutch border. It is strange that everyone claims to have heard about it through the English transmitter. Even the doctors lie about it just as much. In any case, it shows that people here still know how to fantasize.

THURSDAY, SEPTEMBER 7, 1944—Last night it was very quiet here, and all the patients slept in their beds. Today Maxie and Loetje turn three years old. I have given Theelen an assignment to deliver cake to the foster parents and I sent along letters from Lena and me. I'm curious to know if he's already done this. This evening I got to know an Indian painter and a mayor who are both recent arrivals here as patients. Today, for the first time in a while, there were no air raid sirens all day.

INGE JANSEN,
WIDOW, AMSTERDAM

SATURDAY, SEPTEMBER 9, 1944—Got myself a food ration card[*] and had the electrical meter fixed, so I can save some money when bathing. Had a nice lunch at Kempinski's. They still had all sorts on offer. How is it even possible! I'm so happy to live alone quietly, and not disturbed by anxious acquaintances. If I had had a telephone, then surely I would have been called all the time.

SUNDAY, SEPTEMBER 10, 1944—Mr. and Mrs. Van der Deen over for coffee, and sat outside in the sun, which was lovely. There is general outrage about how all the male members of the NSB are forsaking their duty; it is shameful for the Movement. Van der Zaande, Van

---

[*] For rations.

Balen, and the Spierenburgs* are gone. Luckily, Miep was sensible and came to drink tea, just like Mrs. Wijnmalen, who is trying too hard to stay friends with everyone, which doesn't feel nice.

MONDAY, SEPTEMBER 11, 1944—The situation is becoming critical. There is only enough coal to last a very short while. I have exchanged my ration cards [for food etc.], but my groceries can't be delivered. Starting tomorrow, the trams don't run between 10 a.m. and 4 p.m., and large factories will be closed. I went by Mrs. Voûte's home,[†] I heard that the Reichskommissar is so angry over the abandonment of so many men that he wants to fire them. Dr. Reuter made it known that the Allies plan to stage their decisive battle in the Netherlands. My poor country, God grant that the Führer will receive his new weapons in time! Received a very unhappy letter from Hermien; she feels threatened. I wrote to Ans,[‡] asking her to help her. Today delightful autumn weather. Drank tea with Miss Lindenberg. Bought some shallots and flower bulbs. Backer and Plekker have also fled, bah!

WEDNESDAY, SEPTEMBER 13, 1944—Today Alex made quite a bit of progress; the house is becoming cozier by the day. I picked up an emergency rations card. Not for meat, that's only for the sick, but I did manage to get a bit of sausage. The situation is the same in Belgium, there is a lot of heavy fighting, especially at Metz, Brest, and Le Havre. Still hope that we will succeed to stabilize the Western Front. Beautiful weather, and I ate at Kempinski's. In the evening bombs were apparently falling somewhere nearby; the house shook several times; very unpleasant!

MONDAY, SEPTEMBER 18, 1944—The so-called Hembrug [bridge] was blown up, Schiphol,[§] Schellingwoude, I could go on, a wish come

* Names have been changed.
† Probably wife of Amsterdam's mayor.
‡ Surnames redacted.
§ Airport.

true. What's really stupid, [however,] is that now there is a railway strike, so everything is going haywire. People apparently don't think about their stomachs.

THURSDAY, SEPTEMBER 21, 1944—I am largely fine, but idle; dined at the Westers tonight. I feel exhausted nowadays, maybe because of the great tension. The losses are enormous, it is almost impossible to fathom that a great battle is taking place so close to here. We hear that there are "only" 10,000 evacuees coming. I was just miserable every time I heard blasts coming from the harbor, which is thoroughly destroyed.

WEDNESDAY, SEPTEMBER 27, 1944—These are upsetting, hard days. I recalculated all payments since Adriaan's passing, and now I must go to the notary for the inheritance. Does our furniture in Nijmegen still exist? All those poor people there and in Arnhem; there is still heavy fighting. I feel desperately lonely, crying way too much, but I don't understand why I had to be left here alone in this hostile world full of evil spirits. People are blind to Bolshevism. I think it's shameful that anyone supports it—they will regret it one day. In Italy, Romania and Bulgaria they finally know what it means. I long for nice get-togethers, where I can meet a variety of people for a change, and not only women!

INA STEUR,
FACTORY OFFICE CLERK,
AMSTERDAM

LATE SEPTEMBER, 1944[*]—No one has gas and therefore no one can cook anymore. Or you must have a coal stove. Father has found a

---

[*] Undated entry.

way to make stoves. He can make them out of pretty much anything. After just a few days, everyone has heard about it. Neighbors, friends and family members of neighbors all come to our door with garbage cans, buckets, washing kettles and soap boxes. Can father perhaps make a stove out of this? Daily, father tells at least twenty people: "Yes, sure, that's good. Come back Monday to pick it up." And if they come on Monday, of course, it's not finished yet. Father can make two stoves a day at most. Still, he promises, "Come back Monday to pick it up." Then he gets into a fight. First with one, then with another. Until all the stoves are delivered and everyone is satisfied.

Ever since September 12 the trams haven't run from nine in the morning until four o'clock in the afternoon. That too. At the factory, there is a sign that says: everyone is requested to bring their own checkers and chess boards, because we aren't allowed to use the machines. Only the light is allowed to burn. There is a lot of idleness.

INGE JANSEN,
WIDOW, AMSTERDAM

THURSDAY, OCTOBER 6, 1944—I did everything at a leisurely pace this morning, and Justa came by; she was also not doing particularly well. Away for the weekend. Very heavy fighting is expected soon. The Allies are making every effort to march into the Rhineland and the Saar region as soon as possible. As of this coming Monday, no more trams will be running for passenger travel—nor in the rest of North Holland. They say that starting on October 15 the emergency kitchens will be operational and as of Monday we won't be allowed to use electricity! I don't relish the prospect. Well, as long as the war is won!!

INA STEUR,
FACTORY OFFICE CLERK,
AMSTERDAM

WEDNESDAY, NOVEMBER 1, 1944—Already for some time now, we've had no electricity, and every night I find it a little bit harder. At the moment, we have light from a carbide lamp, but we all get a headache from it. If mother is going to milk the goats (we have two large and two small goats), then she takes the lamp with her outside and we must sit gazing for a half hour in the dark. You keep your eyes open as long as possible until it hurts, and then you close them again. If we didn't have the goats, the children would have no milk at all.

Most people sit in the pitch dark. The few who have bicycles connect lamps to a dynamo.* You can also secure a dynamo to a pedal sewing machine, but then you must pedal endlessly if you want light. Or you can make a propeller that you put on the roof so that the wind will give it a little bit of current. Those with guts will try to clandestinely tap into power sources. But woe to those who are caught. That can cost you your head or your freedom.

Sugar and butter aren't available anywhere anymore. We eat dry bread. Bread without butter, cheese, syrup or jam. Brrr, the coffee substitute without sugar and with skim milk. . . . Food comes from the soup kitchen. We go with our bucket to our assigned soup kitchen, where there is always a very long line. There, you receive your three-quarters of a liter of food. After three days, we receive only a half liter. On Monday we eat thin cabbage mash. The day after, it's porridge, but if nobody told you it was porridge you would never know it. Only the pea soup is tasty, but even the pigs don't like the rest. You must swallow it down, and it is so little.

---

* Electric generator.

Meijer Emmerik,
diamond cutter, Beringe

MONDAY, NOVEMBER 6, 1944—I still see no real relief for us. It's been six weeks since I left the hospital in Venlo, and in that time, so for a total of 42 days, I have kept my clothes on every night. Every day, every hour, I sit and wait here for the liberation. One moment we are in the middle of the violence of war, and then suddenly the silence of the graveyard. And then back to the waiting. I find this to be the worst time so far in everything that I have experienced.

TUESDAY, NOVEMBER 7, 1944—Last night it was very quiet here and little happened today. Lena and Loetje have both recovered, but I seem to have a stomach ulcer, which is constantly causing me discomfort.

WEDNESDAY, NOVEMBER 8, 1944—Stayed quiet again last night, and this morning there were airplanes flying overhead, but our deliverance still seems far away to me. This afternoon I heard that the family that is caring for Maxie has moved to Ceelen, after the Krauts blew up their house. That is about one and a half hours walking from here, and now it has been five and a half weeks since we've heard anything about Maxie.

Tonight, the Germans came here again to steal a pig. Not a day goes by that some animal isn't hauled away, and if this situation continues for another 14 days, there will not be one farm animal left in Beringe. All of the farmers' houses and stables have been looted and plundered inside and out and have been totally destroyed. Now the Krauts have planted 9,000 landmines on the road, which on the one hand suggests that the Allies will be here soon, but on the other hand poses a great danger to us, because one of the landmines was laid just five-minute's walk from this house. The Krauts who were in the house today declared that if we are blown up, we can blame it only on ourselves because we stayed here. We will just wait and see whether that will happen.

THURSDAY, NOVEMBER 9, 1944—Quiet again last night, and it is unbelievable to me that here on the front there is a complete break in hostilities. Let us hope that it's the quiet before the storm. Tonight, again, I had a great deal of pain in my stomach.

FRIDAY, NOVEMBER 10, 1944—The night was very quiet. There are no signs of war here. Again, I had stomach pains tonight.

Elisabeth van Lohuizen,
general store owner, Epe

SATURDAY, NOVEMBER 11, 1944—Today was a very dark day for us. The forester came this morning and when I asked if he had good or bad news, his answer was "bad." They all have been caught. For a moment it was as if my heart stopped. Does everything we undertake have to be destroyed; can we not help anybody? We so bitterly wished for peace for our people. And now?

All kind of things went rushing through my mind, while in the meantime I tried to grasp what had happened. Very likely, someone betrayed us. Apparently, a number of agents provocateurs lived near [our cottages] and the woods were full of Green Police, according to the forester. All our men, except Hans, were staying in the shelter in the woods, along with Irma and Bep. The poor souls thought they were safer there, but now they've been discovered. It's so distressing, especially that this has happened now, when we're so close to liberation. How will they fare? I just hope they will be strong and believe that it will all end well, then they'll manage. . . .

There's nothing, absolutely no war news about our country. Roosevelt talks about a speedy liberation, but what does he mean by speedy? Most people are expecting an offensive near here just like in Metz very soon. God grant that it doesn't come too late for this small group of people. And so many others. The food supply is still rather poor in liberated Holland. Four planes deliver foodstuffs every day. All rolling stock must be made available for the troops.

SUNDAY, NOVEMBER 12, 1944—It is so strange to be a human being. Your friends gone, and they are suffering under such terrible circumstances, and yet you continue to live. You eat and drink and sleep. This morning in church I had such a hard time, because I could not stop thinking about them. Have they been mistreated? How is K., and how is Bep?

Last night, Els and I discussed all of this, how difficult it is and that you need to do your utmost to remain spiritually strong. Sometimes, I just can't see any light, yet you must continue to hope and believe, in order not to sink into despair.

MEIJER EMMERIK, DIAMOND CUTTER, BERINGE

SATURDAY, NOVEMBER 11, 1944—Last night it remained very quiet here, but we got word that half of Venlo has been burned to the ground. We left there just in time, although nothing happened to the hospital. The Krauts stole a pig and a cow again from here today.

MONDAY, NOVEMBER 13, 1944—The status on the front is still unchanged. Tonight, I had another fight with Marie, who involved some other people in it, including some of the other people in hiding with us. I was ashamed of this and so angry that when I went to bed sometime later, I was spitting up blood. Naturally, Marie was shocked by this and at least it had a good effect, which was that peace was restored, between Marie and Lena as well. That was necessary because lately they have developed an animosity between them. The rest of the evening I was feeling miserable.

TUESDAY, NOVEMBER 14, 1944—Last night I had very little sleep and was quite short of breath, but at least I haven't noticed any more blood. This morning I already felt a bit better, and by midday the doctor came. Lena had made sure of it. This one gave me a full examination and advised me to lie flat on my back in bed for two months. But I know for certain that as soon as I feel better, I'll get out of bed. At night, I ate a little bit of porridge, and until now I haven't seen any more blood. Whatever the situation is at the front, it seems that most of the Krauts here have left. It's said that they've gone back to Germany. This afternoon, a couple of young soldiers, about 19 years old, asked for sandwiches. They said that they'd been cut off from their unit, and so they couldn't get any more provisions. The troops at the front are also on the move and it is generally expected that the English will be here very soon. Let's hope that that is the case.

WEDNESDAY, NOVEMBER 15, 1944—A tolerably good night last night. This morning I was able to get up, which I was pleased with. Tonight, grenades whizzed all around our house, same as this morning. Lena went to Panningen early to pick up my medications, saying she would also try to find Maxie. She succeeded, and she brought him back here with her. I was so surprised! He looks fine and seems to be very healthy.

At one in the afternoon, the Krauts blew up an old and scenic windmill that has stood in that place for at least sixty years, and at 10:30 tonight, they blew up the tower of the church next to the mill. Everything happened just five minutes away from us. We heard a pair of horrible blasts, but the windows remain intact. Still, all these things suggest that we can expect the Allies soon.

FRIDAY, NOVEMBER 17, 1944—Last night there was a lot of shooting and we heard grenades flying over our house. At 8:30 this morning, all of us in hiding started to go downstairs, in the firm conviction that it was finally safe, but then two minutes later we saw Green Police in front of the farmhouse, and we all immediately climbed back up the ladder again. The Green Police were searching for men. They left after a while but of course we are now especially careful because it's clear now that they take all the men they can get their hands on back to Germany with them. While the Green Police were busy searching here, the Allies began their attack.

It is hell here now, and everyone, including us, has crowded into the basement. At 11 a.m., our house got hit. All the windows were blasted out and huge holes were punched through the roof. Just then, it started to rain cats and dogs and water was pouring in all over. My room, where I'd stayed for more than a year, suffered the worst damage. The lamp fell from the ceiling and now there are enormous holes in the walls. It is a ruin. If we had stayed in there, our suffering would have been incalculable.

At 6:30 p.m. all the little ones were put to bed on the straw mattresses in the cellar. The older ones had to stand, all packed in. Through the night we heard firing from both sides, almost continuously. This is certainly the worst day of our lives, the worst day we have experienced so far. We can hear that the English are getting closer, and the Germans are in retreat; they are fighting from the trenches around our house. Everyone here in the cellar is dressed, sitting or standing and awaiting the night. It is, in one word, dreadful.

SATURDAY, NOVEMBER 18, 1944—The night was full of booming. Until now, our house has not been damaged any further. Lena didn't manage a minute of sleep either. In the cellar it is cramped, and it stinks. At nine in the morning, we saw that various houses in Beringe were set on fire, along with many bales of wheat, rye, and oats by the roadside. The sky was tinted red, and there was a great deal of smoke. At around 10 o'clock, one of the *onderduikers* claimed that they saw English tanks on the road. I thought that his imagination was playing tricks on him, or in any case, that it would be too good to be true.

This afternoon, some grenades landed on our house again. When

I took cover behind a weight-bearing wall, shrapnel flew in through a window and hit precisely six inches above my head. There's a big hole punched into the wall where it went in. So, until this moment I have still escaped death. We are in the middle of a Boschian hell[*] and it will be a divine miracle if we all get out of this alive. All the women manage to hold out very well, but I still believe that they don't quite realize the danger we're in.

All of us now lie down in the cellar, fourteen children and eleven adults, and it is an extremely small cellar. We are pressed together like sardines. The noise is almost unbearable, the children cry and scream at the same time. It is a deafening noise. I haven't slept in the last 48 hours and I was only able to leave the cellar once for a toilet break. The atmosphere is terrible, because there are women with awful body odor, and there's a woman who snores so loudly that it's not possible for anyone else to get some sleep. We went through the night amid a hellish noise.

SUNDAY, NOVEMBER 19, 1944—Again, last night there was a lot of shooting. The only pig that the Germans had left behind was killed by a grenade. Around 6:30 a.m., it became a little bit quieter, and people started saying that there were no more Germans in Beringe. At 7:30 I left the cellar and saw various men from Beringe walking on the road. I went to find out what had happened and was told that we had been LIBERATED. The English were already here, and down the road in Panningen.

I went home to bathe and get dressed. Then I left the house and I saw a couple of kids wearing orange winter hats.[†] A few yards from our house, I saw the first English soldier, and I spoke with him a little. It is so hard for me to describe in words what went through my mind at that moment. If I have nothing more to expect from this life, then this will always remain my happiest moment. I will never forget the

---

[*] He writes, "We are in Hertogenbosch in the middle of hell," but I assume he doesn't mean this literally, as they aren't in Den Bosch. I assume this is a reference to a Bosch painting.

[†] In honor of the Dutch Royal House of Orange.

19th of November. Lena will also never forget. When I walked further into Beringe, I saw people in the street, their faces beaming with joy. If these people are so incredibly happy, how do you expect us Jews to feel, those of us who have been reviled and massacred? That is impossible to describe.

WEDNESDAY, NOVEMBER 22, 1944—Last night I slept in a bed for the first time since I left Venlo. And I was able to undress, after sleeping in my clothes for 57 nights in a row. Thank God that is over. All the NSB members here have been arrested. We were incredibly fortunate to have been able to hide at the home of a local farmer, because there have been no groceries available here since September 8, and yet we wanted for nothing all those weeks. The only thing we suffer from is the cold, because all the windows have been shattered and it is impossible to heat the rooms.

24

"WHAT DO YOU HAVE TO KNOW TO *KNOW?*"

What did the general public in the Netherlands *know* about what happened to their neighbors and compatriots, arrested in the night, rounded up in the daytime, in full view in public squares, placed on trains, and never heard from again? What did Jews imagine their own fate would be once they left Dutch soil? What did those who went into hiding believe would become of their deported family members?

Did anyone tell the railway workers who built the tracks where, precisely, they were headed, or inform the train conductors who drove the trains to the German border that their passengers would never return? Did the occupiers tell the police, charged with the roundups, that they would be murdered after they left Holland? And weren't those who cleared Jewish homes, or who took their possessions and businesses clued in?

What went through the minds of those peering out their windows from behind their curtains, as they watched their neighbors forced out with only what they could carry? What information did they have, and how much did they trust that information?

These kinds of questions—boiling down to what was known about the fate of the Jews—are some of the most frequently asked about the Holocaust. What did they know? It's referred to by scholars as "the knowledge question." It is linked to the larger philo-sophical issues, ethics and moral culpability. If they *knew*, why didn't they do more to stop it? And if, on the other hand, they could claim ig-norance of what happened beyond Dutch borders, were they released from moral responsibility?

The "knowledge question" has been a central point of contention in Dutch memory culture in the last two decades, because it is linked to national identity politics. Did three-quarters of the nation's Jews die because non-Jews looked away and allowed it to happen? If so, does this cast a pall of shame over the nation? Was criminal indifference the cause of the Dutch Holocaust?

The term "bystander" is an overly general category with fluid boundaries, but bystanders came in many forms, and took many dif-ferent political positions. "There was a wide variety of responses," wrote late Jewish Dutch politician Ed van Thijn, who as a child was hidden at eighteen different addresses. Although his parents were de-ported, he survived and later became mayor of Amsterdam.

"There were casual passersby who would see a Razzia on their street and deliberately look away, immediately blocking the event from their memory," he wrote. "There were also bystanders, usually neigh-bors, who, after the victims left, entered their homes to see if they'd left anything behind that was worth taking. Some spectators were deeply moved, as they spotted acquaintances among the deportees and tried to exchange a final farewell. For still others, seeing defenseless people taken away was a traumatic event that had a profound impact on the rest of their lives."[1]

Two books that raise questions about bystander knowledge were published in the last two decades, each taking a strong stance on the matter. Their titles alone suggest their positions: In his book, *Against Better Judgment*, Ies Vuijsje wrote of "self-deception and denial in Dutch historiography about the persecution of the Jews." Bart van der Boom's subsequent book, *We Know Nothing of Their Fate*, argued that ordinary Dutch people were uncertain about the Final Solution.

Vuijsje, after analyzing news sources for information, concluded that the claim "we didn't know" was a national myth. "What did the Dutch, Jews and non-Jews, know about the extermination while it was taking place?" he asked. "A lot, and already at an early stage."[2]

In his rebuttal, Van der Boom, using 164 diaries from the NIOD collection as evidence, came to the opposite conclusion. "Did the ordinary Dutch person know about the Holocaust during the Occupation?" Van der Boom asked. "The answer is: No. Knowing was not an option in the absence of clear, frequent and authoritative information." Although this statement sounds unequivocal, Van der Boom added, "They had no certainty, but they did have an expectation."[3] Had they felt *certain,* he suggested, they might have done more.

Vuijsje's book drew widespread criticism in the national press, with some experts dismissing him as an "amateur historian" and others arguing that *information* does not always lead to *knowledge.* Critics argued that media reports often weren't trusted. There were also social and psychological factors that caused many to disbelieve what information they'd heard.[4] Vuijsje didn't just attack "bystanders," who *knew but failed to act*; he also took the nation's leading postwar historians to task for failing to accurately characterize wartime knowledge.

Bart van der Boom spent a half decade working on his rebuttal, working with a team of student researchers to cull bystander perceptions from Dutch diaries, to assess not what "ordinary Dutch people" could have read or heard, but how they processed this information alongside all the other news and rumors they were hearing during the occupation.

Van der Boom was eager to navigate this question, he wrote in his introduction, "because it touches directly on our identity." He added, "The occupation has become a defining moment of our national past—the moment we had to demonstrate our worth."[5] He was concerned that the national identity was in peril, because contemporary historians and writers had replaced the "myth of resistance" with the "myth of the guilty bystander."[6] If "ordinary Dutch people" had known about murder-on-arrival in Sobibor and Auschwitz, and still been passive and indifferent to the fate of the Jews, the moral verdict would be dire.

We Know Nothing of Their Fate won a prestigious Dutch Libris Geschiedenis (Great History Prize) and the book was hailed in rave reviews. The jury praised the work as "brave" for taking "an unusual position," after deep study of original source material.

While Van der Boom's admirers felt that his analysis was a welcome tonic against shaming the population for moral laxity, these conclusions were subsequently met with a great deal of dissension from other historians. Controversy over the book played out for months in Dutch newspapers and international historical journals.

Van der Boom was seen by some as an apologist seeking to exonerate the nation, and give its moral identity a boost. "After the publication of this book the Dutch people were discharged from their collective guilt," Baggerman and Dekker wrote, adding that the book's initial positive reception "tells us more about the present than about the past."[7]

Both books must be situated along the narrative arc of Dutch memory culture,* which has been attempting a slow and bumpy reckoning over decades about the role of the "average Dutch person," or "bystander," in a painful national story.

ON THE MOST profound existential level, the concept of a systematic, industrialized murder of millions of human beings, including elderly, marginalized, and disabled people, as well as newborn infants, in modern Europe remains, in the most basic use of the word, *unfathomable*. That it happened, and it did, is hard to fully comprehend even for the most hardened scholars—which is part of the reason that it remains a source of continual, and often emotional, debate.

There are two separate issues to address when attempting to an-

---

* Sometimes called "collective memory."

swer the knowledge question: First, *what could be known*? What information got out of Germany; what news was circulating in the public, at what point in time, and where?

Secondly, assuming people did receive this information, *what did they make of it*? How did they process reports of genocidal mass murder in the context of other types of information, such as Nazi propaganda, reports from underground sources, rumor, and hearsay? Did they trust or doubt the messengers? And, finally, how did they psychologically process this unfathomable news?

To address the first question, we can explore at least some of the warnings and later news reports that more or less accurately described the Nazis' murderous activities.

Very early on in the war, there was evidence that Hitler's oft-stated plans to rid Europe of Jews could materialize as genocide. Jewish witnesses to violence, and their organizations, were some of the first to warn of German plans for Jewish annihilation, long before the "Final Solution" was officially instituted.

"We shall have to face the fact that under German rule two million Jews will be annihilated," warned Richard Lichtheim, head of the Geneva office of the Jewish Agency for Palestine, in October 1939 in a letter addressed to its London headquarters.[8]

As early as 1941, dozens of international newspapers reported brutal Nazi tactics used against Jews across Europe, as well as large-scale killing operations. The earliest reports came out of occupied Poland, which had been divided in two by Germany and the Soviet Union, forcing the Polish government into exile in London. Word got out of executions by firing squad, as well as gassings in trucks and mass graves at the first Nazi extermination camp, Chełmno nad Nerem. In January 1942, one of Chełmno's forced gravediggers, a man named Szlamek, managed to escape and reach a nearby small town, Grabow, where he informed the local rabbi and residents of what he'd witnessed, and he later made his way to the Warsaw Ghetto, where his story was written down.[9]

The BBC first reported news of mass executions of Jews earlier, on

June 2, 1942, because of a report by the General Jewish Labor Bund, which had been delivered to the Polish government in exile in London a month earlier by Leon Feiner, an underground activist in Warsaw. The report's assertion that the Jewish population was being "systematically annihilated" was also printed in prominent articles in *The New York Times* and *Boston Globe*.

Gerhart Riegner, the head of the Geneva office of the World Jewish Congress, alerted officials on August 8, 1942, in the United States and Britain that reliable informants in Germany had learned of plans for the Final Solution from Hitler's headquarters:

THREE AND HALF TO FOUR MILLIONS SHOULD AFTER DEPORTATION AND CONCENTRATION IN EAST BE AT ONE BLOW EXTERMINATED IN ORDER RESOLVE ONCE FOR ALL JEWISH QUESTION IN EUROPE.[10]

On July 22, 1942, Lichtheim wrote a letter to the organization's Jerusalem office to say: "The Jews in almost every country on this tormented continent live only in fear of deportation for the purpose of slow or swifter physical extermination or of slave labor in unendurable conditions, and their thoughts are focused only on saving themselves by escaping, a hope that can be realized in only a very few cases."[11]

In November 1942, Jan Karski-Kozielski, a Polish government emissary, had arrived in London to report to the British government on German atrocities in occupied Poland. He had twice snuck into the Warsaw Ghetto and witnessed systemized Nazi murder first-hand, after apparently bribing his way into a concentration camp. At that time, his report estimated that the number of Jews murdered in Poland already exceeded one million.

The first official international report that described "extermination camps" is known as the Raczyński Note. Written by Polish diplomat Edward Raczyński, who was at that time the Minister of Foreign

Affairs of the Polish Exile Government* in London, it was sent to all signatory governments of the United Nations Declaration.

On December 10, 1942, it was published in the form of a sixteen-page brochure, with the title *The Mass Extermination of Jews in German Occupied Poland,* printed in red lettering on stark white card stock. It detailed the unfolding Nazi genocide of Eastern European Jews on Polish territory, verified by an eyewitness account from inside German concentration camps.

One week after receiving the Raczyński Note, the Allied nations, including the United States, the United Kingdom, the USSR, Yugoslavia and the French National Committee, Poland, Belgium, Czechoslovakia, Greece, Luxembourg, Norway, and the Netherlands, issued a joint declaration explicitly stating that German authorities were engaging in mass murder in Eastern Europe.

Those responsible for this "bestial policy of cold-blooded extermination," it added, would "not escape retribution."

> Jews are being transported in conditions of appalling horror and brutality to Eastern Europe. In Poland, which has been made the principal Nazi slaughterhouse, the ghettos established by the German invaders are being systematically emptied of all Jews except a few highly skilled workers required for war industries. None of those taken away are ever heard of again. The able-bodied are slowly worked to death in labor camps. The infirm are left to die of exposure and starvation or are deliberately massacred in mass executions. The number of victims of these bloody cruelties is reckoned in many hundreds of thousands of entirely innocent men, women, and children.[12]

---

* In 1939, Poland was attacked by both Nazi Germany and the USSR, which divided the country into two parts, effectively dissolving the Polish state. Poland's legal authorities continued to function as a government-in-exile in Britain. Although concentration camps are often described in the diaries as being "in Poland," technically Poland didn't exist during WWII. The camps were located in German occupied territory.

The New York Times, among many other newspapers, published this statement, and the British Foreign Secretary, Anthony Eden, spoke at the House of Commons that same day, December 17, 1942, reading it aloud. Afterward, the House rose for one minute of silence in respect for the victims. That night, Eden went on the radio to share the same text with the world.

A French-Jewish hairdresser, Albert Grunberg, in hiding in a Paris apartment with no access to information except from a radio plugged into a neighbor's outlet through a hole drilled in the wall, wrote in his diary about Karski's report.

"It's not a complicated calculation for the Jews," he wrote, after hearing the story on the BBC, according to historian Anne Freadman. "They are simply to be totally exterminated so that no trace remains of them on the surface of the Earth! That's why the extermination is systematic and carried out in secret." He warned his sons, "Robert! Roger! Children! Remember! Always remember! Remember your whole life long the martyrdom inflicted on your contemporaries by the enemies of your race and of your nation!"[13]

WHILE THIS NEWS clearly reached some people, especially international political officials, did the average Dutch person read or hear such reports? From a practical perspective, how would they have received the news? Perhaps more importantly, how much credence did they give it?

German occupation forces had a firm grip over national newspapers, which were subject to rigorous censorship and used as a vehicle for Nazi propaganda, much of it anti-Semitic, racist, and misleading about the "labor camps." While we'd like to imagine that most people dismissed propaganda for what it was, in fact it often provided a powerful contradiction to real news, likely confusing and disorienting many people. Given the overwhelming abundance of misinformation that was circulated, how did the public know what news to trust?

Dutch queen Wilhelmina, during an address on Radio Oranje on

November 28, 1941, from London, noted, "Civilized humanity in all lands has been horrified at the horrific massacres inflicted on innocent civilians by Nazism in the occupied territories," without adding specific details. She understood that her people were under immense strain from the occupiers, and "how they arbitrarily carry you and yours into captivity and concentration camps, how they horribly persecute the Jews."[14]

This was one of three times during the war that the Dutch queen used the podium of her radio address to mention, in vague terms, the plight of her Jewish compatriots, according to communications scientist Jord Schaap. The other two were on October 17, 1942, at the height of the deportations from Westerbork, and then on December 31, 1943, in which she noted that the "destruction" of the Jewish community "has unfortunately almost become a fact."[15]

From 1940 to 1945 Wilhelmina gave thirty such public addresses on Radio Oranje, a nightly Dutch-language BBC European Service broadcast, which for most Dutch people was the only direct source of government information. But she never hammered out a message to her people that it was crucial that they do something to protect Jewish civilians or to prevent such "destruction."

"One might wonder why this very informed queen with all her German family connections, who highly regarded the radio medium as a means of reaching her people, did not do everything she could to help her people," wrote historian Nanda van der Zee in 2010, "and to warn them against the occupying forces via Radio Oranje, in connection with the Jews, preferably week in and week out. After all, she had that opportunity."[16]

In addition to hearing from "London," the Dutch public could turn to resistance media. At least 1,300 underground resistance newspapers, magazines, and pamphlets were printed in the Netherlands during the occupation, some for a short period and others for the length of the war.

Historian Jeroen Dewulf argued that the Netherlands had more underground newspapers than any other European country during the war. He wrote that this was because so many Dutch people saw their nation as "a stronghold of liberty against oppression and tyranny."[17] In fact, Dewulf argued, printing, both of underground news and false documents, was one of the *primary* activities of the Dutch resistance. While underground papers certainly had a sizeable circulation, it's unclear from diaries whether those who read them trusted the news they delivered more than they did competing news sources.

The average Dutch person tended to rely on what they called "London" for their information. That typically meant the BBC Dutch Service, which used the same studio in London as Radio Oranje, and broadcast across the English Channel. Jews were required to hand in their radios as early as April 15, 1941, and the occupier also confiscated all manner of radio equipment from non-Jews throughout the war, but still plenty of people, including Anne Frank, were able to get an illegal transmitter.

"If it's that bad in Holland, what must it be like in those faraway and uncivilized places where the Germans are sending them?" she wrote in her diary. "We assume that most of them are being murdered. The English radio says they're being gassed. Perhaps that's the quickest way to die."[18]

The entry is dated October 9, 1942, but only exists in the revised version of Anne's diary, which she began working on in 1944, following Bolkestein's Radio Oranje address. It's possible she'd heard about "gassing" on English radio in 1942. BBC Home Service reported on July 9, 1942, "Jews are regularly killed by machine-gun fire, hand grenades—and even poisoned by gas." But it's also possible she added that knowledge to her diary later.

The term "gas chamber" was used for the first time in a Dutch underground newspaper in September 1943, according to historians Dick van Galen Last and Rolf Wolfswinkel. Three months later, Bob Levisson, a Dutch lawyer who had escaped the country, informed the Dutch government in exile about "the systematic . . . and complete liquidation of all Jews in the whole of the Netherlands."[19]

Diarists excerpted in this book mentioned and quoted news reports from various sources. Douwe Bakker, as previously mentioned, often clipped and echoed Nazi propaganda sentiments taken from both explicit propaganda papers, such as *Het Nationale Dagblad* and *Zwarte Soldaat*, along with mainstream papers that contained German news agency propaganda. Elisabeth van Lohuizen cited underground news articles sometimes; she even quotes and clips a "fake news" item from the *Hamburger Fremdenblatt*, reprinted in the resistance paper *Het Parool* about how the Jews were requesting to leave Holland because of Dutch persecution. She knew enough to mock it instantly.

Meijer Emmerik reported reading resistance papers, such as *Het Volk*, and otherwise getting his news from his helpers. In December 1943, Emmerik wrote that he'd met a "gentleman" who'd "listened to the English radio station yesterday, which reported that the Krauts were now transporting the Jews who are in Poland in animal wagons. They are gassed in these wagons and then they are brought to the border of Ukraine where their bodies are thrown into large limestone pits." In September 1944, Emmerik related that he'd heard English correspondent Paul Winterton describe the Nazi death machinery with great specificity. "There were large gas chambers, incinerators and long stone tables in these buildings, which were used as follows . . ." he recounted.

These reports were actually rather late in coming—by 1944 word of death camps had already got out—and most deported Dutch Jews had encountered this machinery of death already first-hand.

TO MAKE HIS argument that people *knew*, Ies Vuijsje surveyed national media sources from the war era,[20] and found twenty-four mentions of the extermination of Jews in 1942. Three were in what he described as "legal press," while seven were broadcast on Radio Oranje, six appeared in *De Waarheid* (The Truth), a resistance newspaper run by a communist organization, and four were broadcast by London-based transmitter, De Brandaris.

In total, he estimated that somewhere between 750,000 and one million Dutch people had heard about mass murder directly through these sources, representing about 10 percent of the national population, which at the time was approximately 8.8 million people. "In addition, there were doubtless many who heard it from others," he wrote, concluding: "By the end of December 1942 the 'Final Solution' was not a secret anymore."[21]

Van der Boom's research indicated that at least some people were alerted; of 164 diaries his team studied, thirty-five "at one time or another wrote about Jews being gassed." They also mentioned other forms of murder such as mass executions or lethal medical experimentation on Jews. Twenty-nine of his 164 "spoke in relatively concrete terms" about deportations, among these twelve non-Jewish and seventeen Jewish.[22] After examining their comments about where they were going, Van der Boom concluded that they, "expected the worst, but not the unimaginable."

In making his case that people *didn't* know, Van der Boom argued that people heard conflicting reports that made them doubt, and in the climate of fear, confusion, and epistemic instability, they didn't know which sources to trust. Many of these diarists, he added, were skeptical about the reports they had heard, some dismissing it as "atrocity propaganda."[23]

"No one saw the deportations of the Jews as a harmless operation," he wrote. "It was self-evident that they would be poorly treated and that ultimately many people would die. The question was, how badly, and how many, and in what time frame? All of that was highly uncertain."[24]

Van der Boom emphasized the significance of this "uncertainty," arguing that a lack of intervention on behalf of the persecuted had more to do with doubt and confusion than with indifference. "Dutch Jews and Gentiles may have understood the genocidal intent behind deportations of Jews, but did not understand the concrete meaning of 'annihilation,'" Van der Boom wrote in *Holocaust and Genocide*

Studies magazine. "They largely assumed that the Nazis' boasts would take time to realize—time the perpetrators did not have."[25]

Not only did they underestimate the threat, but they also could not work out the appropriate ways to help Jews, because of all the mixed messages. Was going into hiding a better option than going to a labor camp? If you were captured trying to flee, you'd face *Moordhuizen*, be labeled a "punishment case," and shot. Going to a work camp might be arduous, but most people thought it was survivable. For bystanders, an ethical dilemma arose around whether to hide Jews: would it help or put them at greater risk? "People at the time did not know what we know now, which is that deportation meant certain death within a few days," Van der Boom said.[26]

The heart of the matter, however, was a question of Dutch empathy. Was the nation "indifferent" to the fate of the Jews, or merely uninformed? "It's an oversimplification to say that bystanders didn't help the Jews because they didn't care," Van der Boom is certain.

Because the nation struggles with what historian Remco Ensel described as "a bad conscience about the war,"[27] these questions of "passivity" and "indifference" still touch a nerve. Two Dutch historians, Christina Morina and Krijn Thijs, put together a book of essays in 2019, many of them directly responding to Van der Boom's arguments about how much the bystander "cared."

Historians Remco Ensel and Evelien Gans responded with two lengthy rebuttal essays in a progressive magazine, *De Groene Amsterdammer,* arguing that Van der Boom's assertion that people were unaware of the Holocaust because they weren't certain that Jews would be killed immediately is faulty at its core.

"Everything that preceded it—the anti-Jewish ordinances, the isolation, the roundups, the deportations—don't count in this approach," they wrote,[28] adding that the Holocaust didn't begin and end in Auschwitz.[29]

Diary experts Rudolf Dekker and Arianne Baggerman took issue with his use of diaries as source "data." "Diaries never provide direct insight into the thoughts of the writers," they noted. "In fact, it is incomprehensible that anyone who has studied 164 diaries still believes that such texts are an unclouded mirror of what the writer thought or felt."[30]

Dekker, who'd conducted two major inventories of Dutch diaries and other personal documents in the National Archives, added in an interview that such documents "can never be representative of a whole society. You aren't taking a Gallop poll, asking people a set of questions."[31]

IN TRYING TO sort through these various arguments, I'm reminded of Lejeune's observation that diarists must "collaborate with an unpredictable and uncontrollable future." The act of diary writing, in that way, is very much like the process of living life. We can never have absolute certainty about the consequences of our actions, or how terrible situations will play out in the future. While it seems to me that Bart van der Boom made his case that most bystanders couldn't have "certainty" that the deportees would mostly be murdered in the East, his logic doesn't serve as absolution.

Clearly many people, such as the Van Lohuizens and Miss Tini, knew *enough* to risk hiding people, and to work in the resistance, at great peril to themselves. People like Meijer Emmerik, Mirjam Levie, and Philip Mechanicus knew *enough* to do everything in their power to avert being sent to the East.

Based on this small collection of diaries alone, we see how people made choices that had an ethical and moral dimension, living history forward, within a vast sea of uncertainty. Decisions to act on behalf of others were not only based on "knowledge" but on a sense of moral obligation. When cautioned by a friend that hiding so many people was too dangerous, Elisabeth van Lohuizen responded, "Talking does not help; you have to do something . . . We will be careful, but we will continue."

What made the difference between a bystander like Elisabeth van

Lohuizen and others who didn't "do something," and for that matter those who took advantage of the vulnerable and persecuted? Although those who hid, and those who helped, and those who joined the resistance for altruistic reasons alone were indeed rare, they still were mostly "ordinary" Dutch people.

The United States Holocaust Memorial Museum defines "the Holocaust" as, "systematic, state-sponsored persecution and murder"—not merely the Final Solution, nor the successful completion of the Nazis' extermination plans. The decimation of Europe's Jewish community began as early as 1933, with Hitler's appointment as German chancellor, and the rise of the Nazi party. It lasted twelve full years, and encompassed a range of anti-Semitic regulations, beginning with the definition of Judaism as a "race."

Nor was the Holocaust limited to "extermination by labor." It was also intentional malnourishment, exposure, torture, medical experimentation, infectious disease, and a host of other fatal consequences of the camp system. The Holocaust was a process of degradation and pilfering that began with withdrawal of statehood, continued with isolation from the larger community and the enforced "branding" with the Jewish star, harassment, intimidation and humiliation, which left deep psychological scars on those who physically survived. Bystanders in the Netherlands witnessed many of these stages of degradation with their own eyes; other stages—with the possible exception of mass murder on arrival—they could have learned about in other ways.

"Although no one could imagine the gas chambers and the furnaces at the end of the line," wrote historian Nanda van der Zee, "no right-minded person" could sustain the notion that the "almost daily deportations of babies and elderly, handicapped, and insane people, right in front of their eyes, did not raise very serious doubts, even more so when the Germans labeled it as part of the 'Arbeitseinsatz,' the enforced labor-replacement program."[32]

The question is not really, "What did they know?" as Rudolf Dekker probably articulated best in an interview, but "What do you have to know to *know*?"[33]

The claim that one "didn't know," as Mary Fulbrook pointed out so eloquently in *Reckonings*, was used by many people who certainly could have "known," like the teacher, Marianne B., in Oświęcim.

"The assumption behind the claim of having 'known nothing about it' is, moreover, based on a disturbing distortion," Fulbrook wrote. "The 'it' about which nothing was allegedly known is reduced, effectively, to the gas chambers of the east. But the sheer inhumanity of the Nazi regime was visible all around. . . . And more was evident to anyone willing to see."[34]

25

"THE EMPIRE OF THE KRAUTS IS OVER"

November 1944–May 1945

INGE JANSEN,
WIDOW, AMSTERDAM

WEDNESDAY, NOVEMBER 22, 1944—Yesterday, I went to Mrs. Geerlings' house at Zuider-Amstellaan 45.* She had a vision that I would soon work in the hospital, helping the wounded. She saw that it would give me great satisfaction, and that I would feel at home there. She also saw another marriage in my future, which would be very good and would give me company. But she said that I won't stay in Amsterdam. She also had a vision about my financial situation, and it seems that I will receive some money to which I am entitled. So, it seems *very* noteworthy that today I received a letter from Professor Snijder, who advised me to contact the representative. He said he could mediate for me to take up the position of supervising the Dutch personnel of the Luftwaffe hospital. I slept, but only until about 4 a.m. because I was so excited.

---

* Mrs. Geerling seems to be a fortune teller.

THURSDAY, NOVEMBER 23, 1944—What is also remarkable is that a few nights ago I sat with Ma[*] and she told me that my life had come to a turning point; I am going to have a new life soon. And the night after Mad Tuesday,[†] I saw Pa,[‡] who also said, through a bit of a laugh, "But you can't stay here!" because I was so indignant about so many other people leaving. Peculiar, all of this.

SATURDAY, NOVEMBER 25, 1944—Ma[§] told me that my life is at a turning point, and that I'm going to get something new, and a man will come into my life. I see her regularly, and she is adamant about it.

SUNDAY NOVEMBER 26, 1944—I cooked early, took extra care with my appearance and my hands, sat down to read quietly, and then at 1:30 p.m. suddenly there was an air battle right above us, planes flying very low right overhead. Lots of bombing, I heard them whistling.

Later, it seemed like our house on Handelstraat was on fire, the Van Ammers house burned down completely. Mrs. Knierim suffered terrible water damage, very sad. The Euterpestraat[¶] was ablaze, probably because the S.D. building is there, but it was not badly impacted.

MEIJER EMMERIK, DIAMOND CUTTER, EINDHOVEN

MONDAY, NOVEMBER 27, 1944—Last night I slept in a wonderful bed, but that's all I can say about this place. There's no food avail-

---

[*] It seems that she's speaking with her dead mother.
[†] A day in September 1944, known as Dolle Dinsdag, when a rumor spread throughout the Netherlands that the war was over, and people celebrated.
[‡] It appears that her father died many years earlier, so this may be a vision.
[§] Again, a conversation with a ghost, it seems.
[¶] The main offices of the Sicherheitsdienst and the Gestapo, as well as the offices of the Central Office for Jewish Emigration, which organized deportations, were on the Euterpestraat.

able, and there's nothing to buy, not even a warm drink, only a glass of beer. I went out early this morning to try to arrange papers to go to Belgium, and to get some ration coupons.

Going to Belgium is very difficult. They'll only give you permission if it is "in the national interest" or for military purposes, but I persisted until the afternoon. With a great deal of effort, I managed to get admission for 14 days, but now getting there will be the issue, because transportation is only allowed by car, and I am not allowed to rent a car. Now I must wait until someone is going to Antwerp by order of the government, and that's what I'll have to settle for. I am now preparing to leave this Friday, December 1 at 8 a.m. I've arranged a car to go to Hasselt, and from there I must continue by train to Antwerp. I just have to hope that everything goes according to plan.

FRIDAY, DECEMBER 1, 1944—After a somewhat sleepless night, I woke up very early to make it to the appointed place this morning, so I would be taken to Hasselt in Belgium. When I got there, the car wasn't there, and after it finally arrived, I had to wait until 11 a.m. for it to leave, while it had been there at 7:30 a.m. It turned out to be a truck, which was transporting empty boxes, so I took the ride to Hasselt in an open wagon sitting on a couple of boxes. I was very lucky that it didn't rain, but I was still numb with cold by the time I arrived around 2:30 p.m. I found out that I could take a train directly to Antwerp at 3:30 p.m., and if I'd have known then what would happen to me on this journey I would've turned right around and gone back to Eindhoven.

When I bought my rail ticket, I was told that I had to reach Antwerp via Brussels, and when asked what time I could arrive in Antwerp, they said 8 p.m. During the journey, it became clear to me why it would take so long. Someone in Eindhoven had already told me that Antwerp was under heavy V-1[*] fire.

Once I was on the train, I heard so many stories about the V-1 and

---

[*]   V-1s were German unmanned jets or flying bombs.

V-2 that my hair stood on end. I was never afraid during this war, but I must confess that after having coped with all these things, I was not at all at ease. During the trip I became convinced that all these stories were true; I saw twenty-seven V-1 bombs above and around Antwerp. I saw one explode and one crash on fire into the city, where I got on the train. I'll admit that I was quite afraid then, but I couldn't really perceive the effect on Antwerp yet. It must be terrible, but I will see more tomorrow.

As to my journey, the train left Hasselt at 4 p.m. . . . and I arrived in Leuven at 7:30 p.m., where the burning V-1 bomb had fallen; as it turned out, no more than 100 meters from the station, and entire streets were wiped out. At 8 p.m. I left Leuven for Mechelen, where I arrived at 9:15 p.m. I didn't go to Brussels from there, but had to change again at Duffel, which is close to Antwerp. I had to get off the train because a V-1 had destroyed the bridge. I had to lug my suitcases for twenty minutes to another train and left for Oude God, a suburb of Antwerp. . . . From there I caught a tram to the center of Antwerp . . . , and had to haul my suitcases another twenty minutes before I found a hotel. It was almost midnight when I finally got to my room, feeling more dead than alive.

INGE JANSEN,
WIDOW, AMSTERDAM

FRIDAY, DECEMBER 1, 1944—I arrived at the Lazarett with great difficulty, as it was cordoned off. . . . I met Head Field Doctor Bölzich, a tall, handsome man with the sweetest face and true-blue eyes. I hope that I won't fall in love with him. I truly dread it. However, the results were disappointing: my letter was apparently held up with Dr. Schröder for too long, and because of the delay, someone else was already appointed. I came home crying, felt very down.

SATURDAY, DECEMBER 2, 1944—Glerum came for coffee, my house is still a ruin. He was very upset about the coming raid and was also very concerned about the famine. Attended a lovely concert of harpist Phia den Hertog-Berkhout, "Two Dances" by Debussy. Also, wonderful music from Rossini's overture from La Scala di Seta and Dvořák's 4th Symphony, modern music.

Some time later, I found Eva packed, sitting with her baggage on the stairs. We chatted for an hour. She has been transferred to another department, not been sweet enough to her boss. Bah! She has a proper boyfriend now, an army major from Baarn. Good for her. Had some cocktails at the Hermans', where I met an S.D. man named Heijting. . . .

SUNDAY, DECEMBER 3, 1944—This morning, I cooked a lot, tried on various pairs of shoes. Arrived late at the concert, a Beethoven matinée, 8th symphony and Ferdinand Hellmann played the violin divinely. Walked a fair distance with Eva in the pouring rain. Later, the Van der Doesens came for drinks. After Carel Piek's appointment as Secretary General of the Netherlands, the entire board of the Red Cross resigned and Banning went into hiding. Not very pleasant, all of this.

I suspect Olly and Daphne will also be forced to leave Amsterdam. The Jeugdstorm has been re-established in Berlin as "Germanische Jugend,"[*] which is part of the Hajot division. Everything is moving fast toward unification. I don't believe we're going to come under Dutch leadership again. I received a gloomy letter from Mien, who is apparently discouraged since she had greatly hoped for a speedy Allied victory.

MONDAY, DECEMBER 4, 1944—Really enjoyed singing this morning, while the sun was shining into the room, so it was absolutely not cold.

---

[*] A Hitler Youth group that was meant to unite the youth of all Germanic countries.

Lots of planes flying over again this morning and, in the afternoon, heavy shooting all of a sudden. Corrie saw a plane shot down. Finally, the plants are here, great. I retrieved the flared velvet dress and took in an old blue shoe for repair. Otherwise I wouldn't be able to use it anymore. Went briefly out in the cold to Mrs. Matthijssen and called Dr. Schröder in vain. Prof. Snijder had already spoken with him, so I should hear more from him tomorrow. Heard that the potato harvesters also must work on Wehrmacht's territory; some refused to do so and were told they'd be shot if they didn't. Some were sent to Germany. Truus Oltmanns was angry that Bob was not back yet. They burst open the Rijndijk south-west of Arnhem, so that everything between Nijmegen and Arnhem is now under water. Our poor country, everything is being destroyed.

TUESDAY, DECEMBER 5, 1944—

It was out of love that the Almighty sent us suffering
Be patient contending with difficulties and wait for better
  times;
The sorrow is heavy, blessed is its fruit.

—Jacob van Lennep

Today, the air raid sirens sounded several times again. Made it cozy for Snijder's visit. I was very surprised when I saw him; instead of a venerable older man, a young, handsome officer stood before me in German SS uniform. Very pleasant conversation, and he stayed for almost three hours. I could speak very freely with him. I hope that I will see more of him. I seem to have a "man storm" coming; I wonder how it will go at the Lazarett, because I must go to Prof. Hessel. It seems kitchen supervision is necessary. What a beautiful quote above!

THURSDAY, DECEMBER 7, 1944—I am really a little upset at my sudden feelings for Snijder. My, have I told him a great deal! Strange that something like this can happen so suddenly. Elsie came over with sandwiches, which was very nice, but she is certainly a bit wild. I told her a little about Mussert's behavior and his views. Did some wonderfully relaxed sewing, stayed at home. The De Ruiters are in jail cells in Elst. It's just terrible for their children. Such bad things are happening everywhere.

FRIDAY, DECEMBER 8, 1944— . . . Foul weather today, some snow, and quite cold. Went to the salon to have a haircut and a facial, before I went to Prof. Hessel's punctually 12 o'clock. What a genteel man; he picked me up from the waiting room and accompanied me down again with the elevator. . . . They will send me a letter. I received a note from Claartje saying that her house was nearly destroyed by a misfired V-1. How unlucky. There is no more gas or electricity in Delft, only at her father's house of course. In The Hague, stores were looted last week; here, bakery carts this morning. We receive 1,000 grams of bread per week, no flour or grits anymore, 2 kilos of potatoes, half an ounce of cheese, no meat, no jam or sugar. It's becoming dire!

MONDAY, DECEMBER 11, 1944—Just spoke to Eveline Hermans, who has also had enough of sitting in the kitchen and is seeking work as a pharmacist's assistant. Very mild weather. Again and again, it is very cold and then all of a sudden spring temperatures. I have such a great desire to see Prof. Snijder again.

TUESDAY, DECEMBER 12, 1944—Still no news from the Lazarett, enormously annoying and I can't do anything to speed it up. Had tea at the home of Mrs. Tijbout, who may be able to find me a Wehrmacht job as the head of a kitchen. I saw Ma very clearly last night and had a powerful dream about Adriaan, who seemed well.

WEDNESDAY, DECEMBER 13, 1944—Cold today, but the sun did eventually shine through. It's definitely going to freeze, brrr. I paid a guilder for a small bag of kindling. We will return via her tenants in Alphen, who will feed us, probably. I will try to stay over with the Boelens. Today, it appears that a new German offensive has begun. Wonderful, there is movement at last!

TUESDAY, DECEMBER 19, 1944—Adriaan[*] tells me that he finds my enthusiasm for Snijder perfectly logical. He says, "You know how I admire him. He will be loving and caring toward you; she will go.[†] If you marry, you will take care of his children and have your own children together as well." Further, he says, "Prof. Hessel wants to have you although he doesn't yet know how. I was shocked about all of this, but it will all be okay for you." About Schröder, he said, "He wants you as a girlfriend." As for Adriaan, he said he was finding his new life very difficult, but at least he was feeling healthy again.

THURSDAY DECEMBER 28, 1944—For a week already it has been impossible to get vegetables. I was able to get apples, for 6 guilders per kilo, nice price. I called Snijder in vain; he must be in Boekelo. It is very slippery outside—the poor horses.

People keep seeing groups of men taken away, which is very unpleasant. Will I still go to work at the Lazarett? So far, not much of the prediction has transpired. I may well need to leave here soon to stay with Truus, because the situation here is becoming untenable.

FRIDAY DECEMBER 29, 1944—Still no bicycle today. Absolutely scandalous! I walked holes into my soles. No potatoes, but a head of cabbage. Picked up my hats, which were nicely repaired. No coal available at Groenewegen. Just had a chat with Mrs. Visser; the American Hotel is full. Went to the salon and Lebbing. Still frightfully slippery, beautiful weather. There's heavy fighting in Belgium.

---

[*] She seems to be conversing with her dead husband.
[†] Apparently this means Snijder's wife.

MEIJER EMMERIK,
DIAMOND CUTTER, ANTWERP

SUNDAY, DECEMBER 31, 1944—We spent the day together, and tonight we stayed up until 1 a.m. together. Our first New Year's Day since liberation.

INGE JANSEN,
WIDOW, AMSTERDAM

SATURDAY, JANUARY 27, 1945—I went to see Professor Snijder and he said he would get me a German identification card; he is really an angel. How terrible that I have fallen in love with a married man.

SUNDAY, JANUARY 28, 1945—I'm feeling truly miserable and sick. The house feels like a pigsty. Elsie has been a great help to me.

SATURDAY, FEBRUARY 3, 1945—Worked hard; got up early and went at 10:30 a.m. to the bank and the grocers. Afterward, took some borax to Prof. Snijder. It was very pleasant to see him, but he was surprised when I asked him to call me by my first name. He thought it was fatherly [to do so], it was quite annoying. His wife's condition is apparently very bad. He must go to Germany for ten days. I will miss our telephone chats very much. Sometimes I am very down. This relationship will not go anywhere—after all it is not possible, because he is married. . . .

SUNDAY, FEBRUARY 4, 1945—I stayed in bed for a long time this morning. I'm just exhausted; this whole period has been quite wearying. The food has been very nice, though, sauerkraut and potatoes with gravy, plus pudding. I cooked some food myself, and then stopped by

Elsie's house. It seems that Feitsma[*] was apparently shadowed and then shot four times in the back. Elsie is devastated. A memorial service will be held for him at the Concertgebouw.

SUNDAY, FEBRUARY 18, 1945—I was up early again, and did some housework, which I enjoyed. Did some sewing and roasted the beef; it turned out well and I had it with potatoes and lamb's lettuce[†]. . . . I had a feeling that Prof. Snijder was thinking of me. Will he call me tomorrow?

ELISABETH VAN LOHUIZEN,
GENERAL STORE OWNER, EPE

SUNDAY, FEBRUARY 28, 1945—I have been home for a few days, so I will try to record everything that has happened to me in the last few weeks when I was unable to write . . . January 25, was another momentous day for me. I went out early in the morning in the heavy snow, to look after the children from The Hague. . . . At around 11 a.m. I ran into Hendriks, who informed me that the S.D. had arrested Anton van de Roest again. I said to him, "You be careful then." . . .

As I arrived at Vorsthof, I saw a German car approaching. I decided to step aside, seeing the slippery road, but the car stopped, and armed S.D. men stepped out of every door, headed right toward me. That's not good, I thought immediately.

"Are you Madam Van Lohuizen?"

"Yes?"

"You must be aware why we're going to detain you?"

"No, I do not know." . . .

---

[*] Jan Feitsma, an NSB member and attorney general of Amsterdam, was killed by a member of the resistance on the street on February 2, 1945. "Forbidden for Jews" posters that were distributed by the government were all signed in his name, Feitsma.

[†] Field greens, also known as corn salad.

Then I saw Dick in the car, looking very pale and miserable. I remained calm. "We'll put your bags in the car, and your husband can go home with them. He doesn't have to come along." That, at least, made me feel calmer. I didn't know how long they'd been in our house, and what they'd asked my mother and my aunt. Two armed men guided me toward the car. . . . Then suddenly he said, "You can admit everything now because your husband has already told us everything. He said, 'I don't involve myself with that because my wife does it.'"

Then I knew they were lying. I said, "I will tell you something now. My husband never says anything he can't account for, because he loves me too much."

I was pushed into a police van, where I found not only Van de Roest, Lanooy and Welling, but also some men and boys from Heerde. . . . "It is about people in hiding," Anton said to me, "Keep your chin up." . . . He passed me some bread.

Luckily, they sent me to the barracks, not where the heavy cases go. I was taken to Ward 38; I will not soon forget the sight of it. A long hall full of bunk beds, two or three high, and two long tables with benches. . . . The sergeant walked along the benches to the last bed and shouted, "Who is ill here?" Apparently, a pregnant woman had fainted, and she was transferred to the hospital. "I'll pour a pail of water over the head of the first of you who faints."

Everything she said, she shouted. "The dirty laundry has to be ready to collect tomorrow morning at 10 o'clock!" . . . I adjusted quickly; my bed was the second crib, on the bottom close to the window, where it was easy to lie down. There were three or four Jewish women among us, but they were sent on to Westerbork by the evening; about an hour later . . . two more were brought in. Of course, they had been betrayed. All together we were about 30 women. . . . Every day, three women had to do household chores: dusting, mopping the floor, wiping damp off the windows and doing the dishes. Women over age 50 did not have these duties. I did it a few times, the last time it was too tiresome for me. . . .

We received four slices of white bread in the morning, sometimes with some cheese or blood sausage or rye bread, no butter. We'd also get a mug of tea or coffee, sometimes warm, often cold. This was between 9 and 10 a.m. A couple of hours later, we'd get cooked food. The first day the soup was inedible, and we were allowed to throw it away. I had porridge 3 or 4 times in those four weeks, sometimes cooked in skimmed milk, sometimes in water; once a mash of beets and once a mash of marrow fats; soup every day, sometimes thick, sometimes very watery. . . .

In four weeks, I lost seven kilos.* The first Friday I shared with the others. Those who had received something put it on a plate and this was divided among those who had nothing. I got to know several of the women very well, some had been there six to eight weeks already, and soon I felt at home. The first days, all I could think about was the interrogation, what they would ask, but I did not have to wait long to find out.

ON MONDAY, FEBRUARY 29, the door opened, and someone called out, "Liesbeth van Lohuizen." My stomach tensed. They didn't require me to put on my coat, which meant that I was to be interrogated in the building. In the hall, I briefly pressed my hands together and offered something like a prayer: "Don't let me give up any names." I became completely calm after that. In the waiting room, where some of the guards were playing cards and the two female sergeants were flirting with them, a Belgian called me to sit at a table.

"Quickly, tell me who picks you up in that beautiful car," he said.

"There never was any car that came for me."

"You know the car, the one that was used when the distribution center was raided." . . .

"I know nothing, absolutely nothing, about that, and I'll swear

---

* About fourteen pounds.

to it." I had a great feeling of relief, because indeed I did not know anything about it.

"Still, you're not going to be released. . . . You were hiding people at your home."

"No, I wasn't hiding anyone at my home." "You regularly received ration coupons." "I haven't received any ration coupons since my husband was put in Vught; I didn't involve myself with anything anymore." "When did he come back from Vught?" "June 15." "And before that?" "I had just returned from prison myself." After asking why Dick had been in Vught, he looked out of the window for a while. Then he said, "Sign this then."

My signature was far from beautiful, but no matter. I was back in the hall within a quarter of an hour and after that there were no more interrogations. It felt strangely quiet, and I often thought, if that was it, why do they keep me here? They did not say who had given my name. . . .

At night, when the lights were turned off at 10 o'clock, we always sang. "What the future may bring!" "Lord, take both my hands," and many other hymns. It often sounded very moving in the quiet night. But the footsteps of the guards would remind you where you were. Sister Boerema and later sister Bep read from the Bible after lunch and after the evening bread, while we prayed before and after the meals. There was central heating and electric light and three built-in washbasins with running water.

Twice a day, in the morning and in the evening, they opened the door, and we were allowed to go to the washroom. . . . There were two windows that could be opened slightly, and after we had been shut up from 6 a.m. to 10 p.m., we were thankful for fresh air. On parcel day, Friday, the windows were kept closed, which was not very pleasant with 55 women in the room.

Under such circumstances, you live from one day to the next. You hear the police van come and go at all hours of day and night and you know how much misery it brings to so many families. Sometimes, a few days would pass and no one would join us, but then two or three or five at a time. Their ages varied from 17 to 74. Of the 55 women who were there with me, sixteen were over age 50. Rich and poor, young and old, all together, each one with their own history, their own sorrow. There was a lot of sorrow, but these women carried it courageously. No grief for houses that had been destroyed or burned, or for furniture or foodstuffs that had been looted. But there was sorrow for children or husbands who were at home, who had sometimes gone into hiding or were imprisoned in Amersfoort. In Arnhem, I gained respect for these women, and in Apeldoorn that feeling only grew. What I saw in Arnhem was child's play compared to what I heard about Apeldoorn, where women, too, were abused by the S.D. brutes.

I think about Grandma Vos, the oldest in our room, who was smacked and punched; they crushed part of her finger with an ax. I think of Mother Boonzaaijer who refused to give up the location of her daughter, and was so badly beaten that she had to lie in bed for eight days. The swelling on her backside was such that she couldn't sit on a bench. She said that they put hats over her head and over her husband's head and smashed their heads together. Or Nel van Rees, who gave birth to a premature baby on December 24, yet was punched, dragged by her hair, thrown in a dark cellar and forced to stand on her knees. Or courageous Eddy Ziel who was beaten so badly that one of her upper arms and one of her buttocks were completely purple. . . .

Fingers were bent back, arms and feet twisted, noses pressed down—those gentlemen applied all these methods, but they didn't obtain any information.

. . . On the first Sunday, Ali Esselink came to me and asked if I would perhaps speak some words of devotion. This was entirely unexpected. She said that "Grandma" Vos would appreciate it. I thought of a verse about "God's armor." I started with a hymn, followed by a Bible passage, prayer, a word of devotion 15–20 minutes, more prayer, another hymn. I did it all by heart, but somehow it worked, because I saw eyes looking at me so full of longing and trust. These women were mostly Christian Reformed and Reformed Associated and they had all missed their Sunday church services. Grandma thanked me so heartily, I did it again the next Sunday.

Then I did it every Sunday. "We're going to church this afternoon," . . . the women would joke when Sunday came around. Sometimes I was afraid that I wouldn't be able to find a particular section, but when I was awake at night the text came to me and I could create a whole sermon in my thoughts. The second time, I spoke about psalm 103, *Praise the Lord, my soul; and do not forget his holy deeds.* The third time, the Samaritan woman at the well, who stopped work to listen to a stranger. . . .

Through this work, I became closer to the women, obtained their trust and tried to help them. Quite soon, I went from bed to bed every evening, offering a few words here, a kiss there. Tilly, a lovely young girl, said to me on the last evening, "Do you know who you look like, Madam? Florence Nightingale." That seemed a bit of an exaggeration, but she meant it so well. Nel, Gerry, Trijn, Dina, Willy, Eddy, oh I will not forget any of those young girls, nor any of the others. What plans we made together, for "whenever we are free again."

MONDAY, FEBRUARY 19, 1945[*]—Dien Schaftenaar came to me after her interrogation today (her voice and hearing gone from the abuse), and told me that Jews were caught in Epe. I was terribly frightened. She said where they'd been hidden and then I knew who was involved. A short while later, Mrs. Grosschalk was brought in. We pretended that we did not know one another so no one was suspicious when I asked her how things were in Epe. Of course, I immediately asked after Siny, Dick and mother. . . . She told me that she'd read of the birth of a baby girl named Elsbeth (Elisabeth Jeanette) in the newspaper on February 17th. That upset me for a while. When little Dickie was born last year, Ger and Dick were in Vught, and now I'm in prison. But everyone in the room was happy for me.

---

[*] The dating is unclear in this section of the diary.

WEDNESDAY, MARCH 2, 1945—As usual, I rested in the afternoon, and since there were four women who had been discharged from the hospital in our room, two of whom were tuberculosis patients, they enforced an hour and a half of quiet, which was wonderful. There is so much talking all day long. I went to look in on Mrs. Rambonnet, who badly needed some attention, and shortly after that one of the guards entered the room and called out, "Lohuizen."

"That's me."

"*Sachen packen. Sie gehen nach Hause, schnel.*"*

I couldn't believe it. A cheer erupted; everyone felt for me with all their hearts. I grabbed my stuff quickly. You're not allowed time to say goodbye, though I would have so liked to do that. So that was the last time I saw them all. . . .

I met Miek at Mrs. Poppel's . . . and we rode together to Epe along a back road. The three of them were seated at the kitchen table and of course they were all very surprised and emotional. . . . I quickly ate some *stamppot* with kale† and a bowl of porridge, which I'd so longed for in prison, and after that we went to see the children. We used our own key to open the door, and there was Ger. He too was so intensely delighted to see me. Upstairs, Siny almost cried from surprise. I felt so close to the children then. Ina was holding the little Elsbeth and she gave her to me at once. She is a lovely baby with blue eyes and curly blond hair. Another wonder.

SUNDAY, MARCH 4, 1945—We can no longer ring the church bells. The Germans have taken control of the church tower; they now have the keys.

SUNDAY, MARCH 11, 1945—It's as if the misery will never end. This morning Dick and I went to church; for me it was the first time in seven

---

* "Pack your bags; you're going home. Hurry!"
† Traditional Dutch dish of mashed potatoes.

or eight weeks. Jan Merkelbach came up to us in the foyer: "What's going on at Ger's house? I saw a lot of bikes." . . .

We left the church and went to Truus van Delden's house. Dick quickly ran home to fetch my diary; later Miek and I went back for the radio, which we hid in a hole in the ground. After a while, we saw Ger walking near Van Koot's house. We went to see Siny.

They had come at 9:45 a.m. Ger was terribly frightened; he was very upset, but he was allowed to say goodbye to Siny. They searched the house, but no one knew what it was about.

They asked, "Does your husband have any close friends who might betray him?"

"Certainly, he has good friends, but there is nothing to betray; my husband is not involved in anything." They arrested Ger, Prinsen, Van Koot, Kunst, Leusveld and his brother-in-law, Kamphuis, both father and son Van Vemde of the Wisselse Veld, and N. van Essen. They discovered a radio at the homes of Prinsen and Van Essen. They were all taken to Hotel Dennenheuvel.

For a moment I was very upset, but I quickly calmed down. I went to see Siny in the afternoon. She was allowed to bring Ger some food at 5 o'clock, and she said that he was calm by then. . . . How long will it last this time? What will the consequences be? I think of Siny with those three children to care for all alone, and Elsbeth only three weeks old. Who here in the village has betrayed us? Ger was not involved with anything. . . . Siny says that she wants to be alone tonight, but to me that does not seem wise. It's strange that one almost gets used to all the arrests. I've only been home for fourteen days, and now it has happened again. But they will not bring us to our knees; they would have to wake up earlier for that. I only wish that I was not so intensely tired.

MONDAY, MARCH 12, 1945—They transferred Ger last night at half past eight from Dennenheuvel to Apeldoorn. We had hoped that he would be set free. We will get through it. Ali ended up staying with

Siny. Surely Ger will be okay. Ger wrote to say that in the months of January and February seven babies had died in 't Klimophuis[*] from the cold. Family members of the mothers and babies there need to give them warm water bottles. In Rotterdam, 75 percent of the babies die.

INGE JANSEN,
WIDOW, AMSTERDAM

FRIDAY, MARCH 16, 1945—Sometimes, I'm really down. I often feel very lonely, and I hear nothing from either Bölzig or Snijder. I don't know how I'm going to survive in the long run. The Hague has been severely bombed, the whole area between Schenkkade, Bezuidenhout and Laan van N.O. Indie has been burned and destroyed. Van Maasdijk has been appointed as the new mayor, since Westra doesn't seem to be able to handle anything.[†]

SATURDAY, MARCH 17, 1945—Worked so hard that I became quite dizzy. Our food rations have become completely inadequate.

SUNDAY, APRIL 1, 1945—Difficult days. Wollerman has been very depressed because he hasn't received any mail in two weeks. I was also quite down. Things are so hard and the future for Germany looks so dim. When will the turnaround finally come?

I must see if I can get a maid; the house is awfully dirty. I am very much in love with Wollerman, and that is difficult. After all, he is married. Henny came over for lunch and we played a little music. Just took

---

[*] A house covered in ivy.

[†] Seyss-Inquart appointed NSB-er Henri van Maasdijk to replace The Hague's mayor Harmen Westra, who was deemed unable to carry on. Van Maasdijk ended up serving only two months until the war ended.

a walk to the Hermans'; fortunately, he was only taken into custody for a short time.

ELISABETH VAN LOHUIZEN, GENERAL STORE OWNER, EPE

MONDAY, APRIL 2, 1945—I had promised myself that I would just read quietly this afternoon, but things worked out differently. I went to visit Jan and Tiny for a while and returned around half past twelve. I noticed Dick coming toward me right across the fields and I asked him, "Has someone come for me?"

"Yes, Ger has returned home."

It was certainly unexpected. Drank a quick cup of coffee and went to see Siny and Ger. Everyone was so happy. We'd received notice on Thursday that they'd be sent on a transport. Some prisoners had been sent to Delden, but later 400 came back. That night, another 17 had fled. Ger didn't dare. Nothing happened; on Saturday there was an air raid alarm in Deventer. Sunday, a day of rest. . . .

Monday morning, they were woken up at half past five: "Get dressed, guys." The guards were gone, the doors open. . . . It was raining, so he arrived home cold and wet, but calm and happy. He told us that the towns of Lochem, Ruurlo, Vorden, and Enschede have already been liberated. Enschede was a surprise. It was German in the evening, but English by the morning. Will Deventer follow soon and Zutphen? There is heavy fighting every day and we hear anti-aircraft guns; at night we see the lights on the front.

SATURDAY, APRIL 7, 1945—Why does waiting take so long and how long do we still have to wait for the liberation? It is in the air, and the front is so close and yet still unattainably far away. The days pass by and we live on, hoping, longing, but calm and full of faith.

INGE JANSEN,
WIDOW, AMSTERDAM

WEDNESDAY, APRIL 18, 1945—Exhausted and upset. Snijder may have been able to get to Germany, but I doubt it. The province of North Holland will be defended to the end. Saw the Beauftragte[*] drive away, so he's gone back. The Reichskommissar[†] is said to be here. There are some SS divisions in the Veluwe. Near Eemnes, the dike has been breached, so we will be deluged. How the hell are they going to arrange for food delivery? I got one kilo of meat. The silver is not there yet. Bolzig was in a hurry again. How miserable to be alone constantly, I can hardly bear it anymore.

WEDNESDAY, MAY 2, 1945—Tonight it was officially announced that Hitler is dead, fallen among his soldiers. I can't understand it. It's a terrible shock, but his ideas live on. Goebbels committed suicide immediately afterward. Göring[‡] is ill and Grosz Admiral Dönitz[§] is now in command. There seem to be negotiations.

In the afternoon, I went in search of old Mr. and Mrs. Snijder, and heard a lot about "Geert." They are lovely people; I feel sorry for them. This evening, I went to a literary reading by Fischer; it was good but a little long. Lüche played piano. Returned home under gunfire, which was scary.

THURSDAY MAY 3, 1945—Today I'm very tired. I got a tonic from Prof. Hessel. Ellen and Fischer have both been a wonderful help to me. I'm a little less sad; I so hope that Bölzig will be sweet to me. I spoke to him today, he is warm, and that does me good. When is Snijder go-

---

[*] Probably Hans Böhmcker.
[†] Seyss-Inquart.
[‡] Hermann Göring, Hitler's second in command.
[§] Karl Dönitz, a German admiral, briefly succeeded Adolf Hitler as head of state in May 1945.

ing to return, and how? I'm afraid that if I see him again, my eyes will betray me. Yesterday there was a meeting of the Reichskommissar, Bölzig, the Beauftragte, and others with Bernard and several British officers. The English behaved well, the Prince stood by with his hands in his pockets. For the time being, it seems the German occupation continues. Today, for the first time, I have the feeling that the war is over.

ELISABETH VAN LOHUIZEN, GENERAL STORE OWNER, EPE

FRIDAY, MAY 4, 1945—I was busy ironing tonight when I heard somebody say, "There's peace." We couldn't believe it. It was half past nine, and I biked over to the village. The Dutch flag was already flying from City Hall. There weren't many people there, but they suddenly started to flow in from all directions. Members of the NSB got their guns, there were gunshots; flares and fireworks shot up into the sky. Everybody congratulated me. People were thankful and so happy. The church bell rang, and everyone cried, "Finally, complete capitulation." Everybody was electrified. My thoughts went to the fallen soldiers. There are so many. . . .

We saw so little of the war, really. Nor did our village suffer, and now so busy with everything, you do not have time to rest. The capitulation is scheduled for 8 o'clock tomorrow morning. How will those in the west of the country experience all of this—finally some light at the end of the tunnel; a hope of getting food.

Oh, there is so much to think about now. We've been under such strain for almost five years, it is unbelievable. And why all this misery, all that bloodshed? Will we be free of war in the future? I hope that God will grant it. We must exert every effort to make that so.

PART IV

THE WAR IN MEMORY

MAY 1945–MAY 2022

26

"AN ARCHAEOLOGY OF SILENCE"

Liberation Day

On May 5, 1945, the church bells pealed at eight in the morning throughout the Netherlands, signaling the German capitulation. The war was officially over. Although some regions had experienced liberation earlier, the country was reunified, and celebration erupted across the land. People ran out into the streets dressed in royal orange, waving Dutch flags, singing, crying, shouting, and climbing into the tanks of the Allied soldiers to kiss their liberators.

"Hallelujah, Hallelujah, Hallelujah," wrote a thirty-eight-year-old tax collector in Amsterdam. "So is the song we sing to welcome Fifth Sunday after Easter. We are free. We are redeemed. I still my pen to reflect on the joy and gratitude I feel and to reflect on the feelings that rush over me. We are delivered from an evil foe, delivered from the scourge of hunger, delivered from fear of a terrifying future."[1]

Anticipation had been building for months, as much of the south had been freed in late 1944. By the spring of 1945, Allied forces had begun delivering emergency food and aid, even amidst the continued fighting, to starving populations of the western Netherlands, where the Hunger Winter caused by German supply blockades had caused an estimated 16,000 to 20,000 deaths. Some people found it difficult to absorb the new reality.

"I expected the end would bring relief, like taking off a lead suit," wrote Anton Frans Koenraads, a thirty-nine-year-old teacher in Delft, in his diary. "Things turned out differently yet again. I find it difficult to get used to the idea that we really are free now. Every time I think of how many things that used to frighten me have now disappeared, my heart is touched with happiness."[2]

Those who had supported the German Reich, whether voluntarily or not, now found themselves in treacherous limbo. "We ourselves no longer know how or what is about to happen, and there is no misery imaginable that is greater than patiently waiting to see what will happen to us," wrote one Dutch soldier, who'd deployed with a German SS unit in Woudenberg on May 5, 1945. "In any case, the outlook is not very rosy, and the number of options is limited . . . The tide has turned, and our fate is in the hands of our enemies."[3]

Little sympathy was spared for NSB members, whose party was immediately outlawed. Known party members and other collaborators were grabbed from their homes, marched into public squares with their hands above their heads and sometimes beaten in public. Women who'd had relationships with Germans or NSB-ers were humiliated as *moffenmeiden* (Kraut girls) or worse, *moffenhoeren* (Kraut whores), and forced to kneel while their heads were shaven.

Meanwhile, camp survivors were on their way home. On April 12, 1945, the Canadian army had already opened the gates of Westerbork, finding the last remaining 750 Jewish residents of the camp. Among them was Jozef Vomberg, who recalled being "exalted, happy," when he was one of the first to be released—"#55 to be precise."[4]

He was one of the very few extraordinarily lucky Jewish survivors from the Netherlands. Only 5,200, out of the more than 107,000 who had passed through Westerbork to killing centers in the East, would return home alive. They trickled back over the coming months from various parts of Eastern Europe. Some 2,000 returned from Bergen-Belsen, 1,500 from Theresienstadt, 1,150 from Auschwitz. A few hundred more were liberated from other miscellaneous camps. A sum total of nineteen survivors returned from Sobibor.

SURVIVORS, MANY OF them still on the verge of death, slowly emerged from the ruins. They came home to barren houses, in decimated neighborhoods, to find most of their relatives gone. Or they returned to their homes to find them occupied by strangers, who were in many cases unwilling to give them back. Anti-Semitism had not diminished in the Netherlands during the war, but had only increased, found historians Dienke Hondius and Evelien Gans.[5]

Returning survivors faced cruelty from neighbors and former friends who no longer wanted to associate with them. The Dutch government took the position that Jews should not receive "extra help" because this would replicate part of Nazi ideology that Jews were "different" from others—a new form of passive anti-Semitism, as Gans has convincingly outlined. This distortion of logic morphed into Kafkaesque bureaucratic policies in the post-war period. For example, in Amsterdam and The Hague, survivors were billed for delinquent property taxes accrued while they were in concentration camps, making it complicated, and sometimes impossible, to reclaim their homes.

Non-Jews complained openly that returning Jews were "greedy" for seeking the return of valuables and furniture they'd left for safe-keeping with neighbors or former friends before they were deported. Some who had hidden Jews groused about their "bad manners" or failure to pay more for their care.[6] When they tried to convey what they'd been through during the war, they were often told by their neighbors, "we suffered too."[7]

In the Netherlands, as across Europe, survivors fell silent.

"We had to tell our story but we couldn't yet," wrote Renata Laqueur, who was liberated from Bergen-Belsen by the Soviet Army on April 23, 1945, spent weeks in a Displaced Persons camp near Kassel, and returned to Amsterdam in July.[8]

"We will never really 'return,' we will never be among the 'others' again," wrote Greet van Amstel, a Dutch sculptor and painter, member of the Jewish resistance, and Auschwitz survivor.[9]

Those who had managed to come out of the camps, to emerge from hiding, to claw back to life from the edge of disease and starvation, those who had been tortured, those with horrendous images trapped behind their eyes, wanted an audience for their suffering. Who would listen?

"Only a very few survivors were lucky enough to have a listener in the immediate post-war period," wrote Robert Krell, a Dutch Jew who'd survived in hiding, and later became a professor of psychiatry, who treated concentration camp survivors and their families. "There were as yet no *reasons* to hear the accounts of survivors."[10]

The "reasons" to listen would emerge later: to bear witness; to register evidence; to inform future generations; to teach values of tolerance, for "Never Again!"; and most recently and worryingly, to counter Holocaust denial.

The sense of silent "otherness," the human experience locked in a chest, lasted a long, long time. "The two decades following the war can be characterized as a period of virtual silence about the Shoah," wrote Czech-born historian Saul Friedländer. "The consensus was one of repression and oblivion."

Survivors often chose to remain silent, he added, "since very few people were interested in listening to them (even in Israel) and since, in any case, their own main goal was social integration and a return to normalcy."[11]

QUIETLY, AND MOSTLY independently, however, a few scattered historians began the work of collecting testimonies. As early as 1944, members of the Historical Commissions of the Central Committee of Polish Jews had gathered 7,300 oral interviews in occupied territories.

Moshe Feigenbaum, a former bookseller who had survived in hiding, extended the project to Displaced Persons camps in Germany, where tens of thousands of survivors were temporarily housed after the war. Working with Israel Kaplan, a documentarian who had survived several camps in Germany and Eastern Europe, he set up a network of more than fifty "historical committees" to take depositions from more than 2,500 survivors. When they both emigrated to Israel, they took the testimonies and established another major archive, which later became Yad Vashem.[12]

Latvian-American Jewish psychologist David Boder also decided on his own to fly from his home in the United States to Paris in 1946. From there, he traveled from one Displaced Persons camp to another in France, Switzerland, Italy, and Germany, carrying a makeshift recording device of carbon and steel wires. Boder wasn't yet familiar with the names of the concentration camps, and had to ask his interviewees to repeat the word "Auschwitz."[13]

In preparation for the journey in 1945, Boder had noted his intention to collect stories from as many perspectives as possible, "'in their own language,' and 'their own voice' for 'psychological and historical reasons.'"[14] Boder spoke seven languages, and, with an assistant, was able to conduct 119 interviews in three months in nine languages (none in Dutch), composing ninety hours of tape.[15]

Boder acted as both psychologist and ethnographer, not only collecting interviews but also capturing sound files of Jewish folk music, religious and resistance songs. He also tried to record peoples' memories of life in Jewish communities before the war. This was a precursor, one might say, to a new form, or genre, of war documentation still to be born: Holocaust survivor testimony, although both the term "Holocaust" and the specific usage of the word "survivor" in this context had yet to be coined.

The title of Boder's published collection of 1946 post-war interviews, *I Did Not Interview the Dead*, invoked the vast numbers of victims who could no longer "bear witness." But interviewing the living also became such an overwhelmingly emotional task that he rather quickly abandoned it.

Recording the testimony of a mother who had been forced to abandon her newborn by the side of a road in Poland, in hopes the baby would live, he broke down in tears, and could not go on. He ended his project and returned home, feeling defeated. He transcribed about fifty of the interviews but was unable to do the rest before he died in 1961. For more than a half a century the archive was virtually forgotten. But a group of archivists resurrected it in 2002, and today it is an interactive website, Voices of the Holocaust.[16]

In September 1946, diggers in Poland began an "archeological expedition," to search through the rubble of the Warsaw Ghetto for the Oyneg Shabes archive that Emanuel Ringelblum and his team of documentarians had buried. Nearly two years had passed since the Nazis had razed the city, following the Jewish revolt and the Warsaw uprising. One of Ringelblum's few surviving coworkers, Hersch Wasser, who'd jumped from a Treblinka-bound train and lived, was directing the rescue effort, with Jews and Poles working side by side.

"They dug deep tunnels under the debris, built ventilation shafts, and pushed long metal probes through the rocks and bricks," wrote historian Samuel D. Kassow. "And then a probe hit something solid: a tin box covered in clay and tightly bound in string—and then nine more."[17]

They unearthed only part of the Oyneg Shabes[*] archive, ten metal boxes and tin milk canisters full of evidence of Polish Jewry, lovingly collected and preserved diaries, photographs, witness statements, last wills and testaments, letters, drawings, illegal newspapers, written reports of life inside the ghetto, as well as historical accounts of Jewish life in Poland before the war.

Only the first two parts of the archive were rediscovered, and a third tragically lost; still, they contained 1,692 files with a total of 30,000 pages, covering a period of three years, from the German invasion of Poland in 1939 to the end of 1942.[18] Currently held at the Jewish Historical Institute in Warsaw, Oyneg Shabes is still considered "one of the most important collections of documentation about the fate of Polish Jewry in the Holocaust."[19]

Isaac Schiper, one of its archivists, wondered despairingly to a fellow inmate at Majdanek concentration camp before he died there in July 1943, whether even this material would convince future generations of the facts of the genocide. "If we write the history of this period of blood and tears—and I firmly believe we will—who will believe us?" he said. "Nobody will want to believe us, because our disaster is the disaster of the entire civilized world."[20]

---

[*] Sometimes also spelled Oneg Shabbat, meaning "Joy of the Sabbath."

Little by little, however, evidence of these millions of lost lives was being collected. By the late 1950s, Polish Jewish historian Philip Friedman, a pioneer in indexing the testimonies collected by various documentarians, told historian Raul Hilberg that the "writings of the survivors had become too numerous to catalog."

At that point, there were eighteen thousand testimonies.[21]

MANY CONCENTRATION CAMP memoirs published immediately after the war might be thought of as "diaries that could not have been written" under the harsh conditions of the extermination camps. Abel J. Herzberg's diary, composed as notes in the more "privileged" barracks of Bergen-Belsen, *Between Two Streams,* was intended as draft material for a book, but he published it in its entirety in Dutch in 1950.

Primo Levi wrote that he had also conceived of his book, *If This Is a Man,* while still in "the Lager," camp barracks. "The need to tell our story to 'the rest,' to make 'the rest' participate in it, had taken on for us, before our liberation and after, the character of an immediate and violent impulse, to the point of competing with our other elementary needs," he wrote. "The book has been written to satisfy this need: first and foremost, therefore, as an interior liberation."

This "interior liberation" didn't yet have an audience, according to Levi's biographer Ian Thompson, who wrote that it was rejected by many publishers. Editors argued it was too early for such an account. Finally, it found its publisher, Francesco de Silva, which produced an initial print run of 2,500 copies. Even with such a limited risk, sales were poor. It was republished in 1958 in Italian, after Anne Frank's diary had already gained some traction.

Elie Wiesel, an Orthodox Jewish boy from impoverished northern Transylvania, who'd been arrested at age fifteen, sent to Auschwitz, torn away from his mother and sister, and forced to watch as his father was beaten to death, emerged an "eloquent witness" for millions more voiceless victims. The Nobel Peace Prize winner became a professor and charismatic lecturer, author of several dozen books, and a "messenger to mankind," as his Nobel citation read, for "peace, atonement and human dignity."

But before any of that happened, Wiesel lived in silence for nearly a decade. In the aftermath of the war, he would say later, he discovered "an archeology of silence," a "geography of silence," and a "theology of silence." Silence, he added, can be a "form of testimony."[22]

"You can be a silent witness, which means silence itself can become a way of communication," he said, explaining that decade. "Job was silent after he lost his children and everything, his fortune and his health. Job, for seven days and seven nights he was silent, and his three friends who came to visit him were also silent. That must have been a powerful silence, a brilliant silence. . . . My intention simply was to be sure that the words I would use are the proper words. I was afraid of language."[23]

He explained in a 1996 interview about winning the Nobel Peace Prize that he wrote his most famous book, *Night,* "not for myself really"—unlike Primo Levi, not for the purpose of "internal liberation."

"I wrote it for the other survivors who found it difficult to speak," he said. "And I wanted really to tell them, 'Look, you must speak. As poorly as we can express our feelings, our memories, . . . we must try. We are not guaranteeing success, but we must guarantee effort.' I wrote it for them, because the survivors are a kind of most endangered species. Every day, every day there are funerals. And I felt that there for a while they were so neglected, so abandoned, almost humiliated by society after the war."[24]

Wiesel's turning point came while he was interviewing one of France's most revered authors of the era, François Mauriac. A devout Catholic, Mauriac frequently invoked the name of Jesus in the interview, and Wiesel, who had lost his own faith in Auschwitz, suddenly found the invocation intolerable, and shouted at Mauriac, "Ten years or so ago, I have seen children, hundreds of Jewish children, who suffered more than Jesus did on his cross and we do not speak about it." Then he walked out of the room. Mauriac followed, and the two men ended up weeping together. "You know, maybe you should talk about it," Mauriac concluded.[25]

Wiesel first wrote in Yiddish, his mother tongue—and the language of European Jewry that had been decimated along with its people—creating a manuscript of nearly 900 pages, entitled *Un die welt hot geshvign* (*And the World Kept Silent*), a title that transferred the silence from the survivors to the bystanders who knew, but did not act. It was first published in Argentina.

Later, he compressed the work into a 127-page French adaptation, *La Nuit*, and tried to get it published in French, with the help of Mauriac, who remained his dear friend and endorsed it by writing a preface. They tried "publisher after publisher" but had little luck, finally settling on Les Éditions de Minuit, which produced a single print run of 1,500 copies. In 1960, after another major effort to shop it in English, it was rejected by more than fifteen publishers in the United States before the small press Hill & Wang finally printed it as *Night*.

Henry Greenspan, a Harvard-Brandeis trained psychologist and playwright who started informally interviewing survivors he'd met in the 1970s, told me that those coming out of the camps in the 1940s probably would have spoken more if they'd found willing listeners.

"You wake up from a nightmare, a terrible nightmare, and you're in bed next to someone who is intimate, someone who cares, and the first thing you want to do is share that nightmare," he told me. "We all have this instinct. This was a literal nightmare, a lived nightmare. It was a natural instinct to tell someone how you felt."[26]

No matter how great their urge to convey some of their experience to others, however, few survivors found willing listeners in the post-war decades, he added. "Most of the survivors I knew remember a period where people either actively silenced them—often it was relatives and sometimes even other survivors—or weren't interested," Greenspan continued.

"There were others who said that they were made to feel ashamed," he added. "People identified survivors of the camps with these skeletal figures immersed in a sea of corpses. The assumption was they were either dead, or mostly dead, or would soon die. And if they had survived they were guilty of, well . . . The idea was that if you survived that, you must have done something . . . They were asked, 'What did you *do* to survive?'"

Survivors often asked themselves the same question: Why me? This existential question gave rise to many post-war memoirs exploring the very nature of existence and the meaning behind survival. Viktor Frankl's 1946 *Man's Search for Meaning,* part concentration camp memoir and part psychological treatise, attempted to describe how individuals could maintain a sense of identity, of spirituality, and of dignity, amid the many depredations and degradations of camp life.

For Frankl, the only way out of the camp was through the heart and through his memories. While undergoing torturous experiences, he was able to summon up an image of his beloved wife, and often played out conversations with her in his mind or imagined that they were holding hands. The "intensification of inner life helped the prisoner find a refuge from the emptiness, desolation and spiritual poverty of his existence, by letting him escape into the past," he wrote.[27]

Yet to merely close one's eyes and live only in the past ultimately made life meaningless. To survive, one also had to believe that a future lay ahead. That there was a reason to go on. "Woe to him who saw no more sense in his life, no aim, no purpose, and therefore no point in carrying on," continued Frankl. "He was soon lost."[28] For Frankl, there were two reasons to go on: the imagined reunion with his wife (who, unbeknownst to him, was tragically already dead), and the book he planned to write about the psychological impact of camp life.

Frankl wrote that the book was originally "composed" in his mind while he was an inmate in Auschwitz, because he was unable to obtain the necessary materials for writing. He jotted down notes for the book, but lost them in a disinfecting chamber. He tried his best to salvage the ideas as he "scribbled the key words in shorthand on tiny scraps of paper." Doing so, he wrote, helped him to rise "above the situation, above the sufferings of the moment."[29]

In the Netherlands, one of the first literary accounts of the war was Marga Minco's *Het bittere kruid* (*Bitter Herbs*), published in 1957, a novel loosely based on the events of her life. Minco, a twenty-year-old journalist for a local newspaper in Breda before the war, escaped through the garden gate when the police came to arrest her family in Amsterdam, and she survived in hiding. Her parents, her brother and sister, and both their spouses were all deported and murdered.

In her epilogue, "The Tram Stop," she wrote about an uncle who, in the post-war years, would stand at the local tram stop every day, in case his brother returned from the camps, although the Red Cross had already informed him that he wouldn't. Minco's first-person protagonist, at the end of the story, finds herself at the tram stop as well.

"I stopped to look at the people getting out, as if I were waiting for someone," she wrote. "Someone with a familiar face who would suddenly be standing right in front of me. But I lacked my uncle's faith. They would never come back. Not my father, not my mother, not Bettie, not Dave and not Lotte, either."[30]

LOE DE JONG described the first fifteen years after the war as a period of "immense suppression," or a "collective locking up." That era would come to an end, most scholars agree, with the Jerusalem trial of Adolf Eichmann in 1961. The architect of the "Final Solution" had been discovered in Argentina and flown to Israel to answer for his crimes against the Jewish people. Unlike prosecutions of other Nazi leaders at the International Military Tribunal Trial at Nuremberg, which focused on the Reich's responsibility for World War II in general, and which relied heavily on documents, the Eichmann trial would focus specifically on the Holocaust, and it would be based on eyewitness testimonies.

Gideon Hausner, leader of the team of prosecutors, said this "oral evidence" would help bring the abstract reality of six million deaths home to the worldwide audience. "The only way to concretize it," according to Hausner, "was to call surviving witnesses, as many as the framework of the trial would allow, and to ask each of them to tell a tiny fragment of what he had seen and experienced."

A total of 118 first-hand accounts, told mostly chronologically, he said, would "superimpose on a phantom a dimension of reality."[31] One survivor after another took to the witness box to recount the process of genocide, from transport to crematorium. The trial was, for many people both inside and outside of Israel, the first detailed account of the Holocaust. It shattered the silence, and the world was listening.

Historian Sara Horowitz found that once Hauser had treated survivors' memories as a form of "oral evidence" akin to official documentation, "testimonies" were taken more seriously in the context of history writing as well. Survivor accounts, she wrote, had been previously "deemed too subjective, too fallible, and too limited to be useful for empirical research and, in juridical contexts, unreliable as evidence."[32]

Once they were deemed worthy of judicial and historical attention, more people would listen. This rich source material had yet to be collected in a broadly systematic way.

"In the United States there are over 50,000 survivors of the Holocaust," lamented Israeli historian Yehuda Brauer, head of the department of Holocaust studies at Hebrew University in Jerusalem in an article in *The New York Times* in 1970. "No work at all has been done to collect their testimonies."[33]

That would change dramatically in the next two decades.

"SUFFERING AND STRUGGLE, LOYALTY AND BETRAYAL, HUMANITY AND BARBARISM, GOOD AND EVIL"

Loe de Jong recording the national television series *De Bezetting*

The resounding voice of Dutch authority on the war in the post-war period, who remains its most influential historian today, was Loe de Jong. As the director of the National Institute for War Documentation, his mandate was clear: he had to work with all the newly collected material to help establish a national understanding of the Nazi occupation period. His work, along with that of others from the Institute, would define the nation's "collective memory" of the war for decades to come.

The staff of the Institute, mostly young Jewish people who had lost family during the war, collected important archives of the Reichs-kommissariat, recorded post-war collaborator trials, and conducted interviews with scores of eyewitnesses. "Within a spectacularly short time, the Institute had managed to build up an enormous collection," wrote historian Jaap Cohen. It held nearly two miles of files.[1]

The notion was that they'd produce a *hoofdwerk*—a single, major, authoritative Dutch war history. De Jong appointed a team of four renowned historians to write it, with an anticipated publication date of 1958. Despite considerable expenditure, the group could not complete the assignment. They threw up their hands in 1955, and De Jong himself was appointed as the author.

A smaller project took shape in the meantime: a compilation of the diaries that had been collected. De Jong instructed his staff, led by Jitty Sjenitzer-van Leening, to cull the diary archive for illuminating excerpts that could, taken together, tell the country's story of the war. In 1954, NIOD published what some people today still consider to be its first singular accomplishment, a 700-page Dutch book,

Dagboekfragmenten 1940–1945 (Diary Fragments), featuring texts from a vast range of social, economic, and political perspectives.

These various excerpts would be published as a multitude of voices, telling the story of the occupation, in chronological order. Due to concerns about privacy, the Institute made the decision not to name or describe the various authors, and each contributor was identified only briefly, by profession, age, and location. No pictures, background information, or historical context was added, either. But as the war had so recently ended, it was reasoned that such information was not not necessary for most readers. *Dagboekfragmenten 1940–1945* was widely praised as giving voice to an entire generation, and it was reprinted twice before 1955.[2]

But the *hoofdwerk* was still incomplete. While De Jong asked staff members to start assembling all the necessary sources, he had another major project underway: from 1960 to 1965, he composed and hosted a monumental television series called *De Bezetting* (The Occupation), which chronicled the war in twenty-one episodes that aired across five years, appearing on national TV about once every three months.

The show was phenomenally successful, becoming one of the first national "TV events," wrote historian Frank van Vree, who would become the director of the Institute later. Families stayed home or got together at the homes of their neighbors who owned a TV set, when it was broadcast—always on a Sunday evening. Hundreds of letters flooded the broadcaster's offices after each broadcast, and it was discussed widely in schools the next day. According to one poll, the final two episodes were watched by approximately 65 percent of Dutch people with a TV set. The national newspaper *De Telegraaf* called it "a monumental television series," and *De Volkskrant* described it as "no less than a national commemoration, the likes of which had never been held before."[3]

The series was clearly a product of its era. De Jong was seated at a desk with a board behind him, which featured helpful maps, and projected pre-recorded interviews. He spoke in the manner of Walter

Cronkite, with a resonant, pedagogical tone. Dispersed throughout the series were 169 testimonies, in which eyewitnesses described what they'd experienced, often reading from written statements.

De Bezetting captivated an entire generation, and many people who were alive then still remember it as formative to their understanding of the war. But critiques of De Jong's approach—notably, its glaring omissions—surfaced almost immediately as well.[4] Some critics pointed out that Dutch collaboration, specifically the rise and power of Dutch Nazis, was a mere sidebar. Others decried the fact that the Jewish persecution, and the horror of the death camps, was either treated too summarily or glossed over, perhaps to shield viewers from the shock of its imagery.

Moreover, wrote Van Vree, the series tried to create a single coherent narrative about "an assaulted but undivided and unbroken nation," an epic tale of resilience that emphasized the Netherlands' heroism, the persistence of good Dutch values in the face of evil, that "came from the outside," while obfuscating the widespread complicity, and ignoring the "possible consequences of passivity and adaptation."

He continued, "'De Bezetting' reveals itself from the start as a dramatic narrative about suffering and struggle, loyalty and betrayal, humanity and barbarism, good and evil," he wrote. "It is a story with a victor, a narrative that ends with the restoration of the original order."[5]

Two years after the TV series ended, De Jong started to publish his similarly monumental historical account of the war, *The Kingdom of the Netherlands in the Second World War,* a multi-volume, 18,000-page encyclopedic history of the occupation period, which is still, without exception, the most significant historical account of the Dutch war period ever written.

The dichotomies of good and evil, homeland and enemy, strength and cowardice, among others, were carried over from *De Bezetting* into his historical writings, setting the tone for many other Dutch historians for years to come. Two types of individuals emerged from this period of history writing: those who were *"goed in de oorlog"* in Dutch and *"fout in de oorlog"* literally meaning, "good in the war" and "wrong in the war." The vast majority of Dutch people had stood on the side of righteousness, innocent bystanders attempting to cope with the extraordinary pressure placed on them by the Nazi occupiers. Only a small minority, this logic asserted, were *fout*: those who were NSB members, or who worked directly for the Germans.

The story of the persecution and subsequent murder of nearly three-quarters of the country's Jewish population—among them members of De Jong's own family—was included in his historiography but was certainly not the dominant narrative. In *De Bezetting,* four of the segments were either wholly or partially devoted to the Jewish persecution in the Netherlands.[6] But as Van Vree and other critics have pointed out, even in these segments the "un-Dutch" nature of this exclusion and violence is emphasized. It is described as a kind of "natural disaster" that Dutch people could not imagine and had no power to prevent.

"One is struck by the factual absence of the individual victims on the one hand and the enormous emphasis on the resistance of non-Jews on the other," wrote Van Vree. "In this respect, 'De Bezetting' was very much in line with the prevailing views on these events, at the time."[7]

THE STORY OF wartime Jewish history was considered, until the mid-1960s, as something of a separate matter, a niche story, that didn't fit neatly into the overarching narrative of Dutch resilience, resistance, and triumph against evil. How was it possible, I have frequently wondered, that De Jong, a Jewish journalist and historian who had suffered great personal tragedy, glossed over that part of the story in his grand narrative of World War II, and contributed to a heroic national "mythscape"?

Although he wrote about Jewish persecution in two of his "Kingdom" volumes, his attention to that aspect of the war was subsidiary rather than central. To be the "nation's historian" it seems that he had to rather strenuously maintain a posture of disinterested objectivity, to remain remote from its losses.

Was there a great deal of pressure on him to not question the actions of his queen, his government, his countrymen, or their responses to the Jewish disaster? Why, for him, was the loss of 75 percent of the Jewish population—among them his parents, sister, brother, and other extended family members—not the main question? Was it possible that he didn't want to appear to identify as Jewish, rather than as an objective historian? Had he internalized the anti-Semitic attitudes of the era? Or was it a matter of trying to reach the broadest popular audience?

As it happened, De Jong outsourced that "other" story, which eventually found its place in post-war historiography. In 1950, on behalf of NIOD, he commissioned University of Amsterdam professor Jacques Presser to write a book specifically covering the persecution of the Jews. This astonishingly challenging assignment, which both parties hoped would be published by 1952, would instead take Presser fifteen years to complete.

Jacques Presser was born in 1899 to socialist parents on the Waterlooplein market in the Jewish Quarter. As an adult, he'd taught at Vossius Gymnasium in Amsterdam, a high school for university-bound students, but during the occupation he was forced to relinquish his position and teach at the Joods Lyceum, a segregated school for Jewish students, who'd been barred from attending public school.

His wife, Debora Suzanna Presser-Appel, was arrested for not wearing a Star of David. She was deported to Westerbork and sent to Sobibor, where she was murdered at age twenty-nine in March 1943. Jacques went into hiding following her arrest and survived.

After the war, Presser went back to teaching and wrote articles, poetry, short stories, as well as detective novels. He was regarded as a public intellectual, popular among his students and his peers. All along, he tried to work on the book De Jong had commissioned him to write for NIOD; he considered it his magnum opus.

In hopes that the book would resonate in a highly personal way, he made the choice to "confront the reader continually" with first-hand eyewitness accounts from diaries and letters. He coined a scholarly term for such first-person sources: "ego-documents." He taught university classes on them for two decades, and published articles about "ego-documents" as well. But still no book on the Jewish persecution.

Presser struggled, he would explain later, because the Dutch Holocaust was "history," but it was also his life experience; the events of the occupation years had impacted him deeply as an individual. He'd been a witness, and he'd lived through its torments; the victims were not distant, anonymous figures, but his wife, his family, his friends, his community. He had a moral reckoning in trying to approach the material.

Ondergang (Destruction) was finally published in 1965. A tome of more than 1,000 pages, it was a stinging indictment not only of the Nazi genocidal program, and the cruelty and violence committed by the occupying forces in the Netherlands, but also of Dutch complicity and indifference—a subject that had been heretofore taboo. Its landmark publication was experienced as a tsunami in the culture, and as a moment of popular social change, said Van Vree.

Writing "To the Readers," in his introduction, he explained that during the fifteen years he'd worked on the project, he'd been sustained by a sense of duty "to speak up for all those thousands now doomed to eternal silence, whose last cries of despair went unheard, and whose ashes no one was allowed to gather up."[8] Rather than writing about "the Jews," he often used the pronoun "we."

Ondergang's first print run, issued in late April, was sold out within four days.[9] In November, an inexpensive paperback edition was published, which immediately sold 40,000 copies.[10] Within a year, it had sold a hundred thousand copies, an extraordinary success for a Dutch nonfiction title. Many of the responses to the book were "very emotional," noted the *Algemeen Handelsblad,* and Presser said he found that to be no great surprise. "This is a historical work about people from our own time, who we, in large part, knew personally," he said.[11] Some of the "emotional" response came from members of the Jewish Council, in particular the children of Abraham Asscher, who objected to Presser's attacks on the institution.

The book was translated into English by Arnold Pomerans and published in 1968 as *The Destruction of the Dutch Jews*, reissued in 1988 and 2010 as *Ashes in the Wind*. It remains a seminal text, paving the way for several other historical works that would appear in Dutch in the later part of the 1960s. Frank van Vree described *Ondergang*, as "a decisive factor in anchoring the Final Solution in the collective memory,"[12] of the Dutch population, and it indeed opened space to voices that had not been heard to that point. It allowed the next generation to create a different framework through which to understand the history of their country.

Some historians of his own era were less impressed, however. "Presser was not seen as a serious scholar in the Netherlands," former NIOD researcher David Barnouw told me in an interview. "He was too emotional. People said this book is famous, famous, but it's not scholarly." He added, "It's written in anger. You could say he was 'too close,'" to his material.

Two of Presser's academic acolytes, Arianne Baggerman and Rudolf Dekker, agreed that, within the world of scholarship, *Ondergang* was not taken entirely seriously. "Presser's subjective history was frowned upon," they wrote. "His emphasis on individual experiences received a rather critical response from his Dutch colleagues."[13]

Because Presser saw the war as a story about human cruelty, culpability, and suffering, while De Jong cast it as a battle of political ideologies, wrote historians Saskia Hansen and Julia Zarankin, the two historians created a schism that might be at the root of the "basic dichotomy in Dutch memory."[14]

This "basic dichotomy" in the writing of history, established in the aftermath of the war, has shaped memory culture in the Netherlands since then. In the 1950s, the post-war generation could still count on the idea that the "essential goodness" of the Dutch population was intact, but by the late 1960s, a new generation, the children of the war survivors, called this fundamental belief into question. Their skepticism reflected the rebelliousness of the era, and the emerging culture of resistance, that pushed back against their parents' stolidity and silence. Younger historians, journalists, and social activists started to explore what really happened in the wartime and asked how the society had allowed it to happen.

Van Vree argued that it would be "too easy" to reduce lack of public attention to the persecution and extermination of the Jews to "a deliberate effort to repress painful memories." In the post-war period, he wrote, the manifold reasons for "social forgetting," included a "deeply felt search for continuity and reconstruction," and a traditional ideology "stressing the idea that all this suffering had not been in vain."[15] Presser's book introduced "radical changes in the dominant memory culture," wrote Van Vree.

Presser and De Jong's individual interpretations of the war reflected not just their emotional distance from the drama, but also their physical proximity. Presser survived at home, while De Jong was across an ocean, in exile. This distance, physical and emotional, allowed De Jong to maintain a judicious veneer. But he must have been carrying a tremendous emotional burden.

DURING THE GERMAN invasion in 1940, Loe, then editor in chief of *De Groene Amsterdammer* news magazine, had rushed with his family to IJmuiden harbor, where a handful of steamships were departing for Dover and other British ports. In the chaos of the harbor, they were separated from his parents and his little sister, Jeanette, twelve years old by that time. All three returned home, and later died in Sobibor. Loe and his wife were among the lucky few to board a ship.[16]

His twin brother, Sally, a doctor, had also stayed behind because he was serving in the Dutch military, as did his wife, Elisabeth van Male, or Liesje, and their baby boys, Abel and Daniël. Sally would die in Buchenwald, and Liesje in Auschwitz. Abel and Daniël, placed in hiding with separate families, survived. They grew up in different households, when their parents didn't return, but they maintained contact with their their famous historian uncle, who rarely spoke to them about their parents.

"Loe felt uncomfortable when we asked something and replied, 'Leave the past alone. Focus on the future,'" Abel said. "Actually, [it was] bizarre for a historian."[17]

Here is where it gets complicated: When Loe died in 2005, his stepdaughter discovered a large envelope stuffed behind a drawer in his bureau. It contained photographs of Sally, letters written by Sally, and lots of other personal materials about his twin brother that Sally's sons had never seen. Why had Loe failed to share these materials with his nephews?

After serving from 1942 to 1943 as a physician at Westerbork, Sally understood the meaning of deportation when he and his wife finally received their own call-up notices. They made two unsuccessful attempts to escape the country, and were arrested. Sally was sent to Auschwitz. There, according to some sources,[*] he was forced to work as an assistant to Josef Mengele, the notorious Nazi doctor who carried out horrific medical experiments on twins.

Loe may have wanted to spare Sally's sons this tale, or else he didn't believe it, but when the envelope full of Sally documents was discovered, Abel and Daniël became bitterly angry with their uncle, and a family struggle ensued that became the subject of a documentary made by Loe's granddaughter, Simonka de Jong, a filmmaker.[†]

It managed to inflame tensions even more. One of Loe's sons, Roel, called it "a nasty film" and said that neither Loe nor he believed Sally was involved in Mengele's medical experiments. The conflict led to a major family rift. Roel said there was an "obvious" reason that Loe had not handed the envelope over to his nephews: "His archive was the only tangible reminder of his past. He simply couldn't part with it."[18] Abel published his own book, *Had het anders gekund?* (Could It Have Been Different?), in 2019, and more debate ensued.

I met Simonka at an outdoor café in Amsterdam in 2020, just a week after Abel had died in Israel. Daniël had passed away two years

---

[*] There is still controversy about the veracity of this narrative.
[†] *Het zwijgen van Loe de Jong* (The Secrets of Loe de Jong), 2011.

prior. Despite the family crisis that ensued from making the film, she felt it had been "a good way to go through it," Simonka said. "I allowed myself to feel the pain." She wasn't angry with Loe, she added. In fact, making the film helped her develop empathy for him. "He just wasn't able to talk about emotions or to be interested in your emotions," she said.

I asked Simonka whether she thought De Jong and Presser had been on either side of an historical divide—one emotional, one detached? Did she think they had contributed to a "basic dichotomy in Dutch memory?"

She thought for a while before she answered: "There's a story about the two of them my father used to tell."

She shared it with me: Loe had completed his PhD at the University of Amsterdam after the war, and young Abel had attended the ceremony. Opening remarks were presented by Jacques Presser, who'd been De Jong's academic advisor. While sharing the extraordinary story of Loe's life, Presser began to cry. Both Loe and Abel were terribly embarrassed, said Simonka. "My grandfather also couldn't deal with it, with showing his emotions," she said. "Presser was someone who could do that. But my grandfather hated it. It felt to him like weakness."

Simonka said she spent a lot of time at her grandfather's house when she was young; but he was "always going back to his room and working. He was not someone who would sit down and ask you, 'How are you doing?'

"Maybe he really wanted to be 'objective,' which is why he had to cut himself off from his emotions," she continued, getting back to my question. "My personal feeling is that it was just too painful for him. For me, his drive to work as hard as he did originated from that trauma."

"OBJECTIVISM," A CONCEPT introduced in the nineteenth century by German historian Leopold van Ranke, had already become an almost sacred value in history writing by the mid-twentieth century, and it was adopted by other socio-scientific fields like anthropology, sociology, and journalism, to a lesser extent. Ranke introduced the concept because he wanted to turn "historiography" into a scientific discipline, which meant expunging it of its moral dimension.[19] Facts were central to "objective" history writing, and to maintain a scholarly distance from facts, historians should eliminate personal bias and take a neutral attitude.[20]

It's no great surprise that for Presser's era, *Ondergang* lacked a certain historical "seriousness" because of its emphasis on subjective accounts, and because Presser, as an author, evidenced a clear personal identification with the victims in his story.

But an important German historian of the post-war era, Reinhart Koselleck, who had been trained as a Hitler Youth, sent by the Nazis to the Eastern Front, and survived Stalin's Gulag, understood that in the aftermath of two calamitous world wars, humanity needed new forms of history writing. "Dismantling the concept of history and coming up with a new theory of how histories actually unfold—chaotic, contingent, messy and ferocious, yet with discernible patterns—was therefore the most important task for historians," he wrote.[21]

Koselleck distinguished between two forms of historical truth, one objective and another subjective, and argued for an open-ended discourse between these forms of history. The professional historian who reconstructs history impartially can claim the domain of "objective" truth, but individuals also have a right to claim their own subjective truths, drawn from specific, distinctive, and authentic memories. By forcing these different types of truth into conversation with one another, he suggested, history could close the wide gap between the two, which leads to the dangerous formation of "ideologies."[22]

Presser clearly chose to keep his historical interpretation personal, subjective. In his "Note to Readers" he explained, "No single Jew who has lived through that period can think dispassionately about the events here recorded. At best, the terrible experiences have been repressed, but never completely forgotten; the wound in the psyche has not had time enough to heal."[23]

In fact, he "did much more than use ego-documents and personal testimonies as illustrations," wrote Baggerman and Dekker. "Autobiographical material is, in fact, at the center of the book."[24]

Barnouw saw the value of diaries, not as the foundation of historical writing, but "just something extra," he said. "De Jong, a real scholar, was using a lot of diaries in his whole series, not as evidence, but as a kind of coloring."

One could tell an epic tale, an overarching objective narrative of a national history without emotional, painful recollection. But to narrate the story of persecution, social abandonment, degradation, and loss, one had to include the sorrow, pain, anger, and sense of tragedy. Presser wrote from a drive to give voice to people who had been forever silenced, a cry from the grave. His story, as Van Vree wrote, was both an "in memoriam" and a "J'accuse." He wanted his compatriots to understand that it was time for all of them to feel the pain, to grieve, and yes, even to cry.

28

"A GRADUAL LIFTING OF COLLECTIVE REPRESSION"

Ralph Polak and Miep Krant in Dam Square in
Amsterdam on the day they got engaged

The landmark television miniseries *Holocaust* was released in 1978, the same year that Loe de Jong's Volume 8 of the *Kingdom of the Netherlands in the Second World War,* entitled "Prisoners and Deportees"—his first explicitly devoted to Jews and resisters—was published. The four-part, eight-hour miniseries, starring Meryl Streep, became a worldwide sensation that cemented the very word "Holocaust" in the popular imagination as synonymous for the murder of European Jewry. Together, these two factors were pivotal elements in changing memory culture in the Netherlands.

First broadcast on the NBC network in the United States, *Holocaust* later made its way onto European television screens, and though it was criticized as overly commercial—Elie Wiesel called it "cheap"—it nevertheless marked a sea change in the cultural reception of the Jewish genocide. It was followed by the 1985 release of the documentary *Shoah,* directed by French filmmaker Claude Lanzmann, a nine-and-a-half-hour film made up almost entirely of filmed testimonies and footage from camps. Reigning American TV critic Roger Ebert described it as "an act of witness," and although it was difficult to watch, millions of people did so, making it a "cultural moment."

Taken together, these films of the late '70s and '80s broke down what was left of the wall of silence. The era Saul Friedländer called "the period of 'amnesia,'" was ending. To him, it was "a gradual lifting of collective repression, induced by the passage of time."[1] Frank van Vree described it as a moment of cultural "rupture," after which the process of "social forgetting" came to an end, and there were "radical changes to the dominant memory culture."[2]

The 1980s became known as the Age of Witness, a period marked by a massive production of survivor testimony. This coincided with the arrival of inexpensive handheld video cameras, which were used to record family members, in the comfort of their own homes. Survivors who by then had been holding on to memories for thirty-five years suddenly had an audience. Such videos were collected by museums, archives, historical institutes, commemorative centers, and private foundations established to collect Jewish heritage.

World War II survivors, and in particular camp survivors, with a capital S, soon became seen not just as sources, but as educational resources, invited to speak to the public on television and at community centers about their experiences, and to visit school classrooms to present their "living histories." Young people like me, in Long Island in the '80s, were taught history through these narratives—in some cases teachers left it primarily to such witnesses to convey the history of the Holocaust, relieved to relinquish this harrowing task.

There was a commemorative and memorializing aspect to this voicing of tragic narratives. Through survivor testimonies, we could not only learn about history, "so as not to repeat it," but simultaneously honor the people who had made it through and remember those who died. Listening to survivor testimony was presented as a kind of inoculation against bias and ethnic hatred of all kinds. Once we'd heard these stories, the logic went, we couldn't possibly wish such a fate on anyone else. We would understand, implicitly, what ethnic, religious, social bias expressed as hate could lead to.

One of the first American archives to start collecting testimonies was the Fortunoff Video Archive for Holocaust Testimonies in New Haven, now at Yale University, which has about 4,400 testimonies recorded in a dozen languages.

After making the groundbreaking film *Schindler's List,* Steven Spielberg in 1993 established a foundation to preserve Holocaust

narratives, the Visual History Archive at the Shoah Foundation Institute. Now at the University of Southern California's Institute for
Visual History and Education, it contains more than 55,000 recorded
testimonies from fifty countries, in dozens of languages.

The United States Holocaust Memorial Museum's collection of
videotaped testimonies includes more than 25,000 interviews, about
a third produced in-house, and the rest "in all shapes and sizes, digi-
tally, as tapes, digital or cassettes, from a middle schooler interviewing their grandparents to fully produced interviews for documentary
films," said Nancy Cooey, the museum's archivist.[3] Other important
collections include Yad Vashem's archive of 200 full-length survivor
testimonies, the Yahad-in-Unum trove of more than 4,000 testimonies
from eyewitnesses to the "Holocaust in bullets"—mass murders of
Jews by firing squad.

Taken together, these archives alone hold 100,000 audio-visual
testimonies. Historian Annette Wieviorka, in her 1998 book, *The Era
of the Witness*, suggested that there could be legions more, "perhaps
hundreds of thousands, for which no exhaustive bibliography exists,"
she wrote. "No other historical event, not even World War I—when
the practice of recording testimonies first became common—has given
rise to such a movement, which is so vast and long-lasting that no researcher can pretend to master it in its entirety."[4]

The testimonies are still being recorded, with a surprising alacrity.
Even during the Covid lockdowns of 2020 and 2021, Ina Navazelskis,
the Holocaust Memorial Museum's lead interviewer, kept conducting
Zoom interviews from her home in Falls Church, Virginia. There was
urgency, Navazelskis told a *Washington Post* reporter. "By the time
this pandemic is over, a lot of these people may not be here."[5]

These individual memories are harvested to supply the "collective memory" of the future. Words of eyewitnesses to the Holocaust
and to the wider destruction of World War II are meant to serve as a
barricade against future "social amnesia" or "social forgetting," and
especially against denialism, when the survivors are no longer around
to give first-hand evidence.

All of these are noble aims. But some historians worried, even in the 1980s, about the growing emphasis on the implied "intimacy" of individual memory. Sociologist Dominique Mehl observed that relying so heavily on testimony signaled "a crisis of expert discourse and a calling into question of the pedagogical authority of the learned and of specialists," while Wieviorka pointed out that such testimony "appeals to the heart and not the mind."[6]

Psychiatrist and psychoanalyst Dori Laub questioned whether anyone who had lived through the camp system could truly serve as a witness, proposing that the Holocaust was an "event without a witness."

"No observer could remain untainted," he wrote, "that is, maintain an integrity—a wholeness and a separateness—that could keep itself uncompromised, unharmed, by his or her very witnessing." The victim's exposure to a brutal and delusional ideology, he wrote, "eliminated the possibility of an unviolated unencumbered, and thus sane, point of reference in the witness."[7]

Could the witness be believed to be "sane" after such traumatic experiences?

This power of testimony, Wieviorka argued, "troubles historians," not because historians are insensitive to suffering or don't feel compassion for the storytellers. Her concern was that the broader, "coherent historical" narrative was in competition, or perhaps even undermined "by another truth, the truth of individual memory." She added, "the historical event becomes fragmented into a series of individual stories." This fragmentation was a concern, she felt, because it teaches us more about "the violence inflicted by certain traumas and their irreparable character," but may not, in fact, teach us much about history.[8]

But it's worth asking the question: How will future generations make sense of these documents? Will they be a representation of the war? Or will they merely reflect the interests of the time—from the 1980s to the present—in which they were made?

Memory is not stable. For one thing, as everyone knows, memory can fade as we age, but even without that process of mental decay, memories are in a constant state of revision, even from the moment they are first created.

Memories shift as we recount events and retell them, crafting and polishing them into more "entertaining" narratives, as my mother did with her war stories, or making them more somber in a commemorative context. They shift depending on who we tell them to and where we tell them. Inevitably, memories morph somewhat when we relate them to other sources of information—photographs, for example, or other peoples' competing memories.

"Individual remembering, as psychologists tell us, does not preserve an original stimulus in a pure and fixed form," wrote historian Aleida Assmann, "but is a process of continuous re-inscription and reconstruction in an ever-changing present."[9]

One of the difficult aspects of asking Holocaust survivors to recount history through personal memory, for example, is a phenomenon known as "source amnesia." People don't always accurately log where or when they acquired a certain memory or learned a certain fact, and sometimes they link these memories to stories where they don't quite fit.

David Barnouw pointed out, for example, that many Auschwitz survivors described seeing Nazi doctor Josef Mengele upon arrival at the death camp. In addition to conducting his horrific experiments, he was part of the team of doctors who made "selections"—those who would be immediately gassed and those who would be sent to labor and starvation. Many survivors remember that Mengele himself conducted their selection, but it's implausible that he would have done so in each case. However, some people may have seen post-war Holocaust documentaries that identified Mengele as the man who made the selections, and added his name to their memories. "Mengele couldn't be there twenty-four-seven," Barnouw told me. "And he definitely wasn't introducing himself. And yet everyone was selected by Mengele himself."

The same anecdote was related to me by Nancy Cooey, the U.S. Holocaust Memorial Museum archivist. "We have a lot of people who were in Auschwitz who report that they were selected by Mengele," she said. "It may not have been Mengele; it may have been someone else." This disputable fact among their memories doesn't mean that the rest of their story is unreliable, she quickly added. "Sometimes people can add a detail like that, which may be a mistake, but the rest of what they say is valuable."

Another way of saying this is that "personal memories include much more than what we, as individuals, have ourselves experienced," wrote memory theorist Aleida Assmann. They are more socially determined than we might like to believe, in part because they help us figure out our place in society or a particular community. They can be "a dynamic medium for processing subjective experience and building up a social identity," wrote Assmann.[10]

The act of "bearing witness" is not usually a pure recounting of memories. There are two players in the process of recording survivor testimonies: the one who remembers, and the one who listens. The interviewer plays a role in shaping the oral history, giving it form and structure. The situational dynamics of the interview, the relationship between the two individuals, and the setting in which the conversation takes place, can all be factors that influence the outcome.

Just as a prosecutor's questions to an accused perpetrator will influence his or her answers, the interviewer's approach to a victim's testimony—whether compassionate or indifferent—contributes to the story that is told. The interviewer also doesn't exist in a vacuum; he or she usually poses questions that are particularly relevant to the time in which he or she lives.

Testimonies gathered by David Boder in Displaced Persons camps in Europe, by this logic, would have a completely different tone and tenor than "survivor" testimonies gathered in the 1990s in the United States, not only because the setting, expectations, or conditions have changed, but also because society and its concerns have altered dramatically.

In Boder's interview with Bella Zgnilek, a twenty-two-year-old Polish-Jewish Auschwitz survivor, for example, he questioned how the

Polish Jews were assembled and taken to camps, and how they were treated. He asked what had happened to various members of Bella's family. Since this was August 1946, in most cases she replied, "I don't know anything." He also asked her to sing some songs she and other inmates had sung at the camp, which she knew well.

In a nearly three-hour interview that Judy Schwartz conducted with Jozef Vomberg for the Shoah archive in the late 1990s, by contrast, topics included Jewish life in the Netherlands before the war, the role of the local rabbis, specific means of survival in hiding, and the family's post-war life in Holland.

"Testimonies, particularly when they are produced as part of a larger cultural movement, express the discourse or discourses valued by society at the moment," wrote Wieviorka. And they are delivered, "in response to questions and expectations motivated by political and ideological concerns," of their own moment.[11]

WHAT MAKES DIARIES different from testimonies? Diaries as sources suffer from many of the same pitfalls that are endemic to testimony. Although they are fixed in time, and can no longer be revised, updated, or muddied by "source amnesia," they also cannot be read as "pure" memory. They, too, are memories shaped by political ideologies, by emotions such as fear and grief, by wishful thinking and spiritual aspirations, and by social context and communal experience. Diaries, too, can be "a dynamic medium for processing subjective experience and building up a social identity." A diary can also be fictionalized, to a greater or lesser degree; it can be written, as we've seen with Douwe Bakker, to create a sense of social identity or connection to a cause. It can be a place where people express their intimate thoughts and little of the world outside of their mental landscape, or, as with Philip Mechanicus, a meticulous form of journalistic reportage.

Whether strictly based on fact or not, writing is always a process of choice. A diarist can never report exactly what occurred in a day or an hour; he or she has begun the process of selecting moments to record, and thereby, remember. These moments have been plucked like leaves from a relentless, rushing current.

The reader of a diary, like one who records testimony, is "in conversation" with the words the diarist scribbled down. Their reading, too, will necessarily be shaped by their own interests.

But diaries do differ from testimony in two substantial ways. One is that testimonies are, by definition, the stories of survivors—and the arc of the narrative of all survivor stories bends toward an uplifting ending. Whatever horrors have occurred, they have been endured, and the narrator made it through to share this story. This does not necessarily mean that the story is in any way less painful and tragic; it only means that the story is intricately bound up with issues of individual triumph, survival, life itself.

The tens of thousands of diaries the culture has collected, on the other hand, include the stories of those who did not survive. Although this point may seem axiomatic, we also need to read narratives that aren't bound up with survival—since so many didn't survive the same trials. We need to hear from the dead—preferably in their own words and not only through surrogates.

The other way diaries differ from testimonies is that they are an immediate response to events or circumstances. Diary writers did not record events precisely while they unfolded, but they attempted to do so hours, or sometimes even minutes, after they transpired. Their memories are still vivid, detail oriented, and potent. Their brightness has only just begun to fade. In this way, I think that they should be read not as a form of history, or as a form of eyewitness accounting. Diaries should be read as a first draft of memory.

Conclusion

"THERE WERE MORE"

Dutch Holocaust Memorial of Names in Amsterdam

On a frigid but magnificently sunny day in early March 2022, I biked across town to meet Rebecca Emmerik at the National Holocaust Names Monument, a new memorial to more than 102,000 Jews and 220 Roma and Sinti men, women, and children from the Netherlands who were murdered in the Holocaust. The commemorative site, designed by Polish-American architect Daniel Libeskind, has a mirrored roof that spells out the Hebrew word לזכר, "le-zekher," which translates to "in memory of." On this day, it glinted in the sun like a celebratory halo.

Rebecca and her husband, Ronald Spierenburg, had driven into the city from Amersfoort, and I watched them both tentatively descending the stairs from street level, into the labyrinth of brick walls bordering the Weesperstraat. This was Rebecca's first time visiting the monument, which had been unveiled to the public eight months earlier.

Libeskind's memorial is made up of more than 102,163 individual bricks, each inscribed with a name, a birth date, and the age of the victim when he or she died. Rebecca had come equipped with a list of 144 names she planned to visit—those with the surname Emmerik plus other relatives who had married into the family. And she had a pocket full of stones.

Victims of the Nazi genocide were denied respectful burial, tossed into mass graves or burned in crematoria, their names often replaced with numbers, tattooed into their skin. Jewish traditions of internment, mourning, and grieving were all desecrated in the process— yet another form of Nazi denial of humanity. One of the traditional

Jewish customs of grieving is to leave stones or pebbles at a gravesite. Flowers are pretty, but stones don't wither and die. Some believe that this practice helps to ground the soul before it leaves the body; others feel it is a way of keeping the soul of the departed close to those they loved, who they've left behind.

At the center of the memorial site, between the labyrinth of walls, Libeskind included a garden of white stones, where visitors could collect rocks to place below the names of the dead. I, too, filled my pockets with small white stones, and followed Rebecca and Ronald through the winding walls of the memorial, looking for Emmeriks.

THE FIRST TIME I'd been to this site was in 2013, when it was just a large, lifeless square behind the Amsterdam Hermitage's lovely flower garden, the Weesperplantsoen.

Then, I'd been accompanying Holocaust survivor Jacques Grishaver, chairman of an organization called the Netherlands Auschwitz Committee, which proposed to build the Names Monument here, just across a canal from the Jonas Daniël Meijerplein, where the statue of the heroic February Strike dockworker stands with his fists clenched.

By his count, Grishaver had lost at least fifty Dutch relatives in the war. He had survived as a child in hiding and was troubled by the general public's unwillingness to recognize the breadth of the Jewish tragedy.

"When I talk to younger people, I tell them I'm the same as Anne Frank," he told me at the time. "That's always where I start, because I want to tell them that it wasn't only Anne Frank. There were more."[1]

Grishaver's committee, founded in 1956, had been advocating for a monument to honor all victims of the Dutch Holocaust for fifteen years. It had attracted one of the world's leading architects, Łódź, Poland–born Libeskind, designer of the Jewish Museum in Berlin and the Ground Zero memorial on the former site of the Twin Towers in New York City.

While the city of Amsterdam had long backed the project, the committee had not had an easy time convincing the public of the necessity of the monument. Libeskind's earlier design for a previous site had to be tossed after protests by neighbors, who said they didn't want to have to look out of their windows and be reminded of this "black chapter" of their country's history. Several other alternative sites were also proposed and dispatched.

The Netherlands Auschwitz Committee, under Grishaver's tireless leadership, had nevertheless continued to fight for the project, and ultimately the plan was ushered through its final permissions. In 2016, the city signed off, and six months later, Libeskind shared his new design for a 1,550 square-foot monument.

"It's time," he said. "It's timely, it's urgent."[2]

Before the Names Monument, a different, painfully maladroit commemorative statue stood in its place. The "Monument of Jewish Recognition" was installed in 1950, in the name of "the Jews of the Netherlands to their protectors" during the occupation years. The white stone wall of five reliefs in the shape of gravestones, and topped with a Star of David, was meant as "an expression of gratitude for the sacrifice and solidarity of Jews and non-Jews."

Ostensibly conceived by a group of prominent Jewish survivors, one former committee member, Bob Nijkerk, suggested in the 1980s that it had in fact been created on Queen Wilhelmina's "royal command." He quoted the Queen as saying, "Would you Jews show no gratitude?"[3] Although some historians feel this assertion is dubious, at least a few committee members understood that the Queen sought a permanent marker of appreciation from the Jewish survivors.[4]

There was a sincere desire to leave the Nazi past behind and move forward as a single, unified nation, without "racial," religious, or other divisions. If the Jews could show gratitude, or forgive and forget, the logic seemed to be, that would serve the nation's broader interests.

Maurits de Hartogh, committee leader, member of the city council, and a Holocaust survivor, expressed his ambivalence about the Gratitude Monument in a speech to the council in November 1945.

"Certainly, our people have not been able to prevent the vast majority of Dutch Jews from being dragged out of the country, of which only a small fraction, unfortunately, have returned," he said. However, if some Dutch non-Jews had not helped, he added, "perhaps none of them would have survived."[5]

The demand for Jewish demonstrations of gratitude in the postwar era did not come from the queen alone. Several newspapers ran articles warning the surviving or returned Jews to show appreciation to resistance helpers, lest they elicit additional antisemitism, wrote historian Dienke Hondius.

"They should continually bear in mind that they should be grateful and should express that gratitude first by making amends to those who became victims on behalf of the Jews," read an article in the former resistance magazine *De Patriot* in July 1945. "They may thank God that they themselves have not lost their lives. It is also possible to lose sympathy. They are probably not the only ones who have had it hard, nor have they suffered more."[6]

When the Gratitude Monument was unveiled in 1950, however, the major Jewish organizations did not seem to agree; none of their representatives were among the hundreds of attendees. Amsterdam's mayor at the time, Arnold d'Ailly, recognized the inherent awkwardness of the situation even as he unveiled the statue.

"The municipality accepts it with pride, but also with shame," he said, because the resistance had actually "fallen short."[7]

For Amsterdam's 2022 mayor, Femke Halsema, "Only the shame remains."[8]

She oversaw the relocation of the Gratitude Monument to make way for the Names Monument. Rather than remove it, the city opted to place it back in its original location on the Weesperplein, nearby, with an explanation. The accompanying text now reads, "The Monument and its history show how complex it was to come to terms with the Second World War and the Holocaust in the Netherlands."

Still, for years, it was the only public monument that referred directly to the Holocaust, and it told a story of resistance and heroism,

rather than tragedy and loss. We can understand this type of commemoration as an effort to assuage the guilt and shame of non-Jews,
or we can categorize it as a strategy of Holocaust deflection and white-
washing as defined by anti-Semitism expert Manfred Gerstenfeld.[9]
"Holocaust deflection entails admitting that the Holocaust happened
while denying the complicity or responsibilities of specific groups or
individuals," he wrote. "Many nations have tried to present themselves as victims of the Germans and denied or diluted their responsibility or that of their nationals for the Holocaust." Either way, the
Gratitude statue was not designed as a place of mourning for the dead,
or as a comfort to Jewish survivors, who had no other location to remember those they'd lost.

The first memorial expressly devoted to the Jewish dead was created at the Hollandsche Schouwburg, the former theater that had been
used as a site of deportation. The building had been abandoned after
the last transport of Jews left the theater for Westerbork on November
19, 1943. After liberation, its new owners (who had purchased it at
auction from a looting firm) attempted to resurrect it as a performance
venue, but were prevented by protestors who decried the indecency of
those plans. A public fundraising campaign raised 200,000 guilders to
purchase the theater from its owners, but after that no one seemed
to be able to agree what should be done with it. Some Jewish leaders
argued for its demolition, saying it elicited too much pain to become
a suitable memorial. But many people continued to visit the site on
Remembrance Day, leaving flowers for loved ones last seen alive there,
even while it was shuttered and fell to ruin.[10]

After seventeen years of disunity and debate, the former theater
was finally converted into the first national site of Holocaust commemoration in 1962. Its nineteenth-century façade was preserved
while its interior was strategically gutted, and a sculptural structure
put in its place. At the center of the space was a monumental obelisk,
mounted on a foundation formed in the shape of the Star of David.[11]

Starting in 1966, members of the remaining Jewish community
celebrated *Yom Hashoah,* Holocaust Remembrance Day, there.[12] In

the 1990s, the Jewish Historical Museum took over management of the space, turning it into an "educational monument," adding modest exhibition and historical programming for children. In the downstairs entry hall, a dark gray stone wall listed 6,700 surnames of Jewish victims from the Netherlands, lit by an eternal flame.

A single last name etched into the wall, however, stood for many victims who may have been relatives, or who just happened to share the same surname. Hundreds of unrelated victims had the last name Cohen, for example. The Schouwburg's wall of names thereby compressed the true number of victims. Ultimately, although some people grew attached to the space, many others found it to be inadequate. Because it included scant explanatory text about the war, or the victims, as the years wore on the site also became increasingly indecipherable to people who were unfamiliar with the specific circumstances of the Nazi occupation.

LIBESKIND'S NAMES MONUMENT was unveiled in mid-September 2021. King Willem-Alexander was in attendance, as well as Prime Minister Mark Rutte, Amsterdam mayor Femke Halsema, and many other national notaries, along with Jacques Grishaver and other Holocaust survivors, and scores of other representatives of Jewish organizations.

"This monument says 102,163 times: No, we will not forget you," said Rutte. "No, we won't accept that your name is erased. No, evil does not have the last word."[13]

He described it as "a memorial for every individual, for every life story," a single name inscribed on each brick.

The bricks are not a uniform color, but rather a range of warm mustardy, rust and brown hues, mimicking the colors of Amsterdam's brick houses. The visitor must slow down to read each name, one by one, and in this process he or she can understand that the Jewish community of the Netherlands was made up of both many individuals and large and dispersed clans.

- Simon Berg, 3.7.1934, 8 years
- Sonny van den Berg, 8.10.1942, 7 months
- Sophia van den Berg, 27.5.1890, 53 years
- Theo Berg, 20.5.1932, 10 years
- Gracia van den Berg-Ereira, 10.3.1849, 94 years
- Saartje van den Berg-Flesschedrager, 14.8.1881, 63 years

In the space of ten bricks, one reads the name of a seven-month-old child and a ninety-four-year-old woman. An infant and a great-great-grandmother, perhaps. Or some other relationship, because these names represent not just families, or family trees, but generations and diasporic kinships. The oldest of the dead were born in the nineteenth century, the youngest may have been born into hiding or in a concentration camp at the very end of the war. So much life, and the heritage that came with it, erased—the majority in the span of a mere fifteen months.

Libeskind's monument makes conspicuous something that the public had a hard time visualizing in the past. The name Cohen, for example, repeated hundreds of times on various hues of bricks, takes up more than thirty columns on a single wall. The name De Vries makes up 29 columns. The name Polak, over and over, the name Levie, again and again, the name De Jong. Brick after brick after brick.

THE LIBESKIND MEMORIAL arrived just ahead of another new landmark: a National Holocaust Museum, which broke ground in August 2021 and is expected to be completed in 2023. It is nearby, on the Plantage Middenlaan, and the two sites (at the time of writing) plan to coordinate activities so that people can visit them in tandem, commemorating and learning at once.

Taken together, these new additions to the Amsterdam landscape represent a profound step forward in the process of recognizing a history that was reduced to silence for decades, and since then frequently minimized, and often misrepresented.

"There's this process of dehumanization that took place during the war, but there's also a process of re-humanization," said Emile Schrijver, director of the National Holocaust Museum. "We are trying to help people understand that this happened to totally normal citizens of the Netherlands, their neighbors."

When the idea for a National Holocaust Museum was initially floated in 2015, the public was, similarly, reluctant to support it, but Schrijver said that the Dutch government embraced the idea "relatively swiftly." He felt that the nation's leadership today is largely in line with the museum's educational goals.

Indeed, the government's attitude has changed. "Since the last survivors are still among us, I apologize today in the name of the government for what the authorities did at that time," Prime Minister Rutte said during the seventy-fifth anniversary of Liberation in 2020. "Our government did not act as the guardian of justice and security."

The acknowledgment was a comparatively long time in coming, considering that French president Jacques Chirac admitted to France's role in the World War II murder of Jews in 1995, Belgian prime minister Guy Verhofstadt in 2002, even Austria, which not only joined the Reich, but supplied it with some of its most vicious Nazi leaders, acknowledged, in 2000, and again in 2006, responsibility for its failures.[14]

Many in government recognize that there is a greater urgency to address the ongoing repercussions, especially as anti-Semitism is increasing in Europe once again. CIDI, a Dutch organization that monitors anti-Semitic incidents in the Netherlands, in 2020 reported a dramatic rise, from 2013 to 2019, in anti-Semitic vandalism, online harassment, verbal abuse, and "real life incidents" involving violence or cruelty.

Its study found a decline of such "incidents" (from 182 to 135) during the first year of the COVID-19 pandemic, while the public stayed home, but concurrently, "a steep rise in the number of conspiracy theories" in which "Jews are portrayed as the cause and/or beneficiaries of the coronavirus with an alarming and growing frequency, in the Netherlands and worldwide."[15]

Schrijver sees the uptick in anti-Semitic incidents across Europe and locally as another good reason to open the museum's doors. "There's a stronger need for awareness, a stronger need to be warned, than there was before," he said. "There's also a lot more to talk about."[16]

One thing to talk about is a spike in denialism and false Holocaust equivalencies in Europe. Just a few weeks before the Names Monument was unveiled in Amsterdam, Dutch right-wing activists protesting public health measures, including a requirement to wear masks on public transportation and show a QR code as proof of vaccination, wore T-shirts with the Star of David printed on them, and the word #ongevaccineerd (#unvaccinated) in the center.

Protesters argued that the unvaccinated were being persecuted like Jews, or "like Anne Frank," under the Nazi occupation regime, and right-wing members of Dutch Parliament both justified and promoted the use of this imagery, as well. Populist far-right party Forum for Democracy used the same imagery and slogan in its street posters.

Thierry Baudet, the Forum's leading national representative, defended his own security team during a parliamentary debate for wearing the T-shirts, by arguing that Jews "cannot claim" World War II. He reasoned that left-leaning parties had invoked the war for their political purposes; why shouldn't the populists defend "the freedoms that we lost in 2020/2021. What hypocrisy."[17]

He didn't stop there. In a tweet, he addressed Jewish organizations directly, writing, "The war is not yours but all of ours." In the same tweet, he put the word Holocaust in quotation marks. Other politicians scolded Baudet for his "insensitivity," but no one pointed out to him the absurdity of appropriating the symbol of Jewish persecution, the star, while simultaneously engaging in Holocaust denial.

Baudet is no mainstream politician and his party had just two seats in Parliament, but his Instagram feed has 274K followers, and he is regularly featured on Dutch television talk shows, with many acolytes. Appreciation for his sentiments indicates that there are still many Dutch people who echo that old *Patriot* magazine, claiming that

Jewish people were "not the only ones who had it hard, nor have they suffered more."

While one part of the culture is making progress in articulating the scope of the tragedy, another part is busily forgetting, distorting, and misappropriating it.

I wish it went without saying but, in fact, by almost any measure, those who were Jewish as defined by the Nazi racial laws, certainly did "suffer more." The brunt of the violence, cruelty, persecution, looting, economic hardship, and death resulting from the Nazi occupation was experienced by Jews. Although they amounted to about only 2 percent of the population before the war, they suffered about one-third of the country's combined financial losses.[18] Once they were torn from their homes, humiliated, degraded, and shorn of all their rights, they were more than 50 percent of the Netherlands' war dead.[*]

There are still many people who would love to dismiss this reality, and gloss over the significance of this history, convert it into an abstraction or political metaphor, or simply silence it again because they feel they've heard it enough or it's time to move on to other issues. But it remains a source of pain, sensitivity, and controversy, because the wound has not healed. The Names Monument, at long last, acknowledges the enormity of the loss—every single name—but grasping the poignancy of the names requires knowing their stories.

"What ultimately matters in all processes of witnessing, spasmodic and continuous, conscious and unconscious," wrote Dori Laub, "is not simply the information, the establishment of facts, but the experience itself of *living through* testimony."[19] The healing part of the equation, however, is the listening.

REBECCA EMMERIK WANTED to start her trip through the Libeskind monument by visiting the names of relatives who had married into

---

[*] Approximately 187,000 Dutch civilians died during World War II, according to World Population Review, 2020. The estimated 104,000 Jewish victims included about 102,000 who were murdered and about 2,000 who committed suicide.

the family. "I need to do this in steps," she explained. We started with the name Polak, a man who had married a distant cousin, and went on to a distant relative with the surname Neftalie. Ronald stayed by Rebecca's side, and I followed. We searched together, sometimes finding ourselves bewildered by the order of the walls. The names are arranged alphabetically along each wall, but we'd often arrive at the end of one wall and not know which way to turn next. A wall of Plukkers turned a corner and became a wall of Kruijers. I assumed that this sense of disorientation, of leaving off and not being able to find one's way forward, was by design. It seemed an appropriately resonant metaphor for the process of mourning.

I had a few people of my own to visit. I wanted to pay my respects to the Bolles and the Levies. To the Vombergs who hadn't made it, to Simon de Jong and the men of the February Razzia who'd gone to Mauthausen and Schloss Hartheim. I wanted to see if I could find Rudolf Breslauer, and to check if there were any Siegals here, by chance. I also stopped by to visit diarist Etty Hillesum, and the Frank family, Margot, Esther, and Anne, to add some more stones to their piles.

I turned myself around several times looking for my journalist friend, before I found him on a mustard colored brick: "Philip Mechanicus, 17.4.1889, 55 years." He was surrounded by Markus, age 28, Max, age 32, Rika, age 20, Sara, age 23, and Sarah, age 3. None of these young people were relatives I'd heard of, but they might have been part of his extended family.

I reached out to touch his brick, and discovered how much I appreciated its rough tactility. I felt grateful that it was a rugged material object, something tangible that I could feel under my fingertips. I closed my eyes for a moment, wishing I had memorized the Kaddish prayer, and instead silently thanked Philip for his eloquence and fortitude. Then I laid a white stone beneath his name.

A memorial of this kind provides room for remembrance, but one has to bring something to the space for it to have meaning. Rebecca had come with her list, and I had come with my thoughts full of diaries. I wondered how I might feel if I'd come here without the diaries;

what kind of experience would such bricks evoke? Diaries had provided me with a sense of intimate connection, and the memorial gave me a physical location where I could express grief.

When I looked for Rebecca and Ronald again, I saw that they had found the wall with Emmeriks. She had her hand pressed against the bricks, reflecting, while Ronald stood beside her. Taking a step back and letting out a deep sigh, Rebecca unzipped her jacket as her face began to redden, and the tears came. Ronald reached out and grasped her shoulder to give her support.

"You can appreciate that they each have a place now," he said, gently.

"That's what makes it beautiful," she said, through tears. "But it's also what makes it so intense."

This wall was inscribed with the names of more than fifty Emmeriks—but only a third of the names on her list. We all realized then that the rest must be dispersed throughout the memorial site. All the women who'd married and either changed or hyphenated their maiden names would be listed under their husband's names—as would their children. Our journey wasn't finished. Rebecca dipped into her coat pockets and drew out many stones, distributing them at the bottom of the wall.

After taking a deep breath, Rebecca told me she wanted to find Rebecca Emmerik. For a second I thought she was making some kind of existential joke. But no, she was serious. There was another Rebecca in the Emmerik clan. The other Rebecca was Rabekka, spelled slightly differently, who had died at age twenty-one. In her final days at Camp Westerbork, she had married a man she'd fallen in love with, Leendert Brilleman, who was twenty-six. We searched and found Rabekka Brilleman-Emmerik's squash-colored brick, not far from her beloved Leendert's brown one.

"They were married on Monday, and on Wednesday, they went on the transport to Sobibor, where they were killed on arrival," Rebecca told me.

After that, the wind was knocked out of Rebecca. She said she couldn't keep looking for names, she just didn't have it in her any-more. I understood, and I suggested we get something warm to drink at the café behind the museum, and she and Ronald agreed.

The host at the café, however, informed us that the indoor seat-ing was fully booked. We were welcome to sit at one of the picnic tables outdoors in the garden. When our drinks were ready, he'd call our name. In spite of the frigid weather, the sun was welcoming, and Ronald placed our order.

While waiting, I asked them both what they felt about the memo-rial.

"It's a beautiful monument," said Ronald. "It's not screamy, like some other very impressive monuments. It's big but it's not . . ." He trailed off, and Rebecca chimed in.

"Yes, it's impressive but it doesn't come at you," she said. "You don't feel cramped because it's open. There are so many names, but they can all get the respect they deserve."

"It's not something you can take in all at once," Ronald said. "It's overwhelming the first time. We'll have to come back."

"Yes, definitely," said Rebecca. "We'll come back."

We sat chatting for a little while, feeling the warmth of the sun, before we heard someone call out, "Emmerik! Emmerik!"

We all shouted back, "Emmerik!" And then, because we'd said it simultaneously, we all started to laugh. In this most unlikely way, I was brought back, once again, to my grandfather. He'd been with me through the whole journey, and now here he was again.

We soundlessly clinked our paper coffee cups across the picnic table. "L'chaim," we said in unison.

A toast: To life.

A NOTE ON TRANSLATIONS

The diaries in this book were all originally submitted to the NIOD Institute for War, Holocaust and Genocide Studies in Amsterdam after the liberation of the Netherlands in 1945. They exist in a wide variety of forms. Some have since been published in Dutch, and some have been translated into English; others are only in their original, raw, handwritten form.

All the translations of excerpts from the diaries are mine, with the exception of the diary of Mirjam Bolle. Her letters were translated into English by Laura Vroomen and published by Yad Vashem in 2014 as *Letters Never Sent: Amsterdam, Westerbork, Bergen-Belsen*. Bolle and Yad Vashem granted ECCO/HarperCollins permission to re-use excerpts of these selected translations.

I used a number of digital tools to assist with my translations: Google Translate, Deepl Translate, Reverso, and the Glot app, in addition to an old fashioned *Van Dale* Dutch-English dictionary. My translations of the diaries of Douwe Bakker, Meijer Emmerik, Elisabeth van Lohuizen, Inge Jansen, and Philip Mechanicus were checked and polished by Amsterdam-based translator Susan Ridder.

Philip Mechanicus' diary was published in Dutch as *In Dépôt* in 1964 by VanGennep Amsterdam, and it was transcribed onto the DBNL.org website, now in public domain. I used that version as the basis of my translation.

Douwe Bakker's diary existed only in its "raw" form, 3,300 pages of handwritten notebooks in Dutch. I had help transcribing the excepts into typewritten form from both Martien de Groot and Susan Ridder.

Elisabeth van Lohuizen's diary was transcribed by Martien de Groot, as part of the NIOD's Adopt-a-Diary program. I used both his transcription and Jozef Vomberg's English translation of the original to create my own translation, which was checked and polished by Susan Ridder.

Inge Jansen's diary, which was written in a single book, but not in chronological order, was ordered and typed by an anonymous somebody, who unfortunately I can't thank by name for their help—but that was very useful, thanks.

Meijer Emmerik's diary was transcribed by his relative, Rebecca Emmerik, as part of the Adopt-a-Diary project at NIOD, and she checked my translations, granted me permission to use his text, and provided me with supplementary photos and information.

Ina Steur's daughter, Anneke Dijkman, transcribed her mother's diary for the NIOD and it was published in Dutch, as *Als het weer eens vrede was* (If only there was peace again), by Gooibergspers Bussum Publishers in 2017. Anneke granted me permission to use the selected excerpts, and she also fact-checked my translations. She also provided me with supplementary photos and information.

Additional diary excerpts, including those of Cornelis Komen and Salomon de Vries Jr., were published in the book *Dagboekfragmenten 1940–1945,* published by NIOD in 1954, and translated by me. These were also checked by Susan Ridder.

Although the transcribers who work for NIOD are instructed to reproduce the diary text precisely as it was written, including mistakes and antiquated spellings, I decided not to attempt a formal, literal translation of all the diaries. For example, I have standardized the date formatting (day of week, month, day, year) in an American English style, for ease of reading, although each diarist did this in his or her individual way. I have often changed the formatting of numbers, writing out three, for example, rather than keeping the numerical form, for consistency and ease of reading. Each diarist used their own form for writing numbers and dates, but I felt that mimicking these idiosyncratic individual styles to the letter would be unnecessarily distracting for the reader. Similarly, I have not duplicated abbreviations in names (when Van Lohuizen wrote *D.* for Dick, I wrote out Dick instead) for clarity's sake, and I have avoided replicating grammatical errors or misspellings in the original texts, and instead corrected them.

Although I have tried to keep most of the individual diary entries largely intact, I made the decision to trim parts of text that were irrelevant or that might need too much additional explanation, so as not to unduly confuse the reader. In such cases, I have used ellipses (. . .) to indicate where I've removed text.

More broadly, I had to make a great many choices about which excerpts to use and which to leave out. When working with diaries of hundreds, and sometimes thousands of pages, these decisions could be quite difficult. Someone else reading and translating these same diaries would have made vastly different choices, and maybe someday someone will. My choices were driven by a desire to stick to the central narrative of the individual diarist's story: What were the main events of the war for them, and how did they make sense of these experiences?

ACKNOWLEDGMENTS

This book grew out of an article that I wrote for *The New York Times* called "The Lost Diaries of War," which was published in April 2020. Kevin Flynn, Investigations Editor with the Culture Desk of *The New York Times,* saw merit in my pitch about the NIOD diary collection in 2019, and across several months he helped me develop the story into an interactive multimedia feature, both online and in the newspaper.

Digital production editor Josephine Sedgwick created a beautiful online and print layout for the piece, working with a team of designers and technical experts in the New York headquarters of *The New York Times,* including turnable diary pages on the *Times'* website, as well as a visually stunning four-page spread in the print edition, which helped the work garner a great deal of attention. I'd like to thank Kevin, Josie, and all the other people involved in making my original piece shine in the *Times*.

I would never have encountered the diaries in the first place without NIOD researcher René Kok, who introduced me to the archive in April 2019. He also gave me early and ongoing guidance for finding the kinds of diaries I would use, first for the *New York Times* piece and later for this book. He guided me to Jitty's summary pages and discussed with me which diaries might fit my goals.

Similarly, René Pottkamp, who coordinates NIOD's "Adopt-a-Diary" transcription program, introduced me to the digital archive, connected me with diary transcribers and family members of the diary writers, and helped me locate diaries in the system, and photographs in the NIOD image bank. I'm deeply grateful for the help of both Renés.

The following people either fact-checked or vetted sections of the book prior to publication: David Barnouw, Fran Bender, Mirjam Bolle, Bart van der Boom, Koert Broersma, Anneke Dijkman, Rebecca Emmerik, Bep Fontijn, René Kok, Wally de Lang, Joggli Meihuizen, Dan Michman, Guus Meershoek, Elisabeth Oets, René Pottkamp, Susan Ridder, Benjamin Roberts, Margriet Schavemaker, Emile Schrijver, Elisabeth Vomberg Shapiro, David Siegal, Dawn Sworsoreski, Laurien Vastenhout, Willem Veldkamp, and Frank van Vree.

A lot of my research, especially during the Covid lockdowns, would have been impossible if not for several incredible digital public research resources. I want to credit De Digitale Bibliotheek voor de Nederlandse Letteren (DBNL), a digital library of Dutch texts that are in the public domain; Delpher, a digitized databank of articles from Dutch newspapers, books, and magazines; the United States Holocaust Memorial Museum's website, which contains an extraordinary wealth of information, documents, and archival material; the Stadsarchief, the Amsterdam City Archives' digital records; and Joods Monument, an online memorial to Dutch Jews who were persecuted during the occupation.

My most important tool was NIOD's online portal, which, thanks to the Adopt-a-Diary program, contained, as of April 2022, digital transcriptions of more than 250 diaries. The amazing team of volunteer transcribers are adding to it every day. During the Covid lockdowns of 2020 and 2021, I wouldn't have been able to continue my work without this digital resource.

For helping me gain real-world access to archival materials and photographs, I'd like to thank the Stadsarchief in Amsterdam, the

Dutch National Archive in The Hague (in particular, Rivka Baum), and the NIOD (the workers in the Studiezaal, Hubert Berkhout, René van Heijningen, and Bram Schamhart, and photo archivist Harco Gijsbers, in addition to the other NIOD researchers previously mentioned).

I would like to thank Humanity in Action and its terrific leader, Judith Goldstein, for granting me a Research Fellowship in 2020, which provided me with support for translating the diaries.

The final stage of research and writing would not have been possible without the 2021 Whiting Foundation Creative Nonfiction Grant, an extraordinary fellowship, which came at precisely the right moment to give the time and focus to develop the book from a draft to the final product you hold in your hands now. I'm profoundly grateful for their recognition and the support.

Family and friends have, in various practical, emotional, and other sympathetic ways, supported this writing process over the last few years, including Stuart Acker Holt, Rebecca Sakoun, Bajah Freeman, Itamar Gilboa, Rhiannon Pickles, Taco Dibbits, Marian Krauskopf, David Siegal, Rebecca Webb, Carol Crigler, Alex Suarez, Joshua Blau, and (most of all) Gabriela Roa.

I'm especially grateful for the extraordinarily useful feedback from my readers, Jenn Ben-Yakov, Benjamin Moser, and Leslie Jamison, who took the time to read drafts and comment on my pages as I was working on them, and who generously engaged in deep conversation with me about the subject matter.

My agent, Marly Rusoff, must be the world's greatest literary agent. She has had such a deep, abiding belief in this project from the beginning and provided me with unceasing, spontaneous, and any-time-of-day support (even on weekends) over all kinds of matters, large and small. I feel very fortunate to have found her many years ago, and our relationship has only become stronger over the years. Marly, you're amazing.

My editor, Gabriella Doob, and publisher, Helen Atsma, have helped me develop the book along the way with great encouragement and faith in its outcome, and I'm grateful to Allison Saltzman, who designed its beautiful cover, and to senior production editor Rebecca Holland, who worked valiantly with me through the final drafts.

Finally, I am profoundly grateful for the love, encouragement, and support I always receive from my dad, Frederick P. Siegal, and my incredible daughter, Sonia, my sweet darling angel, who inspires me with her brilliance, curiosity, and sparkling good nature every single day.

NOTES

Prologue: Searching for Emerich

1. Estimate is based on the landmark Steven M. Cohen, Ph.D., Jacob B. Ukeles, Ph.D., and Ron Miller, Ph.D., UJA-Federation of New York, "Jewish Community Study of New York: 2011 Comprehensive Report," *Jewish Policy & Action Research* (June 2012) and "American Jewish Population Estimates, 2020," published 2021 by Brandeis University's Cohen Center for Modern Jewish Studies, 2021.

2. Pim Griffioen and Ron Zeller, "Comparing the persecution of Jews in the Netherlands, France and Belgium, 1940–1945: similarities, differences, and causes," in *The Persecution of the Jews in The Netherlands, 1940–1945* (Amsterdam: Vossiuspers UvA, 2012), 55.

3. (Witness No. 733, interviewed in Bibrka, on January 9, 2009) Yahad in Unum, In Evidence: "The Map of the Holocaust by Bullets, Execution of Jews in Bibrka," https://www.yahadmap.org/#village /bibrka-bobrka-boyberke-boiberik-lviv-ukraine.20; Yahad in Unum, In Evidence: "Execution of the Bibrka Jews in Volove," videotaped testimony of witness, Evstafi I. https://www.yahadmap.org/#village /volove-lviv-ukraine.333.

4. Mauthausen Memorial website, "The Subcamps, Gunskirchen," https://www.mauthausen-memorial.org/en/History/The-Subcamps #map‖16.

5. Nina Siegal, "Witnessing the Holocaust," *The New York Times,* May 22, 2019.

6. Frank van Vree, *Als de muren konden spreken. De onwaarschijnlijke geschiedenis van Herengracht 380–382* (NIOD).

7. Siegal, "Witnessing the Holocaust."

8. René Kok and Erik Somers, *De Jodenvervolging in foto's, Nederland 1940–1945* (Zwolle: W Books, NIOD, 2019).

Introduction: "Vast quantities of this simple, everyday material"

1. Translation of Bolkestein speech from Patricia Hampl, "The Whole Anne Frank," *The New York Times*, March 5, 1995.
2. *The Diary of Anne Frank, The Critical Edition* (Amsterdam: NIOD, 1986), 59.
3. Anne Frank, *The Diary of a Young Girl*, The Definitive Edition (New York: Penguin Books, 1997), 244.
4. Boudewijn Smits, *Loe de Jong 1914–2005, Historicus met een missie* (Amsterdam: Boom, 2005), 128–129.
5. P.J. van Winter, *"Herdenking van Nicolaas Wilhelmus Posthumus (26 february 1880–18 april 1960)*, (Overdruk uit het Jaarboek der Koninklijke Nederlandse Akademie van Wetenschappen, 1960–1961), 6.
6. "A detailed History of the IISH," International Institute of Social History website.
7. Boudewijn Smits, *Loe de Jong,* 129–130.
8. René Kok, "De eerste jaren van het Rijksinstituut voor Oorlogsdocumentatie," *Documentaire Nederland en de Tweede Wereldoorlog. De oorlog na de oorlog* (Zwolle, 1991).
9. Samuel D. Kassow, *Who Will Write Our History: Rediscovering a Hidden Archive from the Warsaw Ghetto* (London: Penguin Books, 2009), 210–212.
10. Kassow, *Who Will Write,* 210.
11. Henry Rousso and Jane Marie Todd, *The Latest Catastrophe: History, the Present, the Contemporary* (Chicago: University of Chicago Press, 2016), 83–84.
12. Peter Fritzsche, *An Iron Wind: Europe Under Hitler* (New York: Basic Books, 2016), xi–xiii.
13. Rousso and Todd, *The Latest Catastrophe,* 70.
14. He used Louis de Jong for English publications.
15. Annemieke van Bockxmeer, *De oorlog verzameld: Het ontstaan van de collectie van het NIOD* (Amsterdam: De Bezijge Bij, 2014).
16. Rousso and Todd, *The Latest Catastrophe,* 85.
17. Bram Mertens, "An Explosion of Vitality and Creativity? Memory and Historiography of the Second World War in Belgium and the Netherlands," *Dutch Crossing,* 37: 1, 42–43.
18. Duncan S.A. Bell, "Mythscapes: memory, mythology, and national identity," *British Journal of Sociology,* vol. 54, no. 1 (March 2003), 63–81.
19. Bockxmeer, "De oorlog verzameld," 316.
20. Bockxmeer, "De oorlog verzameld," 317.
21. René Kok interview.
22. Philippe Lejeune, *On Diary*, edited by Jeremy D. Popkin and Julie Rak, trans. by Katherine Durnin (Honolulu: University of Hawai'i Press, 2009), 208–209.

The Diarists (in alphabetical order)

1. *Biographical Dictionary of the Netherlands: 1880–2000,* Huygens ING.

Chapter 2: "One should make the best of it"

1. Lucas Lichtenberg, *Mij krijgen ze niet levend: De zelfmoorden van mei 1940* (Amsterdam: Uitgeverij Balans, 2017), 17.
2. L. Ph. Polak, *Documents of the Persecution of Dutch Jewry, 1940–1945* (Atheneum, Polak & Van Gennep, Jewish Historical Museum Amsterdam, 1969), document 138, 37 (trans. 36).
3. Bob Moore, *Victims & Survivors: The Nazi Persecution of the Jews in the Netherlands 1940–1945* (London: Arnold, 1997), 63.
4. Dick van Galen Last, "Chapter 7: The Netherlands," in *Resistance in Western Europe*, edited by Bob Moore (Oxford: Berg Publishers, 2000), 193.
5. Jennifer L. Foray, *Visions of Empire in the Nazi-Occupied Netherlands* (Cambridge University Press, 2011), 28–29.
6. Katje Happe, *Veel valse hoop, De Jodenvervolging in Nederland 1940–1945* (Amsterdam/Antwerpen: Atlas Contact, 2017), 46.
7. Foray, *Visions of Empire*, 23, 31.
8. Van Galen Last, *Resistance*, 192.
9. Hein Klemann and Sergei Kudryashov, *Occupied Economies: An Economic History of Nazi-Occupied Europe, 1939–1945* (Oxford: Berg Publishers, 2012), 303–304.
10. Jan Herman Brinks, "The Dutch, the Germans, & the Jews," *History Today* 49, no. 6 (1999): 17–23.
11. Joggli Meihuizen, *Noodzakelijk kwaad: de bestraffing van economische collaboratie in Nederland na de Tweede Wereldoorlog* (Amsterdam: Boom, 2003), 753.
12. Meihuizen, *Noodzakelijk kwaad*, 323.
13. Foray, *Visions of Empire*, 24.
14. Geert Mak, *Amsterdam: A Brief Life of the City*, trans. Philipp Blom (London: The Harvill Press), 235–237.
15. Hanneke de Wit, "De nazi's paten mij mijn jeugd af," *Het Parool*, 25 Feb. 1995, reprinted in Ina Steur en Anneke Dijkman, *Als het weer eens vrede was* (Bussum: Gooibergpers, 2015), 58–59.
16. Ina Steur en Anneke Dijkman, *Als het weer eens vrede was* (Bussum: Gooibergpers, 2015), 79.
17. Steur and Dijkman, *Als het weer*, 85.
18. Jacques Presser, *The Destruction of the Dutch Jews*, trans. Arnold Pomerans (New York: E.P. Dutton & Co., Inc. 1969), 19.
19. Dan Michman, *The Emergence of Jewish Ghettos During the Holocaust* (Cambridge University Press, 2011), 96.
20. Guus Meershoek, *Dienaren van het gezag. De Amsterdamse politie tijdens de bezetting* (Amsterdam: Van Gennep, 1999), 131–137.
21. Kok and Somers, *De Jodenvervolging*, 141.
22. Ben Braber, *This Cannot Happen Here: Integration and Jewish Resistance in The Netherlands, 1940–1945* (Amsterdam: Amsterdam University Press, 2013), 103–104.

Chapter 4: "No graves, no gravestones"

1. Wally de Lang, *De razzia's van 22 en 23 february 1941 in Amsterdam: Het lot van 389 Joodse mannen* (Amsterdam/Antwerp: Atlas Contact, 2021), 25–26.
2. Mirjam Bolle, *Letters Never Sent: Amsterdam, Westerbork, Bergen-Belsen* trans. by Laura Vroomen (Jerusalem: Yad Vashem Publications: 2014), 32.
3. De Vries dagboek, *Dagboekfragmenten 1940–1945* ed. T.M. Sjenitzer-van Leening (Amsterdam: NIOD/Veen Uitgevers, 1954), 69.
4. Annet Mooij, *De strijd om de Februaristaking* (Amsterdam: Balans, 2006), 18.
5. De Lang, *De razzia's*, 142–143.
6. Levie, *Letters*, 33 (written in retrospect, on January 31, 1943).
7. De Lang, *De razzia's*, 214.
8. De Lang, *De razzia's*, newspaper clippings (illustration), 274.
9. Meershoek, *Dienaren van het gezag*, 134–135.
10. BeeldbankWO2.nl-NIOD.
11. Presser, *Destruction*, 49.
12. From the Minutes of the Feb. 13, 1941, meeting at Asscher's factory; NIOD archive, 182.3 (Commissies van de Joodsche Raad), Jewish Council for Amsterdam.
13. Mirjam Bolle interview August 12, 1999, NIOD archive.
14. Bob Moore, *Refugees from Nazi Germany in the Netherlands 1933–1940* (Dordrecht: Martinus Nijhoff, 1986), 79–80.
15. Speech before Tweede Kamer, November 15, 1938, in Corrie K. Berghuis, *Joods vluchtelingen in Nederland 1938–1940* (Kampen: J.H. Kok), 25–27. Translation from Jan Herman Brinks, *The Dutch, The Germans, and the Jews,* 21.
16. Erik Somers, *Voorzitter van de Joodse Raad, De herinnering van David Cohen (1941–1943)* (Zutphen: Uitgeversmaatschappij Walburg Pers, 2010), 11.
17. Somers, *Voorzitter,* 12–14.
18. Henry L. Mason, "Testing Human Bonds Within Nations: Jews in the Occupied Netherlands," *Political Science Quarterly* Vol. 99., Number 2 (Summer 1984): 334.
19. Mason, "Testing Human Bonds," 332.
20. Interviews with Somers and Vastenhout.
21. Bolle, *Letters*, 33.
22. Nina Siegal, "She Discovered What Happened to 400 Dutch Jews Who Disappeared," *The New York Times*, March 16, 2022.
23. De Lang interview.
24. De Lang, *De razzia's*, 110–111.
25. De Lang, *De razzia's*, 175–204.
26. Geert Mak, *Amsterdam: A Brief Life of the City*, trans. Philipp Blom (London: The Harvill Press), 258.
27. Dan Michman, "Explaining the Formation of Ghettos under Nazi Rule

and Its Bearings on Amsterdam. Segregating 'the Jews' or Containing the Perilous 'Ostjuden'?" in *Borders and Boundaries in and around Dutch Jewish History*, edited by Judith Frishman, David J. Wertheim, Ido de Haan and Joël Cahen (Amsterdam: Amsterdam University Press, 2011), 35.

28. Louis de Jong, *The Netherlands and Nazi Germany* (Cambridge: Erasmus Lectures, Harvard University Press, 1990), 9.

Chapter 5: "Now the games can begin"

1. Johannes Boot diary, as cited by Peter Romijn in *Persecution of the Dutch Jews* (originally from Boot, J.J.G. *Burgemeester in bezettingstijd*, Apeldoorn, 1968), 84.

2. Peter Romijn et al., *The Persecution of the Dutch Jews* (Amsterdam: Vossiuspers, UvA), 13.

3. Meihuizen, *Noodzakelijk kwaad,* 323.

4. Report of the Procureur-Fiscaal bij het Bijzonder Gerechtshof in Amsterdam concerning Werkspoor, May 14, 1949, in Nationaal Archief in Den Hague, Centraal Archief Bijzondere Rechtspleging (CABR), copy in archive J.P. Meihuizen, Amsterdam.

5. Typist, 25 years old, Amsterdam, from *Dagboekfragmenten 1940–1945,* (NIOD) 74.

6. Piet de Rooy, ed. *Geschiedenis van Amsterdam: Tweestrijd om de Hoofdstad 1900–2000* (Amsterdam: SUN, 2007) (chapter by Guus Meershoek), 257–259.

7. Guus Meershoek, "Policing Amsterdam during the German Occupation: How Radical Was the Break?" (Chapter 16), in Clive Emsley et al., *Social Control in Europe: Volume 2, 1800–2000* (Ohio State University Press, 2004), 331–333.

8. Willy Lages Proces-verbaal, Bakker CABR file NIOD Amsterdam Doc. I-53, 30 october 1945.

9. Meershoek, *Dienaren van het gezag,* 109.

10. Nina Siegal, "Echoes of Nazi Propaganda in a Collaborator Diary: The Case of Dutch Police Investigator Douwe Bakker," in *Witnessing, Memory and Crisis: AHM Annual Conference 2022,* ed. Ihab Saloul et al. (Amsterdam: Amsterdam University Press, 2022), 34.

11. Willy Lages testimonies; Getuigenverhoor van Willy Lages 30 october 1945 naar G. Th. C. Clement and F.N. Baderhuizen, CABR file NIOD; also Proces-verbaal, Willy Lages, 26 September 1946, CABR file in Den Haag, Nationaal Archief.

12. Na-oorlogssche Rechtspraak 1946, No. 510; Bijzonder Gerechtshof Amsterdam, 16 August 1946, CABR file, NIOD, Amsterdam.

13. The series of images of the raid were taken by German photographer Bart de Kok, and are part of the Stadsarchief's collection.

14. Bart de Kok, photo series of April 27, 1942, Amsterdam Stadsarchief, Collectie Bart de Kok en Jozef van Poppel.

15. Nicolaas Cornelis Jonker, Proces-verbaal, CABR file in the Nationaal Archief, Den Haag, 51–56.

16. Douwe Bakker, commendation letter dated February 20, 1942, from Nationaal Archief, CABR file, Den Haag, 8.

17. Bakker, Politie Amsterdam Bureau Inlichtingendienst, No. 901D/1941 Dossier 60–203, CABR file NIOD D1–53, 5.

18. Johan Ros Proces-verbaal, CABR file, Nationaal Archief, Den Haag, 44–45.

19. Elisabeth Roeland Proces-verbaal, CABR File, National Archief, Den Haag (testimony of van Hamme's wife).

20. Getuigenverhoor van Kurt Döring, 8 november 1945, naar G. Th. C. Clement and F.N. Baderhuizen, CABR file NIOD; geneven naar G.Th.C. Clement and F. N. Badenhuizen, detectives in the police department.

21. Willy Lages, Proces-verbaal, CABR file National Archief, Den Haag.

22. Bob Moore, *Victims & Survivors*, 203.

Chapter 7: "Like a good gardener"

1. J.C.H. Blom, R.G. Fuks-Mansfeld, I. Schöffer, *The History of the Jews in the Netherlands* trans. Arnold J. Pomerans and Erica Pomerans (Oxford, Portland, Oregon: The Littmann Library of Jewish Civilization, 2002), 318.

2. "Kam. dr. REDACTED over zijn taak," *Het Nationale Dagblad*, DATE REDACTED.

3. Katharina von Kellenbach, "God's love and women's love: prison chaplains counsel the wives of Nazi perpetrators," *Journal of Feminist Studies in Religion* (Vol. 20, Issue 2), Indiana University Press, 2004.

4. Gudrun Schwarz, *Eine Frau an seiner Seite: Ehefrauen in der SS-"Sippengemeinschaft"* trans. Kári Driscoll (Berlin: Aufbau-Taschenbuch-Verl., 2001).

5. Schwarz, *Eine Frau,* 102.

6. Von Kellenbach, "God's love."

7. Von Kellenbach, "God's love."

8. Jan Meyers, *Mussert, Een politiek leven* (Amsterdam: De Ardbeiderspers, 1984), 122–123.

9. Hans Olink, "Oorwarmers voor het oostfront," *Elsevier*, 4 August 1990 (NIOD Knipselcollectie KB1–11765).

10. Zonneke Matthée, *Voor Volk en Vaderland, Vrouwen in de NSB 1931–1948* (Amsterdam: Balans, 2007), 12.

11. Matthée, *Voor Volk*, 88.

12. Kees van der Linden, "Oud en fout in huize Wilhoef," *Haarlems Dagblad*, 15 november 1997.

13. Matthée, *Voor Volk*, 14–16.

14. Hans Olink, "Oorwarmers."

15. Wendy Lower, *Hitler's Furies: German Women in the Nazi Killing Fields* (Boston: Houghton Mifflin Harcourt, 2013), 3–4.

16. Von Kellenbach, "God's love."

17. Susanne C. Knittel, "Stand by Your Man: (Self-) Representations of SS Wives after 1945," in *Probing the Limits of Categorization,* eds. Christina Morina and Krijn Thijs (New York/Oxford: Berghahn Books, 2020), 297.

Chapter 8: "Was this forced labor or slaughter?"

1. De Lang, *De razzia's*, 355.
2. Gemeente Amsterdam Stadsarchief, Abraham Emmerik bio, https://www
   .amsterdam.nl/stadsarchief/themasites/razzia/abraham-emmerik/.
3. De Lang, *De razzia's*, 355.
4. Bianca Stigter, *De bezette stad: Plattegrond van Amsterdam 1940–1945*
   (Amsterdam: Atheneum—Polak & Van Gennep), 208.
5. Bolle, *Letters*, 36.
6. Presser, *Destruction*, 95.
7. Erik Somers, *Voorzitter van de Joodse Raad, De herinneringen van David
   Cohen (1941–1943)* (Zutphen: Walburg Pers, 2010), 133–134.
8. Somers, *Voorzitter*, 134.
9. Presser, *Destruction*, 137.
10. Bolle interview, NIOD archive.
11. Moore, *Victims & Survivors*, 120.
12. Edwin and Thea Sluzker, *Herinneringskamp Westerbork* (https://bevrijd
    ingsportretten.nl/portret/edwin-sluzker/).
13. Meershoek, *Dienaren van het gezag*, 234.
14. L. Ph. Polak, *Documents of the persecution of the Dutch Jewry
    1940–1945* (Amsterdam: Athenaeum–Polak & Van Gennep, Jewish
    Historical Museum, 1969), sample call-up notice from, document 213,
    85 (trans. 98).

Chapter 9: "A kind of gathering place"

1. Kok and Somers, *De Jodenvervolging in foto's*, 235–249.
2. Koert Broersma and Gerard Rossing, *Kamp Westerbork Gefilmd: Het
   verbal over een unieke film uit 1944* (Assen: Uitgeverij Koninklijke Van
   Gorcum, 2021), 9, 26.
3. Nina Siegal, "Children of the Holocaust Who Are Anonymous No
   More," *The New York Times*, May 18, 2021.
4. Broersma and Rossing, *Kamp Westerbork Gefilmd*, 134–141.
5. Siegal, "Children of the Holocaust."

Chapter 11: "If only there were more places for these poor people"

1. Els Hendriks, unpublished memoir, (trans. J. Vomberg, courtesy of Willem Veldkamp) 42.
2. Hendriks memoir, 45.
3. "Na geslaagde acties nam hij bloemen mee," *Het Parool*, Amsterdam, 4
   Mei 1979 (Delpher archive).
4. Willem Veldkamp interview.
5. Braber, *This Cannot Happen Here*, 146–147; also Willem Veldkamp,
   *Zoo Menschonteerend: Het lot van de Joods Epenaren tijdens de Tweede
   Wereldoorlog* (In eigen beheer, 2020).
6. Veldkamp, *Zoo Menschonteerend*, 20.
7. Willem Veldkamp, "Voor de oorlog gingen we dansen . . ." (*Ampt Epe*,
   September 2014), 21–22.

8. Veldkamp, "Voor de oorlog," 22.
9. Ter Braak and his wife, Martha Helena ter Braak–Derksen, were honored by Yad Vashem as Righteous Among the Nations in April 2022.
10. Veldkamp, *Zoo Menschonteerend*, 14.
11. Veldkamp interview.
12. Hendriks memoir, 28.
13. Hendriks memoir, 29.
14. Willem Veldkamp, *Verzet in Epe* (In eigen beheer, 1995), 14.
15. Veldkamp interview.
16. Veldkamp, *Zoo Menschonteerend*, 191.

Chapter 12: "The time had come to go into hiding"

1. Presser, *Destruction*, 391–392.
2. Gerard Aalders, *Nazi Looting: The Plunder of Dutch Jewry During the Second World War*, trans. by Arnold Pomerans and Erica Pomerans (Oxford and New York: Berg Publishers, 2004), 211–213.
3. Dawn Skorczewski and Bettine Siertsema, "The kind of spirit that people still kept": VHA testimonies of Amsterdam's Diamond Jews, *Holocaust Studies*, 2020, vol. 26, no. 1, 62–84.
4. Skorczewski and Siertsema, "The kind of spirit," 62–84.
5. Josephina Lewijt, "Shoah Foundation Video Testimony. Amsterdam June 3, 1996 Interview Code #16037," Visual History Archive of the Shoah Foundation Institute at the University of Southern California, 1996. Dutch as quoted in Skorczeski and Siertsema.
6. Aalders, *Nazi Looting*, 212.
7. Skorczewski and Siertsema, "Spirit," 66–67.
8. Albertina Maria van de Bilt was recognized by Yad Vashem as one of the Righteous Among the Nations in 1980.
9. Guus Meershoek interview.
10. Abel J. Herzberg, *Kroniek der Jodenvervolging, 1940–1945*, 5th edition, (Amsterdam: Em. Querido's Uitgeverij B.V., 1985) 142-143.
11. October 22, 1942.
12. Emsley et al., *Social Control*, 333.
13. Christopher R. Browning, *Ordinary Men: Reserve Police Battalion 101 and the Final Solution in Poland* (New York: HarperPerennial, 1993).
14. Ad van Liempt, *Kopgeld: Nederlandse premiejagers op zoek naar joden, 1943* (Amsterdam: Uitgeverij Balans, 2002), 113–116.
15. Ad van Liempt, *Hitler's Bounty Hunters: The Betrayal of the Jews*, trans. S.J. Leinbach (Oxford and New York: Berg, 2005), 25–34.
16. Van Liempt interview.
17. Van Liempt, *Hitler's Bounty Hunters*, 58–59.
18. Van Liempt, *Hitler's Bounty Hunters*, 63.
19. Marnix Croes, "The Holocaust in the Netherlands and the Rate of Jewish Survival," *Holocaust and Genocide Studies* 20.3 (2006): 490–491.
20. Moore, *Victims & Survivors*, 210, 199–200.
21. Van Liempt, *Hitler's Bounty Hunters*, 47.

22. Pinchas Bar-Efrat, *Denunciation and Rescue, Dutch Society and the Holocaust,* trans. from Hebrew by Naftali Greenwood (Jerusalem: Yad Vashem, 2017), 21.
23. Bar-Efrat, *Denunciation,* 125.
24. Bar-Efrat, *Denunciation,* 159–160.
25. Van Liempt, *Hitler's Bounty Hunters,* 47–55.
26. Bar-Efrat, *Denunciation,* 183, 149.

Chapter 14: "The man who goes about with his notebook"

1. Koert Broersma, *Buigen onder de storm: Philip Mechanicus Verslagger tot in de dood 1889–1994* (Assen: Koninklijke Van Gorcum, 2019), 117.
2. Broersma, *Buigen,* 130–131.
3. Broersma, *Buigen,* 117.
4. Broersma, *Buigen,* 132–133.
5. Jacques Presser introduction, *Waiting for Death, a diary by Philip Mechanicus* trans. Irene R. Gibbons (London: Calder and Boyars, 1968), 11.
6. Bettine Siertsema, *Uit de Diepten: Nederlandse egodocumenten over de nazi concentratiekampen* (Vught: Uitgeverij Skandalon, 2007), 173.
7. Broersma interview.
8. Koert Broersma, *Buigen onder de storm: Levensschets van Philip Mechanicus 1889–1944* (Van Gennep, 1993), 21.
9. Philip Mechanicus, *"Ik woon, zoals je weet, drie hoog,"* Brieven uit Westerbork (Amsterdam: Uitgeverij Balans, 1999), 5.
10. Interviews with Koert Broersma and Elisabeth Oets.
11. Johanna Heinsius was honored by Yad Vashem as one of the Righteous Among the Nations in 1995.
12. Oets interview.
13. Mechanicus, *Waiting for Death,* 12.
14. Broersma, *Buigen,* 110–111.
15. Oets interview.
16. Mechanicus, diary entry, September 14, 1943.
17. "April-Meistaking," Kennisbank, Verzets Resistance Museum website vertzetsmuseum.org.
18. *Gids van den Joodsche Raad voor Amsterdam*, 15 Maart 1943 (NIOD, Ned 9.61Gid).
19. Notes of the Central Meeting of the Joodse Raad, no. 94 (May 21, 1943); also Bolle, *Letters,* 138.
20. Bolle, *Letters,* 140–141.
21. Bianca Stigter, *Atlas van een Bezette Stad: Amsterdam 1940–1945* (Amsterdam/Antwerpen: Atlas Contact, 2019), 412.
22. Nina Siegal, "Photos That Helped to Document the Holocaust Were Taken by a Nazi," *The New York Times,* July 29, 2022.
23. "Netherlands Jews Ousted by Nazis" (no byline), *The New York Times,* June 23, 1943, 8.

Chapter 16: "She just had a very large heart"

1. Raul Hilberg, *The Destruction of the European Jews* (Chicago: Quadrangle Books, Inc., 1961), 365.
2. J.C.H. Blom, R.G. Fuks-Mansfeld, I. Schöffer, *The History of the Jews in the Netherlands* trans. Arnold J. Pomerans and Erica Pomerans (Oxford, Portland, Oregon: The Littmann Library of Jewish Civilization, 2002), 323–324.
3. Moore, *Victims & Survivors*, 190.
4. Marnix Croes and Peter Tammes, *Gif laten wij niet voortbestaan? Een onderzoek naar de overlevingskansen van joden in de Nederlandse gemeenten, 1940–1945* (Nijmegen: Radboud University Nijmegen, 2004).
5. Marnix Croes, "The Holocaust in the Netherlands and the Rate of Jewish Survival," *Holocaust and Genocide Studies* 20.3 (2006): 486.
6. Croes, "Holocaust," 494.
7. Aart Visser, *Onderduikers op de Veluwe: Overleven in oorlogstijd* (Wezep: Bredewold, 1990), 4.
8. Jozef Vomberg, Interview 25346, Tape 2, 0:50–1:18, interview by Judy Schwartz, USC (Shoah Foundation Visual History Archive. USC Shoah Foundation, 1997). Accessed August–September 2021.
9. Jozef Vomberg, Interview 25346, Tape 2, 2:20–3:00, interview by Judy Schwartz, USC (Shoah Foundation Visual History Archive. USC Shoah Foundation, 1999). Accessed August–September 2021.
10. Jozef Vomberg, Interview 25346, Tape 2, 1:24–2:13, interview by Judy Schwartz, USC (Shoah Foundation Visual History Archive. USC Shoah Foundation, 1999). Accessed August–September 2021.
11. Jozef Vomberg, Shoah Interview 25346, Tape 2, 4:05–6:15, interview by Judy Schwartz, USC (Shoah Foundation Visual History Archive. USC Shoah Foundation, 1999). Accessed August–September 2021.
12. Jozef Vomberg, Shoah Interview 25346, Tape 2, 9:50–11:58, interview by Judy Schwartz, USC (Shoah Foundation Visual History Archive. USC Shoah Foundation, 1999). Accessed August–September 2021.
13. Jozef Vomberg, Shoah Interview 25346, Tape 2, 16:44–20:50, interview by Judy Schwartz, USC (Shoah Foundation Visual History Archive. USC Shoah Foundation, 1999). Accessed August–September 2021.
14. Jozef Vomberg, Shoah Interview 25346, Tape 3, 5:30–6:14, interview by Judy Schwartz, USC (Shoah Foundation Visual History Archive. USC Shoah Foundation, 1999). Accessed August–September 2021.
15. Jozef Vomberg, Shoah Interview 25346, Tape 3, 6:40–7:25, interview by Judy Schwartz, USC (Shoah Foundation Visual History Archive. USC Shoah Foundation, 1999). Accessed August–September 2021.
16. Vomberg, unpublished memoir.
17. Vomberg, unpublished memoir.
18. Vomberg, unpublished memoir.
19. Vomberg, Shoah Interview 25346, Tape 3, 15:30–16:00, interview by Judy Schwartz, USC (Shoah Foundation Visual History Archive. USC Shoah Foundation, 1999). Accessed August–September 2021.
20. Jozef Vomberg, Shoah Interview 25346, Tape 3, 13:45–13:47, interview

by Judy Schwartz, USC (Shoah Foundation Visual History Archive. USC Shoah Foundation, 1999). Accessed August–September 2021.

21. Shapiro interview.

22. Vomberg unpublished memoir.

Chapter 18: "The diary becomes a world"

1. Siegal, "Echoes of Nazi Propaganda," 37.

2. René Vos, *Niet voor publicatie: De legale Nederlandse pers tijdens de Duitse bezetting* (Amsterdam: Sijthoff, 1998).

3. Heidi Tworek, *News from Germany: The Competition to Control World Communications, 1900–1945* (Cambridge, Massachusetts: Harvard University Press, 2019), 189.

4. Gerrit Bakker, Investigation report, Politieke Recherche Afdeling Amsterdam, CABR file, Nationaal Archief, Den Haag, 62.

5. Proces-verbaal, Henri Trend van Hilten, Politieke Recherche Afdeling Amsterdam, September 24, 1946, from CABR File, Douwe Bakker, Nationaal Archief, Den Haag, 63.

6. Arrest record by police agent A. Den Hartog, CABR file, Nationaal Archief, Den Haag.

7. *De Nieuwe Dag*, August 10, 1946, "Berucht politie-inspecteur staat terecht" (Knipselcollectie personnel KB1–282, NIOD DI–53).

8. Proces-verbaal Kurt Döring, Bakker CABR file, NIOD Amsterdam, 8 november 1945.

9. *"Douwe Bakker, de domme handlanger van de S.D.,"* De Volkskrant, 13 August 1946 (Knipselcollectie personnel KB1–282, NIOD).

10. "Douwe Bakker krijgt 7 jaar R.W.I.," *De Volkskrant*, 27 August 1946 (Knipselcollectie KB1–282, NIOD).

11. "Douwe Bakker, 'moffenknecht' van wie men walgt," *De Volkskrant*, 30 Mei 1947 (Knipselcollectie KB1–282-NIOD).

12. Proces-verbaal Emanuël Antonius Stellingwerff, CABR NIOD Amsterdam, Doc. I-53, 51–52.

13. Proces-verbaal Evert Philip Frederiking, Bakker CABR file, NIOD Amsterdam Doc. I-53, 53–54.

14. "Douwe Bakker noteerde zijn misdaden in een dagboek," *Het Parool*, 31 Mei 1947 (Knipselcollectie, KB1–282 NIOD).

15. Proces-verbaal Douwe Bakker, Vrijdag 16 Mei 1947, CABR file NIOD Doc. I-53, 76–77.

16. Proces-verbaal Douwe Bakker, Vrijdag 16 Mei 1947, CABR file NIOD Doc. I-53, 76–77.

17. Garbarini interview.

18. Garbarini interview.

19. Sibylle Schmidt, "Perpetrators' Knowledge: What and How Can We Learn from Perpetrator Testimony?" *Journal of Perpetrator Research* 1.1 (2017), 87–88.

20. Schmidt, "Perpetrators' Knowledge," 89.

21. Ann Tusa and John Tusa, *The Nuremberg Trials* (Skyhorse, 2010).

22. Thijs B. Bouwknegt and Adina-Loredana Nistor, "Studying

'Perpetrators' through the Lens of the Criminal Trial," in *Perpetrators of International Crimes* (Oxford: Oxford University Press, 2019), 104.

23. *De Volkskrant*, "Douwe Bakker, 'moffenknecht van wie men walgt,'" 31 Mei 1947 (Knipselcollectie personnel KB1–282, NIOD).

24. *De Volkskrant*, "Moffenknecht" (NIOD Bakker Knipselcollectie).

25. "Acht jaar R.W.I. voor Douwe Bakker" *Algemeen Handelsblad*, 13 Juni 1947 (Knipselcollectie personnel KB1–282, NIOD).

26. Voordewind Rapport, 23 September 1946, Bakker CABR file NIOD Amsterdam, 57–59.

27. https://meitotmei.nl/nsber-douwe-bakker-bijna-zaandamse-korpschef/.

28. No. 1204 Bijzondere Raad van Cassatie, 5 Januari 1948, van Naoorlogse Rechtspraak (NOR).

29. Raul Hilberg, *Perpetrators Victims Bystanders: The Jewish Catastrophe 1933–1945* (New York: Aaron Ascher Books/HarperCollins, 1992), ix.

30. Christopher R. Browning, *Ordinary Men: Reserve Police Battalion 101 and the Final Solution in Poland*, Revised Edition (New York: Harper-Collins, 2017), 162.

31. Christopher R. Browning, "Perpetrator Testimony: Another Look at Adolf Eichmann," in *Collected Memories: Holocaust History and Postwar Testimony* (Madison: University of Wisconsin Press, 2004), 5, 11.

32. Browning, "Perpetrator Testimony," 36.

33. Katharina von Kellenbach, *The Mark of Cain: Guilt and Denial in the Post-War Lives of Nazi Perpetrators* (Oxford University Press, 2013), 206.

34. Mary Fulbrook, *Reckonings: Legacies of Nazi Persecution and the Quest for Justice* (Oxford University Press, 2018), 411–412, quoted from DTA Emmendingen, 463, Marianne B., "Bericht uber die Dienstzeit als Gymnasiallehrerin in Auschwitz" (1.9.43–21.1–1945).

35. Fulbrook, *Reckonings*, 417.

36. Fulbrook, *Reckonings*, 423.

37. Stadsarchief, Douwe Bakker registration card.

38. Nationaal Archief, Douwe Bakker CABR file.

Chapter 20: "A journalist in heart and soul"

1. Philip Mechanicus, *"Ik woon, zoals je weet, drie hoog,"* brieven uit Westerbork (Amsterdam: Uitgeverij Balans, 1987), 71.

2. Mechanicus, *"Ik woon . . .,"* 72–73.

3. Broersma, *Buigen*, 206–207.

4. Renata Laqueur, *Dagboek uit Bergen-Belsen, Maart 1944–April 1945* (Amsterdam: Meulenhoff, 2021), 24.

5. Broersma, *Buigen*, 206.

6. Laqueur, *Dagboek*, 25.

7. Loden Vogel, *Dagboek uit een kamp* (Amsterdam: Prometheus Publishers, 2000), 11.

8. Broersma, *Buigen*, 218–219.

9. Vogel, *Dagboek*, April 25, 1944, 12.

10. Mechanicus, "*Ik woon . . . ,*" 74.
11. Broersma, *Buigen*, 221–222.
12. "Ph. Mechanicus Gefussilleerd," *Algemeen Handelsblad*, 5 november 1945 (NIOD knipselmap, KB1–8438).
13. NIOD archief 703/14–15 Analyses.
14. Dirk Mulder en Ben Pinsen, *Bronnen van herinnering* (Herinneringcentrum Kamp Westerbork, Van Gorcum and Comp. B.V., 1993), 77.
15. S. Lillian Kremer, *Holocaust Literature: An Encyclopedia of Writers and Their Work; Volume 2, Lerner to Zychlinsky* (New York: Routledge, 2003), 817.

Chapter 22: "All the trivial things"

1. Helmuth Mainz, "A report on the arrival of 222 transport to Palestine, written on arrival in 1944," in Oppenheim, *The Chosen People*, Appendix 2, 183.
2. Mirjam Bolle interview, August 12, 1999, NIOD archive.
3. Oppenheim, *The Chosen*, 183.
4. Ya'acov Yannay (Jacob de Jong) was one of the 222 Dutch people on the transport, interviewed by Suzanne Glas in 1994.
5. Oppenheim, *The Chosen*, 184.
6. Email exchange with Mirjam Bolle.
7. Oppenheim, *The Chosen*, 165.
8. Michman, Introduction to *Letters Never Sent*, 11.
9. Katja Happe, "The Role of the Jewish Council During the Occupation of the Netherlands," in *The Holocaust and European Studies: Social Processes and Social Dynamics*, edited by Andrea Low and Frank Bajohr (London: Palgrave Macmillan, 2016), 215.
10. Laurien Vastenhout, "The 'Jewish Councils' of Western Europe: A Comparative Analysis" (Sheffield: University of Sheffield, dissertation, September 2019), 4.
11. Laurien Vastenhout interviews.
12. Happe, "The Role," 216.
13. Henry L. Mason, "Jews in the Occupied Netherlands," *Political Science Quarterly*, Summer 1984, 333–334.
14. Happe, "The Role," 215.
15. Isaiah Trunk, *Judenrat: The Jewish Councils in Eastern Europe Under Nazi Occupation* (Macmillan, 1972).
16. Vastenhout, "Jewish Councils," 1.
17. Vastenhout, "Jewish Councils," 282.
18. Trunk, *Judenrat*, 394.
19. Trunk, *Judenrat*, 399.
20. Trunk, *Judenrat*, 400.
21. Trunk, *Judenrat*, 420.
22. Trunk, *Judenrat*, 421.
23. Trunk, *Judenrat*, xxxv.
24. Piotr Wróbel, "The 'Judenräte' Controversy: Some Polish Aspects," *The Polish Review*, vol. 42, no. 2 (University of Illinois Press, 1997), 229.

25. Vastenhout, "Jewish Councils," 19.
26. Wróbel, "Judenräte," 226.
27. *Patterns of Jewish Leadership in Nazi Europe 1933–1945; Proceedings of the Third Yad Vashem International Historical Conference, Jerusalem April 4–7, 1977,* published by Yad Vashem, 1979; opening remarks.
28. Wróbel, "Judenräte," 232.
29. Laura Jockusch and Gabriel N. Finder, *Jewish Honor Courts: Revenge, Retribution, and Reconciliation in Europe and Israel after the Holocaust,* (Detroit: Wayne State University Press, 2015), 130.
30. Evelien Gans, *De kleine verschillen die het leven uitmaken. Een historische studie naar joodse sociaal-democraten en socialistisch-zionisten in Nederland* (Amsterdam: Uitgeverij Vassallucci, 1999), 618.
31. Piet H. Schrijvers, "Truth Is the Daughter of Time: Prof. David Cohen as Seen by Himself and Others," in *Dutch Jews as Perceived by Themselves and by Others,* Proceedings of the Eighth International Symposium on the History of the Jews in the Netherlands Series: Brill's Series in Jewish Studies, Vol. 24 (Jan. 1, 2000), 356.
32. *Patterns of Jewish Leadership in Nazi Europe 1933–1945, Proceedings of the Third Yad Vashem International Historical Conference—April 1977* (Jerusalem: Yad Vashem, 1979), 13–15.

Chapter 24: "What do you have to know to *know*?"

1. Ed van Thijn, "Omstanders, een bruin vermoeden," in *Machteloos? Ooggetuigen van de Jodenvervolging* (Amsterdam: Athenaeum/Polak & Van Gennep, 2007), Anna Timmerman, 7–8.
2. Vuijsje, *Tegen beter* (my translation; the word *vertekend* can mean "distorted" or "biased"), 14.
3. Van der Boom, *"Wij weten . . . ,"* 385.
4. Hella Rottenberg, "Voor de gemoedsrust van de natie," *Trouw,* 24 Juni 2006.
5. Bart van der Boom, *"Wij weten niets van hun lot": Gewone Nederlanders en de Holocaust* (Amsterdam: Boom, 2012), 9.
6. Van der Boom, *"Wij weten . . . ,"* 9–14.
7. Dan Michman, *Egodocuments in Dutch Jewish History,* 37.
8. Jürgen Matthäus, *Predicting the Holocaust: Jewish Organizations Report from Geneva on the Emergence of the "Final Solution," 1939–1942* (Washington D.C.: Rowman & Littlefield in association with the United States Holocaust Memorial Museum, 2019), 2.
9. Fulbrook, *Reckonings,* 1.
10. Matthäus, *Predicting the Holocaust,* 1.
11. Matthäus, *Predicting,* 177–178.
12. "Declaration Regarding German Atrocities Against Jews in German Occupied Countries," issued December 17, 1942, *The United Nations Review* III, no. 1 (1943): 1.
13. Anne Freadman, *Holding On and Holding Out: Jewish Diaries From Wartime France* (University of Toronto Press, Scholarly Publishing Division, 2020), 5.

14. Queen Wilhelmina radio address, November 28, 1941, public domain.
15. Jord Schaap, *Het recht om te waarschuwen over de Radio Oranje-toe-spraken van koningin Wilhelmina* (Amsterdam: Anthos, 2007), 136–138.
16. Nanda van der Zee, *Om erger te voorkomen* (Soesterberg: Aspekt, 1997).
17. Jeroen Dewulf, *Spirit of Resistance: Dutch Clandestine Literature During the Nazi Occupation* (Rochester: Camden House, 2010), 102.
18. Anne Frank, *The Diary of a Young Girl, The Definitive Edition,* edited by Otto H. Frank and Mirjam Pressler, trans. by Susan Massotty (New York: Penguin Books, 1997), 54.
19. Dick van Galen Last and Rolf Wolfswinkel, *Anne Frank and After* (Amsterdam University Press, 1996), 111.
20. Ies Vuijsje, *Tegen beter weten in: Zelfbedrog en ontkenning in de Neder-landse geschiedsbeschrijving over de Jodenvervolging* (Amsterdam/Antwerp: Augustus Publishers, 2006).
21. Ies Vuijsje, *Tegen beter,* 79–80.
22. Van der Boom, *"Wij weten . . . ,"* 263.
23. Bart van der Boom, "The Auschwitz Reservation: Dutch Victims and Bystanders and Their Knowledge of the Holocaust," in *Holocaust and Genocide Studies* 31, no. 3 (Winter 2017): 393.
24. Van der Boom, *"Wij weten . . . ,"* 386.
25. Van der Boom, "Auschwitz Reservation," 385.
26. Bart van der Boom interview.
27. Remco Ensel, "Holocaust Commemorations in Postcolonial Dutch Society," in *The Holocaust, Israel and "The Jew": Histories of Antisemi-tism in Postwar Dutch Society,* edited by Evelien Gans and Remco Ensel (Amsterdam: Amsterdam University Press, 2017), 492.
28. Remco Ensel and Evelien Gans, "Over 'Wij weten iets van hun lot,'" De *Groene Amsterdammer,* December 12, 2012, and February 6, 2013.
29. Christina Morina and Krijn Thijs, *Probing the Limits of Categorization: The Bystander in Holocaust History* (New York: Berghahn Books, 2019). (From Chapter 6, "The Dutch Bystander as Non-Jew and Implicated Subject," by Ensel and Gans).
30. Arianne Baggerman and Rudolf Dekker, "Egodocumenten als bron," *De Groene Amsterdammer,* 24 Januari 2013.
31. Dekker interview.
32. Nanda van der Zee, "The Recurrent Myth of 'Dutch Heroism' in the Second World War and Anne Frank as a Symbol," in *The Netherlands and the Nazi Genocide: Papers of the 21st Annual Scholars' Conference;* edited by G. Jan Colijn and Marcia S. Littell., 7.
33. Dekker interview.
34. Fulbrook, *Reckonings,* 406.

Chapter 26: "An archaeology of silence"

1. P.A. van der Kamp, Belastambtenaar dagboek, *Dagboekfragmenten 1940–1945* (NIOD, 1954), 617.
2. Nina Siegal, "The Lost Diaries of War," *The New York Times,* April 15, 2020; translation of diary text by Susan Ridder.

3. Nederlander bij SS-eenheid, ca. 30 jaar dagboek, *Dagboekfragmenten 1940–1945* (NIOD, 1954), 616.

4. Jozef Vomberg, Interview 25346, Tape 5, USC (Shoah Foundation Visual History Archive. USC Shoah Foundation, 1997). Accessed August–September 2021.

5. Evelien Gans, "'They Have Forgotten to Gas You': Post-1945 Antisemitism in the Netherlands," in *Dutch Racism* 27 (2014), 71, 77–81.

6. Gans, "They Have Forgotten," 79; De Wagt, *Vijf honderd*, 53.

7. Evelien Gans (co-author and co-editor with Remco Ensel), *The Holocaust, Israel and "the Jew": Histories of Antisemitism in Postwar Dutch Society* (Amsterdam University Press, 2017).

8. Dick van Galen Last and Rolf Wolfswinkel, *Anne Frank and After: Dutch Holocaust Literature in Historical Perspective* (Amsterdam University Press, 1996), 127.

9. Van Galen Last and Wolfswinkel, *Anne Frank and After*, 124.

10. Robert Krell, "On Listening to Holocaust Survivors: Recounting and Life History" (Book Review), *Holocaust and Genocide Studies* (2000) 457.

11. Saul Friedländer, "History, Memory and the Historian: Dilemmas and Responsibilities," *New German Critique,* Spring-Summer 2000, No. 80, Special Issue on the Holocaust (Durham: Duke University Press, 2000), 5.

12. Wieviorka, ix–x, citing Lucy S. Dawidowicz, *From That Place and Time: A Memoir: 1938–1947* (New York: W.W. Norton, 1989), 304ff.

13. "Mr. Boder Vanishes," This American Life podcast, episode 197: Before It Had a Name, October 26, 2001.

14. Alan Rosen, *The Wonder of Their Voices: The 1946 Holocaust Interviews of David Boder* (Oxford: Oxford University Press, 2010).

15. Accessible online as "Voices of the Holocaust" at the University of Illinois, Boder's alma mater, https://voices.library.iit.edu/.

16. Voices of the Holocaust (https://voices.library.iit.edu/david_boder).

17. Kassow, *Who Will Write*, 1–2.

18. Frank van Vree, "Writing as Resistance. Emanuel Ringelblum and the Ghetto Archive," speech delivered February 25, 2022, at the Mauthausen Commemoration.

19. The Oneg Shabbat Archive, "Let the world read and know," Yad Vashem website (https://www.yadvashem.org/yv/en/exhibitions/ringelblum/index.asp).

20. Kassow, *Who Will Write,* 210.

21. Annette Wieviorka, *The Era of the Witness*, translated from the French by Jared Stark (Ithaca and London: Cornell University Press, 2006), x–xi.

22. Elie Wiesel, video interview 1996, Academy of Achievement, "Keys to Success, In Their Own Words," part 9 (achievement.org/video/elie-wiesel-9/).

23. Wiesel, Academy of Achievement interview 1996, part 9.

24. Wiesel, Academy of Achievement interview 1996, part 7 (https://achievement.org/video/elie-wiesel-7/).

25. Wiesel, Academy of Achievement interview 1996, Academy of Achievement, part 9.

26. Greenspan interview.
27. Viktor E. Frankl, *Man's Search for Meaning*, trans. Ilse Lasch (London: Rider, 2011), 32.
28. Frankl, *Man's Search*, 62.
29. Frankl, *Man's Search*, 117.
30. Marga Minco, *Bitter Herbs: A Short Chronicle*, trans. Jeannette K. Ringold (London: Penguin Random House UK, 2020), 142.
31. Gideon Hausner, *Justice in Jerusalem*, 292–296, as quoted in Wieviorka, *The Era of the Witness*, 69.
32. Henry Greenspan et al., "Engaging Survivors: Assessing 'Testimony' and 'Trauma' as Foundational Concepts," September 2014, *Dapim Studies on the Holocaust* 28(3):190–226.
33. Israel Shenker, "Israeli Historian Denies Jews Yielded to the Nazis 'Like Sheep,'" *The New York Times*, May 6, 1970.

Chapter 27: "Suffering and struggle, loyalty and betrayal, humanity and barbarism, good and evil"

1.   Jaap Cohen, "In de spiegel van de geschiedenis," *De Groene Amsterdammer*, no. 20, 13 mei 2020.
2.   A.H. Paape, "Inleiding," *Dagboekfragmenten 1940–1945*, v–xiii.
3.   Frank van Vree, *In de schaduw van Auschwitz: Herrinneringen, beelden, geschiedenis* (Groningen: Historisch Uitgeverij Groningen, 1995).
4.   Van Vree, *Schaduw*, 60.
5.   Van Vree, *Schaduw*, 63–65, 69.
6.   Van Vree, *Schaduw*, 68–69.
7.   Van Vree, *Schaduw*, 69.
8.   Presser, *Destruction*, xiii.
9.   Van Vree, *Schaduw*, 83.
10. "Goedkope uitgave verschenen van Pressers Ondergang," *Algemeen Handelsblad*, 16 november 1965 (Delpher archive).
11. "Goedkope uitgave verschenen van Pressers Ondergang," *Algemeen Handelsblad*, 16 november 1965 (Delpher archive).
12. Van Vree, *Schaduw*, 102.
13. Arianne Baggerman and Rudolf Dekker, "Jacques Presser, Egodocuments and Jewish History," in *Egodocuments in Dutch Jewish History: Emotions, Imaginations, Perceptions, Egos, Characteristics*, ed. Dan Michman (Amsterdam: Amphora Books, 2021), 18.
14. Hansen and Zarankin, "Founding Myth."
15. Frank van Vree, "Absent Memories," *Cultural Analysis* 12 (2013): 6.
16. Boudewijn Smits, "Opgejaagd door de furiën der historie: Het vluchtverhaal van Loe de Jong," *De Groene Amsterdammer*, May 4, 2010; nr. 18.
17. Hanneloes Pen, "De 'geheime' tweelingbroer van chroniqueur Loe de Jong," *Het Parool*, 20 november 2019.
18. Chris van der Heijden, "Het verhaal van een zoon: Een ander portret van Loe de Jong," *De Groene Amsterdammer*, no. 10, March 9, 2011.

19. Jouni-Matti Kuukkanen, "Learning Lessons from History—or Not?" *Journal of the Philosophy of History* 13 (2019), 139.

20. X. Chen, "That Noble Dream: Analysis of the 'Objectivity' Question of the Historiography of Ranke," *Advances in Historical Studies* 9 (2020), 92–97.

21. Stefan-Ludwig Hoffmann, "Repetition and Rupture," *Aeon*, September 2020, (https://aeon.co/essays/reinhart-kosellecks-theory-of -history-for-a-world-in-crisis).

22. Aleida Assmann, "Re-framing memory. Between individual and collective forms of constructing the past," in *Performing the Past: Memory, History, and Identity in Modern Europe*, eds. Karin Tilmans, Frank van Vree, and Jay Winter (Amsterdam University Press, 2010), 38.

23. Presser, *Destruction*, xiv.

24. Michman, *Egodocuments*, 30.

Chapter 28: "A gradual lifting of the collective repression"

1. Saul Friedländer, "History, Memory, and the Historian: Dilemmas and Responsibilities," *New German Critique*, no. 80 (2000): 7.

2. Van Vree, "Absent," 6–7.

3. Nancy Cooey interview.

4. Annette Wieviorka, *The Era of the Witness* trans. Jared Stark (Ithaca and London: Cornell University Press, 2006), xi.

5. Michael E. Ruane, "Pandemic forces Holocaust survivor interviews onto Zoom," *Washington Post*, December 20, 2020.

6. Wieviorka, *The Era*, 142–143.

7. Shoshana Felman and Dori Laub, *Testimony: Crises of Witnessing in Literature, Psychoanalysis, and History* (New York/London: Routledge, 1992), 80–81.

8. Wieviorka, *The Era*, 143–149.

9. Aleida Assmann, "Re-framing Memory. Between individual and collective forms or constructing the past," in *Performing the Past: Memory, History, and Identity in Modern Europe*, eds. Karin Tilmans, Frank van Vree, and Jay Winter (Amsterdam: Amsterdam University Press, 2010), 39.

10. Assmann, "Re-framing," 40.

11. Wieviorka, *The Era*, xii.

Conclusion: "There Were More"

1. Nina Siegal, "Beyond Anne Frank: The Dutch Tell Their Full Holocaust Story," *The New York Times*, July 17, 2016.

2. Nina Siegal, "Holocaust Memorial Is Closer to Reality in Amsterdam," *The New York Times*, December 16, 2016.

3. Hartogh, as quoted by Emile Schrijver in "Opinie: 'Voorzie waar mogelijk omstreden erfgoed van de juiste context,' " *Het Parool*, 2 maart 2022 (text of speech at the relocation ceremony).

4. Wim de Wagt, *Vijf honderd meter namen: De Holocaust en de pijn van de herinnering* (Amsterdam: Boom, 2021), 53.

5. Schrijver speech.
6. Dienke Hondius, *Terugkeer: Antisemitisme in Nederland rond de bevrijding* ('s-Gravenhage: SDU-uitgeverij, 1990), 96.
7. De Wagt, *Vijf honderd*, 72.
8. Lotte Rigter, "Monument van Joods erkentelijkheid na 50 jaar weer op het Weesperplien," *NH Nieuws*, 2 maart 2022.
9. Manfred Gerstenfeld, *The Abuse of Holocaust Memory Distortions and Responses* (Jerusalem Center for Public Affairs, 2009), 60–61.
10. Frank van Vree, Hetty Berg, and David Duindam, *Site of Deportation; Site of Memory: The Amsterdam Hollandsche Schouwburg and the Holocaust* (Amsterdam: Amsterdam University Press, 2013), 155–156, 174.
11. Van Vree, Berg, and Duindam, *Site of Deportation,* 176.
12. Van Vree, Berg, and Duindam, *Site of Deportation,* 172–178.
13. Mike Corder, "Dutch king unveils Holocaust name monument in Amsterdam," *Associated Press*, September 19, 2021.
14. Gerstenfeld, *Abuse*, 136–143.
15. CIDI, "Monitor antisemitische incidenten 2020," Stichting Centrum Informatie en Documentatie Israel; quote from English summary.
16. Schrijver interview.
17. "FvD slammed for saying Covid lockdown is akin to WWII occupation," *NL Times*, May 3, 2021.
18. Gerard Aalders, *Nazi Looting: The Plunder of Dutch Jewry During the Second World War,* trans. by Arnold Pomerans and Erica Pomerans (Oxford and New York: Berg Publishers, 2004), 225.
19. Felman and Laub, *Testimony*, 85.

PHOTO CREDITS

For the photos on these pages, grateful acknowledgment is made to the NIOD Institute for War, Holocaust and Genocide Studies in Amsterdam; the Gemeente Amsterdam Stadsarchief (Amsterdam City Archives); the Vrijheids Museum (Freedom Museum) in Groesbeek; the Joods Museum (Jewish Museum) in Amsterdam; and the author, Nina Siegal.

Cover: Photo by Herman Heukels, a Dutch propaganda photographer and NSB member who shot a series of images of the large Razzia in Olympiaplein on June 20, 1943. None of the individuals in the photograph have been identified. Heukels took the pictures in hopes of publishing them in *Storm SS*, a Dutch Nazi propaganda weekly, but they never appeared there. His pictures are some of the only "official" shots of the round-up of 5,500 Jews in Amsterdam that day. (Courtesy NIOD)

INTERIOR PHOTOS:
Page 1: Courtesy of the author
Page 21: Courtesy NIOD photo archive
Page 39: Courtesy Vrijheids Museum Groesbeek
Page 55: Courtesy Anneke Dijkman, Ina Steur's daughter
Page 81: Courtesy NIOD photo archive

Page 97: Photo by Bart de Kok, dated April 27, 1942. Courtesy Amsterdam City Archives, Collection Bart de Kok and Jozef van Poppel, image KOKBB00016000005

Page 121: Propaganda poster from 1935, courtesy NIOD photo archive

Page 133: Photo by R.G.H. Steinberg; courtesy NIOD photo archive

Page 147: Courtesy NIOD photo archive

Page 179: Courtesy NIOD archive, Elisabeth van Lohuizen diary folder

Page 189: Courtesy of Rebecca Emmerik

Page 209: Courtesy Joods Museum Amsterdam

Page 223: Courtesy NIOD, from Mirjam Levie/Bolle diary folder

Page 251: Courtesy NIOD archive, Elisabeth van Lohuizen diary folder

Page 293: Courtesy NIOD archive, from Douwe Bakker diary folder

Page 325: Courtesy Joods Museum Amsterdam, image F000280

Page 347: Jaap Kaas, Amsterdam City Archives, ANWX00486000515

Page 421: Courtesy NIOD photo archive

Page 435: Courtesy NIOD photo archive

Page 449: Courtesy Joods Museum Amsterdam, photo number F001285

Page 459: Photo by Nina Siegal, courtesy the author

INSERT PHOTOS:

Page 1, Top left and top and bottom right: Photos by Nina Siegal

Page 1, middle left: René Kok

Page 2, top half: Photos by Stuart Acker Holt

Page 2, bottom half: Photos by Nina Siegal; Courtesy of NIOD

Page 3, top half: Photos courtesy of Anneke Dijkman

Page 3, bottom left: Photo by Stuart Acker Holt

Page 3, bottom right: Photo by Nina Siegal

Page 4, top and middle: Photo by Stuart Acker Holt

Page 4, bottom: Photo by Nina Siegal

Page 5, top: Photo by Stuart Acker Holt

Page 5, bottom: Photos by Nina Siegal

Page 6, top and middle left: Photos by Stuart Acker Holt

Page 6, bottom left: Photos courtesy of Lis Vomberg Shapiro
Page 6, bottom right: Photo by Nina Siegal
Page 7, All photos by Nina Siegal, courtesy of NIOD
Page 8, top right and left: Photos by Nina Siegal
Page 8, bottom: Photo by Ronald Spierenburg

INDEX

Note: Page numbers in *italics* indicate photos.